Hiking

New Mexico's Gila Wilderness

Polly Burke and Bill Cunningham

Published in cooperation with The Wilderness Society

FALCON®

HELENA, MONTANA

A **FALCON** GUIDE ®

Falcon® Publishing is continually expanding its list of recreational guidebooks. All books include detailed descriptions, accurate maps, and all information necessary for enjoyable trips. You can order extra copies of this book and get information and prices for other Falcon® books by writing Falcon, P.O. Box 1718, Helena, MT 59624, or by calling toll-free 1-800-582-2665. Also, please ask for a copy of our current catalog. Visit our website at www.FalconOutdoors.com or contact us by e-mail at falcon@falcon.com.

©1999 Falcon® Publishing, Inc., Helena, Montana
Printed in the United States of America.

1 2 3 4 5 6 7 8 9 0 MG 04 03 02 01 00 99

Falcon and FalconGuide are registered trademarks of Falcon® Publishing, Inc.

Cover photo: Laurence Parent.
All black-and-white photos by the authors unless otherwise noted.
Project Editor: Molly Jay
Production Editors: Jessica Solberg and Larissa Berry
Copy Editor: Durrae Johanek
Cartographers: Sue Cary, Joe Menden, and Tony Moore
Page Compositor: Dana Kim-Wincapaw
Book design by Falcon Publishing, Inc.

Cataloging-in-Publication Data is on file at the Library of Congress.

CAUTION

Outdoor recreational activities are by their very nature potentially hazardous. All participants in such activities must assume responsibility for their own actions and safety. The information contained in this guidebook cannot replace sound judgment and good decision-making skills, which help reduce exposure, nor does the scope of this book allow for the disclosure of all the potential hazards and risks involved in such activities.

Learn as much as possible about the outdoor recreational activities in which you participate, prepare for the unexpected, and be cautious. The reward will be a safer and more enjoyable experience.

♻ Text pages printed on recycled paper.

Contents

Re BB Park – good rocks, moonstone off 152 towards hillsboro

*To all of you with enough gumption to lace up a pair of hiking boots
and to venture beyond the roads into the Gila Wilderness, and with
enough heartfelt commitment to fight for the freedom of wild country.
May your spirit, and it, endure forever. And to the timeless
vision of Aldo Leopold, who started it all.*

Acknowlegments

The Gila Wilderness is a vast, complicated landscape with hundreds of miles
of trails criss-crossing some of the most convoluted terrain in the West. A
project of this magnitude, spread over several field seasons, could not have
been accomplished without the help of many folks, some of whom we met
on the trail.

Much of our initial guidance came from Patti Johnston, resource assistant for the Rocky Mountain Ranger District in Montana. Patti worked in
the Gila Wilderness many years ago and cheerfully shared her knowledge
of the country. Other Forest Service professionals who were of immense
help include Tom Dwyer, recreation program manager for the Gila National
Forest, and David Harloff, a wilderness and trails ranger who works out of
the Gila Visitor Center. Tom gave us crucial policy guidance and coordinated agency review of this book, for which we are most grateful. David
provided an indispensable reality check for what is actually out there on the
ground. He patiently put up with our endless questions about trail status
and condition and whether our theoretical idea for a trip was even possible.

We especially enjoyed our philosophical discussions with Glenwood District Ranger John Baldwin about wilderness management. John sees all too
clearly the tenuous balance between use and overuse of this resource. He
feels strongly that continued public support for wilderness hinges on an
increasingly urban population being able to safely enjoy their experiences
in the wild. This book is certainly written with this objective in mind.

There are many other Gila National Forest people who were helpful. We didn't get your names but please know that your commitment to public service is deeply appreciated.

Along the way we met a number of local Gila Wilderness outfitters. Their anecdotal wisdom of the land is wonderful. We especially want to thank Becky and Ysabel Campbell, who grew up in Gila country, and whose father, the late Doc Campbell, knew more about the Gila Wilderness than anyone. They cheerfully and generously shared their knowledge and love of the country, from how best to find a trail that no longer exists to where not to go. When visiting Gila Hot Springs, be sure and stop by Doc Campbell, well-stocked general store. The showers are great!

Several adjacent landowners deserve special mention. Pete Evans graciously allowed us to pass through his Double Springs Ranch on a "wild trail" chase, and educated us on a bit of local history. Art Ordman, who manages the Trails End Ranch for the Albuquerque Academy, was a friendly source of information about trails and places along the East Fork of the Gila River.

A warm thanks is owed to area rancher Sam Luce, whom we have never seen outside the Gila Wilderness. On two different trips in two different years we ran into Sam, on his horse, deep in the Gila. In both instances we enjoyed great camaraderie as he shared his wide knowledge and deep love of the land. "These mountains are my life," he told us.

And a tip of our sun hat to the couple from Texas who donated a pair of dog booties to our faithful lab Philly. This simple act of kindness allowed Philly to negotiate the sticker patches and cobblestones that make up so many of the Gila trails.

Last, we are indebted to our editor Molly Jay and the other Falcon staffers who took our mountain of raw material and somehow transformed it into this book.

"The elemental simplicities of wilderness travel were thrills...because they represented complete freedom to make mistakes. The wilderness gave...those rewards and penalties for wise and foolish acts...against which civilization has built a thousand buffers."

Aldo Leopold (1887–1948) quoted in USFS Southwest Region,
"Wilderness & Primitive Areas in Southwestern National Forests"

The Wilderness Act: An Anniversary Celebration

When Aldo Leopold, Robert Marshall, and six other farsighted citizens founded The Wilderness Society in 1935, passage of the Wilderness Act was still more than a generation away. During the '30s Leopold and Marshall were literally the "commanding generals" of the Wilderness Battle with no legislative tools to work with. Instead of "breaking new ground," as the first Forest Service Chief Gifford Pinchot had done a generation earlier, these wilderness generals were trying to keep some of the wilder ground from being broken. The basic strategy employed by both was to develop and implement the strongest administrative rules possible for interim protection of wilderness. Both Leopold and Marshall held key positions in the Forest Service that enabled them to influence wildland policy. Shortly before his untimely death in 1939, Bob Marshall compared the alarming loss of wilderness to a "snowbank melting on a hot, June day."

The demand for timber after the Second World War effectively turned up the heat lamp on the wilderness "snowbank." By the late 1940s it had become abundantly clear to Howard "Zahnie" Zahnizer, Executive Director of The Wilderness Society, that permanent statutory protection of wilderness was essential if wilderness was to endure forever. Zahnie authored the Wilderness bill and tirelessly led a nationwide grass roots campaign to turn the bill to law. Companion legislation was first introduced in the U.S. House of Representatives and U.S. Senate in 1956 by Rep. John Saylor (R-PA) and Senator Hubert Humphry (D-MN). This unique and far-reaching law contains more prose than legalese, reflecting the vision of Zahnizer, the philosophy of Leopold, and the activism of Marshall.

Bipartisan and Western support finally put the measure over the top. After eight long and demanding years and perhaps the most exhaustive hearing record of any bill debated in congress President Lyndon Johnson signed the bill into law on September 3, 1964. Among other things the Act established the National Wilderness Preservation System with immediate designation of 9.5 million national forest acres, including the Gila, that had been administratively set aside through the actions of Aldo Leopold and Bob Marshall. In the continuing battle for wilderness the Wilderness Act is a "double-edged" sword. Wilderness defenders have the difficult task of passing legislation to secure an "enduring resource of wilderness." But thanks to the Act wilderness can no longer be declassified by the "stroke of a bureaucrat's pen."

This book celebrates the 35th anniversary of the world's most significant land preservation law and system. It all began in 1924 with the vision of a young forester who dared to make a difference.

USGS Topographic Map Index

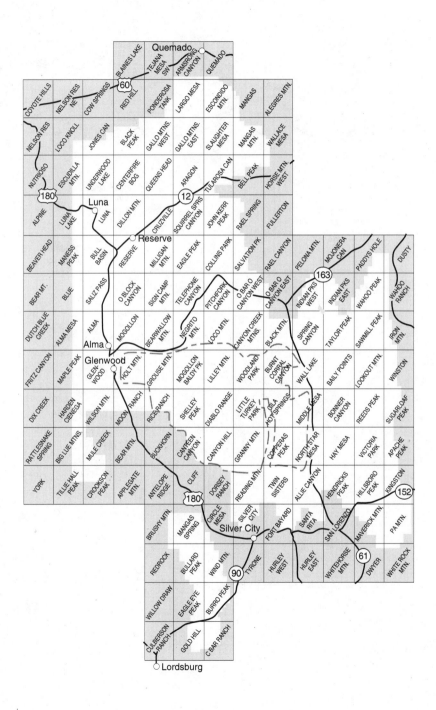

Overview Map

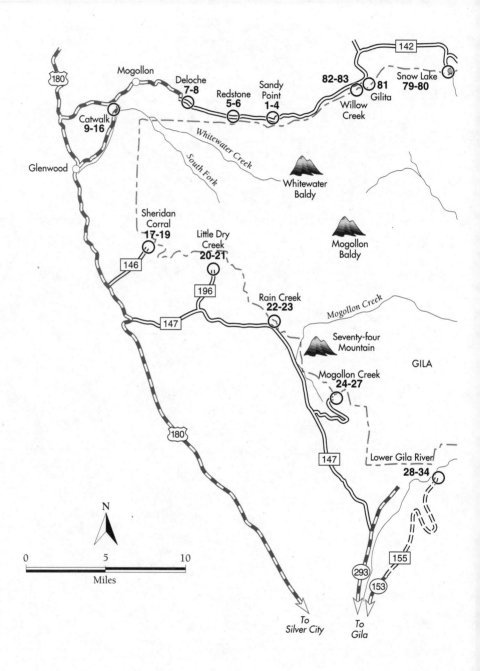

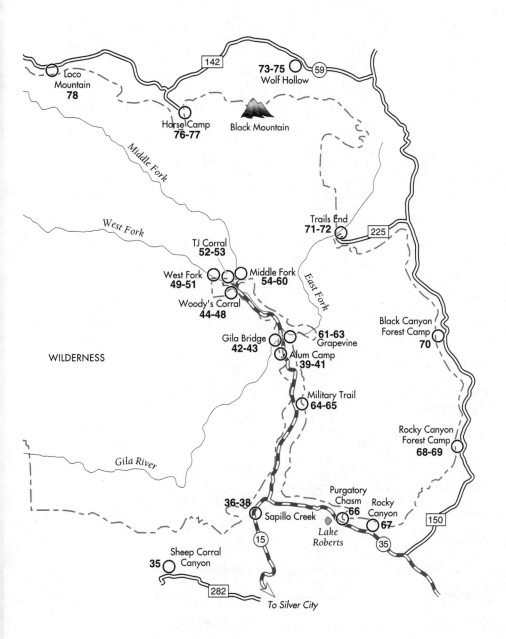

Loco
Mountain
78

142

73-75
Wolf Hollow

59

Horse Camp
76-77

Black Mountain

Middle Fork

West Fork

Trails End
71-72

225

TJ Corral
52-53

West Fork
49-51

Middle Fork
54-60

East Fork

Woody's Corral
44-48

Black Canyon
Forest Camp
70

Gila Bridge
42-43

61-63
Grapevine

WILDERNESS

Alum Camp
39-41

Military Trail
64-65

Rocky Canyon
Forest Camp
68-69

Gila River

36-38

Sapillo Creek

Purgatory
Chasm

66

Rocky
Canyon

67

150

15

Lake
Roberts

35

Sheep Corral
Canyon
35

282

To Silver City

Locator Map

Legend

U.S. Highway	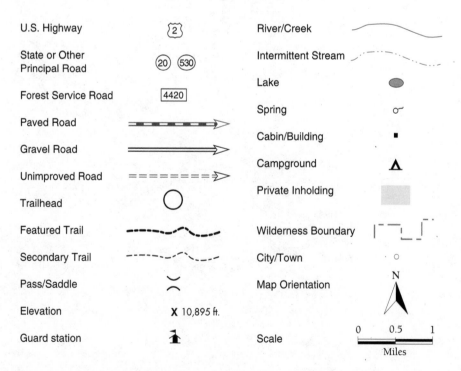	River/Creek	
State or Other Principal Road		Intermittent Stream	
Forest Service Road		Lake	
Paved Road		Spring	
Gravel Road		Cabin/Building	
Unimproved Road		Campground	
Trailhead		Private Inholding	
Featured Trail		Wilderness Boundary	
Secondary Trail		City/Town	
Pass/Saddle		Map Orientation	
Elevation	X 10,895 ft.		
Guard station		Scale	

Introduction

WILDERNESS AND ALDO LEOPOLD

While enjoying the wild majesty of the Gila Wilderness we couldn't help thinking about that remarkable visionary, Aldo Leopold. We wondered if he had axed the blaze on that tree up ahead or set his tent next to the stream where we were camping. In his own quiet but persuasive way, Leopold was the driving force behind the notion that as an enlightened society we should keep some places wild forever.

It was thus through the leadership of Aldo Leopold, Forest Service ranger, writer-philosopher, and the nation's pioneer professor of wildlife ecology, that the USDA Forest Service set aside 755,000 acres in the headwaters of the Gila River as the world's first wilderness area on June 3, 1924. This marked the first time that a large expanse of wildland was to be preserved in its natural state. Management was wonderfully simple: "prohibit roads and hotels, and then leave it alone."

Later on, boundary deletions drove home the need for the lasting legal protection of wilderness that was not achieved until 40 years later with passage of the 1964 Wilderness Act. Meanwhile, in 1930 the Gila Wilderness boundary was reduced along its eastern, northern, and western edges. The following year the Gila was needlessly bisected by construction of the North Star Mesa Road. Ironically, the purpose of the road was to give hunters access to harvest "excess" deer. To Leopold the road and loss of wilderness added insult to injury, for already he recognized that overpopulation of deer was the result of overzealous predator control. Joining forces with Bob Marshall and other leading conservationists, Aldo Leopold cofounded the Wilderness Society in 1935—the nation's foremost wilderness conservation group.

After being downgraded to a "primitive area" in 1933, additional reductions were made in 1936 and 1938 when once again the Gila was designated as wilderness. Six years later, another 5,150 acres were subtracted from the southwest corner to permit the mining of fluorite. In 1953 the 137,388-acre Gila Primitive Area and separate Gila Wilderness of 438,626 acres were formally classified under the stronger Secretary of Agriculture U-1 Regulation. In 1957 the road was extended to the Gila Cliff Dwellings National Monument, removing 4,600 acres from the primitive area. The cliff dwellings had originally been transferred to the National Park Service in 1933 as a national monument. In 1962 another 320 acres were transferred from the Gila Wilderness to the monument.

Upon passage of the landmark Wilderness Act in 1964 the Gila was among the first units in the new National Wilderness Preservation System. Legislation was enacted in 1980 that designated or expanded 12 national forest wildernesses in New Mexico, including an increase of the Gila Wilderness to its present 557,873 acres. Fittingly, the primitive area just east of the

North Star Mesa Road and part of Leopold's original Gila Wilderness was designated the 202,016-acre Aldo Leopold Wilderness in the same legislation. No doubt the unassuming professor would be embarrassed to learn that the smaller Black Range portion of his beloved Gila country had been named for him. So, despite the unfortunate bisection of the Gila by a road, Congress has at least restored the wilderness to the original size envisioned by Aldo Leopold more than 75 years ago.

Today the National Wilderness Preservation System (NWPS) contains about 104 million acres. New Mexico's share of this wild legacy consists of 24 units totaling more than 1.6 million acres. A full appreciation of the meaning and value of wilderness will enhance your enjoyment of the Gila Wilderness while lessening your impact on the wildness of this special place.

Those of us who love wild country have our own heartfelt definition of wilderness as, indeed, Aldo Leopold did when he defined it as "a continuous stretch of country preserved in its natural state . . . big enough to absorb a two weeks' pack trip." But because Congress reserved to itself the exclusive power to designate wilderness, it is important to understand the legal meaning of wilderness.

The basic purpose of the Wilderness Act is to provide an enduring resource of wilderness for this and future generations so that a growing, increasingly mechanized population will not occupy and modify every last wild niche. Just as important as preserving the land is the preservation of natural processes that shape the land, such as naturally ignited fires. After suppressing fire for the past 70 years the Forest Service is finally restoring natural fire to the Gila Wilderness. A return to natural fire frequency will reduce the threat of catastrophic fire by reducing fuel buildup. Other benefits of natural fires include an increase in secondary ground cover for wildlife and for better moisture retention that will decrease flooding.

The act defines "wilderness" as undeveloped federal lands "where the earth and its community of life are untrammeled by man, where man is a visitor who does not remain." Or, to paraphrase Leopold, the Gila is meant to play in, not stay in. The word trammel means "net" in Old English, so that "untrammeled" land is "unnetted," or uncontrolled by humans. Congress recognized that no land is completely free of human influence, going on to say that wilderness must "generally appear to have been affected primarily by the forces of nature, with the imprint of man's work substantially unnoticeable." Further, designated wilderness must have outstanding opportunities for solitude or primitive and unconfined recreation, and be at least 5,000 acres in size or large enough to preserve in an unimpaired condition. Last, wilderness may contain ecological, geological, or other features of scientific, educational, scenic, or historical value.

The moment you set foot in the Gila Wilderness you'll realize that this wild remnant of Aldo Leopold's Southwest more than meets these criteria.

In general, wilderness designation protects the land from development: roads, buildings, motorized vehicle and equipment use, and most commercial uses. Four federal agencies are empowered to administer land in the NWPS: the National Park Service, the U.S. Fish and Wildlife Service, the

Bureau of Land Management, and, in the case of the Gila Wilderness, the USDA Forest Service. These agencies can and do make recommendations, as any citizen can, but only Congress can set aside wilderness on federal lands. This is where politics enters, as epitomized by the kind of grassroots democracy that brought about the restoration of much of the original Gila Wilderness in 1980. The formula for wilderness conservationists has been, and continues to be, "endless pressure endlessly applied."

Once an area has been designated wilderness, the unending job of stewardship is just beginning. The managing agencies have a special duty to administer wilderness areas in "such manner as will leave them unimpaired for future use and enjoyment as wilderness." In a speech marking the 75th anniversary of the Gila Wilderness as the first natural preserve of its kind it was gratifying to hear Mike Dombeck, chief of the Forest Service, call for better management of wilderness areas. Leopold would have been especially pleased to hear the chief state the need for more ecosystems to be preserved as wilderness, from old-growth forests to grasslands to deserts. Dombeck went on to say, "Unlike the jargon-filled legalese of most laws, the Wilderness Act says that the best that remains is worth preserving for future generations. That in a world of compromises, insincere gestures, and half-measures, there are lands and waters where we will not allow expediency to override conviction."

Indeed, wilderness is the only truly biocentric use of land, where the needs of native flora and fauna take precedence over human desires. As such, preservation of wilderness is our society's highest act of humility. It is in places like the Gila where we deliberately arrest our impulse to cut down the last great ponderosa pine forest or to dam the chasms of the Gila River forks. The explorer of the Gila Wilderness can take pride in reaching a remote summit under his or her power, traversing a narrow, serpentine canyon, or walking across the expanse of a high mesa. Hiking boots and self-reliance replace motorized convenience, allowing us to find something in ourselves we feared lost.

NATURAL HISTORY

If you hike several miles or more into the Gila Wilderness, you can't help but experience a variety of forest types and landforms. The natural diversity in this vast, untrammeled space is mind boggling. While the 558,000-acre number might not mean much, think of a swath of land without roads or permanent human settlements that is 40 miles east to west and 30 miles north to south. This rugged, elevated landscape is a mixing zone between the southern end of the Rocky Mountains, the northern extension of the Sierra Madre Mountains from Mexico, and the Sonoran and Chihuahuan Deserts. "Gila" is the Spanish-spelled version of a Yuma Indian word meaning "running water which is salty." This describes the water downstream in Arizona but not in the cold, clear headwaters of the Gila forks within the wilderness. The upper basin of the Gila River drains more than 85 percent of the area, with the remainder in tributary drainages flowing southwesterly to the San Francisco River.

3

The Gila Wilderness is deeply dissected by the spectacular canyons of the Gila River, its three major forks, and hundreds of twisting tributaries. Some of this country, without trails or hikable terrain, is so rough and remote that humans never visit it. The major landform of the wilderness is the Mogollon Range, rising to nearly 11,000 feet through the western half in a southeasterly direction. Smaller ranges include the Jerky Mountains and Diablo Range, situated north and south of the West Fork Gila River, respectively. The Pinos Altos ("tall pines") Range parallels the southern boundary.

Some of the hikes presented in this book begin in upper Sonoran Desert vegetated with cholla and agave and climb a vertical mile to lush subalpine spruce-fir forests. Along the way, the routes pass by great spires and cliffs of lava, dry pinyon-juniper woodlands, ponderosa parks, meadows, high mesas, and aspen parklands.

Sedimentary formations with fossils tell of a time when much of southwestern New Mexico was beneath warm seas. Then came a period of active volcanism about 65 million year ago. A second volcanic period probably took place here 30 to 20 million years ago. As a result, two monumental calderas formed, then collapsed. The resulting volcanic layers from the calderas are blanketed with a thick Gila conglomerate mix of mudstone, sandstone, and alluvial material. Meanwhile, flat-topped mesas continue to erode while some of the mountains are still uplifting. Widespread faulting from earthquakes has produced today's impressive vertical relief of thousands of feet.

The most distinctive features of the Gila Wilderness include the pinnacles and spires of volcanic escarpments along major streams and rolling virgin ponderosa pine forests, the largest in the world protected as wilderness. By far these pine woodlands are the most predominant habitat type, and are found mostly in midelevation uplands above canyons between 6,000 and 7,500 feet. A second major vegetative community includes spruce-fir forests above 9,000 feet, sprinkled with aspen, grassy parks, and wet meadows. Your wanderings through the Gila will also take you across brushy south slopes, vast mesa grasslands, and woodlands dominated by oak, pinyon-juniper, or deciduous trees along streams. Wherever you hike in the Gila look carefully at the surrounding forest and how it got there. It is largely determined by exposure to the sun, elevation, available soil moisture, and the presence or absence of fire. Natural fire is especially important to the perpetuation of fire-dependent pine forests that make up most of the Gila Wilderness.

Expect to see a blend of Engelmann spruce, Douglas-fir and Southwestern white pine high in the Mogollons. Midelevation uplands are the home of open pine parks along with pinyon-juniper woodlands on south-facing hillsides. The greatest plant diversity exists along major fast-moving streams. A typical hardwood mix includes sycamore, cottonwood, alder, boxelder, ash, mountain maple, walnut, and several kinds of willow. Imagine the flourish of colors in the fall!

The fauna is correspondingly varied. There are up to 280 species of birds, 81 types of mammals, 51 reptiles and amphibians, and a couple dozen fish

species. Several threatened and endangered species, such as the reintroduced Gila cutthroat trout, find refuge in small tributary streams. Many of
the following hikes traverse the high country home of elk and blue grouse,
all the way down to low canyon bottoms, inhabited by gila monsters and
coral snakes. Coyotes, turkeys, and javelinas are commonly seen. Black bears
and mountain lions are more reclusive, but chances are they've seen you
first from the security of a high rock ledge or dark thicket.

So, as you explore the world's first wilderness, think of it as gigantic
patchwork of virtually unlimited forest types, climatic conditions, and topography. As an alert hiker you'll thrill to the discovery of something new
around every bend in the canyon or trail.

HUMAN HISTORY OF THE GILA

The Gila area has been the scene of human activity for only a few centuries. Paleo-Indians traveled across the mesas and along the river valleys in
their nomadic pattern of life. Hunters sought game and found refuge in
large alcoves. The Mogollon migrated to the West Fork in the 1200s, perhaps fleeing from enemies or famine. A small group built their dwellings
high on canyon walls and raised crops in the river valleys. Their residence
was temporary, but extraordinary dwellings remain to impress us with their
elaborate engineering and construction skills.

Later groups of Native Americans, most notably the Apache, hunted and
fished in the Gila region for centuries, but left no permanent trace of their
presence. Much of the nineteenth-century traffic in the Gila consisted of
Army attempts to eradicate the Apache and their leaders, Victorio and
Geronimo. Names from this era remain in the wilderness today (Lookout
Mountain, Prior, McKenna, Cooney), as does the military trail, built to supply Army posts.

In the homestead era of the early twentieth century, intrepid settlers found
the Gila lands inviting. The short growing season and the lack of transporta-
tion to markets limited their success. All you find now are traces of their
cabins, or their names. Nat Straw Canyon, Lilley Park, and the Trotter Trail
represent some of the heritage preserved by place names. Ben Lilley, for
example, had the dubious distinction of being the Southwest's leading exter-
minator of bears and mountain lions. Miners came also, but found few riches
outside of Mogollon. Evidence of their activities remain on the trail to Windy
Gap, and on the Golden Link Trail on Dry Creek. The Catwalk itself is an
artifact of the mining era.

Ranching remains a dominant commercial activity in the Gila region.
Grazing is permitted in the wilderness where it existed before designation.
Cattle can be found in the eastern and northeastern sections of the Gila on
the ranchers' grazing allotments. Elsewhere, you frequently come across
corrals and stock ponds, dating back 80 years and more. And word has it
that there are rogue cattle roaming wild in the remote canyons of the lower
Gila, still avoiding capture after decades of freedom. In fact, one of the side
canyons along this stretch of the Gila River is aptly named "Wild Cow
Canyon."

5

Hiking in the Gila

The Gila Wilderness has steep, rugged mountains, rough, deep canyons, flat mesas, and rushing mountain streams. The elevation of the Gila ranges from 4,800 feet on the lower Gila River to 10,895 feet on Whitewater Baldy. Water is a primary concern when planning a trip in this exciting country. There's often either too much of it, or not enough.

Hikes along river corridors, specifically the Forks of the Whitewater, the Forks of the Gila, the Gila and Mogollon Creeks involve many wet-foot crossings. Flash flooding is a danger in the summer rainy season or during spring runoff if there's a good snowpack in the high country. Before embarking on any trip along the Gila's main streams, check with the USDA Forest Service office in Glenwood (for Whitewater Creek) or the Gila Visitor Center (the Gila River and its forks) for current and anticipated water levels.

The scarcity of water seriously limits your itinerary away from the rivers. Don't be fooled by the springs and stock ponds that appear on Forest Service maps or USGS topographic maps. Not all springs are reliable, and most stock ponds are too muddy and mucky for human use. Check with the Forest Service district office in Glenwood or the Gila Visitor Center for the current status of springs you are counting on.

CLIMATE AND WEATHER

The temperature and precipitation graphs are useful for planning your trip to the Gila. Notice that the data were gathered at Gila Hot Springs. On the

Climatic Data The temperatures shown are averages for Gila Hot Springs (Elevation 5,616'). Most of the areas you will travel through will probably be much higher in elevation and therefore cooler. Frost often occurs at higher elevations during the summer months. Always be prepared for the unexpected.

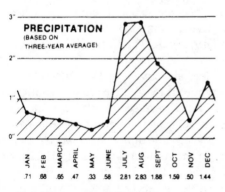

Gila Wilderness Map (1984) USFS

Mogollon Crest, it may be 15 degrees or more cooler, especially at night. Regardless of elevation, nights are cool throughout the Gila, even in the summer. Up-to-the-minute weather reports are located at www.weather.com. Also consult Falcon Publishing's book *Reading Weather*.

From July through August, you can expect to experience nearly 3 feet of rain. Flash flooding, lightning, and wildfires are also dangers during July and August. You need to know how to deal with these potential dangers.

September through November is a delightful time of year in the Gila, with lower precipitation, warms days and cool nights, and spectacular fall colors on the aspen slopes and along the river corridors. Hunting season brings a lot of backcountry users. It is wise to wear hunter's orange if hiking then. Make sure your pets are properly attired, too.

Winters are mild in the Gila corridor, often in the 50's and 60's during the day, but dropping to below 20 degrees F at night. Snowstorms can temporarily stop travel on New Mexico Highway 15 from Silver City. The forest roads north and east of the wilderness are not open or maintained until late in the spring.

March through June is prime time for visiting the Gila. Nights are still cold, especially in the higher country, but the warmer days are excellent for hiking, without insects and without many other hikers. The only concern is the impact of spring runoff on the rivers. The Forest Service can provide you with accurate information on daily river volumes.

June through July is the period of highest visitation. The size of the densely forested Gila, however, means you can still find wilderness solitude. Away from the Gila Cliff Dwellings National Monument or the Catwalk you are likely to be totally alone, even at the busiest season.

WILDERNESS MANAGEMENT

The Wilderness Ranger District manages most of the Gila Wilderness. The Glenwood District manages the smaller Mogollon Mountain region in the western end of the wilderness. To its credit, the Forest Service has adopted a relaxed management posture in the Gila Wilderness. For example, no permits or visitor registration is required. Several of the trailheads in the Glenwood District have voluntary sign-in sheets. For the most part, visitor management consists of random user contacts and educational information about minimum-impact hiking and camping at trailhead kiosks. This low-key management style is certainly conducive to maintaining the spontaneity of the wilderness experience. It is therefore even more important for hikers and other visitors to respect and help protect wilderness values in the Gila. For only in so doing will the wilderness and the freedom to enjoy it remain.

OVERVIEW OF RECREATIONAL USE

The Gila Wilderness is accessed by 58 trailheads that serve 658 miles of trails. Some of them have been abandoned, whereas others that haven't been maintained for years may as well be. The best current mileage estimate of open, maintained trails is about 500. In the early 1980s, visitor use information was collected from every Gila Wilderness trailhead. The practice has been discontinued, but some interesting visitor-use data were compiled in a 1985 study by Scott Steinberg titled, "Gila Wilderness Visitor Distribution and Use." According to the study, an astounding 51 percent of day use originated from only 5 of the 58 trailheads, 4 of which are within 2 miles of the Gila Cliff Dwellings National Monument. In contrast, 23 trailheads showed fewer than 100 visitor days per year. The average group size was three people, who stayed an average of 3.5 days. The high season of May, June, and July attracted 51 percent of the visitors. In contrast, only 0.3 percent of the annual visitation took place in January. So, solitude and snow seem to go together.

Gila Area Logistics

HOW TO GET THERE

The Gila is protected by its wilderness designation and its remote location. Silver City, the gateway city for the Gila, is about 160 miles northwest of El Paso, Texas, which has the nearest commercial airport. Tucson, Arizona, is 200 miles away, and Albuquerque, New Mexico, is about 250 miles from Silver City.

From Silver City to the Gila Visitor Center, it is a 2-hour drive on New Mexico Highway 15, a narrow, winding paved road through the Gila National Forest and over the Pinos Altos Mountains. Drivers of large motor homes are advised to approach the Gila corridor on NM 35 via Mimbres to avoid crossing the Pinos Altos Range on NM 15. On the western side of the wilderness, Glenwood, the gateway town for the Mogollon Mountain region, is an hour from Silver City on U.S. Highway 180. This highway is a major two-lane road.

The forest roads that border the wilderness on the north and east are improved gravel. Under normal conditions they are passable by passenger vehicles. The Bursum Road on the north is high enough to be snowbound and gated into June in some years. Even when the temperatures in the lower country are in the 70s, Silver Creek Divide can have heavy snow on the road. Forest Road 150 (North Star Mesa Road) on the east is also closed by snow, especially in its higher southern end where it crosses the Continental Divide. In early spring, erosion damage can make this road impassable until the road crew gets there. The mesa roads on the northwest (FR 141 and 142) are usually in good condition and are rough only in the few sections where they cross a drainage.

NEARBY SERVICES

Silver City (pop. 10,700) is a full-service city. Little towns around the Gila provide a variety of goods and services, but these are quite limited.

Glenwood: This small town has a café, a pizza parlor, and a tavern, which is also the liquor store. There are limited groceries at the general store at the gas station. The nearby motel sells showers and also has a laundromat. The Los Olmos guest ranch across the street from the gas station serves elegant meals at reasonable prices. Immediately north of town the Forest Service's Big Horn Campground (no fee) has a vault toilet and picnic tables. The Glenwood Ranger District Office is 0.25 mile south of town on US 180. Water is available there, along with information and maps.

Mogollon: On the Bursum Road, 6 miles east of US 180, the town of Mogollon is a lightly inhabited settlement. Formerly a thriving mining town in its heyday, it is now almost a ghost town.

New Mexico 35 to Lake Roberts: There are a couple of commercial establishments on the highway along Sapillo Creek near the southeastern edge of the Gila. The Grey Feather Motel at the NM 15/NM 35 intersection has a café and a gift shop. A general store at Lake Roberts offers a few groceries, beer, ice, and gas, unleaded regular and diesel. It also has pay phones and a mailbox.

Gila Hot Springs: About 40 miles north of Silver City, this tiny community has around 30 permanent residents. Doc Campbell's Trading Post, the local general store, bookstore, and museum, has been in the same family for over 60 years. It has a selection of canned and freeze-dried foods, ice, and milk, but carries no produce or beer. If you like a cold beer after a hike, you've got to bring it with you. Laundry facilities and showers are available at Campbell's. The only pay phone in the valley is on the front porch, along with the only mailbox. Only regular unleaded gas is sold at the store. Campbell's carries an impressive selection of books on the region's natural history, history, geology, and archeology.

There is no garbage collection in the Gila corridor. There are no trash containers at any of the trailheads, at the visitor center, or at the monument. Be prepared to carry your trash all the way home with you.

Lodging is available at a small motel or a bed and breakfast at Gila Hot Springs. The Forest Service campgrounds in the Gila corridor are currently no-fee facilities. The Scorpion campgrounds near the monument were former picnic areas; they have paved parking, flush toilets, water, and picnic tables. South of Gila Hot Springs, along the river, are the Grapevine and the Forks forest camps. The term "forest camp" is used to denote a no-fee site at which amenities are few. In this case they have vault toilets. Access roads to both are improved gravel, and neither has drinking water available. There are no prohibitions about camping on national forest land along the NM 15 corridor. Consult your wilderness map to verify the location of public land amid all the private inholdings in the river valley.

Campgrounds and forest camps: Forest Service campgrounds (or forest camps) are scattered around the perimeter of the Gila Wilderness. Except for the campgrounds at Lake Roberts and Snow Lake, these are no-fee sites. They do have pit toilets and, in some cases, picnic tables. Consult the Gila National Forest map for the location and facilities of these campgrounds and forest camps.

Safety and Preparedness

Statistically, your backcountry outing is safer than your drive to and from the trailhead. There are, however, hazards you need to be aware of in the Gila. If you are prepared, you will be much safer. The following "Treacherous Thirteen" are in no particular order.

Meningitis: The water in hot springs is the home of the amoeba *Naegleria fowleri*, which can enter your brain via mouth or nasal passages. Do not submerge your head or splash hot spring water on your face in order to avoid potential contamination.

Rattlesnakes: The Gila is home to several species of rattlers that may be out as early as April and as late as October. They are most active in the hot summer months. Do not sit or put your hands anywhere before looking. Use a walking stick to prod a trail covered with leaves or vegetation. Snakes are terrified of humans and will usually flee if you warn them of your approach. If you get bitten, seek help as quickly as possible. Use a venom extractor kit only when you are far from medical assistance.

Rabies: Stay away from any wild animal that behaves unnaturally. Friendly behavior is not normal and should be considered suspect. Control your pet so it won't tangle with a rabid wild animal, and make sure its shots are current before visiting the Gila.

Mountain lions: The Gila is outstanding habitat for mountain lions. This is their home and you are only a visitor. Avoid hiking at night when lions are often hunting. Instruct your children on appropriate behavior when confronted with a lion: Do not run. As a precaution, keep your children in sight.

Lightning: Especially during summer months, lightning is a very real hazard in the Gila. Stay off ridges and peaks when storms threaten. Seek shelter in dense woods, a grove of young trees, or a deep valley or canyon. Avoid large or lone trees. If caught in the open, discard any metal products—like your backpack—stay away from fences, and sit or lie down separately.

Wildfire: Fires are frequent in the Gila. If naturally ignited by lightning, wilderness fires are usually allowed to burn, unless they threaten structures or grow too huge. If you encounter a fire, stay upwind from the blaze. In mountainous terrain, fires tend to run uphill, so stay below a fire, out of its path. If a trailhead is closed by fire, sometimes the case in August, find an alternate route.

Poison ivy: This nasty plant is common in riparian areas. Be vigilant.

Stream crossings: Before embarking on any trip along the Gila's main streams, check with the Forest Service for water levels. Sturdy footwear is necessary for backpacking along Whitewater Creek, the Forks of the Gila, and the main Gila. Flimsy sandals are hazardous on the uneven slippery rocks of the swiftly flowing streams. A pair of lightweight hiking boots ("sacrifice boots") are best, worn both in the streams and on the trail between crossings. A sturdy walking stick is also handy for stability.

Hypothermia: Even in moderate temperatures, hypothermia is a danger. It results from a combination of exhaustion, moisture, and wind, which cool the body faster than it can replace the lost heat. These conditions can occur after a spill in a stream or on a mountain ridge in a summer storm. Symptoms include shivering, slurred speech, lack of coordination, drowsiness, and poor judgment. Keep an eye on your companions when hypothermic conditions exist; victims are unaware of their situation, denying that a problem exists. The solution is immediate warmth. Get the hypothermic hiker out of wet clothes and into something warm and dry, or into a sleeping bag. Seek shelter. Provide warm drinks and food.

Heat-related illness: Protect yourself from sun and heat with proper clothing. Avoid exertion during the hottest part of the day, especially if you are not yet acclimated to the heat. Seek shade. Drink plenty of water, both before and during your outing. Avoid alcoholic beverages when exercising in hot weather.

Flash floods: Warnings are posted in some slot canyons (Little Bear and Purgatory Chasm), but nearly all Gila canyons are potentially dangerous during the July–August thunderstorm season when several inches of rain can fall in a matter of hours. Don't schedule trips in narrow canyons when the danger is high. Camp only on high ground during the rainy season.

Water contamination: All natural water in the Gila should be treated by pumping or boiling or with iodine tablets. Don't jeopardize your trip by developing a debilitating case of diarrhea.

Hantavirus: Deer mice are carriers of this deadly disease. Don't stir up dust in areas where rodent droppings exist, such as old cabins. The virus is transmitted by inhaling the dust of mouse urine and droppings.

On a more cheerful note, there are several pointers that can improve the quality of your trip.

Trail etiquette: Horse parties have the right of way on the trail. It is easier for hikers to step off and allow livestock to pass than it is to reroute a bunch of half-ton animals. When livestock approaches, have your entire group step off the trail on the same side, preferably on the downhill side if there is a slope. If possible, shed your backpacks. Horses can be spooked by your unusually large silhouette. Do not attempt to pat passing horses, but do say something to the riders. The horses will realize that you are humans rather than scary monsters if you speak.

Downfall: When hiking, especially with only a day pack, help the Forest Service and your fellow travelers by flinging fallen branches off the trail where possible. Backcountry users cannot assume this service will be done for them.

Solitude: Whenever possible, camp away from other wilderness users. It is seldom the case that you need to camp close to anyone else. There's plenty of space in the Gila to allow for solitude.

Zero Impact

The Gila Wilderness is beautiful and primeval. Human visitors need to keep it that way. Travel lightly, leaving only footprints in your path.

Plan ahead: Have the appropriate maps, food, and equipment. Desperate hikers are usually not concerned with protecting the resource. If possible, avoid high-use areas and peak seasons. Keep your group small and your pack light. Overburdened hikers are less considerate about what they leave behind.

Prepare: Repackage food to reduce your trash load. What you don't consume you will be carrying out, with all the packaging material.

Toileting: Carry a trowel to bury human waste 6 to 8 inches deep. Toileting must be done 200 feet away from streams or any other body of water. If you are traveling in a canyon, try to get above the floodplain for your communion with nature. Pack out your used toilet paper and feminine hygiene products in zip-locked bags. Burning toilet paper is discouraged in the Gila due to fire danger.

Tread lightly: Stay on existing trails wherever possible. Avoid cutting switchbacks.

Camp lightly: If possible stay at an established campsite. Don't leave any traces of your stay on your site—no initials on trees, no cut or broken limbs, no trenches around tents.

Campfires: Open campfires are often prohibited in the Gila because of fire danger. Notices will be posted at trailheads if there is a fire restriction in effect. Use gas stoves when possible to reduce impact on the campsite. If you have a campfire, keep it small. Use only small, already downed branches. Do not cut down trees, even dead ones. The pesky Gila winds surge to life in the afternoon. Never leave a fire unattended. When you leave camp, douse your fire thoroughly and spread the dead embers. Finally, cover the cold embers with earth and naturalize the site. Remove any rock ring construction. These structures are ubiquitous in the Gila, and usually are large.

Protect the water: Water is a precious commodity for both humans and wildlife. Treat it accordingly. Never bathe or wash dishes directly in a water source. Move at least 100 feet away from springs and streams to do your washing. Food scraps and even biodegradable soaps pollute streams. Never throw garbage in streams.

Food: Carry all food and garbage out with you. Skunks, raccoons, and bears will dig up buried trash and learn to associate food with campsites, not a pleasant experience for later parties. Hang your food at night and whenever you are away from camp—10 feet off the ground and 4 feet away from the tree trunk. Always keep a clean camp.

Wildlife: Do not disturb or harass wildlife. If you hike with your dog, keep it under control at all times.

Pack out trash: If you packed it in, pack it out! All of it—cigarette butts, pop bottles, chewing gum, dental floss, fishing line, beer cans, candy and gum wrappers. Don't be a slob hiker. If your exit trailhead is in the Gila corridor, bring a trash bag for the drive home. There is no garbage service in the Gila River valley.

Artifacts: This is the big exception to the pack-it-out rule. Leave all historic and prehistoric artifacts in place. The federal Antiquities Act prohibits removal from federal land of any item more than 50 years old. Common courtesy also requires you to leave these treasures so your successors can enjoy the thrill of discovering them. The Austin Roberts Vista above Lake Roberts on NM 35 has a display of local artifacts, with an emphasis on their value when left untouched. These "whispers of the past" retain their spiritual value only if left in place.

The bottom line is to make your passage through wild country wholly invisible to your successors. Savor the beauty of the Gila, and leave it for others to enjoy. Wildness is a precious resource, in short supply, that will only endure with your help.

How to Use This Guidebook

The Gila Wilderness is huge, with well over a half-million acres of canyons, river valleys, mesas, and lofty peaks. Potential hikes are virtually unlimited, but we have put together trips in this book that are surely among the best. The descriptions of the 83 hikes presented here will prepare you for your exploration of the Gila. Following is some additional information to help you get the most out of this book.

All of the hikes presented here are complete, self-contained trips with essential information needed for the suggested route. Every hike begins and ends at one of 29 established national forest trailheads that can be driven to. The hikes are numbered in sequence, starting from the Sandy Point Trailhead and going counterclockwise completely around the Gila Wilderness, ending at the Willow Creek Trailhead. So, if you're basing your hike from a single trailhead, this book offers several good trip ideas for you to choose from or to combine in various ways as options. The two major topographic provinces of the Gila Wilderness are the Mogollon Range in the west end (Hikes 1 through 27) and the upper basin of the Gila River to the east (Hikes 28 through 83).

You'll find in the following pages many, but not all, of the best hikes in the Gila Wilderness. We wanted to save a few for you to discover, although every hike in this guide presents unforeseen wilderness discoveries.

TYPE OF HIKES

The three basic types of hikes are:

Out-and-back: Traveling to a specific destination or into a general region, then retracing your route back to the same trailhead.

Loop: In general, loop trips explore new country throughout all or most of the route by starting from and then circling back to the original trailhead. Loops include "lollypops" with an outer circle and hikes that end with a short walk on a road to get back to the trailhead. This type of hike also has a base camp at one location for several nights with long day hike loops.

Shuttle: A point-to-point hike that begins from one trailhead and ends at another. This may require shuttling a vehicle to the exit trailhead, having two vehicles (one left at the other end of the hike), or a prearranged pick-up at a designated time and place. Logistics can sometimes be simplified with a midtrip key exchange. When the trip is completed, the two parties drive each other's vehicles home.

DISTANCES

Distances in the Gila Wilderness tend to be underestimated on Forest Service trail signs, but not always. We used Forest Service distance estimates whenever we determined that they were accurate. In all cases, the total distance and key point mileage are our best field estimate. Distances are often less important than difficulty.

DIFFICULTY RATINGS

To help you select and plan your trip, hikes are rated as to difficulty. By necessity, these ratings are subjective and are only a general guide. The variables that determine actual difficulty at a given time on the ground are numerous and, well, variable. Here are some general definitions:

Easy: Anyone in reasonable condition can do easy hikes given enough time. These hikes generally have gentle grades. However, there may be short rocky sections and a few shallow stream crossings.

Moderate: These hikes are challenging to inexperienced wilderness travelers. The hike may have several stream crossings, steep pitches, and short sections where the trail is hard to follow. These hikes are suitable for hikers who have some experience and at least an average fitness level.

Strenuous: These hikes are suitable for experienced hikers with above average fitness. Frequent river crossings are likely along with steep trails, loose rock, and lots of elevation gain and loss. Some parts of the hike may be hard to follow, requiring route finding with a topo map and compass.

BEST MONTHS

The "best" time for a particular hike, from the standpoint of comfortable hiking conditions, is as variable as Gila weather. Typically, the beginning and ending months are marginal transition periods in terms of weather. Be sure to check local conditions prior to your trip.

MAPS

Please keep in mind that the maps in this book are general schematics designed to get you to the trailhead and give you a good visual impression of the route. You need to take along more detailed maps for the actual hike, as indicated in the map information block. See Appendix A for ordering information.

SPECIAL CONSIDERATIONS

These are "red flags" that could be troublesome, but not necessarily hazardous. The information presented is important to consider before embarking on the hike.

KEY POINTS

These are usually trail junctions or key natural features that will confirm your location and serve as an indicator of your progress during the hike.

ELEVATION PROFILES

Elevation profile graphs are provided for each hike. The graphs approximate the vertical ups and downs in relation to the distance between key points. They show major elevation changes along the route. Because of scale limitations, small changes, especially those less than 200 feet, may not show up on the graphs.

"...the wilderness is the one thing on earth which was furnished complete and perfect."

Aldo Leopold, Outdoor Life, *November 1925*
"A Plea for Wilderness Hunting Grounds"

Gila Wilderness Hike Finder

	EASY	MODERATE	STRENUOUS
Short Day Hikes (up to 6 miles)	9 The Catwalk 22 Rain Creek	41 Gila Forks 42 Gila River Hot Springs 44 Little Creek 49 Grudging Grave 50 Cliff Dwelling 52 Adobe Canyon 54 Middle Fork Hot Springs 61 SA Canyon 66 Purgatory Chasm 68 Caves 70 UpperBlack Canyon 76 Sam Martin Spring	

Long Day Hikes (over 6 miles)	28 Lower Gila River
	82 Iron Creek
		1 Whitewater Baldy
		5 Redstone Park
		7 Deloche Canyon
		20 Windy Gap
		24 Bud's Hole
		30 Turkey Creek Hot
		    Springs
		53 Jordan Hot Springs
		64 Military Trail
		65 Gila Flat
		67 Rocky Canyon
		70 Upper Black Canyon
		71 Trails End-Whiterocks
		    Loop
		73 Black Mountain
		74 Black Mountain–
		    Christie
		79 Trotter
		81 Gilita Creek
			12 South Fork Whitewater
			17 Skunk Johnson Cabin
			19 Holt Mountain
			27 Mogollon–Rain Creek
			35 Sheep Corral Canyon
			36 Sapillo Box
			55 Whiterocks
			62 Lower Black Canyon
			69 Big Timber Canyon
			75 Black Mountain–Indian
			    Creek

Shorter backpacks (up to 6 days)	78 Aeroplane Mesa
	82 Iron Creek
		2 Mogollon Crest
		5 Redstone Park
		14 Catwalk–Deloche
		    Canyon
		15 Catwalk–Redstone
		43 Murdocks Hole
		47 Granite Peak
		53 Jordan Hot Springs
		72 Trails End–Middle Fork
		79 Trotter
		80 Snow Lake–Willow
		    Creek
			3 Hummingbird–Willow
			    Creek
			4 Sandy Point–Sheridan
			8 Grouse Mountain Loop
			12 South Fork Whitewater
			13 Nabours Mountain
			16 Catwalk–Sandy Point
			17 Skunk Johnson Cabin
			18 Sheridan-Catwalk
			21 Apache Cabin
			23 Snow Park
			25 Trail–Gobbler Loop
			26 Mogollon–McKenna
			    Loop
			27 Mogollon–Rain Creek
			33 Turkey–Little Spring
			34 Turkey Creek–Little
			    Turkey Park
			37 Sapillo–Gila Bridge
			38 Sapillo–Lower Gila

	EASY	MODERATE	STRENUOUS
Shorter backpacks (up to 6 days)— continued			48 Little Creek–White Creek Flat Loop 56 Little Bear Canyon Loop 57 Meadows–Big Bear Loop 63 Grapevine to Middle Fork 77 The Meadows 83 Jerky Mountains Loop
Longer backpacks (more than 6 days)			10 Whitewater Loop 11 Whitewater–Dry Creek Loop 29 Gila River 31 Turkey–Mogollon Loop 32 Turkey–Gila Loop 51 West Fork–Willow Creek 58 Meadows–Hells Hole Loop 59 The Forks via Trotter 60 Middle Fork–Gilita
Mountain peaks and high ridges		1 Whitewater Baldy 2 Mogollon Crest 20 Windy Gap 47 Granite Peak 73 Black Mountain 74 Black Mountain–Christie	6 Redstone–Baldy Loop 8 Grouse Mountain Loop 19 Holt Mountain 23 Snow Park 31 Turkey–Mogollon Loop 75 Black Mountain–Indian Creek 83 Jerky Mountains Loop
Hot springs	54 Middle Fork Hot Springs	30 Turkey Creek Hot Springs 42 Gila River Hot Springs 53 Jordan Hot Springs	
Cultural and historical sites	9 The Catwalk 28 Lower Gila River 49 Grudging Grave 50 Cliff Dwelling	2 Mogollon Crest 20 Windy Gap 39 Alum Camp 79 Trotter	11 Whitewater–Dry Creek Loop 12 South Fork Whitewater 17 Skunk Johnson Cabin 21 Apache Cabin 29 Gila River 80 Snow Lake–Willow Creek
Deep narrow canyons	9 The Catwalk 66 Purgatory Chasm	14 Catwalk–Deloche Canyon 15 Catwalk–Redstone 53 Jordan Hot Springs	12 South Fork Whitewater 36 Sapillo Box 48 Little Creek–White Creek Flat Loop 51 West Fork–Willow Creek 56 Little Bear Canyon Loop 57 Meadows–Big Bear Loop 58 Meadows–Hells Hole Loop 59 The Forks via Trotter 60 Middle Fork–Gilita

	EASY	MODERATE	STRENUOUS
Big river canyons	28 Lower Gila River	43 Murdocks Hole 71 Trails End–Whiterocks Loop 72 Trails End–Middle Fork	29 Gila River 32 Turkey–Gila Loop 37 Sapillo–Gila Bridge 38 Sapillo–Lower Gila 63 Grapevine–Middle Fork
Ponderosa parks and meadows	44 Little Creek 82 Iron Creek	47 Granite Peak	23 Snow Park 26 Mogollon–McKenna Loop 48 Little Creek–White Creek Flat Loop 80 Snow Lake–Willow Creek
Dry-foot hikes	9 The Catwalk 22 Rain Creek 44 Little Creek 52 Adobe Canyon 66 Purgatory Chasm 68 Caves 82 Iron Creek	1 Whitewater Baldy 2 Mogollon Crest 20 Windy Gap 65 Gila Flat 73 Black Mountain 74 Black Mountain–Christie	4 Sandy Point–Sheridan 19 Holt Mountain 67 Rocky Canyon 69 Big Timber Canyon 75 Black Mountain–Indian Creek

1 Whitewater Baldy

Highlights:	Vistas of Whitewater Canyon and Mogollon Mountains from crest ridge, ascent of highest peak in the Gila Wilderness.
Type of hike:	Out-and-back day hike, or 1-night backpacking trip.
Total distance:	12 miles.
Difficulty:	Moderate.
Best months:	May through October.
Maps:	Forest Service Gila Wilderness map (1984); Grouse Mountain USGS quad.

Special considerations: Bursum Road often remains closed by snow into May. Dry trail; springs at 1.8 miles (Bead Spring) and 5.2 miles (Hummingbird Saddle).

Finding the trailhead: To reach the Sandy Point trailhead, drive 4 miles north of Glenwood on U.S. Highway 180. Turn right (east) on New Mexico Highway 159, also known as Bursum Road, toward Mogollon. NM 159 changes from pavement to improved gravel after 9 miles. Drive east 22 miles to Sandy Point Trailhead. Bursum Road is closed in the winter and often remains snow-blocked into May.

Parking and trailhead facilities: There is a large gravel parking area right on Bursum Road. There are no other facilities and no water. There is an information board and a registry at the trailhead. Camping is permitted, but a more comfortable site is located a mile east on Bursum Road at the Bursum Forest Camp (no fee, no water, no facilities).

Key points:
0.0 Sandy Point Trailhead for Crest Trail 182.
1.9 Side trail to Bead Spring.
5.0 Hummingbird Saddle and junction with Trail 207.
     (0.2 mile down Trail 207 to Hummingbird Spring)
6.0 Summit of Whitewater Baldy.

The hike: This is a popular trail into the Mogollon Mountains, used by hikers in the spring and summer and by hunters in the fall. From the high-elevation trailhead (9,132 feet) the highest peak in the Gila is only 1,693 feet higher. There is moderate use on the Crest Trail.

From the Sandy Point trailhead, the trail climbs steadily to the signed wilderness boundary, and on to the signed Bead Spring junction. Descend 0.1 mile on the Bead Spring Trail to the east to the spring, which provides a scenic resting spot after the initial rocky section of the journey. The bubbling spring supports lush ferns and mosses as it cascades down to Willow Creek. As always, pump or treat your water. There is plenty of horse use at Bead Spring. If you feel like exploring further, the Bead Spring Tail winds on

Whitewater Baldy

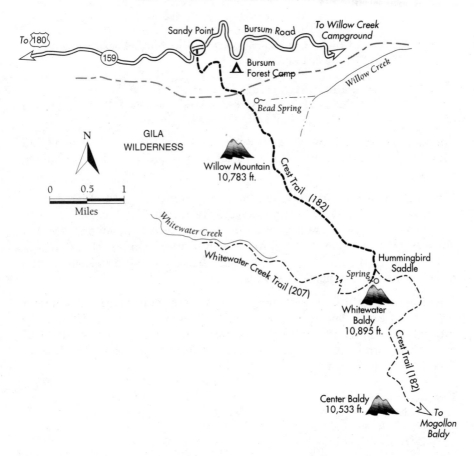

GILA NATIONAL FOREST

To 180

159

Sandy Point

Bursum Road

To Willow Creek Campground

Bursum Forest Camp

Willow Creek

Bead Spring

N

GILA WILDERNESS

0   0.5   1
Miles

Willow Mountain
10,783 ft.

Crest Trail (182)

Whitewater Creek

Whitewater Creek Trail (207)

Spring

Hummingbird Saddle

Whitewater Baldy
10,895 ft.

Crest Trail (182)

Center Baldy
10,533 ft.

To Mogollon Baldy

down the hillside, eventually getting lost in the marshy valley. Horses do better than hikers.

Back on the Crest Trail, continue south. Snowbanks linger late in the spring on the north slopes, shaded by dense ponderosa pine and Douglas-fir. This is windy country, so you can also expect blowdown on the trail in the early spring. The pine-fir forest, with patches of aspen marking sites of old forest fires, is especially vulnerable to gusts along the ridge between Willow Mountain and Whitewater Baldy.

A side trip up Willow Mountain (10,783 feet) is tempting. Be warned that the going is tough. Jackstrawed trunks obstruct travel and snowbanks linger into June. The rounded top of Willow is heavily forested and doesn't permit much of a view.

On past Willow, the Crest Trail climbs steadily through wind-dwarfed

Hiking in Hummingbird Saddle with lingering snowbanks in June.

aspen, periodically breaking into small meadows. The openings here provide sweeping views to the west into Whitewater Creek country. The trail is periodically very rocky due to erosion on its steeper sections. After traversing patches of dog-hair fir, the trail switchbacks down to Hummingbird Saddle on a very rocky segment.

There are excellent campsites in the saddle area. Hummingbird Spring is a little over 0.2 mile southwest of the saddle via Trail 207, the Whitewater Trail. The trail junction of 182 and 207 is marked with a bizarre red metal ladder, as well as a trail sign.

For the hike up Whitewater Baldy, go straight south of the saddle, following the mountain's north ridgeline. Faint game trails lead to the rounded, forested mountaintop. There's a huge pyramidal cairn on the southern edge of the summit, but the dense spruce forest blocks any view from the spot. To remedy this problem, follow the rough-use trail that drops to the cliffs on the southeastern edge of the peak, about 0.1 mile beyond the cairn. Here's the mountain's bald spot. Perch on the volcanic outcropping and watch for golden eagles soaring above the slopes. From this aerie you have a sweeping view of the Mogollon Range of the Gila and much of southwestern New Mexico. Return by the same trail, either to your campsite at the saddle or back to the Sandy Point Trailhead.

2 Mogollon Crest

Highlights:	The crest of the Mogollon Mountains, spectacular vistas; the three highest peaks in the Gila Wilderness.
Type of hike:	3- to 4-day backpacking trip, out-and-back.
Total distance:	24 miles.
Difficulty:	Moderate.
Best months:	May through November (depending on snow).
Maps:	Forest Service Gila Wilderness map (1984); Grouse Mountain and Mogollon Baldy Peak USGS quads.

Special considerations: Bursum Road often remains closed with snow into May. Limited water at springs on the crest (Bead Spring, 1.8 miles; Hummingbird Saddle, 5.2 miles; Hobo, 9 miles; Little Hobo, 9.3 miles; West Fork Saddle, 10 miles; Blacktail, 11.2 miles). High elevation means exposure to storms and lightning, and the risk of hypothermia.

Finding the trailhead: To reach the Sandy Point Trailhead, drive 4 miles north of Glenwood on U.S. Highway 180. Turn right (east) on New Mexico 159, also known as the Bursum Road, toward Mogollon. New Mexico Highway 159 changes from paved to improved gravel after 9 miles. Drive east 22 miles to the Sandy Point Trailhead. Bursum Road is closed in the winter.

Parking and trailhead facilities: There is a large gravel parking area right on the road. There are no other facilities, and no water. Camping is permitted, although the site is not ideal. Bursum Forest Camp, a primitive no-fee area, is a mile east on Bursum Road.

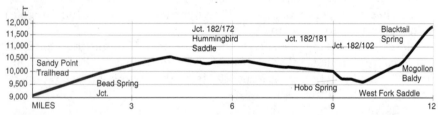

Key points:
- 0.0   Trailhead on Bursum Road at Sandy Point; Trail 182.
- 1.9   Bead Spring turnoff.
- 5.0   Hummingbird Saddle and Hummingbird Spring, 0.2 mile off trail and side trip to Whitewater Baldy.
- 6.0   Junction with Iron Creek Lake Trail (172).
- 7.8   Junction with Holt–Apache Trail (181) and optional side trip to Center Baldy.
- 9.0   Junction with Turkeyfeather Mountain Trail (102).
- 9.4   Hobo Spring.
- 9.7   Little Hobo Spring.
- 10.0   West Fork Saddle; junction with West Fork Mogollon Creek Trail (224); spring.
- 11.2   Trail to Blacktail Spring.
- 12.0   Mogollon Baldy Guard Station and Lookout.

Mogollon Crest

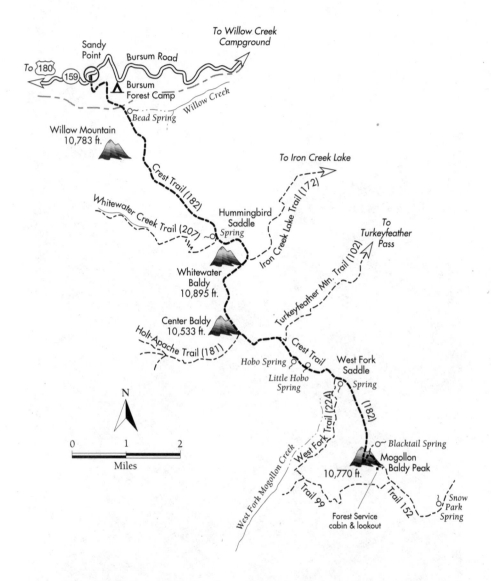

The hike: This is a popular route into the high country of the Mogollon Mountains. The Crest Trail (182), has moderate use, with hikers in the summer and hunters in the fall. The views are magnificent. The peaks of the three baldies (Whitewater, Center, and Mogollon) are short walk-ups. The drive to the trailhead allows your vehicle to do the work of gaining elevation to this high mountain country.

From the trailhead on Bursum Road, the Crest Trail climbs quickly to 10,000 feet and contours around Willow Mountain's northwest flank. Here

Packing up in the fog at Hummingbird Saddle.

you can expect snowbanks to linger into spring. You may also find frequent fallen trees across the trail. The Forest Service suggests that early season horse parties carry axes and crosscut saws. Hikers are expected to be more agile. The steeper sections of the trail to Hummingbird Saddle are quite rocky due to erosion.

After passing Willow Mountain the trail breaks into a saddle at 10,500 feet with wind-stunted aspens and periodic views of Whitewater Canyon stretching to the west. Continue southeast to another dense north-slope forest of pine and fir before arriving at another vista point in a meadow (10,400 feet) with a sweeping view of Whitewater Baldy to the south. After cresting at 10,510 feet the rocky trail switchbacks down to Hummingbird Saddle.

There are plentiful campsites at the saddle, in the open as well as in the timber on the east and west, so there's protection depending on the wind's direction. The spring is 0.2 mile down the Whitewater Trail (207) from the junction in the saddle, which is marked with an odd red metal sculpture of two stacked Z's. Follow the Whitewater Trail, sloping to the west through the aspen to the spring. An evening ascent of Whitewater Baldy (10,895 feet), just south of the saddle, is a perfect end to the day (see Hike 1 for details).

From Hummingbird Saddle, the Crest Trail drops gently through a spruce-fir forest for about 0.9 mile to the signed junction with the Iron Creek Lake Trail (172) in a grassy park on the east slope of Whitewater Baldy. This is an easy segment of the Crest Trail; the only obstacle may be snowdrifts, which we encountered in early June of a good snow year.

From the Iron Creek Lake junction, the Crest Trail rises and falls gently though the dense spruce-fir forest, with aspen groves marking sites of ancient forest fires. The well-blazed trail winds along the crest to the junction with the Holt–Apache Trail (181). Center Baldy lies to the southwest of this junction. It is an easy walk to the summit (10,535 feet) from Trail 181, a short detour from your route. Take the Holt–Apache Trail for 0.3 mile southwest to an open saddle where a faint-use trail on the right leads to the grassy opening of Center Baldy. From this viewpoint you can see the Gila mountains and valleys in all directions.

Back on the Crest Trail, the route descends to the junction with the Turkeyfeather Mountain Trail (102) just below an ancient grove of huge Douglas-fir. The Crest Trail continues to descend to Hobo Spring at 9,700 feet. The spring is a mere trickle. In most years drinking water can be pumped from a small pool. A modest campsite is perched on the downhill side of the spring in a Douglas-fir and aspen forest. With another tent site above the trail there would be space at the spring for up to four small tents. Downslope is a rocky outcropping from which you can enjoy a grand view of the West Fork of Mogollon Creek, where Gila trout have been recently restocked. Aspen, gnarly snags, and volcanic mounds add to the photogenic qualities of the site.

Continuing toward the lookout you reach Little Hobo Spring in 0.3 mile. It's a signed trickle nestled in the aspen, right on the trail. Located on a steep slope, Little Hobo offers no campsites.

At the West Fork Saddle, 0.3 mile farther, is the junction with Trail 224 from the West Fork of Mogollon Creek. Right in the saddle is a spacious, flat campsite, with a spring nearby. This is a good spot to establish a base camp from which to embark on an out-and-back day hike of Mogollon Baldy.

From the West Fork saddle, it's a steady climb to the peak. You gain 1,150 feet in about 2 miles. Steeply ascending Baldy's ridge from the West Fork Saddle, the trail gets to 10,240 feet in a mile, where it reaches the burned area. This section of the journey is made even more challenging due to the devastating 1996 fire that obliterated the forest on the dry west-facing slope, leaving shaggy brush and lots of loose rock.

A signed path to the left (east) leads to Blacktail Spring, which sits on the eastern side of Mogollon Baldy, 1 mile north of the lookout. The main trail climbs another 0.8 mile to the grassy rounded apex of Mogollon Baldy, site of a historic guard cabin and lookout. The cabin was built in 1923 and the tower in 1948. Unfortunately the practice of tying horses directly to trees next to the cabin has impacted the site with barren rings and exposed roots around the junipers. The 1996 fire was started by lightning and went on to burn 15,000 acres in the wilderness. The lookout was evacuated. Usually lookouts are in residence from May through August. Rain-fed cisterns supply the water for the lookout staff; there is a stern warning posted at that cabin that the water is not for public use, so don't ask. Also there is no camping permitted in the vicinity of the lookout.

On a clear day you can get an incredible view from the bald peak of the entire Gila, as well as most of southwest New Mexico. After enjoying this lofty experience, saunter back to your camp and retrace your steps to the Bursum Road Trailhead.

Option: To extend your backpack, you can easily drop on over the top of Mogollon Baldy into Snow Park, 1.5 miles to the south. There is a spring on the eastern side of the park with water even in dry years. Campsites are plentiful in the vicinity of the spring.

3   Hummingbird–Willow Creek

Highlights:	Start in the Mogollon Mountains, in the Gila highlands, and end at Willow Creek, in the Middle Fork drainage.
Type of hike:	3-day backpacking trip, shuttle.
Total distance:	23 miles.
Difficulty:	Strenuous.
Best months:	May through November, depending on snow.
Maps:	Forest Service Gila Wilderness map (1984); Grouse Mountain, Loco Mountain, and Negrito Mountain USGS quads.

Special considerations: Bursum Road is often closed by snow into May. Dangers of storms and lightning on peaks and ridges during July and August. Dry stretch of 11.5 miles across Turkeyfeather Mountain.

Finding the trailheads: To reach Sandy Point, the entering trailhead, drive 4 miles north of Glenwood on U.S. Highway 180. Turn right (east) on New Mexico Highway 159, also known as the Bursum Road, toward Mogollon. NM 159 changes from paved to improved gravel after 9 miles. Drive east 22 miles to the Sandy Point Trailhead. Bursum Road is closed in the winter, and often remains snow-blocked into May.

To reach Willow Creek, the exit trailhead, continue east on the Bursum Road another 7.5 miles to the Willow Creek Recreation Area. Turn in and drive past the Willow Creek Campground to the Iron Creek Lake Trail (151). Length of car shuttle is 8 miles, all on improved gravel road.

Parking and trailhead facilities: At Sandy Point, there is a large gravel parking area, a trailhead information board and registry, but no other facilities. At Willow Creek is a large grassy parking area and a vault toilet. Water is available in Willow Creek (to be treated, of course). Camping is permitted at both trailheads, but the terrain at Willow Creek is more suitable, and there's a nearby campground.

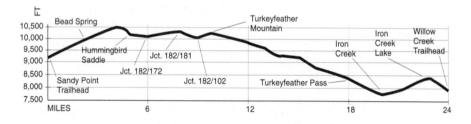

Key points:
- 0.0   Sandy Point Trailhead on Bursum Road of Crest Trail (182).
- 1.9   Trail to Bead Spring.
- 5.0   Hummingbird Saddle.
- 5.9   Junction with Iron Creek Lake Trail (172).
- 7.8   Junction with Holt–Apache Trail (181).
- 9.0   Junction with Turkeyfeather Mountain Trail (102).
- 18.0   Turkeyfeather Pass; junction with West Fork Trail (151).
- 20.0   Iron Creek; junction with Cooper Clayton Trail (141).
- 22.8   Junction with Iron Creek Mesa Trail (171).
- 23.0   Iron Creek Lake.
- 23.1   Junction with Iron Creek Lake Trail (172).
- 24.0   Willow Creek Trailhead.

The hike: This shuttle hike involves a very short car shuttle distance (8 miles). Another positive feature is that the Willow Creek campground is an attractive area for your pick-up party to await your arrival after dropping you off at the Sandy Point Trailhead.

From the heights of the Mogollon Crest you descend the long ridge of

Hummingbird–Willow Creek

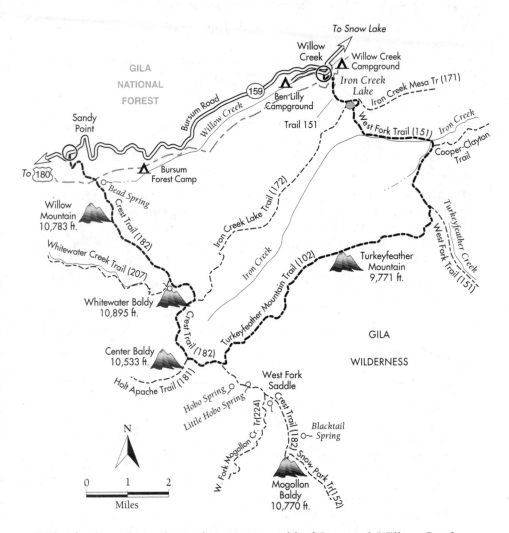

Turkeyfeather Mountain to the wetter world of Iron and Willow Creeks, traveling from an alpine to a riparian ecosystem. While the final 5 miles have plenty of water, water availability is a concern for the rest of the hike. In the high country, your water sources are springs (Bead, Hummingbird, and Hobo) with varying water flows.

From the Sandy Point Trailhead, the Crest Trail climbs steeply, rising 700 feet in the first 1.5 miles on a wide, rocky trail. This entrance to the Gila Wilderness gets moderate use by hikers and hunters. The wilderness boundary is at 1.5 miles. Bead Spring is off the Crest Trail on a side trail to the east (left), 0.1 mile and about 40 feet below the trail. Beyond the spring the Crest Trail levels out more on the east side of Willow Mountain in a dense ponderosa pine–Douglas-fir forest. At the saddle at 3.4 miles, you'll enjoy your first view of Whitewater Creek extending to the west. After a respite at the saddle the trail resumes its climb. A second vista point is reached at 4 miles, with a great view of Whitewater Baldy. The rocky trail goes up to a high point at 10,510 feet through wind-distorted aspen before zigzagging down to Hummingbird Saddle and the junction with Whitewater Creek Trail (207). Follow the Whitewater Creek Trail 0.2 mile to the spring in the aspen thicket on the west side of the saddle. There are many campsites at the saddle. This is also the take-off point for the optional ascent of Whitewater Baldy, the highest peak in the Gila (10,895 feet; see Hike 1).

The hike continues south on the Crest Trail, wrapping around Baldy and meeting the Iron Creek Lake Trail (172) on its shady eastern flank. South of the peak the trail resumes its undulations along the crest of the range to the junction with the Holt–Apache Trail (181) below Center Baldy. From here it's only 0.4 mile to the top of Center Baldy for an optional side trip (see Hike 10).

Continue south on the Crest Trail to the junction with the Turkeyfeather Mountain Trail (102), which takes off sharply up the hill on your left 1.2 miles farther. Hobo Spring lies less than half a mile beyond this turn, so filling water containers there is a wise move. The distance to Turkeyfeather Pass is a bit farther than the sign indicates. There is no water on the route until you get a mile down Cooper Canyon, at least 10 miles away, or in Iron Creek, a mile farther.

With full water bottles you're ready for the journey across Turkeyfeather Mountain. The trail leads you to the high point of the mountain in the first mile, with a steep climb to 10,400 feet. Intermittent openings in the woods or rock outcroppings provide opportunities for pausing to enjoy the view. The Turkeyfeather Trail winds along the forested crest of the mountain, which is a dominant feature of the central Gila skyline. The final 4 miles of the trip are a gentle descent to the towering pines in the park at Turkeyfeather Pass and the junction with the West Fork Trail (151).

There is no water at the pass. Turn left (northwest) on the West Fork Trail to Iron Creek and the Willow Creek Trailhead. The West Fork Trail drops into Cooper Canyon, following its rocky gorge down to Iron Creek and the junction with Cooper Clayton Trail (141) at the confluence of Cooper and Iron Creeks. There are campsites both at the junction and also along Iron Creek after the stream crossing.

The West Fork Trail follows Iron Creek upstream on its sunny north bank. The open ponderosa park along this side of the stream contrasts sharply with the dark, dense forest of spruce and fir, draped with moss, on the less-sunny south side. Iron Creek supports a vibrant population of endangered Gila trout, reintroduced by New Mexico Fish and Game, so it is closed to fishing. At 1.7 miles from the crossing, the trail leaves the creek and climbs along the slope of a ravine to the ridge east of Iron Creek Lake. After the junction with the Iron Creek Mesa Trail (171) to the Middle Fork, stay left to the lake, a rather muddy former stock pond, not suitable for pumping. On the west side of the lake is the junction with the Iron Creek Lake Trail (172) which you met up on the side of Whitewater Baldy. Continue on the West Fork Trail another mile, descending to the Willow Creek trailhead and campground.

Options: In addition to Whitewater Baldy and Center Baldy, you can include an outing to Mogollon Baldy on the route. Camp at Hobo Spring and do it as a day hike (see Hike 2). For a shorter trip, you can take the Iron Creek Lake Trail (172) from Whitewater Baldy to the lake, making it a one-night backpacking trip of 17 miles. Carry extra water on the long dry stretch to Iron Creek Lake because there's no water until you arrive at the Willow Creek Trailhead.

4   Sandy Point–Sheridan

Highlights:	The crest of the Mogollon Range, spectacular vistas; a diverse cross-section of the Gila Wilderness from the highest peaks to lower elevation streams and woodlands.
Type of hike:	3- to 4-day backpacking trip, shuttle.
Total distance:	23.2 miles.
Difficulty:	Strenuous.
Best months:	May through November (depending on snow).
Maps:	Forest Service Gila Wilderness map (1984); Grouse Mountain and Holt Mountain USGS quads.

Special considerations: Sandy Point Trailhead on Bursum Road may be inaccessible due to snow into May or early June. Limited water at springs along the crest. Exposure to possible storms, lightning, and hypothermia on high ridge segments of hike. Two miles of Holt–Apache Trail (181) are extremely steep, rough, and primitive in upper Sheridan Gulch.

Finding the trailheads: Sandy Point Trailhead: Drive 4 miles north of Glenwood on U.S. Highway 180. Turn right (east) on New Mexico Highway 159 (also known as Bursum Road) toward Mogollon. NM 159 changes from paved to improved gravel after 9 miles. Continue east another 13 miles to the trailhead. Bursum Road is closed during winter and may be blocked by snow into June. Check locally. Sheridan Corral (exit) Trailhead: Drive 8 miles south of Glenwood on US 180 to Forest Road 146, which is signed for hiking trail 181. Turn left (east) and continue 4 miles on the improved gravel road to the signed end-of-road trailhead.

The driving distance between the two trailheads is approximately 39 miles, 26 of which are paved.

Parking and trailhead facilities: Sandy Point: The only facilities are a kiosk and large gravel parking area. There is no water at the trailhead, and camping is marginal. The primitive no-fee Bursum Forest Camp is a mile east on Bursum Road.

Sheridan Corral: A large sloping gravel parking area and kiosk with no water and only limited campsites are at the trailhead. There are several flat campsites 0.3 mile back down FR 146 at the Sheridan Corral stock tank.

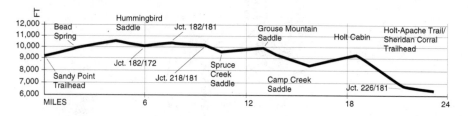

Key points:

0.0	Trailhead on Bursum Road at Sandy Point; Crest Trail (182).
1.9	Bead Spring turnoff.
5.0	Hummingbird Saddle and Hummingbird Spring, 0.2 mile off trail and optional side trip to Whitewater Baldy.
6.0	Junction with Iron Creek Lake Trail (172).
7.8	Junction with Holt–Apache Trail (181) and optional side trip to Center Baldy.
8.6	Saddle at start of abandoned Rain Creek Trail.
9.2	Junction with Little Dry Trail (180) and sign for Trails 218, 182, and 206.
9.4	Junction with Golden Link Trail (218).
9.8	Black Mountain Spring.
10.5	Spruce Creek Saddle and junction with Redstone Trail (206).
13.0	Junction with Grouse Mountain Trail (781) and optional side trip to Grouse Mountain.
13.6	Junction with Nabours Spring Trail.
13.7	Spider Saddle and junction with Winn Canyon Trail (179).
14.0	Junction with East Fork Whitewater Trail (213).
15.7	Camp Creek Saddle and junction with Golden Link Trail (218) and South Fork Whitewater Trail (212).
18.5	Holt Cabin and junction with Holt Gulch Trail (217).
21.2	Junction with Skunk Johnson Cabin Trail (226), which is shown as Trail 225 on the Gila Wilderness map.
23.2	Sheridan Corral Trailhead at end of FR 146.

The hike: This north-to-south traverse of the high west end of the Gila Wilderness provides a superb sample of the country, from the loftiest peaks to brushy woodlands more than 4,000 feet below. With much of the elevation already gained on the Bursum Road, the moderately used Crest Trail (182) from Sandy Point is a popular route into the high, forested country of the Mogollon Range. Short walk-ups to the top of two of the three baldies (Whitewater and Center) provide magnificent vistas. After passing Willow Mountain, the Crest Trail climbs to a 10,500-foot saddle of wind-stunted aspens surrounded by a dense spruce-fir forest. The rocky trail then switchbacks down to 10,370-foot-high Hummingbird Saddle where plentiful campsites exist. Hummingbird Spring is 0.2 mile down the Whitewater Trail (207) from the junction in the saddle. An evening climb of the apex of

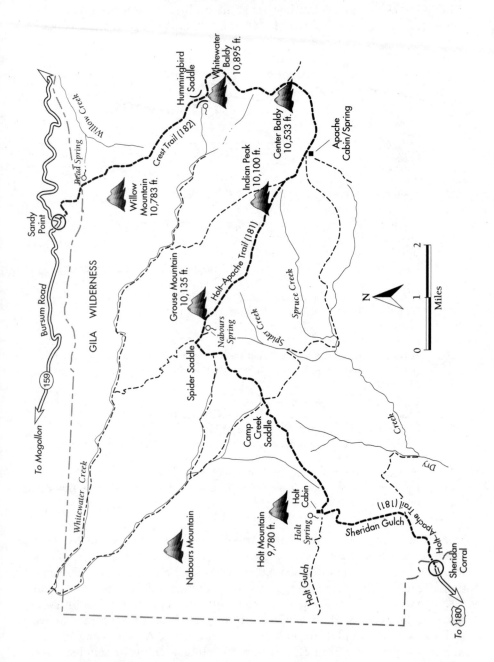

the Gila, 10,895-foot Whitewater Baldy, brings a fitting conclusion to a vigorous day in the mountains (see Hike 1 for details).

From Hummingbird Saddle the Crest Trail drops gently through a spruce-fir forest for nearly a mile to the signed junction with the Iron Creek Lake

Trail (172). Continue right (south) on the well-blazed Crest Trail as it rises and falls through a diverse mix of aspens and conifers to its junction with the Holt–Apache Trail (181). Turn right (southwest) onto the Holt–Apache Trail. For further details about these first 7.8 miles of the hike refer to Mogollon Crest Hike 2.

After 0.3 mile and a slight climb of 100 feet, a low open saddle appears on the right. Look for a faint-use trial up the south ridge of Center Baldy, which provides an easy 100-foot gain in 0.1 mile to this open grassy 10,533-foot mound. Here you'll be treated to a stunning 360-degree vista of wild, forested peaks, ridges, and drainages fanning out in all directions. Especially interesting are the vegetative patterns of fires, old and recent.

From Center Baldy, the trail contours across a north-facing spruce-fir forest to a saddle from where an unmarked abandoned trail drops south to Rain Creek. Soon a sign is reached pointing in different directions to Mogollon Baldy (6.25), Windy Gap (6.5) and onto Spruce Creek Saddle (1.75). This nicely contoured stretch is especially scenic, with grand views south to distinctive 10,658-foot Sacaton Mountain. The trail to Windy Gap (180) leads 0.1 mile downhill to the signed Apache Spring, which is little more than a seep trickling into a small pool adjacent to the tiny Apache Cabin. (Refer to Hike 21 for details about this "open to the public" structure.) The signed junction just east of the cabin points to the Golden Link, Crest, and Redstone Trails. Continue uphill on the Holt–Apache Trail, where a nearby saddle offers campsites in proximity to Black Mountain Spring. The difficult Golden Link Trail heads west over Black Mountain. Stay right (northwest) on the Holt–Apache Trail, reaching the flowing cascade of Black Mountain Spring after another 0.4 mile. For the next 0.7 mile the good trail provides open views of upper Whitewater Creek and Whitewater Baldy before descending to the 9,620-foot Spruce Creek Saddle. Gorgeous campsites abound in this grassy aspen-ringed flat.

To find the wonderful but unsigned Spruce Creek Spring from the saddle, head west toward the head of Spruce Creek veering left (southwest) as you reenter the forest from the opening. Look for a primitive but well-defined use trail marked by ancient ax cuts on logs. Follow the path for about a quarter mile as it drops about 100 feet around the ridge, ending at the spring in a tight draw. From Spruce Creek Saddle, Trail 206 heads north to Redstone Park. Continue northwest toward Grouse Mountain on the good Holt–Apache Trail. The narrow trail is sloped sideways in places but easy to follow. It passes through a dry ponderosa pine forest on the south-facing slopes of Indian Peak, with glimpses into the cliffy buttresses of Dry Creek. Wild turkeys and black bears are plentiful in this stretch as the pleasant trail drops gently down the west ridge of Indian Peak to a saddle marked by an ancient stand of huge Douglas-fir. For the next 0.8 mile the trail steepens to a signed junction with the Grouse Mountain Trail (781) in an aspen-fir forest carpeted with ferns and forbs. A 1-mile round-trip side hike to Grouse Mountain is well worth the time and effort (see Hike 8 for details).

From this junction, the trail overlooks the sheer canyon walls of Spider Creek as it drops steeply down rocky switchbacks, reaching a signed junc-

Backpacking the Crest Trail 182 near Apache Spring.

tion with the Nabours Spring Trail after another 0.6 mile. This primitive side trail ends at the flowing spring after losing 320 feet in 0.4 mile. Be sure and stock up on water if you visit this spring because Rock Spring near Camp Creek Saddle will most likely be dry. The Holt–Apache Trail continues west another 0.1 mile to another signed junction with the Winn Canyon Trail (179). Continuing left (southwest) the trail intersects the East Fork Whitewater Trail (213) after another 0.3 mile. From near this point the rugged Skeleton Ridge branches off to the northwest. If contemplating a side hike on the Skeleton Ridge Trail shown on the USGS quad, but not on the Gila Wilderness map, be advised that this trail has been abandoned and no longer exists. From here stay left as Holt–Apache rises and falls before climbing along the west side of a ridge opening to a scenic overlook into the volcanic spires of Spider Creek. The trail then drops through pine parks, down a gully, and over a low ridge to a four-way signed trail junction in the closed-in 8,460-foot Camp Creek Saddle.

Continue straight ahead southwesterly toward Holt Spring on an excellent 2.8-mile stretch of high country trail to Holt Cabin. The well-graded section passes beneath stately pines with grand vistas to the south and east. Nearby Holt Spring is usually a reliable water source. From here the trail changes from excellent to poor as it plummets southward, becoming extremely rough and primitive as it loses 2,300 feet over the course of 2.7 miles. The rock-strewn jumble and the deeply incised upper waterway are one and the same. The descent is followed by a half-dozen rocky crossings in the lower section. It's a genuine relief to finally reach the signed junction with the Skunk Johnson Cabin Trail. (See Hike 17 for the vigorous hike down to the cabin and old homestead.)

Continuing to the right (south) the trail drops steadily along the draw, vegetated with Douglas-fir, pine, and Gambel oak, to the remains of an old corral that encloses a portion of the stream and cabin ruins. The excellent moderate- to heavy-use trail then climbs to the right (west) out of the gulch to a saddle containing an early Gila Wilderness sign. The actual wilderness boundary is closer to the trailhead. The sign proclaims "pioneers" as being the first explorers of the Gila, but someone corrected the arrogance by scratching in "Indians." For the final 0.6 mile the trail sidehills around the ridge above Dugway Canyon, dropping gradually through a woodland of pinyon-juniper and brush to the Sheridan Corral Trailhead.

Options: If time and energy permit, consider a 1-mile round-trip trail hike to Grouse Mountain along with short off-trail hikes to the summits of Whitewater Baldy (10,895 feet) and Center Baldy (10,533 feet). To extend your backpack you can take the southern route on the Golden Link Trail (218) from Black Mountain to Camp Creek Saddle instead of the higher Holt–Apache Trail (181) to the north. This will add nearly 6 miles to the trip plus significant elevation gain and loss, making this option much more strenuous. (See Hike 11 for further details.)

5   Redstone Park

Highlights: Short hike to upper Whitewater Creek, with good
fishing, a beautiful canyon, and campsites in a
ponderosa pine park along the creek.
Type of hike: Out-and-back day hike, or 2-day backpacking trip.
Total distance: 10 miles.
Difficulty: Moderate.
Best months: May through October.
Maps: Forest Service Gila Wilderness map (1984); Grouse
Mountain USGS quad.

Special considerations: No water at the trailhead or on the trail until
Whitewater Creek.

Finding the trailhead: To reach the Redstone Trailhead, drive 4 miles north
of Glenwood on U.S. Highway 180. Turn right (east) on New Mexico Highway 159, also known as Bursum Road, toward Mogollon. NM 159 changes
from paved to improved gravel after 9 miles. Drive 14 miles on NM 159 to
the Redstone Trail 206 trailhead.

**Parking and trailhead facili-
ties:** There is limited off-road
parking available, as well as a
few shaded campsites, at the
trailhead. Silver Creek provides
water, but it needs to be treated.
There is an information board
and a trail registry, but there are
no other facilities.

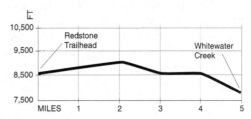

Key points:
- 0.0   Redstone Trailhead on Bursum Road
- 5.0   Junction with Whitewater Creek Trail 207 on the north bank of the creek

The hike: This may not be the straightest route to Whitewater Creek, but it
is the kindest. The steep sections are at the beginning (300-foot climb in 0.4
mile) and the end (700-foot descent via switchbacks in 0.5 mile). The middle
4 miles cruise along the contours of the west flank of Willow Mountain. The
dense forest of fir, aspen, and ponderosa pine provides a shady trail.
Blowdown is not uncommon, especially in the spring before the Forest Service crews have cleared the trail. Rugged volcanic outcroppings also sprout
from the hillside, creating clearings and vistas down the canyon with exhilarating views.

After a dry hike the sound of the falls on Whitewater Creek will be welcome at 4.5 miles. Here the trail switchbacks down the steep north bank to
the creek where it intersects the Whitewater Creek Trail (207).

Redstone Park

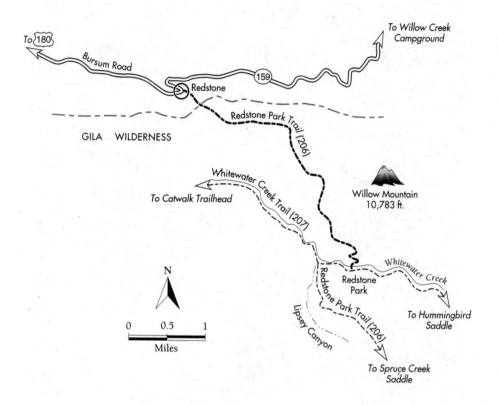

If you are camping at Redstone Park, there are numerous sites on both sides of the creek. Keep an eye out for poison ivy along the river, especially in campsites. As always, treat all water before using.

After an enjoyable stay in Redstone Park, return to the trailhead by the same route.

Option: See Hike 6 for a loop extension of this trip.

Crossing number 43 on Whitewater Creek, graced by red rock and sublime pools.

6 Redstone–Baldy Loop

Highlights:	From riparian to alpine, a trek through the varied landscape of the Mogollon Mountains; canyon of Redstone Park, fishing, solitude on upper Whitewater Creek; ascents of two of the highest peaks (Whitewater and Center Baldies).
Type of hike:	3- to 4-day backpacking loop.
Total distance:	27 miles.
Difficulty:	Strenuous.
Best months:	May through October.
Maps:	Forest Service Gila Wilderness map (1984); Holt Mountain and Grouse Mountain USGS quads.

Special considerations: High water in Whitewater Creek in spring run-off; many stream crossings. Danger of storms and lightning on mountains and ridges in July and August.

Finding the trailhead: Drive 4 miles north of Glenwood on U.S. Highway 180. Turn right (east) on New Mexico Highway 159, also known as Bursum Road, toward Mogollon. NM 159 changes from paved to improved gravel after 9 miles. Drive a total of 14 miles east to the Redstone Trail (206) Trailhead.

Parking and trailhead facilities: There is limited off-road parking and a few shady campsites at the trailhead. Seasonally, water is available in Silver Creek (to be treated). There is an information board and registry, but no other facilities.

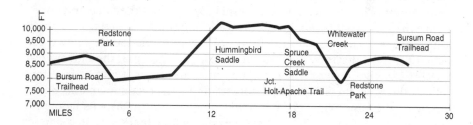

Key points:

0.0	Redstone Trailhead on Bursum Road.
5.0	Redstone Park; junction with Whitewater Trail (207).
12.8	Hummingbird Spring.
13.0	Hummingbird Saddle; junction with Crest Trail (182).
13.9	Junction with Iron Creek Lake Trail (172).
15.9	Junction with Holt–Apache Trail (181).
17.2	Junction with Little Dry Trail (180) to Apache spring and cabin.
17.4	Junction with Golden Link Trail (218).
18.5	Spruce Creek Saddle and spring; junction with Redstone Trail (206).

21.8	Whitewater Creek; junction with Whitewater Trail (207).
22.0	Redstone Park; junction with Redstone Trail (206).
27.0	Redstone Trailhead on Bursum Road.

The hike: This extended backpacking trip in the Whitewater–Mogollon region of the northern Gila Wilderness includes a wide variety of landscape and terrain. While the Redstone Park Trail (207) and the Crest Trail (182) experience moderate use during the summer and fall, the long stretch of the upper Whitewater Trail above Redstone Park has very light visitation. Reliable sources of water along the route will allow you to select campsites at Redstone Park on the creek, Hummingbird Saddle with its spring, and Spruce Creek Saddle with its spring. In addition, both Whitewater Baldy and Center Baldy can easily be climbed from the high end of the loop.

The Redstone Park entrance into the Gila is a popular one. The trail is well marked and is largely shady with periodic views of Whitewater Canyon (see Hike 5 for details). There is no water until you reach the creek at mile 5, so the sight and sound of the rushing stream will be most welcome. The bright red stone and the towering pines add to the visual delights of the location. There are many campsites along the creek both above and below the trail junction.

From Redstone Park, turn left (east) and hike upstream on Whitewater Creek Trail (207). The trail crosses the creek, and frequently; farther up the canyon, unnamed side streams create additional wet crossings. This is a lightly used primitive trail, not manicured by Forest Service trail crews. Windblown pines create hurdles on the trail. Sometimes it's challenging to follow it in the rocky streambed, and it requires some detective work to pick it up after a wet crossing. It's easier just to hike in your wading shoes or boots rather than changing at crossings, but your footwear has to provide sturdy support on this trail.

Small campsites are located at several crossings but they become nonexistent when the trail heads uphill toward Hummingbird. Keep your water bottles full in anticipation of the final dry ascent to the saddle. Shown correctly on the wilderness map but incorrectly on the topo, the narrow trail switchbacks vigorously through aspen, pine, and fir as it climbs the steep slope of the Mogollons. The dense forest often preserves snowbanks on the trail even into June. The spring is a welcome spot in the aspens below the saddle. Above the spring the trail reaches the saddle, marked with a sign for the junction with the Crest Trail, and also with an odd red metal ladder of Z's. There are many campsites at the saddle and in the timber on either side, to provide cover in case of windy conditions. After the ascent, this is an excellent spot to spend the night. For an optional climb of Whitewater Baldy (10,895 feet), see Hike 1. The off-trail route to the summit lies just south of the saddle.

Picking up the Crest Trail at the saddle, turn southeast, contouring around the east side of Whitewater Baldy in a dense spruce-fir forest. Stay on the Crest Trail at the junction with Iron Creek Lake Trail (172), and continue heading south. About 2 miles farther along the Mogollon Mountain ridge you reach the Holt–Apache Trail junction just east of Center Baldy. Turn

Redstone–Baldy Loop

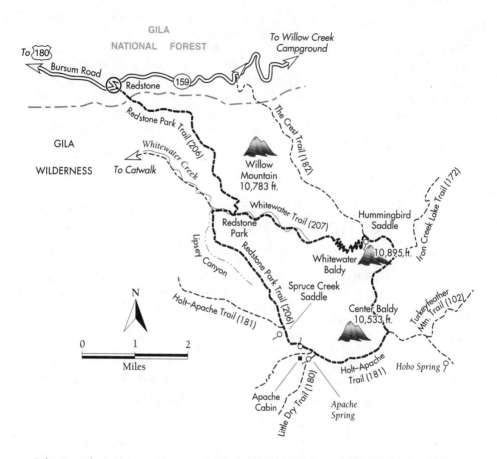

right (southwest), curving around the forested mountaintop. Just 0.3 mile from the junction you will see a faint-use path on the right. This is the route to the peak of Center Baldy (10,533 feet). Drop your pack behind a tree (so as to not frighten any stock that may come by), and walk 0.1 mile to the peak for a panorama of the Mogollon Range from the grassy summit.

Continue on the Holt–Apache Trail to the various junctions near Apache Cabin. The cabin and spring are just west of the first junction on the Dry Creek Trail to Windy Gap. Stay right, unless you want to spend the night indoors. (See Hike 21 for the amenities offered at Apache Cabin and tips on backcountry cabin etiquette.) Just beyond the Apache turnoff, up the hill in a saddle, you reach another junction. Here, too, disregard the trail to the left, which is the Golden Link Trail. Continue on Holt–Apache to arrive at Black Mountain Spring, which is on the trail 0.4 mile from the saddle and is a reliable source of water.

A mile from the spring you reach Spruce Creek Saddle. There are excellent campsites in the grassy aspen-encircled park at the saddle. The spring is downhill to the southwest, toward the head of Spruce Creek. Watch for ax-cut logs and a primitive footpath at the forest edge, and follow it about a quarter mile and 100 feet down from the saddle.

The junction with Redstone Trail is at the saddle. This is your return route to Whitewater Creek. The trail stays high above Lipsey Canyon, following a ridge east of the canyon, dropping slowly. Then in the final 1.5 miles, the trail descends 1,600 feet to meet Whitewater Creek Trail next to a gargantuan house-sized boulder resting in the bottom. Turn right (southeast) on the Whitewater Creek Trail to return to Redstone Park. Turn left (north) at the Redstone Trail junction on the south bank of Whitewater Creek, and return to Bursum Road by the 5-mile section you came in on, relishing the memories of the Gila and its beauty.

7 Deloche Canyon

Highlights:	A quick route to Whitewater Creek, with its fishing, canyon, and water wonderland.
Type of hike:	Out-and-back day hike, or overnight backpacking trip.
Total distance:	7 miles.
Difficulty:	Moderate.
Best months:	March through November.
Maps:	Forest Service Gila Wilderness map (1984); Mogollon, Holt Mountain, and Grouse Mountain USGS quads.

Special considerations: South-facing trail down to Whitewater can be very hot, especially in the afternoon. No water at the trailhead or on the trail until reaching Whitewater Creek.

Finding the trailhead: To reach the Deloche Canyon trailhead for Trail 179, drive 4 miles north of Glenwood on U.S. Highway 180. Turn right (east) on New Mexico Highway 159, also known as Bursum Road, toward Mogollon. NM 159 changes from paved to improved gravel after 9 miles. Drive 2 miles after the pavement ends to Deloche–Winn Canyons Trail 179.

Parking and trailhead facilities: There is limited trailhead parking. Across Bursum Road there is a campsite with shaded parking. There is a seasonal stream from Fanny Spring at the campsite. An informational board and a trail registry are located at the trailhead, but there are no other facilities.

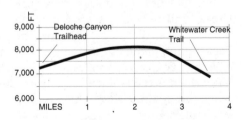

Deloche Canyon

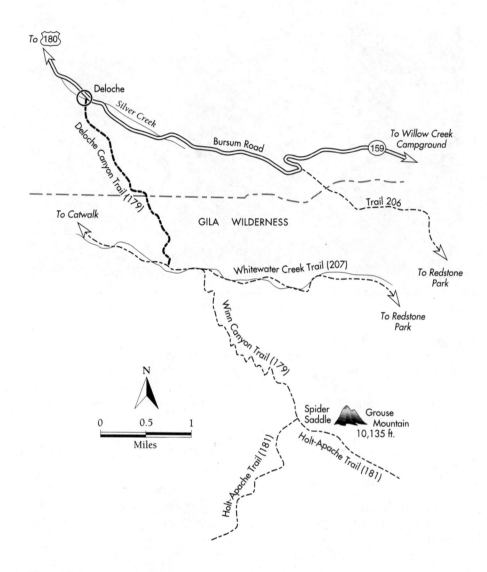

Key points:
- 0.0   Trailhead on Bursum Road.
- 3.5   Junction with Whitewater Creek Trail (207).

The hike: The Deloche Canyon Trail (179) is a short route to the remote watery world of Whitewater Creek. The trail receives moderate use, especially in late spring and summer, and is popular with fishermen.

From the Bursum Road trailhead, you gain 800 feet in elevation in the first 1.5 miles. Shade of ponderosa pine and Douglas-fir provide relief in the first mile, but this vegetation changes into scrub oak and juniper at the dry

Looking southeast into Whitewater Creek country from Deloche Canyon Trail.

ridgetop, providing little shade. The trail levels off on the ridge for more than a mile before switchbacking down to Whitewater Creek.

There are great vistas from the high portions of the trail, with cliffs above and semidesert vegetation sweeping below to the bright green riparian stripe of the creek bottom. The hot, dry south-facing slope of the descent makes Whitewater Creek a welcome relief. The junction with the Whitewater Creek Trail (207) is on the north side of the creek.

There are several campsites along the creek if you're staying overnight. When your visit to Whitewater is over, retrace your steps on the Deloche Trail to the trailhead on Bursum Road.

Option: For a shuttle trip, you can hike on up Whitewater to Redstone Park (5.5 miles) and take the Redstone Trail (207) north to Bursum Road (5 miles). The shuttle distance is 3 miles.

8 Grouse Mountain Loop

Highlights: Quick route to the fishing, deep canyons, and water wonderland of Whitewater Creek, spectacular mountain vistas on high ridges and peaks, wide array of diverse habitats from desert slopes to alpine summits.

Type of hike: 3- to 5-day backpacking trip; loop.

Total distance: 24.8 miles.

Difficulty: Strenuous.

Best months: May through November.

Maps: Forest Service Gila Wilderness map (1984); Holt Mountain and Grouse Mountain USGS quads.

Special considerations: Hot, dry, south-facing trail to and from Whitewater Creek. Stream crossings on Whitewater Creek may be difficult during high water runoff. Sudden storms with lightning may occur along high ridges, producing possible hypothermia conditions. Higher-elevation trails may be blocked by snow into late spring.

Finding the trailhead: Drive 4 miles north of Glenwood on U.S. Highway 180 and turn right (east) on New Mexico Highway 159, Bursum Road, toward Mogollon. NM 159 changes from paved to improved gravel after 9 miles. Drive 2 miles after the pavement ends to the Deloche–Winn Canyon Trailhead. The only sign is the hiker symbol with "Trail 179."

Parking and trailhead facilities: Limited trailhead parking. There is a campsite with shaded parking across Bursum Road along with a seasonal stream from Fanny Spring. A kiosk and trail registry are located at the trailhead. There is no water or other facilities.

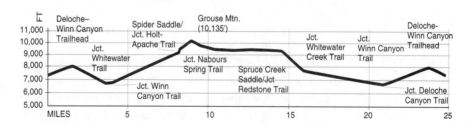

Key points:

0.0   Trailhead for Deloche–Winn Canyon Trail (179).

3.5   Junction with Whitewater Creek Trail (207).

4.0   Junction with Winn Canyon Trail (179).

7.9   Spider Saddle and junction with Holt–Apache Trail (181).

8.0   Junction with Nabours Spring Trail.

8.6   Junction with Grouse Mountain Trail (781).

9.1   Grouse Mountain (10,135 feet).

9.6   Junction with Holt–Apache Trail (181).

Grouse Mountain Loop

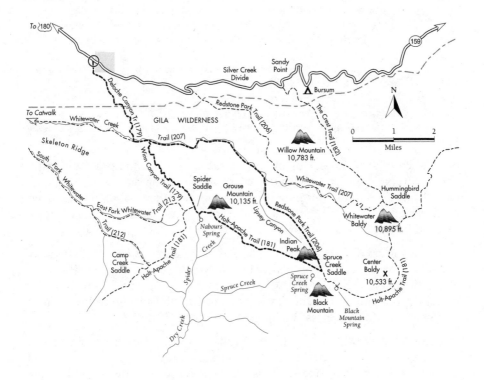

The hike: The central Mogollon summit of Grouse Mountain is a wonderful focal point for this diverse loop into and around the middle reaches of Whitewater Creek. The moderately used Deloche Creek Trail (179) provides a short route into the extremely rugged Whitewater Canyon. Sometimes you have to go up before going down. In this case the trail climbs 800 feet in the first 1.5 miles. Then it leaves the welcome shade of a conifer forest for a dry ridgetop, levels off for a mile, and switchbacks down a desert slope to the watery world of Whitewater. Several campsites invite an overnight respite near the trail junction. To continue on the Winn Canyon Trail to Spider Saddle, follow the Whitewater Trail (207) upstream for 0.5 mile to the signed junction on the south side of the stream.

The Winn Canyon Trail (179) is a bit obscure where it first leaves the

A panoramic view from Grouse Mountain to Whitewater Baldy.

junction in a lovely pine park directly behind the trail sign. The lightly used trail passes along a lush microenvironment of ferns and firs, crosses the tiny stream in Winn Canyon three times, and begins a series of long steady switchbacks through continuous Douglas-fir forest. After intersecting a ridgeline covered with aspen and fir, the trail climbs and contours evenly to the densely forested gap of Spider Saddle. This narrow, windy pass offers semiopen views into the cliffy upper reaches of Spider Creek to the south. A mountain lion may have been the most recent trail user ahead of you. This 4-mile segment displays markedly different worlds between rugged, rocky canyon bottoms and heavily forested ridges that hide the chasms in a green coniferous carpet. The only open vistas appear just northwest of Spider Saddle.

Turn left (southeast) on the Holt–Apache Trail (181) toward Grouse Mountain, climbing steeply 0.1 mile to the signed junction with the Nabours Spring Trail. This primitive path switchbacks steeply downhill, losing 320 feet in 0.4 mile, to a flowing spring. The trail used to continue below the spring but has since been abandoned. The junction with Grouse Mountain Trail (781) is another steep 0.6 mile with rocky switchbacks and overlooks to distant sheer cliffs above Spider Creek.

The 0.5-mile-long Grouse Mountain Trail climbs north to an open grassy swale on the mountain, opening to superb views to the north, and eastward to Whitewater Baldy, Center Baldy, and upper Whitewater Creek. The actual 10,135-foot summit is reached on a primitive overgrown path 0.1 mile north of the grassy opening. Scattered debris from the abandoned lookout includes rusted bedsprings, tin roofing, and even an old phone box, enough to keep a cleanup crew busy for days. A magnificent view down Whitewater Creek unfolds from a jutting slab of rock on the northwest side of the summit. Gigantic rock fins rise above the lower canyon. After savoring the mountain vistas drop back to the Holt–Apache trail and turn left (southeast) toward Spruce Creek Saddle.

For the next 0.8 mile the trail gently descends through an aspen-fir forest carpeted with ferns and forbs to a saddle adorned with huge Douglas-fir. This is a good place to flush a wild turkey or perhaps to see a black bear. The pleasant trail climbs up the ridge and then sidehills along south-facing slopes with views into rugged canyons guarded by rock spires. Two miles southeast of Grouse Mountain the trail intersects the west ridge of Indian Peak with occasional glimpses into the cliffy buttresses of Dry Creek. From this saddle a side trip possibility is an off-trail hike of 1.5 miles round trip with a 600-foot elevation gain to Indian Peak. The Holt–Apache Trail contours up and down over the next 1.2 miles to the grassy aspen-ringed flat of Spruce Creek Saddle. The nearby Spruce Creek Spring, not signed or shown on maps, makes this alpine opening a premier campsite. The spring is about 100 feet below and south of the saddle in a deeply incised draw at the head of Spruce Creek. To find the spring from the saddle, head west down the grassy opening, veering left (southwest) as you enter the forest. Look for a primitive but well-defined use trail marked with a few ancient ax cuts on logs. Follow the trail for about a quarter mile to the spring.

From Spruce Creek Saddle turn left (northwest) on the Redstone Park Trail to Whitewater Creek. The trail climbs slightly through a spruce-fir forest with a path that is sometimes obscure but always well blazed. This upper 1.5 miles of trail drops gently along the eastern slopes of Indian Creek. After leaving the main east ridge above Lipsey Canyon the trail steepens dramatically, losing 1,800 feet over the next 1.5 miles to Whitewater Creek. A rocky overlook 400 feet above and 0.4 mile before Whitewater Creek offers a good excuse for a scenic break.

Aptly named Redstone Park is only 0.3 mile above the Whitewater Trail junction and is well worth a quick side visit. To continue the loop turn left (northwest) and hike down the Whitewater Creek Trail toward Deloche Canyon. This 5.3-mile stretch of the canyon is narrow, rocky, and choked with dense alder, oak, maple, ash, and thorny locust. With barely enough room for the trail campsites are scarce to nonexistent in the deep canyon. Monumental cliffs and spires rise above stream crossings too numerous to count. Enjoy the frequent wadings. After all, they are not dangerous, and they do serve to slow you down to better admire canyon formations and diverse vegetation. During spring and summer evenings the air is alive with swallows and bats.

Upon reaching the junction with the Deloche Canyon Trail, you've completed the basic loop to and around Grouse Mountain and have only the "lollypop" stem to retrace. Carry plenty of water, and, if possible, hike this final 3.5-mile dry stretch to the Bursum Road during a cooler part of the day.

Option: The loop can be turned into a shorter shuttle hike of 21.5 miles by exiting northward on the Redstone Park Trail (206) from Redstone Park. The Redstone Park Trailhead is only 3 miles east of the Deloche–Winn Canyon Trailhead on Bursum Road (see Hike 5 for details).

9 The Catwalk

> **Highlights:** Dramatic gorge of Whitewater Creek and historic structure of ladders, bridges, and walkways.
> **Type of hike:** Day hike; out-and-back.
> **Total distance:** 2 miles.
> **Difficulty:** Easy.
> **Best months:** Year-round.
> **Maps:** Forest Service Gila Wilderness map (1984); Mogollon USGS quad.

Special considerations: The Catwalk lies wholly outside of the Gila Wilderness and is not a wilderness experience in the usual meaning. It is often quite crowded, especially on hot summer weekends.

Finding the trailhead: On the north side of Glenwood on U.S. Highway 180, turn right (east) on New Mexico Highway 174 to the Catwalk and the Whitewater picnic ground. Drive 5 miles to the end of the road at the trailhead parking area.

Parking and trailhead facilities: There is a large gravel parking area. Vault toilets and tables at the picnic area. Water is available in Whitewater Creek (to be treated). No trailhead camping. The nearest public campground is the Forest Service's Big Horn campground (no fee) on US 180 immediately north of the US 180/NM 174 junction on the north side of Glenwood.

Key points:
  0.0   Whitewater picnic ground.
  1.0   Dead end of Catwalk; turnoff to Whitewater Creek Trail (207).

The hike: The narrow gorge of Whitewater Creek is the site of the Catwalk National Scenic Recreation Trail, 2 miles from the Gila Wilderness boundary. This is a very popular trail. With the Whitewater picnic grounds at the trailhead, the Catwalk attracts hundreds of visitors on warm summer weekends and 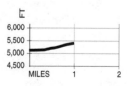 holidays, who enjoy the shade of the sycamores and the cool rushing waters of the mountain stream.

The gorge itself is spectacular with huge cliffs of volcanic conglomerate soaring up, large globular boulders rounded by the rushing waters, and the roar of the captive surf washing through the chasm. More than geology, what really makes this mile-long hike unique is the manmade structure, the

The Catwalk

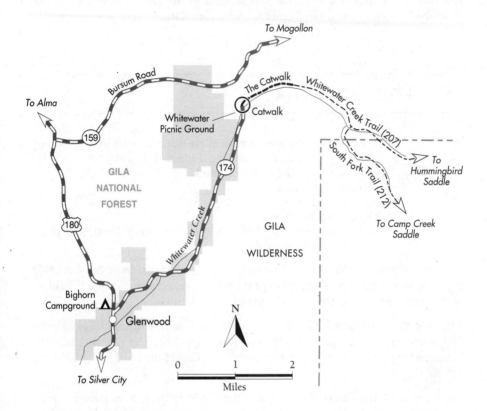

Catwalk, originally built in the 1890s as a pipeline for water to generate power for a local mine. A walkway was developed to allow workers to maintain the pipeline. When the mine closed in 1913, the walkway rapidly deteriorated. During the New Deal of the mid-1930s, the Civilian Conservation Corps (CCC) rebuilt the wooden catwalk. The Forest Service improved it with a metal one in 1961, and in 1986, after repeated floods, raised it and did some rerouting to avoid annual rebuilding.

For today's visitors the Catwalk remains a wonder. Stone steps are carved into canyon walls along the thundering stream. Narrow mesh swinging bridges lead over the wild waters of Whitewater. Metal walkways cling to canyon walls, suspended above the river.

The trail climbs 300 feet in a mile. At times the ascent is quite abrupt, via tight mesh-stepped ladders. The well-marked and labeled trail can be challenging for backpackers on their way up Whitewater Creek. The overhanging canyon walls occasionally prevent passage of heavily laden hikers on the elevated mesh walkways. The mesh grating of the Catwalk sections can also be harrowing for canine hiking companions.

The Catwalk is an awesome sight and a fun adventure, although it is

Backpacking the "Catwalk" through Whitewater Canyon.

somewhat of an anomaly, located at the entrance to the world's first designated wilderness area. Even if your hiking plans do not include a journey up Whitewater, this is a 2-mile hike that will be remembered.

10 Whitewater Loop

Highlights:	Spectacular canyons and mountain streams; fishing; the crest of the Mogollon Range and two of its highest peaks.
Type of hike:	6- to 8-day backpacking loop.
Total distance:	39.4 miles.
Difficulty:	Strenuous.
Best months:	May through October.
Maps:	Forest Service Gila Wilderness map (1984); Holt Mountain and Grouse Mountain USGS quads.

Special considerations: Numerous stream crossings on Whitewater Creek. Storms and lightning in the high Mogollon country. Hypothermia.

Finding the trailhead: On the north edge of Glenwood on U.S. Highway 180, turn right (east) on New Mexico Highway 174 to the Catwalk and the Whitewater picnic ground. Drive 5 miles to the end of the road at the trailhead parking area.

Parking and trailhead facilities: There is a large gravel parking area; the picnic area has vault toilets. Water is available in Whitewater Creek (to be treated). No trailhead camping is permitted. The nearest public campground is the Forest Service's Big Horn campground (no fee) on US 180 immediately north of the US 180/NM 174 junction on the north side of Glenwood.

Key points:
0.0	Catwalk Trailhead.
1.0	Begin Whitewater Creek Trail (207).
2.3	Junction with South Fork Whitewater Creek Trail (212).
2.4	Junction with Gold Drip Trail (810).
3.0	Gila Wilderness Boundary.
6.5	Junction with Deloche Canyon Trail (179).
6.8	Junction with Winn Canyon Trail (179).
12.0	Redstone Canyon Trail (206).
19.8	Hummingbird Spring.
20.0	Hummingbird Saddle; junction with Crest Trail (182).
20.9	Junction with Iron Creek Lake Trail (172).
22.8	Junction with Holt–Apache Trail (181).
23.4	Junction with Little Dry Creek Trail (180).
23.6	Junction with Golden Link Trail (218).

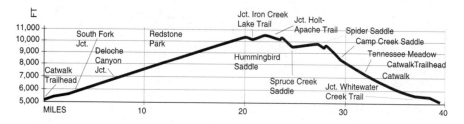

				Jct. Iron Creek Lake Trail	Jct. Holt- Apache Trail	Spider Saddle	

11,000
10,000
9,000
8,000
7,000
6,000
5,000

South Fork Jct.
Deloche Canyon
Catwalk Trailhead
Jct.

Redstone Park

Hummingbird Saddle

Spruce Creek Saddle

Jct. Whitewater Creek Trail

Camp Creek Saddle
Tennessee Meadow
Catwalk Trailhead
Catwalk

MILES   10   20   30   40

24.0   Black Mountain Spring.
24.7   Spruce Creek Saddle; junction with Redstone Trail (206).
27.2   Junction with Grouse Mountain Trail (781).
27.8   Junction with Nabours Spring Trail.
27.9   Spider Saddle; junction with Winn Canyon Trail (179).
28.2   Junction with East Fork Whitewater Creek Trail (213).
29.9   Camp Creek Saddle; junction with Golden Link Trail (218) and South Fork Trail (212).
31.8   Junction with Little Whitewater Trail (214).
32.1   Tennessee Meadow; junction with East Fork Whitewater Creek Trail (213).
35.3   Devil's Elbow in South Fork Canyon.
37.1   Junction with Whitewater Creek Trail (207).
38.4   Junction with Catwalk Trail.
39.4   Catwalk Trailhead.

The hike: This is the supreme do-it-all trip in the Whitewater–Mogollon region of the northwest Gila Wilderness. As the elevation profile illustrates, your journey will take you through a wide variety of ecosystems. The trip can be done in a minimum of six days. It takes two pack days to reach Redstone Park, 12 miles up Whitewater Creek, and another day to climb the 8 miles to Hummingbird Saddle. Both these locations have campsites and water. In the 10 miles along the crest of the Mogollons, from Hummingbird to Camp Creek Saddles, you can camp at Spruce or Spider Saddle, or hike all the way to the South Fork Trail and camp when you reach water in the upper reaches of the drainage. The ridge trails are a lot faster than the river trails! The South Fork leg of the hike will take two days, with the second one including the hike back to the Catwalk Trailhead. You might want to schedule in layover days to fish at Redstone, to climb Whitewater and Center Baldies on the route, or to hike 8.4 miles round trip south on the Crest Trail to visit Mogollon Baldy's peak, lookout, and guard cabin. Travel is slow along Whitewater Creek. Allow yourself plenty of time to enjoy the trip and not be pressured by the setting sun.

The loop can be done in the reverse by heading up the South Fork and then down Whitewater. We enjoyed the challenge of climbing to the highest saddle first and then cruising downward gradually via the South Fork, whose canyon is especially remote, cozy, and intricate.

From the trailhead, wind along the Catwalk bridges, ladders, and walkways to its termination at the upper end of the gorge where Whitewater Creek Trail (207) (with a sign) leads to the left on the north bank. The chaotic crowds of the Catwalk disappear as you hike on up Whitewater Creek.

Whitewater Loop

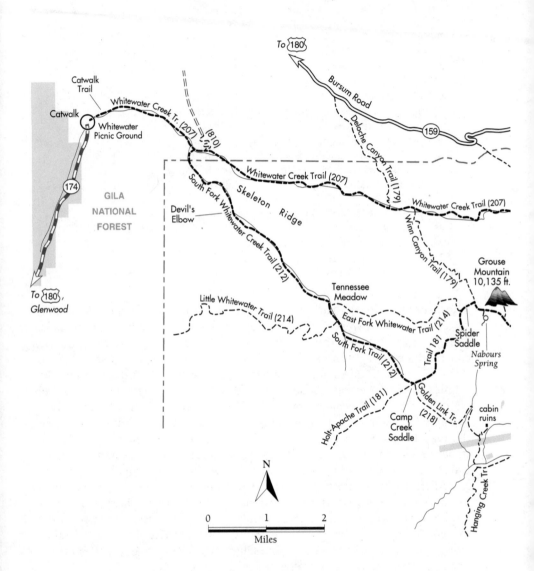

Soon the trail slopes down to the peaceful sycamore and cottonwood groves along the river. There are several campsites in this area as it is a popular spot for fishing for rainbow trout. At the signed junction with the South Fork Trail, your return route, continue up the main river. After passing the Gila Wilderness boundary high on the sunny north bank, the trail stays above the creek for more than a mile, and then drops back to the bottom. The stream crossings begin in earnest here, and will increase in frequency

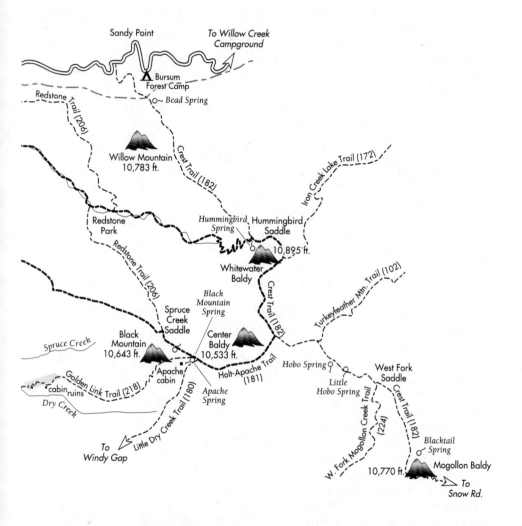

as you go upstream. The most efficient solution to the crossings is to wear sturdy wading footwear all the way up so you don't have to change every few minutes. If you have trouble with cold feet, Neoprene socks are the answer. There are lots of crossings—too many to count. None is hazardous, but they do interrupt the rhythm. Enjoy the crossings. Pause to examine the cliffs, the spires, and the flowers. Swallows are especially busy in the spring and summer, and bats are often working the canyon's air currents in the summer evenings.

Campsites exist near the Deloche Canyon junction, and become scarce on the 5-mile stretch of river from there to Redstone Park. As luck would have it, as soon as you decide it's time to camp, appropriate sites do not exist. The canyon bottom is narrow and rocky and choked with dense alder, oak, maple, ash, and thorny locust. There's not much space even for the trail, which jumps from side to side below the awesome cliffs and spires. If you see a good spot and it's close to the end of the day, it would be a good idea to stop there for the night.

The ravine doesn't widen until you reach Redstone Park at 12 miles. The bright stone announces your location before you reach the trail junction. There are plentiful campsites beneath the ponderosa pines. The botanical zone has shifted, with the conifers and aspen becoming more numerous. Redstone is a popular destination from the Bursum Road; it is likely that you will encounter other hikers here.

Above Redstone, the Whitewater Creek Trail to Hummingbird is lightly used so you are ensured of solitude. The trail narrows to a footpath, seldom used by horse parties, so fallen tree trunks are not uncommon. As the valley narrows again in its climb to the ridge, stream crossings continue, with side streams adding to the total—if you're still counting.

Finally the trail breaks away from the stream and switchbacks up to the spring. On the forested slope of Whitewater Baldy you may encounter snowbanks into June. You reach the spring in the aspen grove at 19.8 miles, and the saddle, at the Crest Trail junction, 0.2 mile farther. There are many campsites in the open saddle, as well as others tucked into the spruce-fir forest on either side of the ridge where you can get protection from the wind. You may want to walk up Whitewater Baldy (10,895 feet), the highest peak in the Gila, as an after-dinner outing (see Hike 1).

From Hummingbird Saddle, pick up the Crest Trail and head south around the eastern side of the mountain, passing the junction with Iron Creek Lake Trail on your left. Your next intersection, 2.8 miles from the saddle, is with the Holt–Apache Trail, just below Center Baldy. Turn right (southeast) on Holt–Apache. Shortly after this turn you may wish to take a side outing to Center Baldy (10,533 feet). Just 0.3 mile from the turn a faint path leads to your right 0.1 mile up to the bald summit and a spectacular view.

Continuing farther down the Mogollon ridge, the Holt–Apache Trail travels through a heavily forested landscape, with openings in the vegetation on the hotter, dry south-facing slopes. There are two intersections close together beyond Center Baldy. Stay right in both cases, unless you want to visit Apache Spring Cabin. They are 0.2 mile south on the first trail, the one to Windy Gap. (See Hike 21 for cabin etiquette in the Gila.)

Beyond the second side trail you will pass Black Mountain Spring; it flows out of the mountainside right on the trail and is an excellent source of cold water. Continue on to Spruce Creek Saddle, about 2 miles from the turn. It also has a spring, nestled in the woods to the southwest. Look for ax cuts and a faint path to lead you to the spring 0.3 mile from the saddle.

Past the saddle 2.5 miles is the trail to Grouse Mountain (10,135 feet).

Trail 207 climbs high above Whitewater Canyon 4 miles above the trailhead.

Here, too, you can take a side jaunt to the peak, 1 mile round trip, and soak up the view. (See Hike 8 for details.) From the Grouse Mountain Trail, the main trail seesaws past the Nabours Spring Trail to Spider Saddle and the Winn Canyon Trail junction. Views of Spider Creek canyon are outstanding from this ridgetop.

Continue on Holt–Apache, passing the East Fork Whitewater Creek Trail on your right. Stay on Holt–Apache to Camp Creek Saddle, with a signed junction for the Golden Link Trail to the left and the South Fork Whitewater Trail on your right. Take the latter, turning northwest (right) off the ridge and dropping into the head of the South Fork drainage. You'll encounter water eventually as you descend the South Fork.

Two miles from the turn down the South Fork you arrive at Tennessee Meadow, a spacious opening in the pine-fir forest on the south bank of the South Fork. Here you are guaranteed water. Heavy horse usage has denuded areas of the meadow, especially around tree trunks. Beware of poison ivy at the edge of the meadow. The meadow is also the junction with the East Fork Trail.

Continue on down the South Fork. The canyon narrows below the meadow. Very different from the main Whitewater, the South Fork does not experience the seasonal flooding of the larger river. This canyon is tighter, the stream smaller and easily crossed, and the vegetation is lush and diverse. Remote and intimate, the South Fork has a 5-mile canyon of abrupt cliffs, alcoves, hoodoos, towers, mushroom rocks, and shaggy columns. Stock parties especially have to be cautious; the twisting trail is too narrow for stock trains in the tight turns. With the babbling stream a constant companion, this is a delightful section in which to take your time. The few campsites are quite tiny, but the scenery is majestic with the cliffs on all sides. Below the Devil's Elbow formation, the bottom widens to accommodate sycamore groves. On the floodplain where the South Fork joins the main Whitewater are the remnants of an old power plant, built in the past century to supply power to mining activities in the region. From this site the trail crosses the main Whitewater Creek to join Whitewater Creek Trail; turn left for the 2.3 miles back to the trailhead via the Catwalk. Joining the merry crowds for the final mile is an unusual conclusion for a wilderness adventure. The scene makes the wilderness part of the trip even more spectacular.

Options: You can take the East Fork Whitewater Creek Trail to cut a mile off your trip. From the Holt–Apache Trail turn right on the East Fork for a 3-mile steep route down to Tennessee Meadow For a longer trip, continue south on the Crest Trail to visit Mogollon Baldy. (See Hike 2 for details and campsites.) You will need the Mogollon Baldy Peak USGS quad for this extension of the basic route.

11   Whitewater–Dry Creek Loop

Highlights:	Three unique canyons (Whitewater, Dry Creek, and the South Fork); the Mogollon high peaks; mining and cabin ruins.
Type of hike:	7- to 9-day backpacking loop.
Total distance:	45.4 miles.
Difficulty:	Strenuous.
Best months:	May through October.
Maps:	Forest Service Gila Wilderness map (1984); Holt Mountain and Grouse Mountain USGS quads.

Special considerations: Countless wet-foot crossings on Whitewater Creek. Long stretches between water sources (two water bottles recommended). Vicious ground bees in the fall on the dry slopes of the Golden Link Trail. Danger of storms and lightning on high ridges and peaks. Hypothermia.

Finding the trailhead: To reach the Catwalk Trailhead, on the northern edge of Glenwood on U.S. Highway 180, turn right (east) on New Mexico Highway 174 to the Catwalk and the Whitewater picnic ground. Drive 5 miles to the end of the road at the trailhead parking area.

Parking and trailhead facilities: There is a large gravel parking area and an information kiosk at the picnic area. There are vault toilets. Water is available in Whitewater Creek (to be treated). There is no camping permitted at the trailhead. The nearest public campground is the Forest Service's Big Horn campground (no fee) on US 180 immediately north of the US 180/ NM 174 junction on the north side of Glenwood.

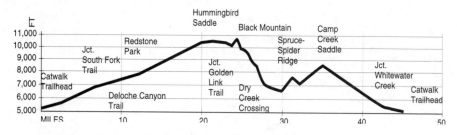

Key points:

0.0   Catwalk Trailhead.
1.0   Begin Whitewater Creek Trail (207).
2.3   Junction with South Fork Whitewater Creek Trail (212).
2.4   Junction with Gold Drip Trail (810).
3.0   Gila Wilderness Boundary.
6.5   Junction with Deloche Canyon Trail (179).
6.8   Junction with Winn Canyon Trail (179).
11.8 Junction with Redstone Trail (206).
12.0 Redstone Park; junction with Redstone Trail (206).
19.8 Hummingbird Spring.
20.0 Hummingbird Saddle; junction with Crest Trail (182).
20.9 Junction with Iron Creek Lake Trail (172).
22.8 Junction with Holt–Apache Trail (181).
23.4 Junction with Little Dry Creek Trail (180) to Apache Spring and cabin.
23.5 Junction with Golden Link Trail (218) to Dry Creek.
29.9 Junction with Hanging Rock Trail to Windy Gap.
30.9 Trail to Spruce Creek cabin ruins.
35.9 Camp Creek Saddle; junction with Holt–Apache Trail (181) and South Fork Whitewater Creek Trail (212).
37.8 Junction with Little Whitewater Creek Trail (214).
38.1 Tennessee Meadow; junction with East Fork Whitewater Trail (213).
43.1 Junction with Whitewater Creek Trail (207).
44.4 Junction with Catwalk Trail.
45.4 Catwalk Trailhead.

The hike: This more strenuous alternative to the basic Whitewater Loop (see Hike 10) takes you via the Golden Link Trail into Dry Creek. In addition to visiting a remote wild canyon, this outing features remnants of mining activities and cabin ruins. The Golden Link route increases the Whitewater Loop hike by 6 miles, and also adds a day to the journey.

Traveling along Whitewater Creek is slow due to the numerous crossings. It is reasonable to take two days to get to Redstone Park, where there are excellent campsites. From Redstone it is a day's journey to hike up to Hummingbird Saddle. Heading south on the Crest Trail and then west on Holt–Apache, it is nearly 10 miles to the first good campsites along Dry Creek near the Hanging Rock Trail junction. To shorten this arduous day's

Whitewater–Dry Creek Loop

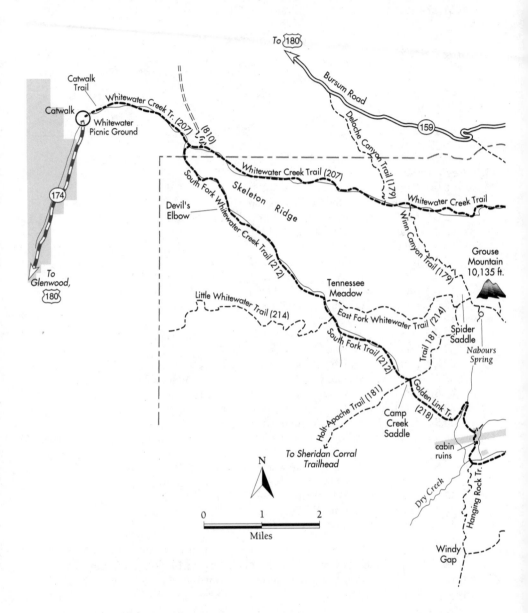

journey, consider stopping at Apache Cabin, 0.2 mile west of the Holt-Apache/Little Dry Trail intersection. This shorter backpack day (only 4 miles from Hummingbird Saddle) provides time for visiting peaks (Whitewater Baldy at 10,895 feet, and Center Baldy, 10,533 feet), as well as for exploring the area south of Apache Cabin (see Hike 21 for details on cabin etiquette in the Gila). Then the 6.3 miles to the camp on Dry Creek won't be so brutal.

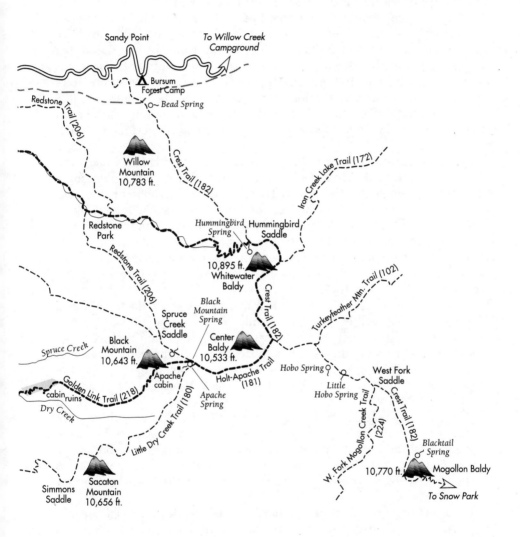

Sandy Point

To Willow Creek
Campground

⛺ Bursum
Forest Camp

Redstone Trail (206)

O~ Bead Spring

Willow
Mountain
10,783 ft.

Crest Trail (182)

Iron Creek Lake Trail (172)

Redstone
Park

Redstone Trail (206)

*Hummingbird
Spring*

Hummingbird
Saddle

10,895 ft.
Whitewater
Baldy

Crest Trail (182)

*Black
Mountain
Spring*

Spruce
Creek
Saddle

Turkeyfeather Mtn. Trail (102)

Spruce Creek

Black
Mountain
10,643 ft.

Center
Baldy
10,533 ft.

Hobo Spring ○

West Fork
Saddle

Apache
cabin

Holt-Apache Trail
(181)

○
*Little
Hobo Spring*

Golden Link Trail (218)

cabin ruins

*Apache
Spring*

Little Dry Creek Trail (180)

W. Fork Mogollon Creek Trail (224)

Crest Trail (182)

Dry Creek

*Blacktail
Spring*

Simmons
Saddle

Sacaton
Mountain
10,656 ft.

10,770 ft.

Mogollon Baldy

To Snow Park

From Dry Creek it's about 7.5 miles to water along the South Fork Trail over Camp Creek Saddle, or 8.2 miles to go to Tennessee Meadow to camp. From there, a long day's backpack will get you to the trailhead (7.3 miles).

From the Catwalk Trailhead, negotiate the gorge via the ladders, bridges, and walkways to emerge at 1 mile at the tiny Trail 207 sign on the left (north) bank. Hike upstream on Whitewater Creek Trail 207 for 20 miles.

Trail crossings grow more frequent as you head east. You will find it easier to hike in your wading boots instead of changing at each crossing. The trail has moderate use below Deloche Canyon at 6.5 miles; then it is lightly traveled beyond that until Redstone Park, which is a popular destination for fishing parties. Above Redstone Park the trail is seldom visited. The Whitewater Creek hike is described in detail in Hike 10.

At Hummingbird Saddle, on the crest of the Mogollon ridge, you have an opportunity to climb Whitewater Baldy, just south of the saddle (see Hike 1). To continue the loop trip, take the Crest Trail from the junction in the saddle south toward Mogollon Baldy. Almost 3 miles south of the saddle is the junction with the Holt–Apache Trail (181). Turn right (west) on Holt–Apache, wrapping around Center Baldy. Just beyond the intersection (0.3 mile) a faint-use trail on your right leads to the bald top of this central peak from which you can enjoy a sweeping view of the northwest Gila Wilderness.

Continue on Holt–Apache to the junction with the Little Dry Creek Trail to Apache Cabin and Windy Gap. This is your turn if you're planning a night at the cabin next to the spring. There aren't any decent tent sites near the cabin, so if the cabin is occupied, continue to the saddle at the Golden Link junction, 0.2 mile beyond on Holt–Apache, where you can camp. There's no water at the saddle, but Black Mountain spring is 0.4 mile farther down Holt–Apache in the spruce-fir forest on the mountain's northeast slope, right on the trail. You should fill your water bottles here anyway before embarking on the Golden Link Trail.

From the junction, the Golden Link Trail goes straight to the top of Black Mountain (10,643 feet) in the first 0.5 mile. Views are breathtaking to the southwest into Rain Creek and the West Fork of Mogollon Creek. The descent is longer, via a multitude of switchbacks through spruce-fir forest and aspen thickets. Thick aspen saplings are trying to dominate the trail, but the rocky path is still bare and visible. Below Black Mountain a fire-cleared saddle provides a view of the Sacaton massif (10,656 feet) and the jagged Dry Creek valley below. The trail then drops to California Park where a sea of jumbled downfall from a recent fire obstructs the path. Cairns mark the makeshift trail through the jackstrawed blackened trunks to the bottom of the ravine where a chortling brook announces the return of vegetation after the fire. You will emerge from this trail segment with charcoaled hands and legs.

The trail contours along the dry slope east of the creek through steeply sloped ponderosa meadows. After a panoramic view from a rocky promontory, the trail begins its descent via tightly packed switchbacks into the green Dry Fork valley. Numerous side paths lead off the steep gravelly trail to deserted mines. This trail was designed by miners and is very steep. The ruins of the Golden Link cabin on the left are located on one of the old patented mining claims in the Dry Creek ravine. From the cabin the trail continues its drop to the creek, with the roar of Dry Creek growing louder.

Enjoy a leisurely wet-foot crossing and a view of the canyon. It's a differ-

Rock spires tower high above Whitewater Canyon.

ent world here at the creek, with broad-leaved deciduous vegetation and a
gurgling stream. The trail then stays on the south side of the creek. Half a
mile downstream are several creekside campsites, unfortunately heavily
impacted by horse parties. On the hillside before the second Dry Creek
crossing is the junction with the Hanging Rock Trail. This trail is no longer
an official Forest Service trail; it is not maintained and has been removed
from the wilderness map. The sign at the junction announces that it is not
recommended for livestock.

Continue on Dry Creek Trail to another crossing. After this second crossing the trail leaves the Dry Creek bottom and begins the hot, dry climb to
the divide between Spruce and Spider Creeks. Switchbacks are minimal on
the steep gravel slope. Scrub oak crowds the trail but doesn't provide much
shade. The views down the Dry Creek canyon to the west provide a good
excuse to pause during the climb.

Near the top of the ridge is a side trail to your right leading to the ruins of
Spruce Creek cabin. Drop your pack behind the shrubbery and follow the
trail 0.5 mile down to the shady creekside glen of the old mining claim. This
patented claim is a private inholding, a vestige of an optimistic prospector
earlier in the century. There are tent sites near the cabin ruins, and Spruce
Creek has water. Endangered Gila trout have been planted in Spruce Creek,
so no fishing is permitted in the stream.

After the interlude on Spruce Creek, the main trail continues up to the
saddle, then plunges into the green shady conifer forest of Spider Creek.

After crossing Spider Creek, the final water for almost 5 miles, it's a winding rocky trek to Camp Creek (dry) and a steep, eroded slope to the saddle and the junction with the Holt–Apache Trail and the South Fork Whitewater Trail.

Continue straight over the saddle, dropping into the head of the South Fork. After 1 mile, water will appear in the rocky streambed. At 2 miles down the South Fork, Tennessee Meadow provides broad flat campsites at the junction with the East Fork Trail. From the meadow to the mouth of the South Fork the canyon winds through dramatic narrows and gorges. There are a few modest campsites nestled along the creek next to the trail. (See Hikes 10 and 12 for details.)

Near the junction with the main Whitewater Creek is the site of the power plant ruins, to the left of the trail under stately sycamores. After crossing Whitewater Creek, turn left (west) on Trail 207, heading back to the Catwalk Trailhead. After your outing in the remote canyons of the wilderness, the crowds at the Catwalk and the Whitewater picnic area will be startling. Savor your experience in wilderness!

12 South Fork Whitewater

Highlights: Deep canyon bound by sheer cliff walls and colorful rock formations with permanent stream, dark trout-filled pools, and lush vegetation; historic mining structures in lower end.
Type of hike: Long day hike or overnighter, out-and-back.
Total Distance: 19 miles.
Difficulty: Strenuous.
Best Months: May through October.
Topo maps: Forest Service Gila Wilderness map (1984); Holt Mountain and Grouse Mountain USGS quads.

Special considerations: Numerous rock-hopping stream crossings, short midsection hazardous to livestock. Poison ivy. Stream intermittent above Tennessee Meadow.

Finding the trailhead: Turn east from U.S. Highway 180 onto New Mexico Highway 174 (Catwalk Road) on the north end of Glenwood and drive to the end of the 5-mile long paved Catwalk Road to the popular picnic ground and trailhead parking area. Hike through the Catwalk and up Whitewater Creek to the start of South Fork Whitewater Trail (212) at the confluence of the main and south forks of Whitewater Creek, 2.3 miles above the Whitewater Trail Trailhead.

Parking and trailhead facilities: Large gravel parking area, vault toilets, and posted trail information at the end-of-the road Whitewater picnic ground.

This day use area, closed to overnight camping, is especially popular because it serves as the entrance to the Catwalk National Scenic Recreation Trail. The nearest public no-fee campground is the Forest Service's Big Horn campground on US 180 immediately north of the US 180/NM 174 junction on the north end of Glenwood.

Key points:

0.0	Whitewater–Catwalk National Scenic Recreation Area Trailhead, Trail (207).
2.3	Junction of Whitewater Trail and South Fork Whitewater Trail (207).
4.1	Devil's Elbow in the South Fork Whitewater Creek Canyon.
7.3	Tennessee Meadow–East Fork Whitewater Trail (213).
7.6	Junction of Little Whitewater Trail (214).
9.5	Camp Creek Saddle; junction with Trails 212, 181, and 218.

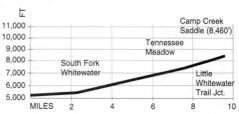

The Hike: After negotiating the Catwalk and hiking 2.3 miles up the main Whitewater Creek canyon on Whitewater Creek Trail (207), turn right (south) onto the signed South Fork Whitewater Creek Trail (212). Soon after a wet crossing of the main Whitewater Creek the trail reaches a lovely sycamore bottom near the mouth of the South Fork next to historic power house remnants, where both wood and water power were generated for mines in Mogollon. Some 0.4 mile up, a spectacular cathedral rock formation appears on the left (east) near the end of Skeleton Ridge. Soon the shallow canyon narrows dramatically. The vegetation is lush, with a diverse mix of conifers, willows, yucca, and much more. About 2 miles up the South Fork at mile 4.3, the aptly named Devil's Elbow is bound by great angular rock columns and spires with a spacious campsite in the bottom. In places the canyon widens with sheer cliff walls soaring hundreds of feet. To alert people with stock, a sign appears after another 0.6 mile below a steep, cliffy section of the trail notched into the east side of the canyon warning that the trail is hazardous for livestock and that animals should be led single file on foot. Here the trail rapidly gains and loses 100 feet in short, steep switchbacks. Just upstream look for a hole-in-the-wall arch to the right (west).

During the next mile the canyon deepens with alcoves, grottos, moss-covered rocks, and columns of rock towering overhead on the right (west) side. Trout dart into the shady recesses of dark pools. Unlike the main Whitewater canyon, floods don't often scour the South Fork, so lush communities of evergreen and deciduous trees abound. The dozen or more stream crossings through this stretch of the small creek can usually be rock-hopped without getting your feet wet. The canyon continues to close in, deepening the feeling of intimacy. Although rocky in spots, much of the trail is cushioned by a bed of pine needles. The pleasant grassy opening of Tennessee Meadow is 5 miles up the South Fork at mile 7.3. Sadly, stock parties who have tied their horses to trees close to the stream have degraded the mead-

South Fork Whitewater

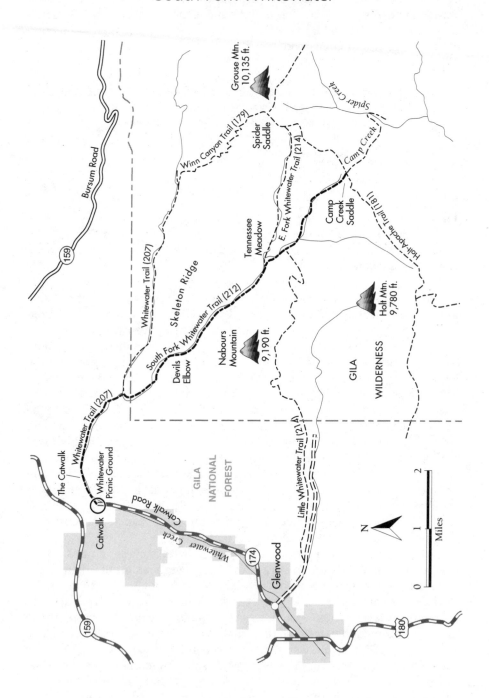

ows. Here the east side is especially dramatic with white rock spires, cliffs, and turrets. The East Fork of Whitewater Creek meets the South Fork just below the meadows. The East Fork Whitewater Trail (213) is identified simply by a primitive sign pointing toward Grouse Mountain and back down to Whitewater Creek. This section of the trail is a delight as it winds through parks of stately ponderosa pine. Fishing can be good as far up as the meadows, but just upstream the South Fork becomes intermittent.

After another 0.3 mile at mile 7.6 the trail reaches the signed junction with Little Whitewater Creek Trail (214), which climbs sharply to the right (west). Continuing uphill another 0.4 mile the trail passes a southern tributary to the South Fork, which enters from the right. The USGS quad shows the "Straight Up" pack trail leading up this right-hand fork, but the trail has long since been abandoned. Nonetheless, a short offtrail exploration up this drainage is enjoyable, with its early season babbling brook, ferns, and large pine trees. Before reaching 8,460-foot-high Camp Creek Saddle at mile 9.5, the easy-to-follow trail becomes steep, brushy, and rough in places, especially where it crosses the dry, rocky streambed. An open pine forest in a deeply incised valley leads up to the saddle and signed four-way trail junction. This wide gap has ample flat tent sites, but nearby Rock Spring will likely be dry in June

If you're hiking the South Fork as a long out-and-back day trip, don't linger long at this view-challenged saddle. Instead, allow plenty of time to enjoy the ever-changing canyon during the downhill return to the Whitewater picnic grounds.

Options: This route is the recommended return (downhill) leg of a 6- to 8-day backpacking loop (see Hikes 10 and 11). Nabours Mountain (Hike 13) is reached by way of the Little Whitewater Trail and is a good side hike if you are camping on the South Fork of Whitewater Creek.

Backpacking in the lower reaches of the South Fork of Whitewater Creek.

13 Nabours Mountain

Highlights: Panoramic vistas from Nabours Mountain; solitude on a lightly visited trail.

Type of hike: 2- to 3-day backpacking trip, out-and-back.

Total distance: 23.4 miles; out-and-back.

Difficulty: Strenuous.

Best months: May through October.

Maps: Forest Service Gila Wilderness map (1984); Holt Mountain USGS quad.

Special considerations: No water along the entire length of the Little Whitewater Trail to Nabours Mountain. Logs may block portions of the trail early in the season. The trail is usually snowbound on the east side of Nabours Mountain into early spring.

Finding the trailhead: To reach the Catwalk Trailhead, drive to the north end of Glenwood and turn east onto New Mexico Highway 174, which is Catwalk Road. Drive 5 miles to the Whitewater picnic ground located at the end of the paved road. This is the trailhead for the Catwalk Trail and Whitewater Trail (207).

Parking and trailhead facilities: Large gravel parking area, vault toilets, kiosk and picnic grounds. Water is available from Whitewater Creek but must be treated. Trailhead camping is not allowed. The nearest public no-fee campground is the Forest Service Bighorn campground on U.S. Highway 180 immediately north of the US 180/NM 174 junction on the north end of Glenwood.

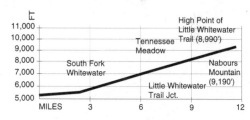

Key points:

1.0   Catwalk Trailhead.

2.0   Beginning of Whitewater Creek Trail (207).

2.1   Junction with South Fork Whitewater Creek Trail (212).

2.2   Junction with East Fork Whitewater Creek Trail (213).

2.3   Junction with Little Whitewater Creek Trail (214).

2.4   High point on Little Whitewater Creek Trail.

11.7   Nabours Mountain.

The hike: After backpacking up the scenic South Fork of Whitewater Creek canyon (see Hike 12), Nabours Mountain is well worth exploring as a day hike from a base camp at Tennessee Meadow or elsewhere in the South Fork of Whitewater Creek drainage. The signed junction for the Little Whitewater Trail (214) is about 0.3 mile above Tennessee Meadow and is accurately depicted on the Forest Service Gila Wilderness map. However, be warned that the USGS topographic map incorrectly shows the trail taking off from Tennessee Meadow downstream. The lower end of the trail seems

Nabours Mountain

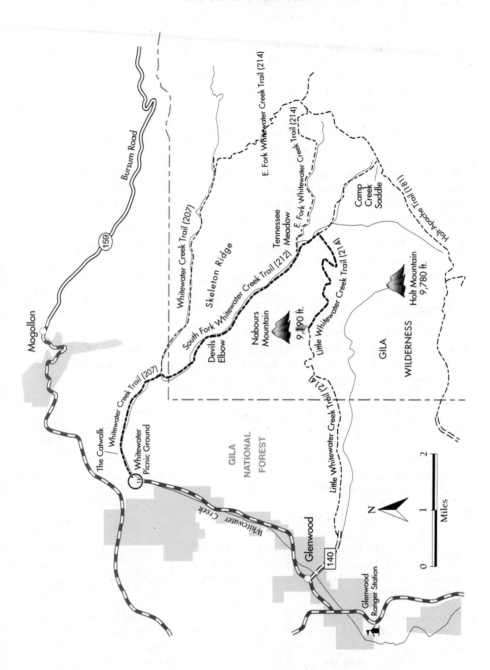

to have a bumper crop of poison ivy, so beware. At first this needle-cushioned trail follows the side drainage for about 0.4 mile. Then it begins a long series of switchbacks, some steep, as it climbs through a dense ponderosa pine–Douglas-fir forest.

After 2 miles a more open forest allows views eastward of the South Fork valley. The trail then follows a narrow oak-lined ridge for a mile on the southeast side of Nabours Mountain before dropping to an open saddle. This rocky stretch of the trail then climbs steeply up the southeast ridge of the mountain for 0.5 mile, reaching the 8,990-foot-high point of the route after climbing 3.3 miles from the South Fork of Whitewater Creek. This open slope offers expansive overlooks into Little Whitewater and southward toward Holt Mountain.

From this high stretch of the Little Whitewater, make the 0.8-mile cross-country trek northward to the 9,190-foot summit of Nabours Mountain. Walk along the east side of the summit ridge through open pine forest. Soon you'll be directly above the rocky cliff face marking the northeast end of the mountain. You'll be rewarded by fabulous views of Sacaton Mountain, Center Baldy, and the lofty Whitewater divide, along with a spectacular look into the rugged canyon of lower South Fork Whitewater Creek—an inspiring perspective on this remote corner of the Gila.

Options: Starting out on the Little Whitewater trail (214) from the 5,200 foot trailhead isn't recommended for an overnight backpacking trip because this tortuous, dry trail gains an average of 1,000 vertical feet per mile to Nabours Mountain. There are easier and more enjoyable ways to access the South Fork of Whitewater Creek. However, Little Whitewater would make a challenging final leg of an extended 3- to 5-day shuttle backpacking trip, whether coming from the canyons of Whitewater and its South Fork or from the high ridges of the Mogollon Range. This route is for those willing to work for solitude, thereby avoiding the heavy hiker traffic on the Catwalk. The one-way distance on the Little Whitewater Creek Trail from the South Fork of Whitewater Creek westward to the Little Whitewater Trailhead is 7.8 up-and-down miles.

14 Catwalk–Deloche Canyon

Highlights:	Vigorous mountain stream; deep canyon of volcanic tuff; fishing; birding.
Type of hike:	1- to 2-day backpacking trip; shuttle.
Total distance:	10 miles.
Difficulty:	Moderate.
Best months:	April through October.
Maps:	Forest Service Gila Wilderness map (1984); Mogollon, Holt Mountain, and Grouse Mountain USGS quads.

Special considerations: Many stream crossings require sturdy wading shoes or boots.

Finding the trailhead: For the entrance at the Catwalk, on the north side of Glenwood on U.S. Highway 180, turn right (east) on New Mexico Highway 174 to the Catwalk and the Whitewater picnic ground. Drive 5 miles east on the paved road to the end of the road at the trailhead parking area.

For the exit at Deloche–Winn Canyon Trailhead, drive 4 miles north of Glenwood on US 180. Turn right (east) on NM 159, also known as Bursum Road, toward Mogollon. NM 159 changes from paved to improved gravel after 9 miles. Drive east a total of 11 miles to Deloche–Winn Canyon Trail (179) trailhead.

The length of the car shuttle is 20 miles, 18 of which are on paved roads.

Parking and trailhead facilities: At the Catwalk, there is a large gravel parking area and a picnic ground with vault toilets but no water other than Whitewater Creek, which is to be treated before using. There is an information kiosk. No camping is permitted at the trailhead. The closest public campground is the Forest Service's Big Horn campground (no fee) on US 180 immediately north of the US 180/NM 174 junction on the north side of Glenwood.

At the Deloche–Winn Canyon Trailhead, there is limited parking; across the road is a small campsite with parking. Seasonally water is available from Fanny Spring (to be treated). There is an information board and a hiker register.

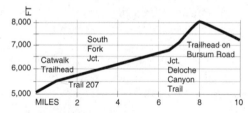

Key points:
1.0   Catwalk Trailhead.
2.0   Whitewater Trail (207) begins.
2.1   Junction with South Fork of Whitewater Creek Trail (212).
3.0   Gila Wilderness Boundary.
3.1   Junction with Deloche Canyon Trail (179).
4.0   Deloche–Winn Canyon Trailhead on Bursum Road.

The hike: The Catwalk area is often crowded with happy picnickers enjoying the cool waters of Whitewater Creek and relaxing in the shade of the sycamore grove. The Catwalk Trail (see Hike 9) can present a challenge for backpackers with large loads; the narrow metal ladders and walkways are quite tight against the leaning canyon walls. The multitude of day hikers on the Catwalk on warm weekends can produce traffic jams.

At the end of the exciting but hectic Catwalk section, where Whitewater Creek Trail (207) commences on the left (north) bank as the Catwalk dead-ends along a narrow metal gangway, suddenly the crowds vanish. The quiet trail to the wilderness climbs above the creek and stays high and dry on the sunny north slope, dropping back to the creek at 2 miles. Always carry water to be prepared for these arid interludes while hiking on the lower stretches of Whitewater Creek.

Catwalk–Deloche Canyon

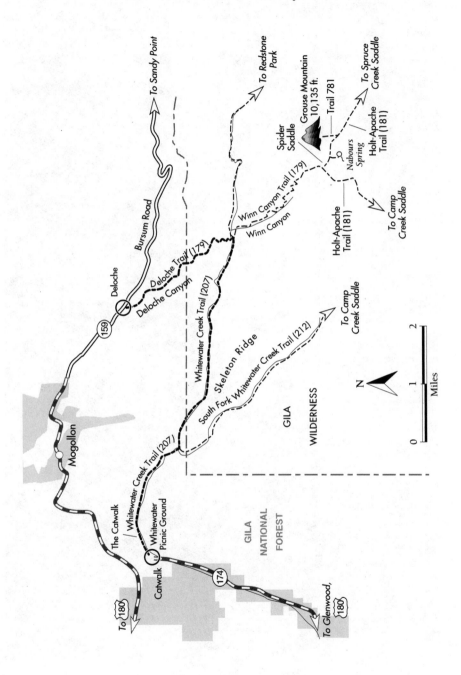

Wading Whitewater Creek just below Winn Canyon.

At the junction with the South Fork Trail, you may wish to take a side trip to the ruins of an old industrial site, 0.2 mile up the South Fork (see Hike 12). Back on the main Whitewater Trail, continue upstream. There are intermittent campsites, usually near crossings. The frequent stream crossings are less troublesome if you can wear your wading shoes or boots for the entire journey. Sturdy footwear is essential, however.

The Gila Wilderness boundary sign is on the north bank after the South Fork junction. After another long, high, dry stretch the trail returns to zigzag in the creek bottom. With the broad-leaved riparian forest, this is a cooler spot, but it is slow traveling along the creek. You will want to enjoy the views of the intricate canyon and towering spires. Watch for swallows at work along the canyon walls, and late in the day bats zoom on the canyon air currents.

At the Deloche Trail junction there are several campsites. If you have planned a layover day to enjoy the canyon, consider a day hike to Grouse Mountain (see Hike 8) for an outing from your base camp at Deloche.

When it's time to leave, fill your water bottle and turn north on the Deloche Trail to Bursum Road. The trail climbs steeply up the dry slope to the ridge above Whitewater Canyon. This trip is much easier with a lightened pack. You then follow the contours of the ridge before descending into Deloche Canyon and arriving at the Bursum Road trailhead.

15 Catwalk–Redstone

Highlights:	The Catwalk and the stunning gorge of Whitewater Creek; fishing; birding; colorful geological formations.
Type of hike:	2- to 3-day backpacking trip; shuttle.
Total distance:	17 miles.
Difficulty:	Moderate.
Best months:	May through October.
Maps:	Forest Service Gila Wilderness map (1984); Holt Mountain and Grouse Mountain USGS quads.

Special considerations: Many stream crossings on Whitewater Creek.

Finding the trailhead: For the entering trailhead at the Catwalk, on the northern edge of Glenwood on U.S. Highway 180, turn right (east) on New Mexico Highway 174 to the Catwalk and the Whitewater picnic ground. Drive 5 miles to the end of the road at the trailhead parking area.

For the exit trailhead at Redstone Trail (206), drive 4 miles north of Glenwood on US 180. Turn right (east) on NM 159, also known as Bursum Road, toward Mogollon. NM 159 changes from paved to improved gravel after 9 miles. Drive east a total of 14 miles to the Redstone Trailhead. Total shuttle distance is 23 miles, 18 of which are on paved roads.

Parking and trailhead facilities: At the Catwalk there is a large gravel parking area. There are vault toilets at the picnic grounds. Water is available in Whitewater Creek (to be treated). There is no trailhead camping. The nearest public campground is the Forest Service's Bighorn campground (no fee) on US 180 immediately north of the US 180/NM 174 junction on the north side of Glenwood.At the Redstone trailhead, there is limited off-road parking. There are a few shady campsites at the trailhead. Silver Creek usually has water, but it needs to be treated.

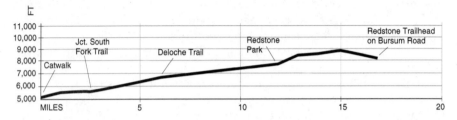

Key points:

0.0	Catwalk trailhead.
1.0	End Catwalk; begin Whitewater Creek Trail (207).
2.3	Junction with South Fork Whitewater Trail (212).
2.4	Junction with Gold Drip Trail (810).
3.0	Gila Wilderness Boundary.
6.5	Junction with Deloche Canyon Trail (179).
6.8	Junction with Winn Canyon Trail (179).
11.8	Junction with Redstone Canyon Trail (206).
12.0	Junction with Redstone Canyon Trail (206).
17.0	Redstone Trailhead on Bursum Road.

The hike: A glance at the elevation profile might convince you to commence the trip at the Redstone trailhead. It is important to consider the idiosyncrasies of the lower Whitewater Creek Trail. We found that starting via the Catwalk, while an unusual environment for a wilderness expedition, was rather exciting. Leaving the chaos of civilization behind, the goal of most Gila adventurers, is dramatically exemplified by the transition from the Catwalk crowds to the solitude of the Whitewater Creek Trail. Returning from several days in the wilderness, on the other hand, we found that the jolly congestion along the Catwalk, especially on a warm summer Sunday, too quickly erased the serenity we had achieved in the solitude of the Gila. In any case, you can easily reverse this trip if you wish.

From the Catwalk trailhead, weave up the intricately engineered series of ladders and bridges. Where the Catwalk dead-ends in the deep canyon, Trail 207 begins, going left (north) and climbing to the side of the ridge above the canyon. After a dry mile the trail returns to the wide Whitewater valley above the canyon. There are numerous campsites in the streamside cottonwood and sycamore groves. At the junction with the South Fork Trail (212) a sign suggests that Redstone Park is 9.5 miles away. Do not be deceived—river miles seem considerably longer than dry land miles. It is a

Catwalk–Redstone

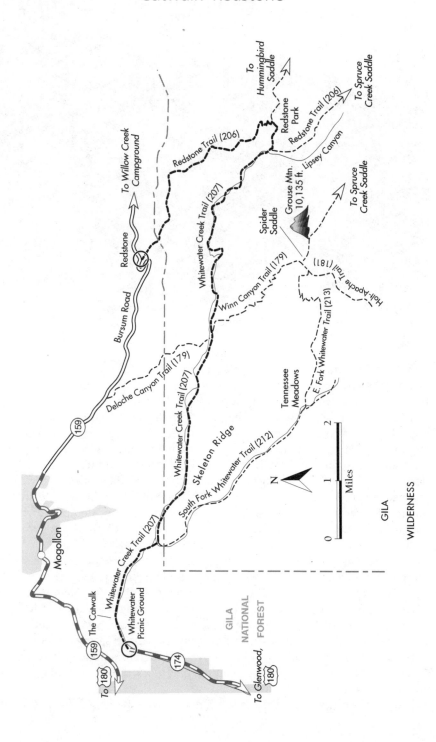

To Hummingbird Saddle

To Spruce Creek Saddle

Redstone Trail (206)

Redstone Park

Redstone Trail (206)

Lipsey Canyon

To Spruce Creek Saddle

Grouse Mtn. 10,135 ft.

Spider Saddle

To Willow Creek Campground

Redstone Trail (206)

Whitewater Creek Trail (207)

Holt-Apache Trail (181)

Redstone

Bursum Road

Winn Canyon Trail (179)

E. Fork Whitewater Trail (213)

Deloche Canyon Trail (179)

Whitewater Creek Trail (207)

Tennessee Meadows

159

Skeleton Ridge

South Fork Whitewater Trail (212)

N

2

Miles

1

GILA

0

WILDERNESS

Mogollon

Whitewater Creek Trail (207)

The Catwalk

Whitewater Picnic Ground

GILA

NATIONAL

FOREST

159

174

To 180

To Glenwood,

180

77

Looking down Whitewater Canyon from Redstone Trail (206).

two-day trip from the trailhead to Redstone Park.

The trail climbs again to the hot, dry north bank, passing the wilderness boundary on a pinyon-juniper slope above the river. Eventually the trail returns to the river bottom and begins the pattern of frequent river crossings. Wearing sturdy wading boots, and hiking in them the whole way upstream, is a lot easier than changing shoes many times an hour. Campsites are frequent to the Deloche Trail, 6.5 miles from the trailhead. The canyon narrows and stream crossings are more numerous above Deloche, where campsites become more rare. If it's getting late, it would be wise to stop at a campsite rather than press on; the next one may be a couple of miles farther upstream. Above Deloche, there are from 5 to 11 crossings per mile.

As the stream valley gains elevation, the botanical zones change. White pine appears at 7,300 feet, with alder thick along the stream bank. In spots, the gorge widens and the stream loses its vigorthen quickly resumes its hectic foamy pace. No crossings are hazardous, but you do have to keep a sharp eye for the trail when it crosses, and a hiking stick is very helpful when carrying a full pack. This is slow hiking country. Savor it, and don't count on covering vast miles in a day. Linger at the crossings to enjoy the canyon, its weeping walls above the river and the cliffs honeycombed with caves. Swallows and, later in the evening, bats work the air currents, swooping after a meal.

Just south of Redstone Park is the junction with Redstone Trail (206) up

Lipsey Canyon to the right (south) to Spruce Creek Saddle. A massive boulder sits in the streambed below the junction. Here the valley is narrow, clogged with fir, aspen, thimbleberry, and thorny locust. A major change occurs just beyond the boulder, when you enter red stone country: Bright cliffs,and spacious towering ponderosas. Plentiful campsites exist on both sides of the river near the junction with Redstone Trail (206) on the north bank.

After a stay at Redstone Park, take the Redstone Trail north to the Bursum Road trailhead. Carry plenty of water; it's a dry trail up out of the canyon. The initial climb is swift, switchbacking up 700 feet to the ridge, then following the contours northwest before descending to Bursum Road. Grand views of the country can be enjoyed from the high exit trail.

Option: At the junction with the South Fork, cross Whitewater Creek and visit the old power plant site, just 0.2 mile from the crossing. (See Hike 12 for details.)

16 Catwalk–Sandy Point

Highlights:	The entire length of Whitewater Creek, from the gorge to the spring on the slopes of Whitewater Baldy; fishing; dramatic canyon; highest peak in the Gila.
Type of hike:	4- to 5-day backpacking trip; shuttle.
Total distance:	25 miles.
Difficulty:	Strenuous.
Best months:	May through October (depending on snow, which can linger into June).
Maps:	Forest Service Gila Wilderness map (1984); Holt Mountain and Grouse Mountain USGS quads.

Special considerations: Many stream crossings; steep ascent to Hummingbird Saddle. The Bursum Road can be closed until quite late in the spring. Check with the Glenwood Ranger Station before taking this trip in May or June in a heavy snow year.

Finding the trailheads: For the entering trailhead at the Catwalk, on the northern edge of Glenwood on U.S. Highway 180, turn right (east) on New Mexico Highway 174 to the Catwalk and the Whitewater picnic ground. Drive 5 miles to the end of the road at the trailhead parking area.

For the exit trailhead, drive 4 miles north of Glenwood on US 180. Turn right (east) on NM 159, also known as Bursum Road, toward Mogollon. NM 159 changes from paved to improved gravel after 9 miles. Drive east a total of 22 miles to the Sandy Point Trailhead. Bursum Road is closed in the winter and often remains snow blocked into May. Call the Glenwood Ranger Station for road information if you're taking this trip in the spring to check on the condition of Bursum Road; even if it's spring in the valley, it can still be winter on Bursum Road! Shuttle distance is 31 miles, of which 18 are on paved road.

Parking and trailhead facilities: At the Catwalk, there is a large gravel parking area. The picnic grounds have vault toilets and an informational kiosk. Water is available in Whitewater Creek, to be treated. Camping is not permitted. The nearest public campground is the Forest Service's Big Horn campground (no fee) on US 180 immediately north of the US 180/NM 174 junction on the north side of Glenwood.

At Sandy Point, there is a large gravel parking area. There is an information board and a trail registry. There is no water. Camping is permitted.

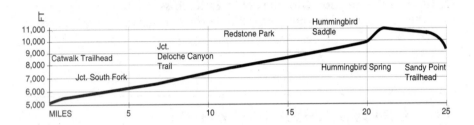

Key points:
- 0.0   Catwalk trailhead.
- 1.0   End of Catwalk; begin Whitewater Trail (207).
- 2.3   Junction with South Fork Whitewater Trail (212).
- 2.4   Junction with Gold Drip Trail (810).
- 3.0   Gila Wilderness Boundary.
- 6.5   Junction with Deloche Canyon Trail (179).
- 6.8   Junction with Winn Canyon Trail (179).
- 11.8   Junction with Redstone Trail (206).
- 12.0   Junction with Redstone Trail (206).
- 19.8   Hummingbird Spring.
- 20.0   Hummingbird Saddle; junction with Crest Trail (182).
- 23.1   Bead Spring Trail.
- 24.0   Sandy Point Trailhead.

The hike: The Catwalk, a fine example of man's engineering ability, is an exciting starting point for this trip. See Hike 15 for an explanation of why we recommend that the journey ends high on Bursum Road, instead of at the Catwalk.

Over a hundred stream crossings along Whitewater Creek make this backpack outing one of the most arduous in the Gila. Don't count on covering vast miles on the zigzag trail back and forth across the rushing stream. Two days of hiking to get to Redstone Park is a realistic goal; there are few campsites between Redstone and Hummingbird Saddle, and Redstone is an idyllic location. After perhaps a layover day for recovery or fishing, it is another day to Hummingbird Saddle. From there it is a 5-mile hike out to Sandy Point for a four-night, five-day wilderness outing, with water at every campsite.

Catwalk–Sandy Point

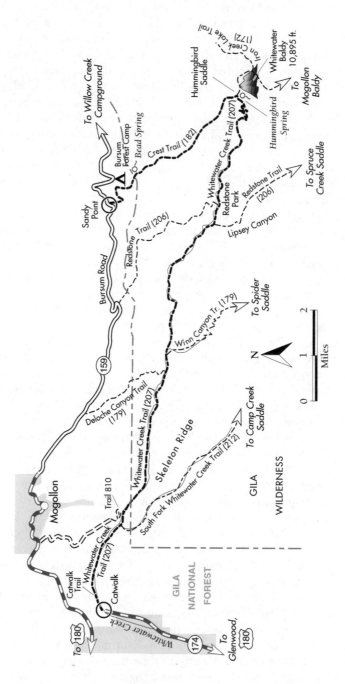

From the Catwalk Trailhead, thread your way up the narrow metal bridges, ladders, and hanging pathways above the Whitewater gorge. Emerge on the north slope at the Catwalk's end to find a tiny Trail 207 sign affixed to a boulder on the left where the Catwalk goes right to deadend in the gorge. Here you'll leave crowds behind. Travel up Whitewater on a dry slope of pinyon-juniper and scrub oak before dropping back to the lush river valley and its towering sycamores, cottonwoods, and campsites.

Fishing parties visit this lower Whitewater region frequently. At mile 2.3 there's a junction with the South Fork Trail. Take a 0.4-mile round trip to visit the old power plant ruins just up the South Fork (see Hike 12 for details), then return to the main trail. Shortly thereafter, you pass the junction with the Gold Drip Trail (used by fishermen on ATVs and trail bikes, as recommended by the Forest Service handout on fishing) and then the wilderness boundary on the north slope of scrub oak and pinyon pine, so now the adventure really begins.

The trail takes up its pattern of stream crossing farther up the canyon. Surprisingly there are some dry stretches in this lower section, so carry water in anticipation if it's a warm day. From 5 miles on, the crossings become increasingly more frequent. There are about a dozen crossings between mile 5 and mile 7; then the trail has from 5 to 12 crossings per mile until you begin the switchbacks to Hummingbird at mile 16. It's best just to plan on hiking in your wading gear, so wear sturdy waders. If cold feet are a problem, Neoprene socks are the solution.

Intricate cliff walls topped with creative spires cause frequent breaks as you need to stop to admire the erosive powers of the stream. The lush foliage of the streambed, the broad-leaved forest, and the noisy sparkling cascades of the creek provide contrast with the semidesert landscape above.

Campsites are at the Deloche junction. Suitable sites become rare between Deloche and Redstone, so if you see a likely spot and it's getting late, it would be wise to camp. The Redstone Park area is unique along the creek with its broad campsites and bright red stone providing stark contract with towering ponderosa pines. Redstone Park is a popular day hike destination and is frequently visited by fishermen. Nevertheless, it is a pleasant halfway spot for a layover day on your trek up Whitewater.

From Redstone Park it is 8 miles to Hummingbird Saddle. The trail sign's low projection of 5 miles must be an "as the crow flies" estimate. Above Redstone, the stream crossings continue, and side streams add to the wet-foot experience. The less traveled trail is often hard to follow in the rocky streambed. The trail narrows to a footpath in places as the dense shrubbery closes in; periodically fallen trees create hurdles in the path. There are a few small marginal campsites here and there, but they are nonexistent in the final 4 miles to the saddle. The journey up the densely forested northwest slope of Whitewater Baldy to Hummingbird Saddle is via long switchbacks. The Grouse Mountain topo map shows the trail running in a straight line right up the ravine; this imaginary route may be shorter, but it doesn't exist. The spring is right on the trail, nestled in the aspen thicket. Campsites are plentiful at the saddle, on the open grassy top, and in the

Entering the Gila Wilderness on trail 207 in Whitewater Canyon.

timber on both east and west, so you can be protected from the wind. In the saddle is the signed junction with the Crest Trail (182) as well as a peculiar red sculpture whose meaning is a mystery.

Take the Crest Trail north (left from the Whitewater Trail from the spring). This is a dry 5-mile section, so fill your bottles before you depart. The Crest Trail to Bursum Road gets moderate use. The trail is wide and rocky in its sloping sections. From the saddle it rises to a high point of 10,510 feet and then weaves along the ridge with excellent views of your Whitewater route stretching to the west. The trail travels through dense ponderosa pine–Douglas-fir forest on the northeast side of Willow Mountain. After the Bead Spring Trail drops off to your right, and the wilderness boundary sign, the trail descends via a rocky steep section to Bursum Road, the Sandy Point Trailhead.

Options: From Hummingbird Saddle it's only a mile to the summit of Whitewater Baldy (10,895 feet), the highest peak in the Gila Wilderness. (See Hike 1 for details.) From Hummingbird Saddle you can extend your backpack along the Crest Trail to Mogollon Baldy (10,770 feet). (See Hike 2 for details.)

17 Skunk Johnson Cabin

Highlights:	Vistas of Sheridan Gulch and Dry Fork Canyon; historic cabin on remote stream; fishing; apples (in season).
Type of hike:	Day hike or overnight backpacking trip;out-and-back.
Total distance:	10.6 miles.
Difficulty:	Strenuous.
Best months:	Year-round (except for occasional snow).
Maps:	Forest Service Gila Wilderness map (1984); Holt Mountain USGS quad.

Special considerations: *Hantavirus* is a danger when exploring cabin ruins. Avoid stirring up dust, which makes the mouse droppings and dried urine airborne and allows you to inhale the deadly virus.

Finding the trailhead: To get to the Sheridan Corral Trailhead, drive 8 miles south of Glenwood on U.S. Highway 180 to the sign for hiking trail 181 at Forest Road 146. Turn left (east) and drive 4 miles on the improved gravel two-wheel-drive road to the dead end at the trailhead.

Parking and trailhead facilities: There is a large gravel parking area and an information kiosk at the trailhead. There is no water. There are a few marginal campsites at the trailhead; additional

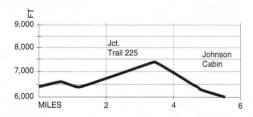

Skunk Johnson Cabin

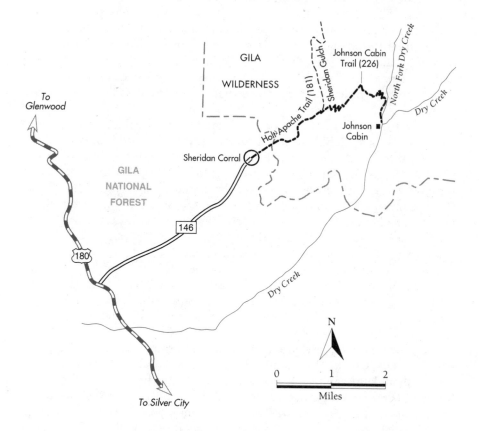

campsites are located 0.25 mile back down Forest Road 146 at the stock tank.

Key points:
- 0.0   Sheridan Corral Trailhead for Holt–Apache Trail (181).
- 2.1   Junction with Johnson Cabin Trail (225).
- 5.0   Cross the North Fork.
- 5.3   Skunk Johnson Cabin.

The hike: This short hike takes you into a deep canyon in the remote southwest corner of the Gila. Its destination is the site of several cabins dating from the 1930s. There are pleasant campsites along the Dry Fork near the cabins, as well as excellent fishing.

From the Sheridan Corral Trailhead, the Holt–Apache Trail (181) is wide and rocky as it slopes up to the saddle where an old wilderness sign stands. This is a unique sign because it gives a lengthy explanation of how the wilderness has been preserved just as it was for the first explorers in the area. These first explorers were identified as "pioneers" in the original version;

they have been scratched out and replaced with "Indians" by a concerned passer-by. From this thought-provoking spot, the trail then drops along the ridge, reaching the bottom of Sheridan Gulch.

An old corral by the trail along the stream probably housed mining burros during the prospecting era in the 30s and before. Continue up the Sheridan Gulch draw to the sign for Big Dry Creek, 3 at the Skunk Johnson Trail turnoff on the right. The Johnson Trail is identified as 225 on the Gila Wilderness map and 226 on the USGS map, resulting in some confusion. We'll stick with the wilderness map since that is the one that hikers are more likely to carry.

The trail cuts across the stream and immediately begins climbing up to the ridge. Long switchbacks make for an easy grade on this steep section, but they do increase the distance significantly. Pause at the saddles for the view. At the top of the ridge, the trail contours along the east side where scrubby vegetation permits a spectacular aerial view of the cliffs of Dry Creek Canyon. The trail drops swiftly, with few switchbacks, to the North Fork, a small tributary in a steep rocky ravine. The trail turns south and follows the North Fork closely downstream 0.3 mile to the cabin on the bench at the confluence of the North Fork and Dry Creek.

The well-constructed cabin dating from the 1930s still stands. The register in the cabin makes good reading; be sure to add your remarks to the historical record. Skunk's orchard flourishes still, with dense ground cover spreading beneath the apple trees. The apples are a fall delicacy for hikers and bears alike. The remains of other buildings are nearby.

It is interesting to prowl around the ruins and think about Skunk and his world on Dry Creek. How unusual for a miner to plant trees or be concerned about landscaping. He must have anticipated being here a long time. Just getting materials, particularly cement, in to construct the cabins meant considerable expense and effort. This was an ambitious, energetic man! Tragically, boorish visitors have disturbed Skunk's dwelling. Be considerate of his spirit, and treat the site with respect.

Fishermen have created footpaths up and down Dry Creek, seeking the wary trout, so it's easy to wander along the creek. There are numerous campsites. This is a sheltered spot to spend a night or two before returning to the modern world.

When your time is up, return to the trailhead by the same route. The hike out of the ravine is the strenuous part of the trip since the trail from the North Fork to the ridge lacks those long switchbacks.

18 Sheridan–Catwalk

Highlights: A diverse cross-section of the Gila Wilderness;
expansive mountain vistas; deep canyons bound by
sheer cliffs and colorful rock formations; trout-filled
pools; historic mining structures; the suspended
Catwalk high above Whitewater Gorge.
Type of hike: 3- to 4-day backpacking trip; shuttle.
Total distance: 17 miles.
Difficulty: Strenuous.
Best months: May through November.
Maps: Forest Service Gila Wilderness map (1984); Holt
Mountain and Grouse Mountain USGS quads.

Special considerations: A 2-mile stretch of the Holt–Apache Trail (181) in
upper Sheridan Gulch is rough and primitive. Numerous wet-foot crossings.
Poison ivy is common along streams in places. Stream is intermittent above
Tennessee Meadow.

Finding the trailhead: Sheridan Corral Trailhead: Drive 8 miles south of
Glenwood on U.S. Highway 180 to Forest Road 146, which is signed for
hiking trail 181. Turn left (east) and continue 4 miles on the improved gravel
road to the signed end-of-road trailhead.

Catwalk Trailhead: On the north end of Glenwood from US 180 turn
right (east) onto New Mexico Highway 174 (Catwalk Road) and drive the 5
miles to the end of the paved road at the Whitewater picnic ground and
trailhead parking area.

The shuttle driving distance between the two trailheads is 18 miles, 14 of
which are paved.

Parking and trailhead facilities: Sheridan Corral Trailhead: large gravel
parking area and kiosk, with no trailhead water and only limited camping.
Additional flat campsites can be found 0.25 mile back down FR 146 next to
the Sheridan Corral stock tank.

Catwalk Trailhead: large gravel parking area, kiosk, vault toilets, and
picnic tables. Water is available from Whitewater Creek but must be treated.
Trailhead camping is not allowed. The nearest public no-fee campground is
the Forest Service's Bighorn campground on US 180 immediately north of
the US 180/NM 174 junction on the north side of Glenwood.

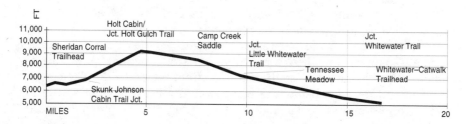

Key points:

  0.0   Sheridan Corral Trailhead at end of FR 146.

  2.0   Junction with Skunk Johnson Cabin Trail (226).

  4.7   Holt Cabin and junction with Holt Gulch Trail (217).

  7.5   Camp Creek Saddle and junction with South Fork Whitewater Creek Trail (212).

  9.4   Junction with Little Whitewater Creek Trail (214).

  9.7   Tennessee Meadow and junction with East Fork Whitewater Creek Trail (213).

12.9   Devil's Elbow.

14.7   Junction with Whitewater Creek Trail (207).

17.0   Catwalk Trailhead–Whitewater picnic ground.

The hike: Despite a tough climb during the first 5 miles, a south to north direction for this shuttle hike is recommended because the varied South Fork Whitewater canyon is better appreciated as a downhill route. Also, the rough section of the trail in upper Sheridan Gulch is easier going up than down. And we suppose that there is satisfaction in achieving the elevation quickly, followed by a long downhill roll to the exit trailhead.

The Holt–Apache Trail (181) is excellent during the first 2 miles to its junction with the Skunk Johnson Cabin Trail. The trail then continues left (north) straight up Sheridan Gulch to Holt Cabin and the junction with the Holt Gulch Trail (217). This extremely rough 2.7-mile stretch of the trail gains 2,300 feet and can best be described as primitive and rocky. It stays mostly in the bottom of the gully, joining the waterway in the upper reaches of the gulch and then makes a steep climb across the headwall of the drainage to the tiny cabin perched high on the southwest ridge of 9,780-foot Holt Mountain. The nearby spring is normally a reliable source of water. Turn right (east) for a delightful stretch of high ridge trail with panoramic views eastward, dropping to Camp Creek Saddle after another 2.7 miles. The saddle is high, dry, and closed in by trees and terrain.

Turn left (northwest) at the four-way junction onto the South Fork Whitewater Trail (212). The trail drops down a narrow gully enclosed in an open pine forest, becoming steep and brushy wherever it crosses the dry, rocky streambed. The main southern branch of the South Fork enters from the left (west) about 1.5 miles below the saddle. The abandoned Straight Up Trail used to head up this draw, which can now only be explored as an off-trail side hike. The South Fork Trail intersects the Little Whitewater Creek Trail (214) after another 0.3 mile on the left (west) side of the creek. (See Hike 13 if interested in a side hike to Nabours Mountain by way of the Little Whitewater Creek Trail.) This upper stretch of the South Fork may be intermittent by midsummer all the way down to Tennessee Meadow, but the trail is enjoyable as it winds through ponderosa pine parks.

The East Fork of Whitewater enters from the right (east) near Tennessee Meadow 0.3 mile below the Little Whitewater Trail junction. Spires, turrets, and cliffs of volcanic tuff rise dramatically from the east side. The canyon closes in and deepens below the meadows, forming a wonderland of alcoves, grottoes, mossy rocks, and great towering rock columns overhead.

Sheridan–Catwalk

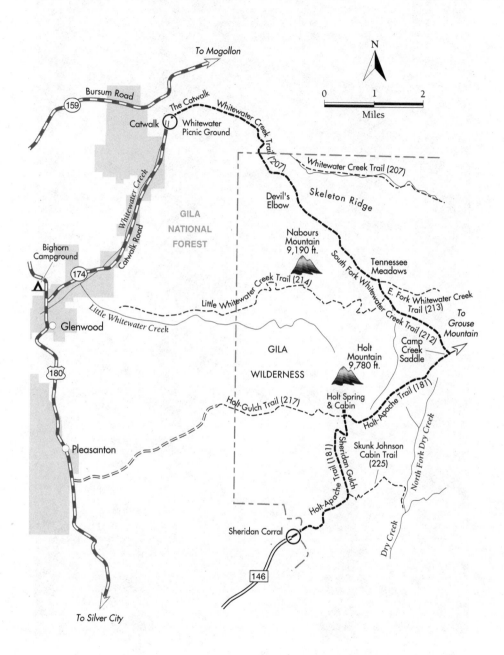

N

0   1   2
Miles

To Mogollon

Bursum Road

159

The Catwalk

Catwalk

Whitewater Picnic Ground

Whitewater Creek Trail (207)

Whitewater Creek Trail (207)

Skeleton Ridge

Devil's Elbow

Nabours Mountain 9,190 ft.

Tennessee Meadows

E. Fork Whitewater Creek Trail (213)

South Fork Whitewater Creek Trail (212)

To Grouse Mountain

GILA NATIONAL FOREST

Whitewater Creek

Catwalk Road

Little Whitewater Creek Trail (214)

Little Whitewater Creek

Bighorn Campground

174

Glenwood

GILA WILDERNESS

Holt Mountain 9,780 ft.

Camp Creek Saddle

Holt-Apache Trail (181)

180

Holt-Gulch Trail (217)

Holt Spring & Cabin

Holt-Apache Trail (181)

Skunk Johnson Cabin Trail (225)

North Fork Dry Creek

Pleasanton

Sheridan Gulch

Holt-Apache Trail (181)

Dry Creek

Sheridan Corral

146

To Silver City

The short section of trail that is signed "hazardous to stock" in the South Fork of Whitewater Creek canyon above Devil's Elbow.

Lush communities of deciduous and evergreen vegetation abound. The contrast of water-loving willows growing within a few feet of desert yucca on nearby dry hillsides is amazing. A steep, cliffy section of the trail is notched into the east side of the canyon about 2.6 miles below Tennessee Meadow with a sign warning that the trail is hazardous for livestock and that animals should be led single file on foot.

A short distance below, the aptly named Devil's Elbow is wedged by great angular rock formations with a spacious campsite in the bottom. The canyon narrows dramatically for the next mile down to a monumental cathedral formation that punctuates the end of Skeleton Ridge on the right (east). As it approaches the main Whitewater canyon the trail exits the wilderness boundary and passes through a lovely sycamore bottom next to power house remnants on the historic superintendent's site. Both wood and water power were produced here for the Mogollon mines.

After an easy wet-foot crossing of Whitewater Creek to the signed junction with the Whitewater–Catwalk Trail (207), turn left (northwest) and continue down the rugged lower Whitewater canyon for the final 2.3-mile stretch to the Catwalk Trailhead. You may find the suspended metal confines of the Catwalk a bit narrow for your backpack in one or two places, but with a bit of maneuvering you'll easily negotiate this final mile-long gorge en route to the exit trailhead.

Options: Do this hike in reverse from the Catwalk to Sheridan Corral if you want to end your trip in solitude. The Catwalk is by far the most popular day-use attraction in proximity to the Gila Wilderness.

19 Holt Mountain

Highlights:	Wide diversity from lower pinyon-juniper brushlands to higher elevation conifer-aspen forests; superb high-country vistas.
Type of hike:	Day hike or overnighter, out-and-back.
Total distance:	12 miles.
Difficulty:	Strenuous.
Best months:	April through November.
Maps:	Forest Service Gila Wilderness map (1984); Holt Mountain USGS quad.

Special considerations: Upper portion of route may be blocked by snow into late May. Limited water at springs along crest. Rough primitive trail in upper Sheridan Gulch south of Holt Cabin. Short off-trail route to the summit of Holt Mountain.

Finding the trailhead: Drive 8 miles south of Glenwood on U.S. Highway 180 to Forest Road 146, which is signed for hiking trail 181. Turn left (east) and continue 4 miles on the improved gravel road to the signed end-of-road Sheridan Corral Trailhead.

Parking and trailhead facilities: The trailhead has a large gravel parking area and kiosk but no water and limited camping. A flat campsite can be found 0.25 mile back down FR 146 next to the Sheridan Corral stock tank.

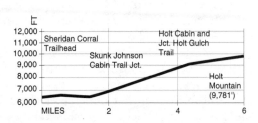

Key points:
- 1.0   Sheridan Corral Trailhead at end of FR 146.
- 2.0   Junction with Skunk Johnson Cabin Trail.
- 4.7   Holt Cabin and junction with Holt Gulch Trail (217).
- 6.0   Holt Mountain (9,781 feet).

The hike: This challenging excursion samples a great western swath of the Gila from rocky canyon to forested peaks. Camping is possible near Holt Spring, which is a reliable water source most of the year. The wide gravel Holt–Apache Trail (181) climbs along the left side of a low ridge above Dugway Canyon and quickly enters the wilderness boundary that wasn't signed when we made this trip. At 0.6 mile the trail joins a small saddle where one of the older wilderness signs proudly proclaims "pioneers" as being the first explorers of the Gila. A modern day explorer scratched in "Indians." The excellent moderate use trail then drops to Sheridan Gulch and works up the draw to a Douglas-fir forest and the signed junction to Skunk Johnson Cabin Trail (226) at 2 miles. Actually the wilderness map incorrectly depicts this trail as 225. The remains of an old cabin foundation and stone patio are tucked away across the gulch in an oak grove.

Continue left (north) on the Holt–Apache Trail. The next 2.7 miles to Holt Cabin and spring is the most difficult segment of the hike. The trail becomes increasingly rough and rocky as it climbs the gulch, crossing repeatedly. In the narrow upper reaches of Sheridan Gulch, the waterway of the gully becomes the trail. The trail is rugged enough to make going up seem a lot easier than going down. The trail is particularly steep near the top, gaining a total of 2,300 feet from the Johnson Cabin Trail junction to Holt Cabin. The tiny Forest Service cabin and nearby spring are just to the left of the junction with the Holt Gulch Trail (217) high on the main southwest ridge of Holt Mountain.

If climbing Holt Mountain, turn right (east) on the Holt–Apache Trail and wrap around the south side of the mountain for 0.7 mile, gaining about 400 to 9,500 feet on a broad south ridge saddle below Holt Mountain. Holt Mountain is mostly closed in by trees but its 9,780-foot summit is well worth a short off-trail walk-up of 0.6 mile to the north of the saddle, if for no other reason than to ramble about on this highest of points in a secluded corner of the Gila.

The Forest Service has long since abandoned the Straight Up Trail in the upper South Fork of Whitewater Creek that used to head down from this

Holt Mountain

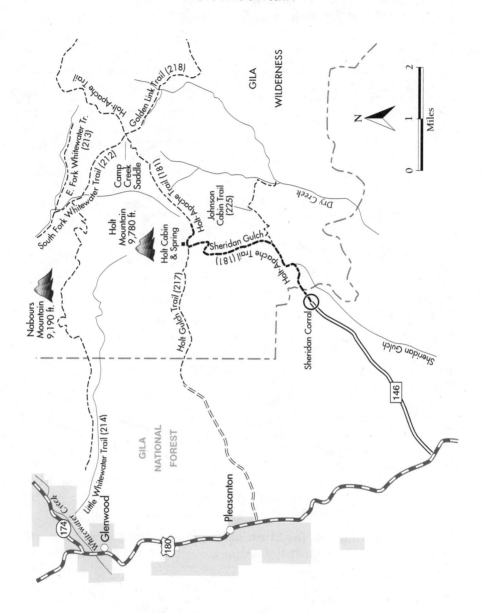

saddle. In addition, the old Holt Mountain Trail used to run from the saddle north over the top of Holt Mountain toward Nabours Mountain, but no longer exists.

Options: Although this hike is suggested as an out-and-back on the Holt–Apache Trail, a shorter day hike shuttle is possible by turning left (west) at the cabin and dropping down Holt Gulch Trail (217). The road to this trailhead climbs east from Pleasanton just south of Glenwood and is rough, requiring four-wheel-drive. Refer to Hike 17 for a side trip from the lower Holt–Apache Trail to the historic Skunk Johnson Cabin on Dry Creek.

20 Windy Gap

Highlights: Remnants of early day mining; scenic portal to the wilderness with year-round accessibility; deep, narrow gorge; breathtaking fall colors in the riparian forest.

Type of hike: Day hike, out-and-back.

Total distance: 9 miles.

Difficulty: Moderate.

Best months: March through November.

Maps: Forest Service Gila Wilderness map (1984); Grouse Mountain USGS quad.

Special considerations: There is no water on the upper portion of the hike after the trail leaves Little Dry Creek.

Finding the trailhead: Drive 11 miles south of Glenwood on U.S. Highway 180 to Forest Road 147, the Sacaton Road, on the left (east). This junction is in the Little Dry Creek valley, just north of the Leopold Vista Historic Monument. FR 147 is a county-maintained improved gravel road. Drive 3 miles east on FR 147 to

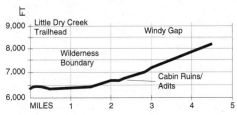

FR 196 on the left (north). FR 196 is also an improved gravel road. Drive north 3.5 miles to the end-of-the-road trailhead for Little Dry–Apache Trail (180).

Parking and trailhead facilities: Large gravel parking area, kiosk, and limited trailhead camping on the sloping ground. There is no water or other facilities.

Key points:

0.0 Little Dry–Apache Trailhead; Little Dry Trail (180).
0.5 Trail sign.
1.8 Private cabin.
2.0 Wilderness boundary.
2.4 Cabin ruins; adits.
4.5 Windy Gap.

The hike: The hardest thing about this hike is turning around, for the coun-

Windy Gap

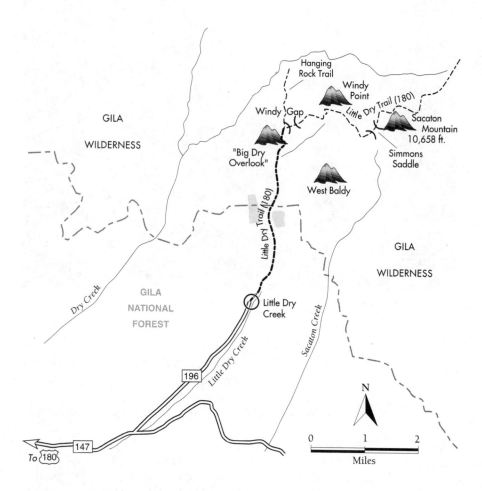

try is truly spectacular and becomes even more so beyond Windy Gap. The nearly 2,000-foot climb to the gap is normally open year-round, but beyond to the higher country expect the moderately used trail to be blocked by snow into late spring.

Little Dry Creek–Apache Trail (180) starts out as a rocky unmaintained four-wheel-drive road that climbs and then drops to Little Dry Creek and a trail sign after 0.5 mile. The sign points onward to Windy Gap. The two-track continues up the left side of the draw, crosses a small scummy stream still suffering from mine leaching and quickly narrows to a singletrack trail. The well-defined trail passes by a constructed stone wall and a private cabin in a canyon bottom of mountain maple, oak, and pine. Cliffs tower above a Douglas-fir forest at the wilderness boundary 2 miles up. The stream slides down bedrock into stairstep pools in a deep gorge as the trail climbs past cabin ruins and adits during the next 0.4 mile. One of the adits has a walk-

Hiking down Little Dry Creek Trail (180) in a spring snowstorm.

in entrance with mine timbers still in place. It sits on the east side of the canyon just below a jumble of large boulders. For safety the adits are best viewed from the outside. The well-built trail climbs out of the bottom several times, only to drop each time to another crossing. The tight chasm is bound by a interesting assortment of formations, from longitudinal walls to isolated spires.

An early prospector trail leads up a ravine on the right (east) at mile 2.8. Continue left up the bottom on the main trail as canyon walls give way to sloping hillsides. At 3 miles the trail climbs right (east) above a flat, gaining 1,000 feet over the next 1.5 miles to Windy Gap. Although there are a few steep brushy pitches, one long, straight section of the trail gains 660 feet without a switchback. An aspen stand graces the head of Rainstorm Canyon just below the gap. Windy Gap is a narrow saddle cloaked in Douglas-fir, with a sign proclaiming 3.5 miles back down to FR 196. Actually, the distance back to the trailhead is closer to 4.5 miles. From the gap the unmaintained Hanging Rock Trail heads north down to Big Dry Creek and is signed "Impassable to Livestock.". The Little Dry–Apache Trail takes a sharp 90-degree right (east) turn uphill. Ironically, this main trail is faint at this point, whereas the abandoned Hanging Rock Trail is much more obvious in its upper end.

Option: For spectacular views into the deep rugged canyon of Big Dry Creek, walk up the west slope above Windy Gap. Within 0.25 mile you'll gain 400 feet and a grand overview of wild scenic canyons in the west Gila.

21 Apache Cabin

Highlights:	A strenuous but rewarding hike with sweeping views of canyons and rugged peaks of southwest Gila Wilderness; display of fall colors in autumn; access to Mogollon peaks from cabin.
Type of hike:	3- to 4-day backpacking trip; out-and-back.
Total distance:	23 miles.
Difficulty:	Strenuous.
Best months:	June through October.
Maps:	Forest Service Gila Wilderness map (1984); Rice Ranch and Grouse Mountain USGS quads.

Special considerations: Snowbanks linger into early summer on the north side of Sacaton Mountain, blocking the trail above Simmons Saddle. This high-elevation trail exposes you to risks of summer storms—lightning and hypothermia. Water may be available in Little Dry Creek. The next source is the spring at Simmons Saddle (7.5 miles).

Finding the trailhead: To reach the Windy Gap–Little Dry Creek Trailhead, drive 11 miles south of Glenwood on U.S. Highway 180 to Forest Road 147, also signed as the Sacaton Road. This is a county-maintained improved gravel road. The junction with the highway is in the Little Dry Creek valley, just north of the Leopold Vista Historical Monument. Drive 3 miles east on FR 147 to FR 196 on the left (north). Turn left at this signed junction and drive 3.5 miles north to the end of the road and the trailhead. FR 196 is improved gravel and negotiable for two-wheel-drive vehicles.

Parking and trailhead facilities: At the end of the road are a large gravel parking area and a kiosk. Camping is permitted, but sites are limited at the sloping trailhead location. There is no water at the trailhead.

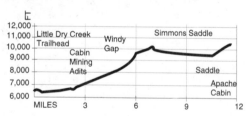

Key points:

0.0	Windy Gap–Little Dry Creek Trailhead.
0.5	Trail sign.
1.8	Private cabin.
2.0	Wilderness boundary.
2.4	Cabin ruins; adits.
4.5	Windy Gap.
7.5	Simmons Saddle and spring.
11.5	Apache Cabin and spring.

The hike: This lightly used trail takes you into the heart of the wilderness amid the peaks of the Mogollon Mountains. The grassy, aspen-encircled

Apache Cabin

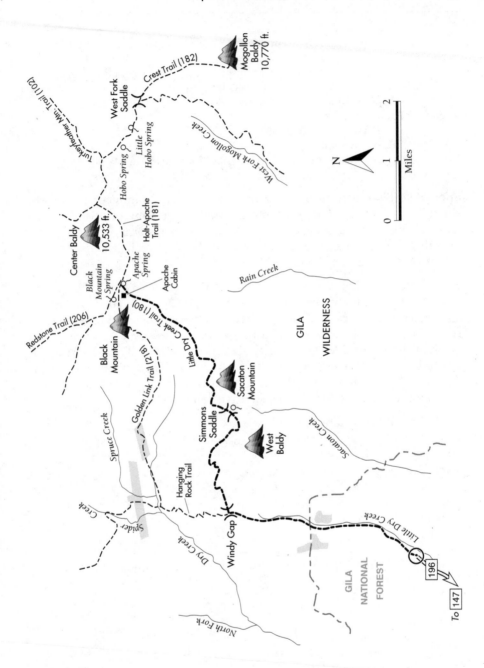

Looking down into the rugged Rain Creek drainage from Trail 180.

slopes of the high ridges provide magnificent vistas of the diving canyons, as well as opportunities to spot elk and deer. From Apache Cabin you can continue your explorations to the Crest Trail, and on to Mogollon Baldy, either as a day hike or an extension of the basic backpack.

The length and elevation gain on the Little Dry Creek Trail make it advisable to divide the trip to the cabin into two days by camping at Simmons Saddle. The spring there is a reliable source of water. This means that your first day is a humdinger, but there are no campsites below the saddle that have water.

The Forest Service has had an open-door policy at Apache Cabin. It is important that visitors do not abuse the privilege for it to continue. The cabin has several squeaky spring beds and a wood stove. If you use firewood, replenish the supply before you depart. You'll be sharing the cabin with a rodent who lives there. He's a daring fellow, and doesn't mind visitors; he is definitely a rat rather than a deer mouse, so it is unlikely that he's carrying *Hantavirus*. There's a supply of food on the cabin shelves, evidently left there by overburdened horse parties since it's mostly canned goods. Don't contribute any food unless it's in rodent-proof containers. When you leave the cabin, close the windows and shutters, and fasten the door. Take all your trash with you, of course, leaving the cabin tidy for your successors. Apache spring is not a gusher. If the water there is too murky for your taste, you can hike 0.8 mile to Black Mountain spring on the Holt–Apache Trail (181). There are limited campsites near Apache Cabin for those preferring outdoor accommodations.

From the trailhead, Little Dry Creek Trail begins as an old jeep track but it very quickly becomes a hiking trail, following the bottom of Little Dry canyon. There's a piece of private land with a cabin adjacent to the trail just south of the wilderness boundary. Just upstream the canyon narrows, crowding the riparian forest into a slender band of greenery between the boulders and cliffs. At 3 miles the trail leaves the bottom and slants swiftly to Windy Gap, in a ponderosa pine–Douglas-fir forest. (See Hike 20 for details on the trip to the gap.)

At Windy Gap the main trail turns sharply east (right) and climbs up the ridge toward Sacaton Mountain (10,658 feet). An unmaintained trail down into Big Dry Creek goes directly north from Windy Gap; this second trail is marked with a "Not recommended for livestock" sign. Hikers have mistakenly surged over the gap and ended up on the Golden Link Trail (see Hike 11), many miles from Apache Cabin.

After turning right at the gap, you begin the strenuous part of the journey. Climb over 600 feet in half a mile, enjoy an undulating half mile of recovery, and then climb 1,200 feet in the next 2 miles. Portions of the trail are quite rocky. When the trail breaks out on the open ridge you'll savor the view while you recover from the ascent. Aspens fringe the meadows, providing cover for elk and deer, and also creating brilliant fall colors.

At Simmons Saddle there is a sign to the spring, down to the southeast about 100 yards. Several campsites are located at the saddle. From here the trail stays on the north side of the Sacaton massif for over a mile. This section of the trail can be blocked by snow long after snow has disappeared elsewhere in the Gila. Even in June, slogging through deep snow here can ruin your outing. There are vast talus slopes from Sacaton extending down into the Big Dry Creek canyon below.

Emerging from the shadow of Sacaton, the trail drops to a saddle 1 mile before the cabin. Here you can enjoy views of Rain Creek and the West Fork of Mogollon Creek off to the south. From the saddle it's a steady climb along the ridge to the cabin. When your outing at Apache Cabin is over, return to the trailhead by the same route you came in on.

Options: The possibilities of additional trips from Apache Cabin are numerous. You can extend your journey with day hikes from the cabin, or move your camp as you travel. From Apache Cabin, you can continue east 0.2 mile to the Holt–Apache Trail (181). Continue east 1.7 miles to the intersection with the Crest Trail (182). From here it is 4.2 miles south to Mogollon Baldy with its lookout and guard station above Snow Park. To break up this 12-mile round trip, consider camping at Hobo Spring. (See Hike 2 for details.)

If you prefer more of a loop trip, you can return via the Golden Link Trail by turning left (west) on Holt–Apache, and then turning left up Black Mountain on the Golden Link Trail. From the low point on Big Dry Creek you will get to climb the rustic Hanging Rock Trail back to Windy Point. Be aware that this option is very strenuous and will require at least another day. The unmaintained Hanging Rock Trail is indicated on the topo map but is not on the wilderness map. (See Hike 11 for details.)

22 Rain Creek

Highlights:	Year-round vehicular access to lower elevation trailhead on south end of wilderness; canyon overlook of spectacular volcanic cliffs and formations.
Type of hike:	Day hike; out-and-back.
Total distance:	2.6 miles.
Difficulty:	Easy.
Best months:	March through November.
Maps:	Forest Service Gila Wilderness map (1984); Rice Ranch USGS quad.

Special considerations: None.

Finding the trailhead: Drive 11 miles south of Glenwood on U.S. Highway 180 to Forest Road 147, the Sacaton Road, on the left (east). This junction is in the Little Dry Creek valley just north of the Leopold Vista Historic Monument. FR 147 is a county-maintained improved gravel road. Drive 10 miles east on FR 147 to a gated road on the left (north), signed Sacaton Trailhead. Close the gate after you. Drive north on the 0.2-mile access road to the road-end trailhead for Rain Creek Trail (189).

Parking and trailhead facilities: There is a kiosk, trail sign, and large gravel parking area. Camping is permitted, but sites are limited at the sloping trailhead. No water or other facilities are available.

Key points:
   0.0   Rain Creek Trailhead for Trail 189.
   0.7   Overlook into Rain Creek canyon.
   1.3   Rain Creek.

The hike: The trailhead sign points northeast to the Rain Creek Trail (189) and toward its junction with the West Fork Mogollon Creek Trail (224). The middle to upper reaches of Rain Creek encompass one of the most wild, rugged, and scenic canyons in all of the Gila Wilderness. The moderately used Rain Creek Trail begins in a pinyon-juniper woodland adjacent to a grassy hillside that was once used as an airstrip. After crossing several small ravines and a side canyon, the good trail drops steadily along the west side of Rain Creek, reaching the stream after 1.3 miles.

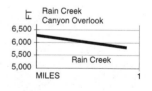

Along the way, at about 0.7 mile from the trailhead, the trail rounds the main west side ridge of lower Rain Creek. Pause here both coming and going for breathtaking vistas of the exceptional cliffs and volcanic formations that define the middle to upper confines of Rain Creek canyon. Overall, the trail drops about 360 feet from the trailhead on Rain Creek Mesa to Rain Creek. The small stream is a good turnaround point for a short hike to the edge of some of the roughest country in the Gila.

Rain Creek

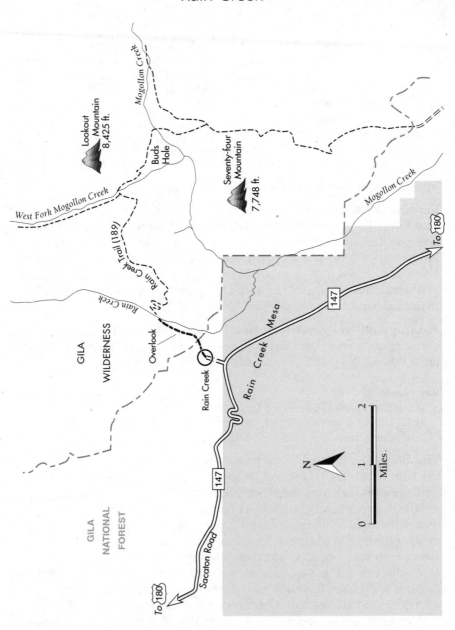

The rugged middle reaches of Rain Creek canyon as seen from Rain Creek Trail (189).

Option: Hike on to the West Fork Mogollon Creek for a long and strenuous 11.4-mile round trip or continue on to the Seventy-four Mountain Trailhead for a reverse shuttle route of Hike 27.

23 Snow Park

Highlights:	Panoramic views of the Mogollon Range; challenging route from rugged canyon bottoms to the rooftop of the Mogollon Mountains.
Type of hike:	4- to 6-day backpacking trip; lollypop loop.
Total distance:	33.8 miles.
Difficulty:	Strenuous.
Best months:	June through November.
Maps:	Forest Service Gila Wilderness map (1984); Rice Ranch, Grouse Mountain, Mogollon Baldy, and Shelley Peaks USGS quads.

Special considerations: Storms and lightning can arise suddenly along higher reaches of the route, bringing possible hypothermia conditions. There are several very steep and rugged sections in the route, particularly between Rain and West Fork Mogollon Creeks, south of Mogollon Baldy Peak, and in upper Gobbler Canyon.

Finding the trailhead: Drive 11 miles south of Glenwood on U.S. Highway 180 to Forest Road 147, the Sacaton Road, on the left (east). This junction is in the Little Dry Creek valley just north of the Leopold Vista Historic Monument. FR 147 is a county-maintained improved gravel road. Drive 10 miles east on FR 147 to a gated road on the left (north), signed Sacaton Trailhead. Close the gate after you. Drive north on the 0.2-mile access road to the road-end trailhead for Rain Creek Trail (189).

Parking and trailhead facilities: There is a kiosk, trail sign, and large gravel parking area. Camping is permitted, but sites are limited at the sloping trailhead. No water or other facilities are available.

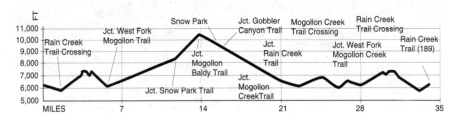

Key points:

- 0.0   Rain Creek (Sacaton) Trailhead–Rain Creek Trail (189).
- 1.3   Trail crosses Rain Creek.
- 5.7   Junction West Fork Mogollon Creek Trail (224).
- 11.5   Junction Snow Park Trail (99).
- 13.7   Junction Mogollon Baldy Trail (152).
- 14.6   Snow Park.
- 14.8   Junction Gobbler Canyon Trail (221).
- 21.1   Junction Mogollon Creek Trail (153).
- 24.9   Junction Rain Creek Trail (189).
- 26.0   Trail crosses Mogollon Creek.
- 28.1   Junction West Fork Mogollon Creek Trail (224).
- 32.5   Trail crosses Rain Creek.
- 33.8   Rain Creek (Sacaton) Trailhead.

The hike: Snow Park and that elevated sentinel of the Gila, Mogollon Baldy, are worthy destinations for this challenging loop from deep, rugged chasms to the crest of the Mogollon Range. The longest sustained ascent is the 8-mile pull from the lower West Fork Mogollon Creek to just below the lookout, averaging more than 500 feet per mile.

The middle to upper reaches of Rain Creek encompass one of the most wild, rugged, and scenic canyons in all of the Gila Wilderness. The moderately used Rain Creek Trail begins in pinyon-juniper woodland adjacent to a grassy hillside that was once used as an airstrip. After crossing several small ravines and a side canyon, the good trail drops steadily along the west side of Rain Creek, reaching the stream after 1.3 miles. Along the way at about 0.7 mile are breathtaking vistas of the exceptional cliffs and volcanic formations that define the middle to upper confines of Rain Creek canyon. Overall, the trail drops about 360 feet from the trailhead on Rain Creek Mesa to Rain

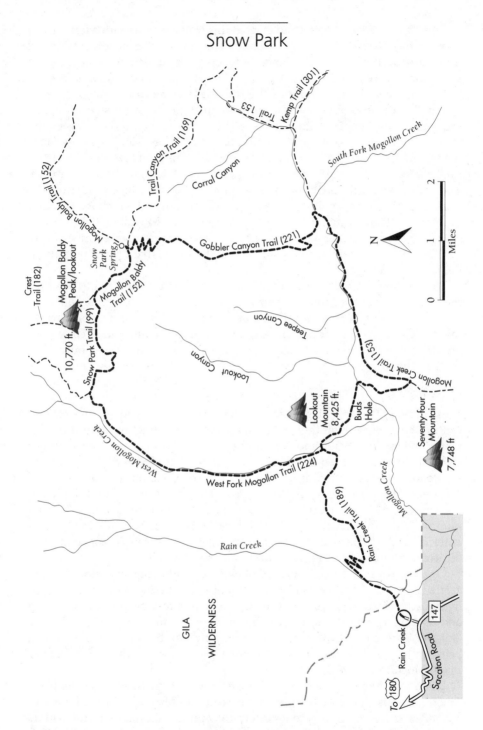

Snow Park

Creek. After a steep series of well-constructed switchbacks to the east rim above Rain Creek, the trail traverses up, down, and around brushy ridges and rocky outcrops before dropping steeply to the West Fork Mogollon Creek.

The 22.4-mile loop begins and ends at this trail junction with a left (north) turn on the West Fork Mogollon Creek Trail (224). The needle-cushioned trail starts up the left bench above the deeply incised stream. The massive 8,425-foot buttress of Lookout Mountain towers thousands of feet overhead to the east. For the next 4 miles the trail stays close to the steep, narrow channel. Cliffs and outcrops rise from steep slopes above a stream of cascades and small pools. At around 6,800 feet, the rugged terrain forces the trail to climb high above the stream bottom on the east slope, gaining more than 1,600 feet over the next 1.8 miles to a junction with the cutoff trail (99) to Snow Park. This trail was reconstructed in 1996 after the lookout fire. The trail goes right (east) and climbs another 500 feet to a saddle on the southwest ridge of Mogollon Baldy. After weaving in and out above Lookout Canyon the trail switchbacks steeply to the main Mogollon Baldy–Snow Park Ridge. Turn left for a short ascent to the lookout and what must surely be the prime mountain vista in all the Gila! (Refer to Hike 2 for details about the lookout and summit.)

To continue the loop, turn right (south) on the Mogollon Baldy Trail for the gently descending mile to Snow Park. The contrast is remarkable between gnarly cliffs on the south side of the park and its north slope, thickly mantled with spruce, fir, aspen, and southwestern white pine. The views are breathtaking. Much of the surrounding canyon country was burned in the 1996 lightning-caused lookout fire. A signed trail in the lower end of the park leads 0.25 mile downhill to a rock-lined spring in a grove of aspen. Snow Park conjures an exhilarating "top of the world" feeling, not only because of its 10,000-foot elevation, but also because of its wide-open expanse.

Proceed downhill another 0.2 mile to the signed junction with the Gobbler Canyon Trail (221) and turn right (south). From the top of Gobbler Canyon the trail descends a long series of well-graded switchbacks with spectacular views southward. White rock formations on the south side of Mogollon Creek are especially impressive. The trail is brushy and sloping in places from fire, but overall it is in good condition. After 2 miles the trail plummets down a narrow gully lined by talus rock. Several side springs enter from the right (west). The descent continues through blackened forest, finally joining the small stream in a narrow notch.

One benefit of the fire is a more open forest, allowing splendid views of castle rock rims on the east side of Gobbler Canyon and white spires highlighting the western skyline. During the final mile to Mogollon Creek the up and down trail passes more scratchy brush en route to July Canyon. The Gobbler Trail ends at the grassy flat trail junction, but only after swinging back up to the east long enough to make you wonder if the trail will ever reach Mogollon Creek.

Upon reaching the junction on the flat turn right on the well-beaten path. The trail drops alongside the pleasant cascades of Mogollon Creek for about 1.5 miles and then climbs moderately for another 2.3 miles to the saddle containing the Rain Creek Trail junction. Make a right (north) turn. The trail begins with a steep descent and a bird's-eye view of rock spires below Buds Hole. An open overlook of more of the rugged country to the west opens after 0.5 mile. After switchbacking steeply the trail reaches a flat ponderosa pine–oak bench just above Mogollon Creek. The trail crossing of the stream after 1.1 miles is marked with blazes on pine trees where it climbs out of the bottom. No trail penetrates Mogollon Creek downstream because of narrow canyon gorges below Buds Hole.

After crossing the stream, the good blazed trail climbs around a brushy slope to a side draw and then across some rocky segments to the narrow east ridge above the West Fork Mogollon Creek. Great white pinnacles dot the far ridge. The trail drops steeply along an eroded gully before climbing to a second ridge with an old stock fence and fine views of the spire-studded west slope of the West Fork at mile 8. After gently contouring the trail plunges down a short white rock section to a level bench of pine and oak and then makes another steep drop to the West Fork. The trail climbs to a grassy bench on the west side of the creek to its signed junction with the West Fork Mogollon Creek Trail (224) and the completion of the basic loop. Retrace the remaining 5.7 miles of the Rain Creek Trail back to the trailhead. These last miles are tough. If it's late in the day and you're already tired, consider camping along the West Fork and getting an early start the following morning.

Option: This hike is equally rewarding if done in reverse by going up Gobbler Canyon and coming down the West Fork Mogollon Creek.

24 Buds Hole

Highlights:	Year-round vehicular access to lower elevation trailhead to Mogollon Creek when high-country routes are still snowbound; panoramic views of the Mogollon Range; exploration of the canyon box of Buds Hole.
Type of hike:	Long day hike or overnighter; out-and-back.
Total distance:	13.6 miles.
Difficulty:	Moderate.
Best months:	March through November.
Maps:	Forest Service Gila Wilderness map (1984); Shelley Peak USGS quad.

Special considerations: No water between the trailhead and Mogollon Creek. South-facing trail may be unpleasantly hot and dry during summer.

Finding the trailhead: From Glenwood drive 11 miles south on U.S. Highway 180 to Forest Road 147 (Sacaton Road) on the left (east). Turn onto the improved gravel FR 147 and drive 16 miles to FR 754, also called Nine-Sixteen Road and signed for Shelley Ranch. Turn left (northeast) and go 6 miles to the right turn to the signed trailhead for Trail 153 located next to FR 754.

Parking and trailhead facilities:
Large gravel parking area, open with no shade and no water. There is a kiosk, a trail sign for the Mogollon Creek Trail (153), a self-registration box, and plenty of flat ground for trailhead camping.

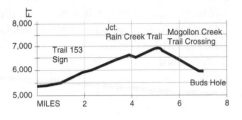

Key points:

- 0.0   Mogollon Creek Trailhead; Mogollon Creek Trail (153).
- 1.9   Sign for Trail 153.
- 5.4   Junction in saddle with Rain Creek Trail (189).
- 6.5   Trail crosses Mogollon Creek.
- 6.8   Upper end of Buds Hole.

The hike: This route penetrates the southwest corner of the lofty Mogollon Range with a chance to explore off-trail to the narrow box of Buds Hole on lower Mogollon Creek. The Upper Sonoran Desert gateway to the Gila crosses several arroyos and then begins a steady climb northward to distant higher ridges. After gaining about 500 feet and nearly 2 miles, the good trail passes a puzzling sign proclaiming what you already know, that this is indeed Trail 153. Great leaning wedges of dark volcanics mark the unnamed canyon to the right (east). The trail steepens up the pinyon-juniper ridge with canyon scenes perfectly framed by agave. After dropping to a gully, the wide rocky trail narrows to a singletrack and passes through a drift fence at mile 3.8. As

Hiking in the upper Sonoran Desert transition zone below Seventy-four Mountain.

Buds Hole

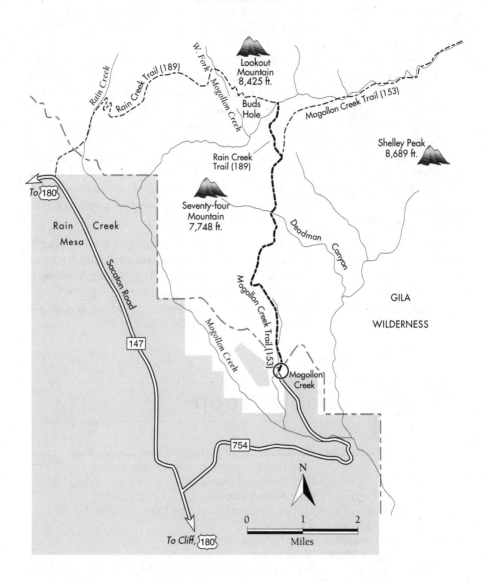

the trail contours to the right (east) the country opens to superb views of the ramparts of Shelley Peak (8,689 feet), a complex canyon network, and Mogollon Baldy (10,770 feet) far to the north.

A genuine "getting into the country" feeling is enhanced by a closer view of the rocky buttress of Lookout Mountain (8,425 feet). The trail drops into the ravine of upper Deadman Canyon and then makes a steep rocky ascent to a level pine bench at mile 4.8. As the trail begins to veer to the northeast it drops slightly and then climbs a bare rock section with wonderful views of the rocky reefs that guard Buds Hole and the West Fork Mogollon Creek. At mile 5.4 the trail drops to a small saddle and the junction with Rain Creek Trail (189). The Mogollon Creek Trail continues right 2.25 miles to its namesake stream. The Rain Creek Trail to the left reaches Mogollon Creek a mile quicker.

Continue left (northwest) on the Rain Creek Trail. The trail begins with a steep descent and a bird's-eye view of rock spires below Buds Hole. An open overlook of more of the rugged country to the west opens after 0.5 mile. After switchbacking steeply the trail reaches a flat ponderosa pine–oak bench just above Mogollon Creek. The trail crossing of the stream at mile 6.5 is marked with blazes on pine trees as it climbs out of the bottom. No trail penetrates Mogollon Creek downstream because of narrow canyon gorges below Buds Hole. The bottom is wide enough for off-trail hiking for about 0.3 mile downstream to the upper end of Buds Hole. Mogollon Creek is well guarded by sheer cliffs above the mouth of its west fork and a rugged canyon gorge both above and below the West Fork.

Options: In addition to, or instead of, exploring the rough rocky chasm of Buds Hole a 4.5-mile round trip can be taken upstream to a more mellow stretch of Mogollon Creek from the Mogollon Creek–Rain Creek Trail junction. From the junction in the saddle, the good Mogollon Creek Trail joins the stream after a well-graded descent of 650 feet over 2.25 miles. If a longer backpack is planned up Mogollon Creek, see Hikes 25 and 26.

25 Trail–Gobbler Loop

Highlights:	Panoramic views of the Mogollon Range; diverse route from rugged canyon bottoms to the highest reaches of the Mogollon Mountains.
Type of hike:	3- to 4-day backpacking trip; lollypop loop.
Total distance:	18.4-mile backpacking trip, plus 16.2-mile day hike.
Difficulty:	Strenuous.
Best months:	June through November.
Maps:	Forest Service Gila Wilderness map (1984); Shelley Peak and Mogollon Baldy USGS quads.

Special considerations: No water between the trailhead and Mogollon Creek. The south-facing trail may be unpleasantly hot and dry during summer. There is another long, dry stretch of the route between upper Trail Canyon and Snow Park. Storms and lightning can blow in suddenly along higher reaches of the route, creating possible hypothermia conditions.

Finding the trailhead: From Glenwood drive 11 miles south on U.S. Highway 180 to Forest Road 147 (Sacaton Road) on the left (east). Turn onto the improved gravel FR 147 and drive 16 miles to FR 754, also called Nine-

Sixteen Road and signed for Shelley Ranch. Turn left (northeast), and go 6 miles to the right turn to the signed trailhead for Trail 153 located next to FR 754.

Parking and trailhead facilities: Large gravel parking area, open with no shade and no water. There is a kiosk, a trail sign for the Mogollon Creek Trail (153), a self-registration box, and plenty of flat ground for trailhead camping.

Key points:

0.0	Mogollon Creek Trailhead; Mogollon Creek Trail (153).
1.9	Sign for Trail 153.
5.4	Junction with Rain Creek Trail (189).
7.7	Mogollon Creek (first water source).
9.2	Junction with Gobbler Canyon Trail (221).
10.7	Junction with Kemp Trail (301) at Trail Canyon.
13.7	Junction with Trail Canyon Trail (169).
19.1	Junction with Mogollon Baldy Trail (152).
19.2	Junction with Gobbler Canyon Trail (221).
25.4	Junction with Mogollon Creek Trail (153).
29.2	Junction with Rain Creek Trail (189).
32.7	Sign for Trail 153.
34.6	Mogollon Creek Trailhead.

The hike: This backpack–day hike combination is a study in contrasts, from rarely visited country along the Trail Canyon Trail to more popular destinations near Mogollon Baldy and along Mogollon Creek. From high desert to primeval spruce-fir forest, the contrasts continue throughout this extended journey into the western core of the Gila Wilderness.

The Mogollon Creek Trail (153) starts at an Upper Sonoran Desert gateway to the Gila, crossing several arroyos followed by a steady climb northward to distant higher ridges. After gaining about 500 feet and nearly 2 miles, the good trail passes a puzzling sign proclaiming what you already know, that this is indeed Trail 153. The wide rocky trail then drops to a gully, narrows to singletrack, and passes through a drift fence at mile 3.8. As the trail contours to the right (east), the country opens to superb views of the ramparts of Shelley Peak (8,689 feet), a complex canyon network, and Mogollon Baldy (10,770 feet) far to the north.

A genuine "getting into the country" feeling is enhanced by a closer view of the rocky buttress of Lookout Mountain (8,425 feet). The trail drops into

Trail–Gobbler Loop

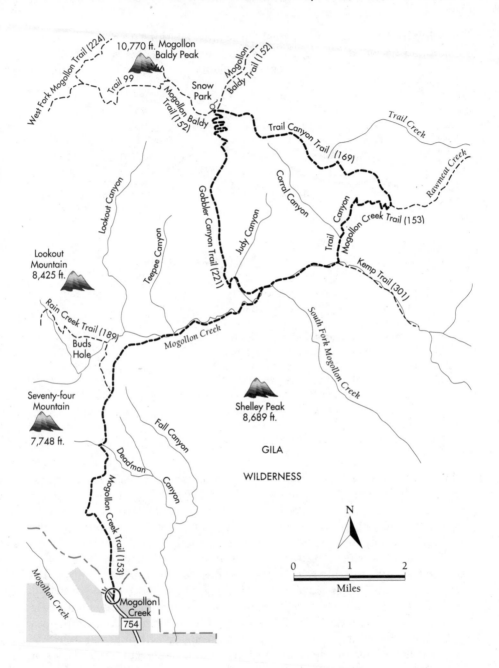

West Fork Mogollon Trail (224)

10,770 ft. Mogollon Baldy Peak

Trail 99

Mogollon Baldy Trail (152)

Snow Park

Mogollon Baldy Trail (152)

Trail Canyon Trail (169)

Trail Creek

Rawmeat Creek

Lookout Canyon

Gobbler Canyon Trail (221)

Judy Canyon

Corral Canyon

Trail Canyon

Mogollon Creek Trail (153)

Teepee Canyon

Lookout Mountain 8,425 ft.

Kemp Trail (301)

Rain Creek Trail (189)

Buds Hole

Mogollon Creek

South Fork Mogollon Creek

Seventy-four Mountain 7,748 ft.

Shelley Peak 8,689 ft.

Fall Canyon

GILA

WILDERNESS

Deadman Canyon

N

Mogollon Creek Trail (153)

0   1   2

Miles

Mogollon Creek

Mogollon Creek

754

the ravine of upper Deadman Canyon and then makes a steep rocky ascent to a level pine bench at mile 4.8. As the trail begins to veer to the northeast, it drops slightly and then climbs a bare rock section with wonderful views of the rocky reefs that guard Buds Hole and the West Fork Mogollon Creek. At mile 5.4 the trail drops to a small saddle and the junction with Rain Creek Trail (189).

From this junction it's a pleasant 650-foot descent to Mogollon Creek in 2.25 miles where good campsites can be found. Then canyon walls close in another half mile upstream before opening again to a large grassy flat at the junction with the Gobbler Trail. Mogollon Creek provides a sharp contrast with the arid land above; its cascades and riffles provide a lovely symphony as the trail winds back and forth across the stream. Camp anywhere along this stretch of Mogollon Creek. The 16.2-mile Trail–Gobbler loop is best enjoyed as a long day hike from a base camp. Several good campsites are available along the stream between the meadow at the lower end of the Gobbler Canyon Trail and Trail Canyon, graced by adjacent waterfalls at its mouth and on Mogollon Creek.

The Mogollon Creek Trail (153) continues left (north) up Trail Canyon. After a gradual climb along the streambed, it makes a steep ascent in the final mile to a saddle and junction with the Trail Canyon Trail (169). From here the entire northwest-trending ridgeline to Snow Park and Mogollon Baldy is in view. Turn left (north) on the Trail Canyon Trail toward Mogollon Baldy. At first the lightly used trail is well blazed. It climbs the forested ridge steadily with several steep pitches on grassy slopes. Past fires and blowdown blacken and obscure the trail in places. When this occurs head straight up the main ridge to intercept the blazed trail. After about 2 miles the trail is partially hidden in thorny brush. Soon the trail improves as it contours through an open pine forest to a large rock cairn. After a steep climb the trail joins a narrow rocky ridgeline with superb views into the rugged confines of upper Corral Canyon. A 300-foot drop into a brushy burn is followed by a 1,000-foot gain through stringers of dead aspen over the next 1.5 miles to an open crest. Snow Park beckons beyond.

The trail penetrates a tangle of aspen and blowdown to a pleasant 0.6-mile stretch to the ridgetop junction with the Mogollon Baldy Trail (152). The right fork leads 8.75 miles to White Creek. Continue left another 50 yards to the signed junction with the Gobbler Canyon Trail (221). Before making another left down Gobber to Mogollon Creek, take a short, scenic walk to the lovely alpine swale of Snow Park and then perhaps onward and upward to the rounded 10,770-foot summit of Mogollon Baldy with its historic fire lookout. (See Hikes 2 and 23.)

From the top of Gobbler Canyon the trail descends a long series of well-graded switchbacks with spectacular views southward. White rock formations on the south side of Mogollon Creek are especially impressive. There is some brush and side sloping from the huge 1996 lookout fire but the trail is in good condition. After 2 miles the trail steepens down a narrow gully lined by talus rock. Several side springs enter from the right (west). The descent continues through blackened forest before the trail finally joins the

Looking down Gobbler's Canyon from the upper end of Gobbler Trail (221).

small stream in a narrow notch. One benefit of the fire is a more open forest, allowing splendid views of castle rock rims on the east side of Gobbler Canyon and white spires highlighting the western skyline. During the final mile to Mogollon Creek the up and down trail passes more scratchy brush en route to July Canyon. The Gobbler Trail ends at the grassy flat trail junction only after swinging back up Mogollon Creek for some distance. The remainder of the hike involves retracing the 9.2 miles from this junction back to the Mogollon Creek Trailhead.

Options: Stash your pack near the Rain Creek Trail junction (mile 5.4) for a short side hike to the upper end of Buds Hole on Mogollon Creek (see Hike 24). A major trip variation is to hike the 22.4-mile Snow Park loop (Hike 23) in either a clockwise or counterclockwise direction from the Mogollon Creek Trailhead instead of the Rain Creek Trailhead. This option is of comparable distance and difficulty, with the loop beginning and ending at the Rain Creek Trail junction.

26 Mogollon–McKenna Loop

Highlights:	A wide variety of ecosystems, from desert to riparian, and terrain, from mountains to deep canyons; in a lightly visited portion of the Gila.
Type of hike:	4- to 5-day backpacking trip; lollypop loop.
Total distance:	35.7 miles.
Difficulty:	Strenuous.
Best months:	April through November.
Maps:	Forest Service Gila Wilderness map (1984); Shelley Park and Diablo Range USGS quads.

Special considerations: Stream crossings on Mogollon Creek. There are long stretches between water sources.

Finding the trailhead: To reach the Seventy-four Mountain Trailhead, drive 11 miles south from Glenwood on U.S. Highway 180 to Forest Road 147 on the left (east). This is signed as the Sacaton Road and is a county-maintained improved gravel road. Drive 16 miles on Sacaton Road to FR 754, also known as Nine-Sixteen Road and signed for the Shelley Ranch. Turn left (northeast) and go 6 miles, then turn right at the trailhead for Mogollon Creek Trail 153.

Parking and trailhead facilities: The trailhead has a large gravel parking area and an information kiosk. There is no water available. Camping is permitted with plenty of flat campsites.

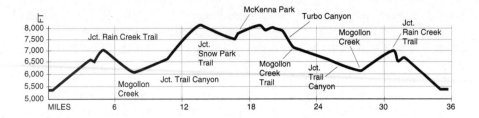

Key points:

   0.0   Mogollon Creek Trailhead; Mogollon Creek Trail (153).
   5.4   Junction with Rain Creek Trail (189).
   7.7   Mogollon Creek (first water source).
   9.2   Junction with Gobbler Trail (221).
  10.7   Junction with Kemp Trail (301) at Trail Canyon.
  13.7   Saddle; junction with Trail Canyon Trail (169).
  16.3   Junction with Langstroth Canyon Trail (302) in lower Rawmeat Creek.
  17.0   McKenna Park; junction with Trail 155 and Trail 158.
  22.0   Mogollon Creek; junction with Cieneg Trail 177.
  22.3   Junction with Woodrow–Sycamore Canyon Trail (158).
  25.0   Junction at Trail Canyon with Mogollon Creek Trail (153).
  26.5   Junction with Gobbler Trail (221).
  30.3   Junction with Rain Creek Trail (189).
  35.7   Mogollon Creek Trailhead.

The hike: This backpack adventure starts in an Upper Sonoran Desert at the trailhead, climbs over the ridges of Seventy-Four Mountain, and then descends to the chattering waters of Mogollon Creek. The loop section of the outing climbs to McKenna Park and returns to Mogollon Creek via Turbo Canyon. The variety of ecosystems cannot be matched elsewhere in the Gila.

The trail to the Rain Creek junction is largely uphill with little shade. The views are magnificent, and the transition from the flat terrain at the trailhead to the incredible volcanic topography of the Mogollon Range is fascinating. In this country it is always a pleasure to pause on the rocky trail and soak up the scenery. From the junction with the Rain Creek Trail at the saddle above Buds Hole it's a 650-foot descent to Mogollon Creek in 2.25 miles. There are campsites along Mogollon Creek before the canyon walls close in at 8.3 miles; another grassy flat occurs at the junction with the Gobbler Trail. Mogollon Creek provides a sharp contrast with the arid land above; its cascades and riffles provide a lovely symphony as the trail winds back and forth across the stream.

At the mouth of Trail Canyon, on a large bench on the south side of the stream, there is a spacious campsite, and a perfect spot for a base camp. From here the loop trip up to McKenna Park can be done with a light day pack. Two waterfalls, one from Trail Canyon and the other on the main Mogollon, provide exceptional acoustics at this location also.

The Mogollon Creek Trail (153) continues on up Trail Canyon; the trail that goes on up the creek is Trail 301. Up Trail Canyon it is a gradual climb

Mogollon–McKenna Loop

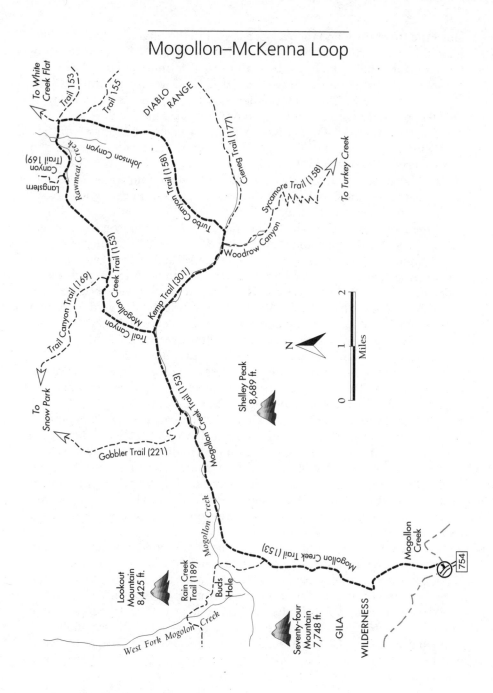

along the streambed, and then a steep ascent in the final mile to the saddle. Here the trail north to Snow Park and Mogollon Baldy is called the Trail Canyon Trail (169), which can be confusing. Continue on over the saddle and along the ridge on the Mogollon Creek Trail toward Rawmeat Creek and McKenna Park. The open ponderosa pines create a soft pathway of needles combined with the pulverized tuff. Within a mile of the saddle, you will reach the bottom of upper Rawmeat Creek in a mixed forest of fir and pine with an understory of thick grasses. The Rawmeat valley is broad and flat, eventually narrowing when it meets the Langstroth Canyon Trail. This is also the location of a spring where you are likely to find water. Here, too, are campsites on the bench above the nascent stream, in case you decided to carry a backpack on the trip.

At the foot of Rawmeat, the trail curls around into Johnson Canyon, going upstream for 0.2 mile and then cutting decisively up the hillside on the left (east) to climb to the plateau of McKenna Park. The trail gets rerouted due to some downed pines, so be sure to cut back to the original pathway in order not to miss the intersection. The first intersection you reach is with the trail north to White Creek Flat. Here you turn right toward McKenna Spring and Turbo Canyon. Within 0.5 mile a second intersection occurs above a dry lakebed, where the trail to Little Creek goes east. Continue south, heading toward Mogollon Creek, 5 miles away.

McKenna Park features rolling ponderosa meadows, stretching away in every direction. There is evidence of many years of patchy fires and the healthy results for the ponderosa pine community. It's a multiaged stand, with lush grass beneath. Groves of Gambel oak create a mosaic and provide a bountiful menu for the plentiful squirrels. The trail is easy to follow, both because of the indentation of the earthen path and conspicuous blazes. The most significant cairns are the cuts in the gigantic downed trunks; these can be spotted from quite a distance, so there is no doubt where the trail is going. It curves gradually south-southwest, running along a narrow rise between two canyons, one of which drains to the Middle Fork of the Gila, and the other to Mogollon Creek.

With an abrupt descent into the rocky head of Turbo Canyon the scenery shifts from pines, grasses, and an earthen trail to the bouldered walls of the canyon and a very rocky pathway. Turbo is a narrow canyon, allowing no space for switchbacks, so the trail plunges directly downward. Only when the Mogollon valley opens in the final 0.5 mile does the trail adopt a more gradual slope. In the valley the trail crosses the main creekbed (usually dry here) and meets the Cieneg Trail (177) on the south side. Turn right (west) and head downstream. The Woodrow–Sycamore Canyon Trail (158) junction is 0.25 mile farther, also on the south side.

Continuing on down Mogollon you will find water between Woodrow and Trail Canyons. You are also likely to encounter a massive amount of blowdown along this section of Mogollon Creek. Enormous winds have converted two hillsides into a jumble of tree trunks, making travel very difficult. The first one you come to occurs right after a stream crossing, where the trail goes to the north bank and is immediately enveloped by the chaos of downed trees. If you stay on the south bank you will discover a crude trail created by desperate hikers avoiding the mess. The next jumble is farther down; this one can be circumnavigated on the uphill slope on the north bank. This stretch of Mogollon is clearly lightly used; you are ensured of solitude.

Returning to Trail Canyon you can pause and reflect on the variety of country that you have visited in your journey. When your treasured time in the wilderness is about up, you can mosey on down the Mogollon and retrace your steps over the flank of Seventy-Four Mountain to the trailhead. This watery world will seem like an Alice in Wonderland experience when you emerge at the flat desert trailhead.

27 Mogollon–Rain Creek

Highlights:	Early spring to year-round vehicular access to lower elevation trailheads when high-country trailheads are still snowbound; spectacular mountain vistas; challenging terrain; solitude in an isolated corner of the wilderness.
Type of hike:	Long day hike or 2-day backpacking trip; shuttle.
Total distance:	14.3 miles.
Difficulty:	Strenuous.
Best months:	April through November.
Maps:	Forest Service Gila Wilderness map (1984); Rice Ranch and Shelley Peak USGS quads.

Special considerations: The Rain Creek Trail portion of the hike has several very steep grades and is rough and rocky in places. The first water is 7 miles into the route on Mogollon Creek. The initial south-facing segment of the route is especially hot and dry during the warmer summer months.

Finding the trailheads: Mogollon Creek Trailhead: From Glenwood drive 11 miles south on U.S. Highway 180 to Forest Road 147 (the Sacaton Road) on the left (east). Turn onto the improved gravel FR 147 and drive 16 miles to FR 754, also called Nine-Sixteen Road and signed for Shelley Ranch. Turn left (northeast) and go 6 miles to the right turn to the signed trailhead for the Mogollon Creek Trail (153) located next to FR 754.

Rain Creek (Sacaton) Trailhead: Drive 11 miles south of Glenwood on US 180 to FR 147 (Sacaton Road) on the left (east). Drive 10 miles east on FR 147 to a gated road on the left (north) signed "Sacaton Trailhead." Close the gate after you. Drive north on the 0.2-mile access road to the road-end trailhead for the Rain Creek Trail (189).

The one-way shuttle driving distance between trailheads is 12 miles, less than the length of the hike!

Parking and trailhead facilities: Mogollon Creek Trailhead: There is a large gravel parking area that's open with no shade and no water. There is a kiosk, a trail sign, a self-registration box, and plenty of flat ground for trailhead camping.

Rain Creek (Sacaton) Trailhead: Here is a large gravel parking area, a kiosk, and a trail sign. Camping is allowed, but sites are limited on the sloping ground. No water or other facilities are available.

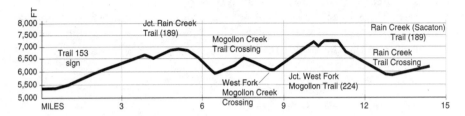

Key points:

- 0.0 Mogollon Creek Trailhead (153).
- 1.9 Sign for Trail 153.
- 5.4 Junction with Rain Creek Trail (189).
- 6.5 Trail crosses Mogollon Creek.
- 8.5 Trail crosses West Fork Mogollon Creek.
- 8.6 Junction with West Fork Mogollon Creek Trail (224).
- 13.0 Trail crosses Rain Creek.
- 14.3 Rain Creek (Sacaton) Trailhead (189).

The hike: This adventurous and highly rewarding sweep across the west-central end of the Gila Wilderness touches, and offers views beyond of, the incredibly rugged south-draining canyons of the Mogollon Mountains. The Mogollon Creek Trail (153) starts out by crossing a series of dry washes before making a long steady ascent of Upper Sonoran Desert ridges. Pinyon-juniper, agave, and clumps of ponderosa pine mixed with brush and oak higher up form the dominant vegetation. After crossing the upper ravine of Deadman Canyon at mile 4.1, the trail makes a steep rocky climb to a level pine bench. Dramatic views of rugged mountains open to the east and north.

The good trail climbs slightly and then drops to a saddle containing the signed Rain Creek Trail (189) junction at mile 5.4. The Mogollon Creek Trail continues right (north). Make a left (northwest) turn at this junction and follow the steeply descending Rain Creek Trail for 1.1 miles to the first water along the route at the Mogollon Creek crossing. During its descent the trail opens to spectacular views of dark volcanic spires guarding Buds Hole and of rugged cliffs above the West Fork Mogollon Creek. (Refer to Hike 24 for more detail about this first stretch of the route.)

After crossing the stream, the good blazed trail climbs around a brushy slope to a side draw and then across some rocky segments to the narrow east ridge above the West Fork Mogollon Creek. Great white pinnacles dot the far ridge. The trail drops steeply along an eroded gully before climbing to a second ridge with an old stock fence and fine views of the spire-studded west slope of the West Fork at mile 8. After gently contouring, the trail

Mogollon–Rain Creek

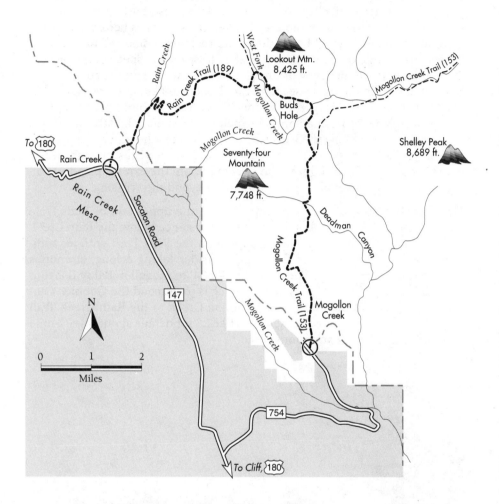

plummets down a short white rock section to a level bench of pine and oak and then makes another steep drop to the delightful small stream of the West Fork. The trail climbs to a grassy bench on the west side of the creek to its signed junction with the West Fork Mogollon Creek Trail (224) at mile 8.6. Massive volcanic buttresses of Lookout Mountain soar thousands of feet above directly to the east. If backpacking, this portion of the West Fork offers plenty of excellent midroute campsites.

A large rock cairn marks the hard left (southwest) turn to continue the hike on the Rain Creek Trail. With a series of steep switchbacks, the trail gains 1,130 feet over the next 1.5 miles to its high point. It then drops steeply through dense brushfields of gray oak, manzanita, and pinyon-juniper, reaching an old corral after another 0.4 mile. The Rain Creek Trail is well defined as it climbs to another ridge with views westward into the remote cliff-walled recesses of Rain Creek—an inspiring panorama from the elevated crest of the Mogollon Range down to the Sonoran Desert. The trail follows the pleasant ridge until cliffs force it to the right (west) down a steep stretch of loose gravel. Then comes an interlude of grassy swales before a series of contours and steep switchbacks down the rocky east slope of Rain Creek. This long 1.6-mile descent offers a chance to savor the spectacular ruggedness of the upper Rain Creek drainage. Overall, the trail is well constructed, but there are some narrow segments with loose rocks on extremely steep side slopes that require extra caution. Cross the babbling brook of Rain Creek, which drops from a parallel bench of pine and oak. After making a long, steady climb along the west side of Rain Creek, the trail crosses a side canyon and several small ravines. Impressive wide vistas of high desert country open southward. From the stream bottom the exit trailhead sits on an open mesa 400 feet above and 1.3 miles beyond the crossing.

Options: If time and energy permit, explore the upper end of Buds Hole and the gorge along Mogollon Creek a short distance below the Rain Creek Trail crossing at mile 6.5. If base camping on the West Fork with an additional two to three days for side trips, consider taking a long, strenuous overnight loop hike up the West Fork Trail (224) to Mogollon Baldy Lookout (10,770 feet) and Snow Park. The return leg is to descend the Gobbler Canyon Trail (221) and then on down Mogollon Creek to the Rain Creek Trail leading back to the West Fork. Refer to Hike 23 for details about this 21-mile addition to an already strenuous route.

Hiking down the Seventy-four Mountain Trail (153) with Mogollon Baldy to the north.

28 Lower Gila River

Highlights:	Spectacular canyon; majestic rock formations and Indian ruins.
Type of hike:	Day hike; out-and-back.
Total distance:	8 miles.
Difficulty:	Easy (low water) to moderate (when higher water makes crossings more difficult).
Best months:	April through October (depending on water levels).
Maps:	Forest Service Gila Wilderness map (1984); Canyon Hill USGS quad.

Special considerations: Crossings on lower section of the Gila are not possible during high water.

Finding the trailhead: From Silver City drive 20 miles northwest on U.S. Highway 180 to milepost 89 and the turnoff for the town of Gila. Turn right (north) on New Mexico Highway 211. Drive north 4 miles to Gila and continue north on NM 153 for 4 more miles to the end of the pavement and the beginning of Forest Road 155. An ominous sign at this point warns of wet weather hazards and difficulties for low-clearance vehicles. With cautious driving FR 155 is negotiable by most vehicles. Only flood conditions or snow make it impassable. Continue northeast on the rocky, unimproved FR 155 for about 6 miles to its boulder-blocked end on the east bank of the Gila River just below Crow Canyon.

Parking and trailhead facilities: Parking is available along the side of the road near the trailhead. Camping is permitted nearby along the river but there are no trailhead facilities. The only water source is the Gila River.

Key points:
- 0.0 Trailhead for Gila River Trail (724).
- 0.2 Gravestone on right (east).
- 1.0 Mouth of Turkey Creek on left (north).
- 2.0 Signed Gila Wilderness boundary.
- 4.0 Prehistoric hunter alcove.

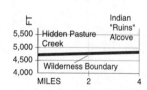

The hike: This excursion into the lower reaches of the Gila River provides an enjoyable introduction to big river canyon country at its finest. Dramatic cliffs define the wide valley on both sides. Large alcoves used by prehistoric Native American hunters are certainly a worthwhile destination. However, a specific destination isn't needed. The lower Gila is a great place to amble up and down for whatever distance you desire. Indeed, the surrounding country makes the trip. The only negative is the sometimes heavy ATV traffic in the first mile or two below the wilderness boundary. If possible, avoid peak use weekends during spring and summer.

Beyond the rock barricade the trail starts out as an old jeep track. The marked grave of Francis E. Jerles (1861–1944) appears on the right at 0.2

Lower Gila River

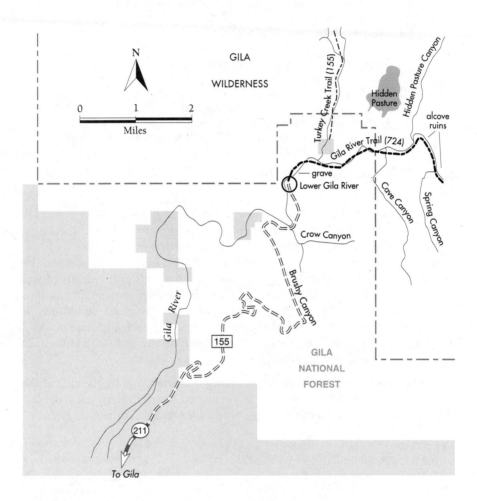

mile. The trail soon crosses the river below an mining adit, reaching the gravel outwash of Turkey Creek on the left (north) at 1 mile. A soft sand and gravel doubletrack of a trail crosses several more times before meeting the wilderness boundary at 2 miles in a sycamore grove. A great rock buttress on the left side complements steep cliffs of fractured sandstone on the right. The canyon deepens with alcoves and ascending layers of cliffs marching high above the river. The rugged gateway of Hidden Pasture Creek enters from the left (north) at 3 miles. Its secluded secrets include the perched mesa of Hidden Pasture. This grassy flat top sits high above the river and is guarded on all sides by sheer cliffs. Every so often the river trail is marked by cairns or tree blazes across benches.

Prehistoric hunters made use of this large alcove along the lower Gila River.

Ridgelines punctuated by dark volcanic cliffs are peppered with shallow caves and lower overhangs. The first large river grade alcove used prehistorically as a hunter cave is hidden by dense vegetation on the north (left) side of the river at mile 4. This is the first of two features indicated on the USGS quad map as Indian ruins. The second ruin is another 0.5 mile upstream on the left (north) side. It is much higher on the rock slope and more difficult to find, let alone reach. Please respect these and all other cultural sites, leaving them untouched. When you have finished your exploration of the Gila, return to the trailhead by the same route.

Option: In addition to hiking upstream beyond the hunter alcove, the lower reaches of Hidden Pasture Creek can be explored as a side hike. Strenuous rock scrambling is required to get very far up the narrow rocky chute.

29 Gila River

	Highlights:	Spectacular canyons; majestic rock formations; Indian ruins; historic cabin sites; pleasant hot springs; a lengthy river valley, offering wild solitude.
	Type of hike:	5- to 7-day backpacking trip; shuttle.
	Total distance:	34 miles.
	Difficulty:	Strenuous.
	Best months:	May through November.
	Maps:	Forest Service Gila Wilderness map (1984); Canyon Hill, Granny Mountain, Little Turkey Park, and Gila Hot Springs USGS quads.

Special considerations: Due to flood danger on the Gila River, trips should be avoided during spring run-off and after heavy rains. High-water river crossings are dangerous and likely impossible. As with all hot springs do not dunk your head and nose underwater. A warm-water amoeba, *Naegleria fowleri,* can enter the brain through the nasal passages, causing a rare form of meningitis that can lead to death.

Finding the trailheads: Lower Gila River Trailhead: From Silver City drive 20 miles northwest on U.S. Highway 180 to milepost 89 and the turnoff for the town of Gila. Turn right (north) on New Mexico Highway 211. Drive north 4 miles to Gila and continue north on NM 153 for 4 more miles to the end of the pavement and the beginning of Forest Road 155. An ominous sign at this point warns of wet-weather hazards and difficulties for low-clearance vehicles. With cautious driving FR 155 is negotiable by most vehicles. Only flood conditions or snow make it impassable. Continue northeast on the rocky, unimproved FR 155 for about 6 miles to its boulder-blocked end on the east bank of the Gila River just below Crow Canyon.

Gila Bridge Trailhead: Drive north of Silver City on NM 15 and turn right (east) onto a gravel road signed "Grapevine Forest Camp" between mileposts 37 and 38 just before crossing the Gila River Bridge. The turnoff is also about 4 miles south of the Gila Visitor Center. Drive 0.1 mile down the steep, rocky gravel road, turning left at the sign for Gila River Trailhead for the Gila River Trail (724) and end of road at the river.

The one-way shuttle driving distance between trailheads is about 75 miles, 6 of which are unpaved.

Parking and trailhead facilities: Lower Gila River Trailhead: Scattered trailhead parking is available along the side of the road near the trailhead. Camping is permitted nearby along the river but there are no trailhead facilities. The only water source is the Gila River. Of course, the water must be treated, as is the case with all open water sources in Gila country.

Gila Bridge Trailhead: There is a large gravel parking area and kiosk. Camping and vault toilets are available in the adjacent no-fee Grapevine forest camp. The Gila River is the only available source of water.

126

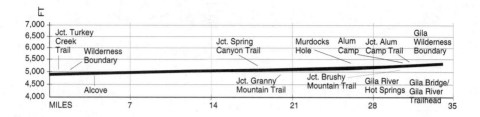

Key points:

0.0	Lower Gila River Trailhead and Gila River Trail (724).
0.2	Gravestone on right (east).
1.0	Mouth of Turkey Creek; junction Turkey Creek Trail (155).
2.0	Gila Wilderness boundary.
4.0	Indian ruins in alcove.
18.0	Mouth of Sapillo Creek; junction Spring Canyon Trail (247).
20.0	Junction Granny Mountain Trail (160).
26.0	Murdocks Hole.
30.5	Junction Brushy Mountain Trail (403).
30.7	Alum Camp.
31.0	Junction Alum Camp Trail (788).
32.2	Gila River Hot Springs.
33.9	Gila Wilderness boundary.
34.0	Gila Bridge Trailhead and Gila River Trail (724).

The hike: The Gila River is one of the few southwestern streams that can be floated during a narrow window in the spring. Of course the best time for floating during higher water is the worst time for hiking because of countless river crossings. If you're making this epic journey up to the Gila Bridge during a marginal in-between time, when you can barely wade and floaters can barely float, you may encounter each other along the way. The irony is that by constantly pulling their boats across gravel bars they'll be working at least as hard as upriver backpackers.

Beyond the rock barricade, the trail starts out as an old jeep track, reaching the gravel outwash of Turkey Creek on the left (north) at 1 mile. A soft sand-and-gravel doubletrack trail crosses several more times before meeting the wilderness boundary at 2 miles in a sycamore grove. A great rock buttress on the left side complements sheer cliffs of fractured sandstone on the right. The canyon deepens with alcoves and ascending layers of cliffs high above the river. Every so often the river trail is marked by cairns or tree blazes across benches.

Ridgelines punctuated by dark volcanic cliffs are peppered with shallow caves and lower overhangs. The first large river grade alcove used prehistorically as a hunter cave is hidden by dense vegetation on the north (left) side of the river at mile 4. This is the first of two features indicated on the USGS quad map as Indian ruins. The second ruin is another 0.5 mile upstream on the left (north) side. It is much higher on the rock slope and more difficult to find, let alone reach. Please respect these and all other cultural sites, leaving them untouched for the ages.

Gila River

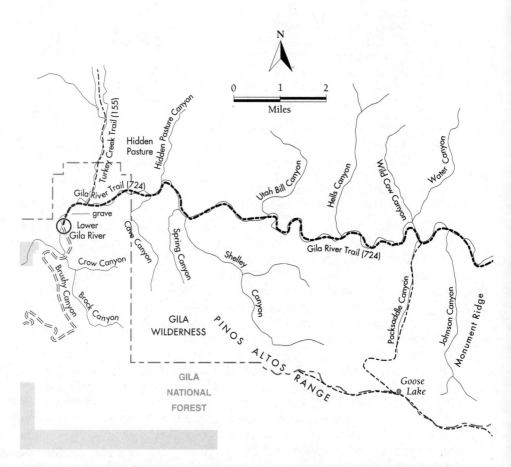

For the next neck-craning 14 miles the twisting canyon is marked by narrows, cliffs, numerous river crossings, and rocky side draws that plunge to the valley floor. There are patches of blazed trail, but at each river crossing the trail is lost on the sand and cobblestone beach in the sticky bushes, so after each crossing you have to look for it again. The ever-shifting wild river, with its periodic floods, rearranges its floodplain and associated trail often enough so that every trip is different. If you've brought your best friend with you, be warned that most of the Gila River is very unpleasant for dogs; their feet seem to attract thorns and briars along the bank.

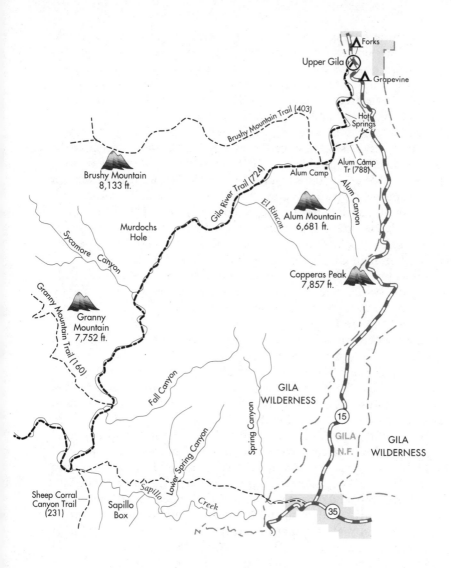

At mile 18 the mouth of Sapillo Creek and the junction with the Spring Canyon Trail (247) is marked only with a rock cairn and sycamores at the low bluff entrance to Sapillo Creek. After another 0.25 mile the trail climbs a brushy pinyon-juniper bench on the right (east) with old blazes, only to fade out as it steepens to nowhere. It's best to stay in the river bottom, crossing alternating alluvial benches. The trail is often faint, but the walking is fairly easy. After 2 miles (mile 20) the signed Granny Mountain Trail (160) leads north from the left side of the river just past an old corral. Continue right toward the Gila Bridge, crossing broad flats with a mix of cottonwoods, ponderosa pine, and juniper overseen by multicolored bluffs of red, gray, white, buff, and black. The riparian off-and-on trail tends to hug the foot of steep sideslopes. Once in a while a rock cairn or blaze will reassure you that you're on the proper path. The trail tends to vanish at the many stream crossings, in part because hikers need to go up or downstream in search of a shallow crossing. Look ahead to the highest, driest bench and you'll soon intercept the elusive trail.

An impressive cliff dominates the west side at mile 21.5. As it crosses open benches the trail is often covered by windblown sand, especially in rough cobblestones near the river. About 4 miles above Sapillo Creek, long benches give way to shorter ones in a tighter canyon, meaning more stream crossings. Sycamores in the intimate canyon contrast with pinyon-juniper hillsides dotted with dark cliffs stacked like cake layers. For the following 2 or 3 miles the canyon deepens on up to a dramatic spot where the river splits around a huge rock, creating an island. The left (west) branch is the only place on the main Gila where sheer cliff walls define both sides.

Another mile (mile 26) brings the rugged amphitheater of Murdocks Hole (Murtocks on the USGS quad map). For at least a mile the hole is wedged by rock formations of every size and shape. Narrow side canyons tempting rigorous off-trail exploration enter from the left (north). As the valley widens again, the trail greatly improves, at crossings and across long benches. The canyon continues to narrow and widen with ever-changing variety. The river is a sparkling serpentine wonder with alternating rapids, lengthy rock gardens, and 90-degree bends into deep, dark pools guarded by sheer cliffs. A huge slide of sulfur-colored rock bracketed by bright red outcrops dominates the right (south) slope at mile 29.5. A grassy bench leads for more than a mile to the Brushy Mountain Trail (403) on the left (north) side at mile 30.5. Continuing upstream to the right, the trail passes by an unsigned cutoff trail to Alum Camp, then crosses the river and joins the Alum Camp Trail (788) at mile 31. Proceed on the right-hand trail past an unsigned cutoff trail to Alum Camp, and cross the river to the Alum Camp Trail junction.

Continue left (north) at this junction and head upstream. The distinct river grade trail soon makes a sharp bend to the right with a prominent rocky ridge jutting eastward from the left. After rounding the bend and before making a second river crossing about 1.25 miles above the trail junction, look for evidence of the Gila River Hot Springs across the river. The telltale sign is sulfur-colored rock. Cross the river and upon reaching the bench, look for a use trail back to the right (southeast) next to a large rock cairn. The use trail follows a gravel bar downstream about 0.1 mile to three spring-fed pools. They sit at the foot of a steep hillside near the east bank of the river. The two lower pools are lined with rocks, one of which is filled with scum. The other is large enough for two people and is endowed with a smooth sandy floor ideal for soaking. The temperature of the pool is delightfully warm, providing a wonderful respite during a cold day or a hot hike.

As it winds upstream, the mostly well-defined river trail makes seven more crossings before reaching the exit trailhead at the Gila River Bridge. Two sets of high cliff faces just below the bridge give the hike a closed-in seclusion to its conclusion.

Hiking along the Gila River above the mouth of Sapillo Creek.

Options: The route can be enjoyed equally in reverse, but the gentle river grade isn't even noticeable, so don't let that determine your direction. Short side hikes along the way include Sapillo Box (Hike 36), Alum Camp and Canyon (Hike 39), and the Gila River Hot Springs (Hike 42).

30 Turkey Creek Hot Springs

Highlights:	Hot springs, swimming hole, and water slide in a remote setting deep in a wilderness canyon.
Type of hike:	Day hike or overnight backpack.
Total distance:	8 miles.
Difficulty:	Moderate.
Best months:	Year-round.
Maps:	Forest Service Gila Wilderness map (1984); Canyon Hill USGS quad.

Special considerations: Spring run-off and heavy rains can make Gila River dangerous to cross; high water after a summer downpour can inundate the hot pools on Turkey Creek. Hot springs users should be aware of the presence of *Naegleria fowleri*, an amoeba that can cause meningitis. Keep water out of your nose and do not submerge your head in hot springs.

Finding the trailhead: To reach the lower Gila River Trailhead, from Silver City drive 20 miles northwest on U.S. Highway 180 to milepost 89 and the turn for the town of Gila. Turn right (north) onto New Mexico Highway 211. Drive north 4 miles to Gila and continue north on NM 153 for 4 more miles to pavement end and the beginning of Forest Road 155. An ominous sign at the pavement's end warns of wet-weather hazards and difficulties for low-clearance vehicles. With cautious driving FR 155 is negotiable by most vehicles; only flood conditions or snow make it impassable. Continue northeast on FR 155 for 6 miles. The trail begins where the road ends on the east bank of the Gila River, a mile north of Crow Canyon.

Parking and trailhead facilities: Trailhead parking is available. There are no trailhead facilities, nor is there a sign or kiosk with information. Camping is permitted. Water is available in the Gila River (to be treated).

Key points:

0.0	Lower Gila Trailhead.
1.0	Junction with Turkey Creek Trail (155).
3.0	Skeleton Canyon.
4.0	Hot springs on Turkey Creek.

FT
6,000 — Turkey Creek — Hot
5,500 — Jct. — Springs
5,000
4,500 — Hot Springs Trail
4,000
MILES   2   4

The hike: The hot springs on Turkey Creek are a magnet to the warm-water set with swimming holes and a slickrock water slide into a deep, heated plunge pool, as well as a couple of hot springs. The

132

Turkey Creek Hot Springs

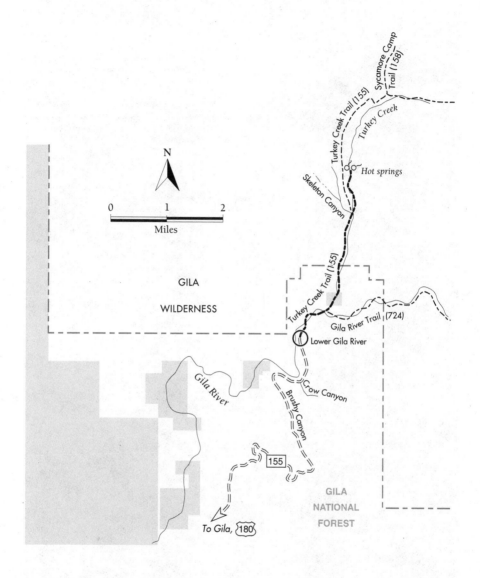

setting is serene in a dramatic bouldered canyon with forested hillsides rising to ridges hundreds of feet above. The area gets heavy use, by Gila Wilderness standards, and it is one of the few places you're likely to run into another party.

From the end of FR 155 on the bank of the Gila River, hike on up the river trail, crossing the river several times. Automotive enthusiasts use the lower Gila as a playground; on weekends you could easily encounter traffic

Irresistible swimming holes next to Turkey Creek Hot Springs.

on your hike to the Turkey Creek Trail. This phenomenon also explains the maze of dirt roads in the area. The trail, now resembling a road, crosses the rocky dry mouth of Turkey Creek and enters a patch of private land isolated here in the Gila National Forest. It's a trashy spot, with deserted buildings and a windmill. Bear left (north) toward the windmill. An opening in a stock fence just north of the windmill marks the beginning of the Turkey Creek Trail and the return to the national forest.

The trail crosses Turkey Creek several times; the first crossings are dry, but eventually water is evident. The trail settles down on the western side of the stream and continues on that side all the way to the hot springs trail junction below Skeleton Canyon.

A couple of miles from the windmill, several campsites lie along the trail adjacent to the creek. If you are staying overnight, it makes sense to camp here rather than carrying a backpack through the boulders on the trail-less route to the springs. This flat, straight stretch of the creek is a signal that the hot springs junction is near. Near the rocky walls of Skeleton Canyon on the left you will arrive at an unmarked fork in the trail. The path to the left angles into the mouth of Skeleton, then begins switchbacking up the steep slope of the ridge that divides Skeleton Canyon from Turkey Creek. If you take this trail to the left you will miss the hot springs. The trail to the right, the more well traveled of the two, dips down into a shady glen of Emery oaks, crosses the dry mouth of Skeleton Creek, and continues up the west bank of Turkey Creek. This is the trail you want.

After the first 0.2 mile, cross Turkey Creek at the sculpted white rock falls, and continue up the east side, picking your way around and over the boulders.

The hike from the junction to the hot springs is about a mile. There is no marked path, although sometimes cairns appear, and there are well-defined footpaths here and there. Many of these use trails are dead ends; a lot of visitors have wandered around seeking the springs. As a general rule, whenever it looks like you have to climb a cliff to get farther upstream, look for a convenient rock crossing and switch sides of the creek. Most of the route is on the east side, and it switches only when it has to. There are a couple of narrow squeezes between huge boulders on the west side, including one spot where it is necessary to scoot under two gigantic tilted boulders.

There are three large alcoves along this section of Turkey Creek—one on the east side of the creek and then two farther up on the west. The springs are after the second one on the west at 5,100 feet. You will not miss the hot springs by walking by them. The first one is a heart-shaped pool right next to the creek on the west bank. Above it, on the next level, are magnificent swimming holes, with a slickrock slide that sends adventurous water worshipers into a heated plunge pool. There's another hot pool on the upper level as well.

After relaxing and cavorting in the toasty water, wind you way back down the canyon. Your journey down will be much faster than your trip up since you know the route. Return to the trailhead on the Gila River by retracing your steps downstream.

31 Turkey–Mogollon Loop

Highlights:	Cascades and pools of Turkey Creek; the remote Diablo Range; wild upper reaches of Mogollon Creek; sweeping views from Sycamore divide; secluded trout pools in Sycamore Canyon.
Type of hike:	5- to 7-day backpacking loop.
Total distance:	59.5 miles.
Difficulty:	Strenuous.
Best months:	April through May; September through November.
Maps:	Forest Service Gila Wilderness map (1984); Canyon Hill, Diablo Range, Little Turkey Park, and Shelley Peak USGS quads.

Special considerations: Several crossings on the Gila River are not to be attempted in high water. Long stretches between water (10 miles, 12 miles) are not recommended in hot weather.

Finding the trailhead: From Silver City, drive 20 miles northwest on U.S. Highway 180 to milepost 89 and the turn for the town of Gila. Turn right (north) on New Mexico Highway 211. Drive north 4 miles to Gila and continue north on NM 153 another 4 miles to the pavement's end and the beginning of Forest Road 155. An ominous sign here warns of wet weather hazards and difficulties for low-clearance vehicles. With cautious driving FR 155 is negotiable by most vehicles, and only flood conditions or snow make it impassable. Continue northeast on FR 155 to its end on the east bank of the Gila River, a mile beyond the mouth of Crow Canyon.

Parking and trailhead facilities: Trailhead parking along the road. Camping is permitted. No trailhead facilities.

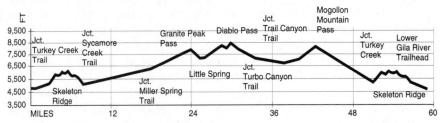

Key points:

0.0	Lower Gila River Trailhead; Gila River Trail (724).
1.0	Junction with Turkey Creek Trail (155) north of windmill.
3.0	Hot springs turnoff; Skeleton Canyon.
5.3	High point on Skeleton Ridge.
7.5	Junction with Sycamore Canyon Trail (158).
16.5	Junction with Miller Spring Trail (159).
24.0	Granite Peak Pass; junction with Granite Peak Trail (150).
25.5	Little Spring; junction with Little Creek Trail (161).
26.2	Junction with Cieneg Trail (177).

Turkey–Mogollon Loop

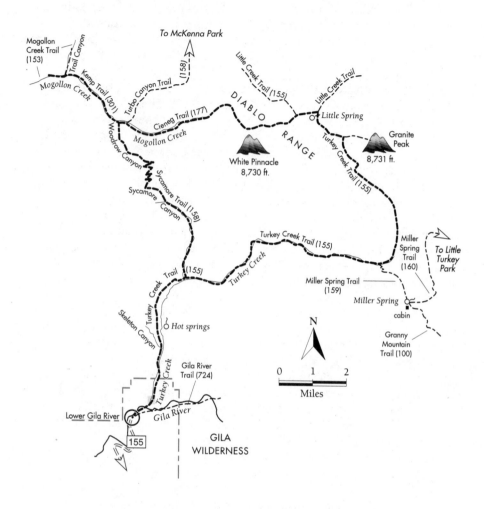

28.7	Diablo Range Pass.
30.5	Junction with old McKenna Spring Trail.
33.7	Junction with Turbo Canyon Trail (158).
34.0	Junction with Sycamore Canyon Trail (158) and Kemp Trail (301).
37.0	Trail Canyon; junction with Mogollon Creek Trail (153).
40.0	Junction with Sycamore Canyon Trail (158).
42.4	Woodrow Canyon–Sycamore Canyon Pass.
51.0	Junction with Turkey Creek Trail (155).
53.2	High point on Skeleton Ridge.
56.5	Skeleton Canyon; hot spring turnoff.
58.5	Junction with Gila River Trail (724).
59.5	Lower Gila River Trailhead.

The hike: This long backpack takes you into three drainages (Turkey Creek, Little Creek, and Mogollon Creek) and over three passes, two in the Diablo Range and the third on the edge of the Mogollons. The trip is made challenging by the scarcity of water over the mountain passes; thus, this hike is not suggested for the hot summer months. The first and last miles of the trek require wading footwear to cross the Gila River. All the other streams can be hopped.

From the trailhead on the Lower Gila, follow the remains of the washed-out old road, also the Gila River Trail, up the river. The several wide crossings have firm gravel bottoms. At 1 mile you will encounter a messy patch of private land strewn with shacks and debris. Off-road vehicles play in this non-wilderness area, and you can expect noisy company on weekends.

The Turkey Creek Trail is due north of the windmill, a conspicuous landmark on the private property. The signed trail begins at the fence on the edge of the property at the national forest boundary. Take the trail north, crossing the wilderness boundary within a mile. The lower crossings of Turkey Creek are dry cobblestones. Farther upstream water is plentiful, forming broad, still pools. Sycamores and oak groves line the trail along the creek, with cliffs soaring over 300 feet. When water appears in the stream, campsites begin to dot the riverbank. There are several sites below Skeleton Canyon, from 2.8 to 3 miles.

At 3 miles the turnoff to Turkey Hot Springs (see Hike 30) is an unmarked trail to the right, going up the Turkey Creek bottom, while the main trail stays on the left, angling into the mouth of Skeleton Canyon and then zig-zagging sharply up the ridge. There is also a use trail up Skeleton Canyon, the remnants of an pack trail, used by hikers searching for the hot springs, which some people are told are up Skeleton Canyon (it seems to be a local prank to send hikers off on wild goose chases). The main Turkey Creek Trail climbs to the crest of Skeleton Ridge; from Skeleton Canyon it is 4.6 miles to the next water and 5 miles to the next campsite.

The trail climbs sharply up Skeleton Ridge between the two canyons. Although the views are spectacular, the steep rocky trail is a tough one, with deceptive rims, and the ridge rising even higher beyond. After 2 miles of climbing, the trail contours up and down along the eastern slope, sidehilling across talus fields before finally descending to the Sycamore Canyon junction on the ridge above Sycamore Creek. Sycamore Creek is the first water you reach; Turkey Creek is 0.2 mile beyond. The first campsites along Turkey Creek are 0.3 mile up from the first crossing.

From Sycamore to the Miller Spring Trail, Turkey Creek is wild and rustic. The path is brushy and very lightly used, and the creek is spectacular. The stream flows on volcanic bedrock, forming pools and cascades in a stairstep pattern, with trout in the deeper pools. It is a slow trail, taking many turns as it travels up the creek. It is 9 miles to the Miller Spring junction from Sycamore.

This is not a trip to be hurried. The area is rich in archeology and geology. The narrow riparian bottom supports cottonwood and sycamore, maple and ash, and lots of dense brush. At 3.5 miles from the Sycamore junction the

Backpacking on the Turkey Creek Trail (151) between Turkey Creek and Skeleton Canyon.

canyon angles sharply east. There's a waterfall on the north canyon wall. The trail climbs over a streamside ridge and then levels out in a totally different landscape in a broad valley of grass and ponderosa pine. Light traffic keeps the trail primitive, but the pace is quicker on the smooth terrain. On the grassy north side you will encounter traces of an abandoned corral, the first evidence of the cattle industry on the journey.

As you approach the Miller Canyon area, the trail becomes obscure from disuse and is overgrown in the mushy bottom. If you lose it temporarily and get on a game trail, just continue up Turkey Creek and you will meet the trail again. Between Miller Canyon and the Miller Springs Trail junction, the water in the creek disappears below the cobblestone-slickrock bottom. Make camp, if possible, at the final water site. The next water on the route is over Granite Peak Pass, at Little Spring, about 10 miles away. Note that water is not always available at Miller Spring. The cabin and stock pond are 2.5 miles up the trail to the east; the pond is muddy, and the spring sinks out of sight in dry conditions.

Continue on up Turkey Creek, where the trail gets more use. In this high and dry region, the foliage is not as well developed; as the drainage broadens, the rocky hillsides support ponderosa pine. The fingers of Turkey Creek diverge, and the trail winds up and down on the ridges as if it can't decide which ridge to take to get up to Granite Pass. After 2.5 miles of indecision, the trail goes straight to the pass in the last mile. Pause here and enjoy the view to the north.

Beyond the Granite Peak Trail, the Turkey Creek Trail descends quickly through ravines and gullies. Eroded mounds of volcanic tuff decorate the Diablo Range hillsides in the ponderosa pine forest. Little Spring is a genuine oasis after the long trip from Turkey Creek. A grassy pine-ringed flat just below Little Spring and the flowing headwaters of Little Creek creates a perfect campsite. It's a soft, gentle spot where three ravines meet.

When you resume your journey, go west from the meadow, up the main Little Creek Trail. The sign in the meadow may be on the ground, the victim of a fallen pine tree. The trail rises in the ravine, following the stream with tiny trout in small pools to a woodsy junction where the trail to the right goes to McKenna Park. Your trail to Mogollon Creek (named the Cieneg Trail) is on the left, partially obscured by downfall and tree clutter. McKenna Park Trail is more heavily used. From the trail sign simply turn left and walk along the left fork of the stream and you'll quickly pick up the trail.

The trail over the Diablo Range to the head of the Mogollon rises and falls constantly. Jagged white pinnacles sprout off the ridgetops; groves of aspen and pine miraculously find sufficient soil amid the rock formations and outcrops. After cresting at the pass, the trail grows more primitive in its descent on the northern slope, following gullies and ravines, with fallen trees frequently obstructing the trail. There's a signed junction with a trail that has been erased from the Forest Service map. From the head of Mogollon Creek the ghost trail goes right, climbing to McKenna Spring. Continue left, toward Turbo Canyon.

Head down the Mogollon ravine; huge boulders sit on the left slope as the canyon narrows with the high walls creating a tight notch for the trail and the dry streambed. The Diablo's rocks are pocketed with dark alcoves and small cave openings. In the dense forest of Douglas-fir and ponderosa pine, the trail is distinct with old blazes but is very rough with downfall and sticky brush; it is not regularly maintained.

Gradually the valley widens; grassy pine benches allow the trail to meander. In this gentler forest you come upon the Turbo Canyon junction. The trail on the right leads to McKenna Park. Continue down the dry Mogollon drainage, passing the Sycamore junction in 0.3 mile. Since the creek is usually dry here, it is necessary to continue down to Trail Canyon to camp. If you aren't too picky about sites, you might find one sooner. This 3-mile section along Mogollon Creek, named the Kemp Trail (301) in the *Wilderness Ranger District's Wilderness Opportunity Guide,* has not been cut out for years.

There are two massive areas of blowdown in the narrow valley, blocking the trail and requiring detours. The first one is in the first mile, just downstream of a crossing from the south to the north bank. Stay on the south bank and you will find a crude bypass trail along the creek, avoiding the trail that is buried beneath the jackstrawed tree trunks. The next chaotic stretch is 0.5 mile farther, also on the north bank, where a cascade of trees is further complicated by talus and thorny brush. Here you have to pick your way around the north side of the mess in order to resume travel on the trail downstream.

When you're ready to resume your journey, retrace your path up Mogollon

Creek to the Sycamore Trail. Carry plenty of water on this leg. After leaving Mogollon Creek you won't encounter water until the upper reaches of Sycamore Creek, at least 6 miles away. Disregard the misleading mileage estimates on the trail signs; it is 11 miles from Mogollon Creek over the divide to Turkey Creek.

Sycamore Trail up Woodrow Canyon follows the streambed, as if reluctant to leave it. You can expect an acrobatic hike up this lightly used trail, climbing over, under, and around burned or downed tree trunks. At 2 miles the trail angles east and finally leaves the ravine bottom, heading up the dry side slope, smoothly and steadily heading skyward. At 2.5 miles you reach the pass, with a magnificent view of the entire southwest Gila. This is one of the few open passes where you can see forever in all directions. Before dropping down the switchbacks in the head of Sycamore, take a side hike to the high point east of the pass for a panoramic view of Mogollon Baldy and Snow Park.

The Sycamore descent is incredible. At the top there are 1.5 miles of steep switchbacks, barely etched into the skiddy, pulverized surface of the nearly vertical mountainside, and held in place by shrubs, some friendly, some hostile. The trail drops 700 feet via lengthy switchbacks, then reaches a high forested valley of ponderosa pine, still far above the creek. It's initially a relief to be out of the sun and the wind, but the joy soon ends. The first mile of the forest presents many challenges; washouts and tangled tree trunks clutter the path, mixed with idyllic soft sections of open trail.

You will encounter an enormous scene of destruction about 3.5 miles from the pass. A high valley above the cliffs released a burst of boulders and tree trunks in a gush, blasting a hole in the floor of Sycamore where the flotsam landed. You have to climb through the flood debris and pick up the trail below the scene of the explosion, on the left. This is the last major obstacle on the Sycamore Trail. By 4.5 miles from the pass, the alpine forest has changed to a stripe of broad-leaved riparian vegetation, and the stream has trout. The trail continues to improve in the lower elevation. Lush deciduous growth contrasts with the arid mountain hillsides above. The narrow canyon drives the trail to repeated crossings of the brook. Eventually the trail climbs high on the west bank far above the stream where the ravine can no longer accommodate it. After you drop bank to the creek, you will pass a couple of small hot spring pools adjacent to the trail by a garden of cholla. The small rock-rimmed pools are hot, but kind of mucky from disuse. Campsites are nearby.

When you reach the Turkey Creek junction, high on the ridge above both creeks, turn right (west) to climb over Skeleton Ridge again. Be prepared, with a full water bottle, for the hike over the ridge. Rejoining Turkey Creek below Skeleton Canyon, continue down to the windmill junction, and then back to the trailhead on the Gila River.

Options: See Hike 30 if you have time for a stop at Turkey Hot Springs, either coming or going. Also you can take a half-hour side trip up Skeleton Canyon. See Hike 47 for the route up to Granite Peak, a worthy side trip between the valleys of Turkey Creek and Little Creek. While at the Trail Canyon campsite, you can spend a layover day exploring Snow Park and Mogollon Baldy (see Hike 25) or hike through McKenna Park (Hike 26).

32 Turkey–Gila Loop

Highlights:	Loop trip up Turkey Creek to Miller Springs; over Granny Mountain; return on Gila River.
Type of hike:	6- to 8-day backpacking trip.
Total distance:	46 miles.
Difficulty:	Strenuous.
Best months:	April through November.
Maps:	Forest Service Gila Wilderness map (1984); Canyon Hill, Granny Mountain, and Diablo Range USGS quads.

Special considerations: Due to flood danger on the Gila River, this trip should be avoided at spring runoff and after heavy rains. There are many stream crossings on the Gila. There's a long stretch without water over Granny Mountain (possibly 11 miles).

Finding the trailhead: To reach the Lower Gila River Trailhead, from Silver City drive 20 miles northwest on U.S. Highway 180 to milepost 89 and the turn for the town of Gila. Turn right (north) on New Mexico Highway 211. Drive north 4 miles to Gila, and continue north 4 more miles on NM 153 to the pavement's end and the beginning of Forest Road 155. An ominous sign here warns of wet weather hazards and difficulties for low-clearance vehicles. With cautious driving, FR 155 is negotiable by most vehicles, and only flood conditions or snow make it impassable. Continue northeast on FR 155 to its end in 6 miles on the east bank of the Gila River, a mile beyond Crow Canyon.

Parking and trailhead facilities: Trailhead parking is along the road. No trailhead facilities. Camping is permitted.

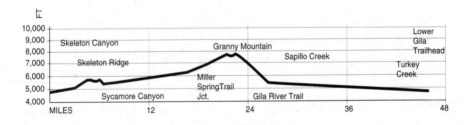

Key points:

0.0	Lower Gila River Trailhead; Gila River Trail (724).
1.0	Junction with Turkey Creek Trail (155) north of the windmill.
3.0	Skeleton Canyon; turnoff to hot springs.
5.3	High point on Skeleton Ridge.
7.5	Junction with Sycamore Canyon Trail (158).
16.5	Junction with Miller Spring Trail (159).
19.0	Miller Spring and cabin; junction with Granny Mountain Trail (160).
26.5	Gila River; junction with Gila River Trail (724).
28.5	Sapillo Creek; junction with Spring Canyon Trail (247).
45.0	Turkey Creek.
46.0	Lower Gila River Trailhead.

The hike: This backpack loop up Turkey Creek, over Granny Mountain, and back down the Gila River has the variety of a broad river valley, a narrow volcanic creek canyon, pinyon-juniper mesa, and a forested mountain ridge. Only in the first 3 miles and the final mile are you likely to encounter other hiking parties.

The Lower Gila area is a mecca for car camping groups, as well as off-road vehicle enthusiasts, especially on warm summer weekends. People heading for the hot springs are numerous year-round. Do not attempt this hike during high water or in flash flood conditions after a heavy rain.

From the end of the road trailhead, hike up the Gila, following the old washed-out road. There are several crossings in this lower section. At mile 1 the trail cuts across a block of private property cluttered with shacks and debris; in the center stands a windmill. The Turkey Creek Trail goes straight north of the windmill, entering the national forest at an open fence where the trail sign is located. Head north here. Turkey Creek is a dry cobblestone bed with the water underground in the lower 0.5 mile, but soon the stream is visible, with riffles and pools, home to trout and ducks. Campsites dot the creek banks.

The trail stays largely on the west bank. In one spot you have a choice of climbing the steep bank to avoid crossing the stream, but Turkey Creek is easily hopped except during high-water conditions. Just below the mouth of Skeleton Canyon is a straight stretch of the trail, with numerous campsites. An unsigned fork in the trail indicates the cutoff to the hot springs. Stay left, following the main trail across the rocky mouth of Skeleton Canyon, and on up the steep ridge that separates Skeleton and Turkey Creek. It's 4.6 miles to water, and about 5 to the next campsites.

The trail up to the ridgetop climbs via switchbacks up the sparsely vegetated ridge. The high point is reached in 2 miles. From here you seesaw along the rocky crest, eventually dropping along the eastern side through talus fields and thorny shrubbery. The views of Turkey Creek are spectacular but it is a tough journey. Finally the trail drops to intersect the Sycamore Canyon Trail, and then drops farther to the creek itself. Campsites are beyond the first Turkey Creek crossing, north of Sycamore Creek.

Above Sycamore, Turkey Creek Trail is lightly used. The path is brushy, wild, and primitive. Travel cannot be hurried because the trail winds back

Turkey–Gila Loop

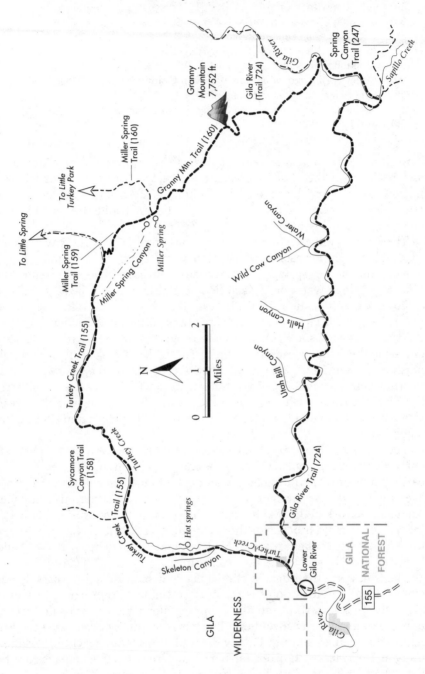

and forth across the stream in the narrow valley. The riparian bottom is crowded with sycamore, maple, ash, and pine. The stream alternates between still pools with rainbow trout and vigorous cascades. Runways of lava make for some slick stream crossings. At 3.5 miles north of Sycamore, Turkey Creek bends sharply east. Listen for a waterfall on the north canyon wall. The trail climbs over a low ridge and then levels out in a totally different landscape, a broad land of grasses and ponderosa pine. An abandoned corral is the first evidence of cattle in the country.

As you approach the Miller Canyon area the trail becomes obscure in the dense foliage. If you temporarily lose the trail and get on a game path, just continue up Turkey Creek and you'll meet the trail again. Watch the water in the creek below the Miller Springs junction. Especially in dry years it will disappear below the rocky streambed. You will want to camp before it vanishes, or stock up for the climb to Miller Springs.

At the Miller Springs junction, turn right to climb the steep south wall of the canyon. In 1.5 miles you reach the mesa and the rolling countryside of pine and juniper. The rocky trail arrives at the New Mexico Fish and Game cabin and spring in 2.5 miles. The stock pond is muddy, but the spring is usually productive, except in very dry years. The Granny Mountain Trail runs alongside the stock pond and up a low draw, climbing steadily toward the wooded summit of Granny Mountain. Although the Granny Mountain portion of the trip is mostly shaded in the forest, the lack of water along the route makes the trip strenuous. The Gila River is a welcome sight. There is a spacious flat and an old corral at the intersection with the Gila River Trail, a delightful spot for a camp.

The final leg of the hike, down the Gila River, is easily a two-day trip. Travel down the broad Gila valley is slow. There are patches of blazed trail, but at each river crossing the trail is lost on the sand and cobblestone beach in the sticky bushes, so after each crossing you have to look for it again. This trip is very unpleasant for dogs; their feet seem to attract thorns and briars along the bank. Two miles below the Granny Mountain junction the river makes a hairpin turn west. At the corner is Sapillo Creek, and the Spring Canyon Trail (247) to NM 15. Continue your meandering journey down the Gila, enjoying the cliffs and canyons, and staying cool in the wide river. The rock formations are enchanting, and you will find traces of prehistoric activity. About a mile above Turkey Creek you cross the wilderness boundary; immediately the river path becomes a doubletrack, taking you back to the trailhead.

Options: If time permits, a side trip to the hot springs is a delightful break (see Hike 30). See Hike 28 for details on the attractions of the Lower Gila. For a point-to-point trip to the Grapevine campground, go upstream from the Granny Mountain trail 13 miles to the bridge on NM 15. Another shuttle option is to leave the Gila at Sapillo Creek; the Spring Canyon Trail is long and dry on most of its 8.5 miles to NM 15. See Hike 37 for both these variations.

Crossing the lower Gila River just above the wilderness boundary.

33 Turkey–Little Spring

Highlights:	Pools and cascades of Turkey Creek in its volcanic canyon; Granite Peak pass in the Diablo Range; rolling pine valley of Little Creek.
Type of hike:	4- to 6-day backpacking trip; shuttle.
Total distance:	38.5 miles.
Difficulty:	Strenuous.
Best months:	March through May; September through November.
Maps:	Forest Service Gila Wilderness map (1984); Canyon Hill, Diablo Range, and Little Turkey Park USGS quads.

Special considerations: Stream crossings on the Gila River—do not attempt the trip in flood conditions. Because of long stretches without water this route is not recommended during hot weather.

Finding the trailheads: To reach the starting trailhead on the Lower Gila River, from Silver City drive 20 miles northwest on U.S. Highway 180 to milepost 89 and the turn for the town of Gila. Turn right (north) on New Mexico Highway 211. Drive north 4 miles to Gila, and continue north 4 more miles on NM 153 to the pavement's end and the beginning of Forest Road 155. An ominous sign here warns of wet-weather hazards and difficulties for low-clearance vehicles. With cautious driving FR 155 is negotiable by most vehicles, and only flood conditions or snow make it impassable. Continue northeast 6 miles on FR 155 to its end on the east bank of the Gila, a mile beyond the mouth of Crow Canyon.

For Woody's Corral, the ending trailhead, drive north of Silver City on NM 15. Turn left (west) after milepost 42 toward the Gila Cliff Dwellings National Monument and the Scorpion campgrounds. This junction is 0.25 mile south of the Gila Visitor Center and 42 miles north of Silver City. Drive west 0.5 mile to Woody's Corral Trailhead on your left (south). Turn left into parking area.

The one-way shuttle driving distance is 80 miles, of which 6 are on unpaved road.

Parking and trailhead facilities: At the Gila River Trailhead, parking is available. Camping is permitted. There are no trailhead facilities. At the Woody's Corral Trailhead, there is a large gravel parking area, a vault toilet, and water; camping is permitted. There is no garbage service in the Gila corridor; be prepared to take your trash with you.

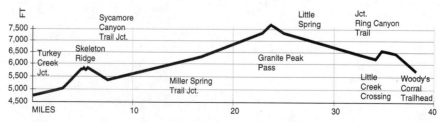

Key points:

Turkey–Little Spring

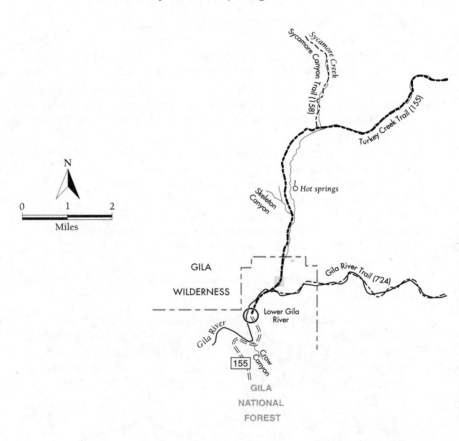

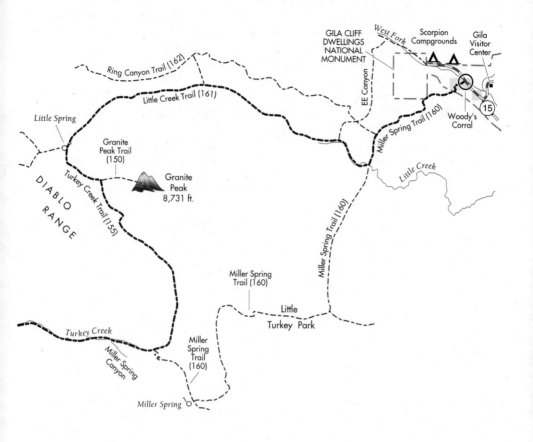

The hike: This outing travels through a variety of ecosystems found in the Gila Wilderness: riparian woodland along Turkey Creek, ponderosa pine forests of the Diablo Range, pine parks of Little Creek, and the pinyon-juniper mesa above Woody's Corral. The trip can easily be done in the reverse, or, to avoid the long car shuttle, you can loop through Little Turkey Park on the Miller Spring Trail (160), returning to the starting trailhead, either at the Gila River or at Woody's Corral.

From the Gila River Trailhead, follow the old washed-out doubletrack upstream. There are several wide crossings, with firm gravel bottoms. In a mile you will reach a block of private property, containing several dilapidated shacks, lots of debris, and a windmill. The Turkey Creek Trail goes north from the windmill, through an open fence, where you once again are on national forest land. Shortly you pass the wilderness boundary, as well as a sign warning of meningitis in hot springs. The trail follows Turkey Creek north. Although its lower reaches are dry, within a mile it is a happily flowing brook, with pools large enough for fish and ducks to enjoy.

Campsites dot the trail, especially on the straight stretch from 2.8 to 3 miles, right before the hot springs turnoff. This unmarked intersection is in an oak grove. A well-worn path goes off to the right, down a little swale, then heads on up Turkey Creek. The main trail stays on the left, angles through the mouth of Skeleton Canyon, and begins climbing steeply up the ridge between these two drainages. There's also a faint trail heading up Skeleton, left no doubt by hikers seeking the hot springs, which aren't in Skeleton Canyon but are a mile up Turkey Creek (Hike 30).

You will not find water for the next 4.6 miles, and the next campsites are about 5 miles away via a rocky steep trail you wouldn't want to negotiate at night. The trail climbs to successive levels of the ridge, always with another one above, until it reaches the high point (5,800 feet) after 2 miles; you stay high, contouring on the eastern side of the ridge, across talus slopes and through thorny shrubs, before finally descending to the ridge above Sycamore Creek and the trail junction. Continue up the Turkey Trail, reaching water in Sycamore in 0.1 mile, and crossing Turkey Creek itself in 0.3. From here to about a mile below the Miller Spring Trail, for the next 7 miles, water is available in the creek. Turkey Creek is spectacular. The volcanic streambed resists erosion, forcing the stream to flow as a sheet on its surface. There are also pools and cascades in the stairstep descent of the waterway, with rainbow trout bunching in the shaded pools.

Above Sycamore the trail is wild and rustic, with light use. Rich in both archeology and geology, the river valley prohibits haste. Furthermore, the trail itself makes travel slow. Sycamore, maple, and ash, as well as lush shrubs, crowd the trail. At 3.5 miles from Sycamore Creek, Turkey Creek angles sharply east. Listen for a waterfall on the north wall. The trail climbs over a streamside ridge and then levels out in a totally different landscape, a broad valley of grass and ponderosa pine. An abandoned corral is the first evidence of the cattle industry since the Gila River. As you approach Miller Springs Canyon, marshy undergrowth temporarily obscures the trail. If you lose the path and end up on a game trail, just continue up Turkey Creek and you'll meet the trail again. About a mile before the Miller Springs Trail junction, the streambed becomes dry. You will find it more convenient to camp before you lose the flowing stream. It is 5 miles round trip to Miller Spring (and a 650-foot climb), which can also be dry.

Beyond the Miller Springs Trail junction, the Turkey Creek Trail has moderate use. This is the route for the Little Turkey Park–Little Spring loop trip out of Woody's Corral. (See Hike 34 for the first half of that trip.) Up to the Turkey–Little Creek divide, the trail stays on the ponderosa pine benches, and then winds up and down over a number of low ridges as it climbs to the pass below Granite Peak, which it reaches 7.5 miles from the Miller Springs junction. From the pass the trail dives swiftly down gullies and ravines to arrive at the oasis of Little Spring in 1.5 miles.

After the dry journey over the Diablo Range, the grassy flat, ringed with towering pines, is a delightful spot. Little Spring creates a flowing stream alongside the meadow. When you are ready to resume your journey, turn east on the Little Creek Trail, down the drainage. It is unlikely that you will encounter water on the 9-mile hike down the Little Creek valley. There are two signed but unnumbered crossover trails that depart on the left, going

Backpacking down the Turkey Creek Trail with upper Skeleton Canyon in the background.

up to the Ring Canyon Trail on the ridge above Little Creek. The main trail splits at times, but is reunited within a mile as one route goes a bit higher on the hillside while the other stays low. Lots of bear, cat, and coyote scat indicates a healthy predator population in the rolling ponderosa grassland. After sidehilling on a ponderosa bench above the rocky stream valley, the trail drops to the open meadow at the Little Creek crossing and the intersection with the Miller Spring Trail (160). There are campsites on either side of the creek.

Turn left (north) and cross the creek to head to Woody's Corral. The trail climbs up a narrow ravine, bounded on the left by a huge lava flow, to reach the junction with the Ring Canyon Trail on the ridge. This area has been hit with repeated lightning fires in recent years. The ponderosa pines are scarred, but are flourishing, with open grasslands beneath. After winding along the ridge at the head of Cliff Dweller Canyon, you reach the pinyon-juniper mesa that slopes to the east. The final mile of the trip is the rocky descent to the corral, on the West Fork floodplain.

Options: If time permits, pause at Turkey Hot Springs, a mile up the creek from Skeleton Canyon. (See Hike 30.) A side trip to Granite Peak is another possibility, either while you are at the pass or from a base camp at Little Spring. (See Hike 47.)

151

34 Turkey Creek–Little Turkey Park

Highlights:	The rugged volcanic canyon of Turkey Creek; Miller Spring and cabin; Little Turkey Park; Little Creek.
Type of hike:	4- to 6-day backpacking trip; shuttle.
Total distance:	33 miles.
Difficulty:	Strenuous.
Best months:	April through November.
Maps:	Forest Service Gila Wilderness map (1984); Canyon Hill, Diablo Range, Granny Mountain, and Little Turkey Park USGS quads.

Special considerations: River crossings on the lower Gila are hazardous in spring runoff or after heavy rain. There may be a long stretch without water from Turkey Creek to Little Creek.

Finding the trailheads: To reach the Lower Gila River Trailhead, drive 20 miles northwest on U.S. Highway 180 from Silver City to milepost 89 and the turn for the town of Gila. Turn right (north) on New Mexico Highway 211. Drive north 4 miles to Gila and continue north 4 more miles on NM 153 to the pavement's end and the beginning of Forest Road 155. An ominous sign here warns of wet weather hazards and difficulties for low-clearance vehicles. With cautious driving, FR 155 is negotiable by most vehicles, and only flood conditions or snow make it impassable. Continue 6 miles northeast on FR 155 to its end on the east bank of the Gila River, a mile beyond Crow Canyon.

For the exit trailhead at Woody's Corral, on NM 14, 42 miles north of Silver City, turn left (west) after milepost 42 toward the Gila Cliff Dwellings National Monument and Scorpion campgrounds. This junction is 0.25 mile south of the Gila Visitor Center. Drive 0.5 mile to Woody's Corral trailhead on your left (south).

The total one-way shuttle driving distance is 80 miles, of which 6 are on unpaved road.

Parking and trailhead facilities: At the Gila River Trailhead, limited parking exists along the road next to the river. There are no trailhead facilities. Camping is permitted. At Woody's Corral there is a large gravel parking area, a vault toilet, water, and an information kiosk. Camping is permitted. The Scorpion campgrounds (no fee) are 0.3 mile up the road.

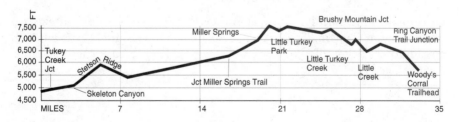

Key points:

- 0.0   Trailhead on the Lower Gila River; Gila River Trail (724).
- 1.0   Junction with Turkey Creek Trail (155) north of the windmill.
- 3.0   Skeleton Canyon; turnoff to Turkey Hot Springs.
- 5.3   High point on Skeleton Ridge.
- 7.5   Junction with Sycamore Canyon Trail (158).
- 16.5   Junction with Miller Spring Trail (159).
- 19.0   Miller Spring and cabin; junction with Miller Spring Trail (160).
- 24.8   Little Turkey Park.
- 25.5   Junction with Brushy Mountain Trail (403).
- 27.5   Little Turkey Creek.
- 29.0   Little Creek; junction with Little Creek Trail (161).
- 29.7   Junction with Ring Canyon Trail (162).
- 33.0   Woody's Corral Trailhead.

The hike: This hike begins and ends at two very busy locations but traverses a wild and primitive region of the wilderness. The hot springs on Turkey Creek are a magnet for visitors, especially on weekends. Likewise, the Gila corridor attracts thousands of visitors at the Gila Cliff Dwellings National Monument. The land in between is quiet and remote, just like it was when Aldo Leopold wandered these trails.

From the east bank of the Gila, begin your trip on the washed-out doubletrack along the river. There are several broad gravel crossings before you reach Turkey Creek. At the dry mouth of Turkey Creek you enter a patch of private property, littered with old shacks and debris. Aim for the windmill that stands in the middle of the property and head north from there. The Turkey Creek Trail begins at the open fence on the north boundary. The trail is signed, as is the national forest boundary at the fenceline.

Although Turkey Creek is a dry cobblestone streambed in its lower 0.5 mile, water is soon plentiful, with deep pools for trout and ducks. Campsites dot the creek bank. The trail is largely on the west bank. At one point the trail splits, with an option to climb the steep west slope in order to avoid a stream crossing. Turkey Creek is crossed with ease, however. In fact, you do not need wading gear after you leave the Gila.

Just below the mouth of Skeleton Canyon, after a straight stretch of the trail, there is an unmarked junction. The trail to the right goes to Turkey Creek and on up to the hot springs. The main trail stays left, winding through the rocky mouth of Skeleton Canyon, and then sharply up the ridge. From here it is 4.6 miles to water, and about 5 miles to the next campsites, so plan ahead. The trail up and along Skeleton Ridge is rocky and steep and unprotected by vegetation. The views, on the other hand, are tremendous, as the southern Turkey Creek drainage stretches below. There are several intermediate false crests, which provide opportunities for sightseeing. The summit ridge is reached in 2.3 miles. The trail stays high, crossing talus slopes and cutting through thorny brush patches until finally dropping to the Sycamore Canyon junction on a ridge above the creek. After crossing Sycamore, curving over another low ridge and crossing Turkey Creek, the trail resumes its streamside rambling.

This middle section of Turkey Creek is wild and primitive. The path is brushy in spots and very lightly used. Turkey Creek has a unique pattern of still pools and waterfalls on a volcanic bed. Often the stream crossings are quite slippery on the flat lava rock. The lush riparian foliage of sycamore, maple, ash, and leafy brush crowds the trail. Rainbow trout hide in the deep shaded pools. Rich in archeology and geology, Turkey Creek canyon requires you to take your time.

About 3.5 miles above Sycamore Canyon, the valley angles sharply east. Listen for a waterfall on the north wall. After the trail climbs over a low

Turkey Creek–Little Turkey Park

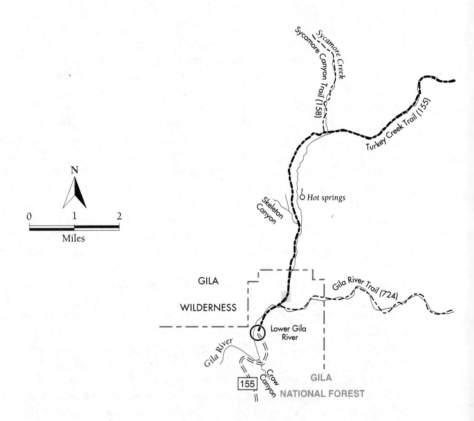

ridge, it levels out in a totally different world, a broad, grassy valley with ponderosa pines. Here are traces of an abandoned corral, the first evidence of cattle in this region. Hiking is a bit faster for a while on the ponderosa bench, then the canyon narrows and the trail winds repeatedly across the smaller stream. Campsites are less frequent in the narrow spots of the canyon. Also, as you near Miller Springs Trail, watch the creek for water. In dry years it vanishes underground about a mile below the junction. You may

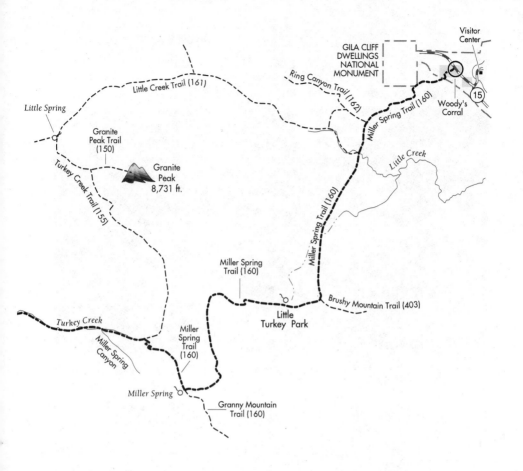

want to camp before the water disappears. Miller Springs is pretty reliable, but it, too, can be dry in a very dry year, and the stock pond there is quite muddy.

Turn right at the sign for Miller Springs and leave Turkey Creek. The trail climbs steeply up the south canyon wall via switchbacks. Upon reaching the mesa, you are in a pine and juniper forest of ridges and ravines. The rocky trail goes up and down to Miller Spring. You drop to the New Mexico Fish and Game cabin and the nearby spring from the north. Your exit trail is on the same northern slope, possibly disguised by a fallen pine tree. There is a sign for the Little Turkey Park Trail on the hillside. The trail adjacent to the stock pond is the Granny Mountain Trail, which will take you to the Gila River.

Heading north, the trail climbs as it wraps around the head of Sycamore Canyon, and then slopes down into Little Turkey Park. The old stock pond there is too muddy to pump. Continue east up from the park to the intersection with the Brushy Mountain Trail. Turn left toward Little Creek and Woody's Corral. The trail follows the ridge off Brushy Mountain down to Little Creek. The deep furrows on the trail make hiking challenging at times.

A muddy pond in the middle of Little Turkey Park.

Little Turkey Creek, which you cross 2 miles from the junction, usually has water. At 1.5 miles farther on the rocky volcanic terrain is Little Creek. Here, too, you can usually find water. The meadow at Little Creek also has numerous campsites, on both sides of the creek.

Cross Little Creek and follow the trail up a narrow ravine to the ridge. The left wall of the ravine is a mass of volcanic conglomerate, which cooled to form a 100-foot wall. On the ridge you meet the Ring Canyon Trail. Near this junction there have been frequent lightning fires recently. The open ponderosa groves demonstrate the positive results of fire in this ecosystem, with flourishing multiaged pines surrounded by lush grass. The trail winds along the narrow ridge above Cliff Dweller Canyon, surrounded by the dense forest. Breaking out onto the more sparsely vegetated pinyon-juniper mesa, the trail slopes to the mesa edge above the trailhead. Here it is a steep, rocky descent to the trailhead in the valley of the West Fork.

Options: This trip can be done in reverse. Looking for the Turkey Hot Springs is traditional for those hiking up Turkey Creek. (See Hike 30.)

35 Sheep Corral Canyon

> **Highlights:** Fastest, most direct hiking access to the remote central reaches of the lower Gila River; scenic valley in a rugged canyon with jagged volcanic formations.
> **Type of hike:** Long day hike or overnighter; out-and-back.
> **Total distance:** 12.4 miles.
> **Difficulty:** Strenuous day hike, moderate overnighter.
> **Best months:** April through November.
> **Maps:** Forest Service Gila Wilderness map (1984); 1997 Gila National Forest map (to navigate forest roads to trailhead); Reading Mountain and Granny Mountain USGS quads.

Special considerations: Carry drinking water. The entire route to Sapillo Creek will probably be dry.

Finding the trailhead: Drive 17 miles north of Silver City on New Mexico Highway 15 or 8 miles south of the junction of NM 15 and NM 35 on NM 15 to the sign for the Sheep Corral Canyon Road 282. Turn west and drive 7 miles to a sizable corral and campsite signed for Sheep Corral and Forest Trail 231. The Sheep Corral Canyon Road is slow, rough, and winding but suitable for two-wheel-drive vehicles. Beyond Sheep Corral the road rapidly deteriorates to four-wheel drive.

Parking and trailhead facilities: The Sheep Corral camp may be occupied by forest workers, a horse party, or grazing permittees. Simply pull off alongside the road and park. There is no water or other facilities at the signed trailhead.

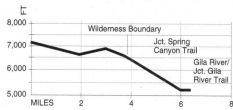

Key points:
- 0.0 Sheep Corral Trailhead for Sheep Corral Canyon Trail (231).
- 2.0 Trail climbs north out of Sheep Corral Canyon.
- 3.8 Gila Wilderness boundary.
- 6.0 Sapillo Creek and junction with Spring Canyon Trail (247).
- 6.2 Gila River and junction with Gila River Trail (724).

The hike: With two-thirds of the route outside the wilderness boundary, there has been some degradation in places from roads that were constructed during a fire in the early 1990s. The trail crosses a road and then follows another road for 0.5 mile to the wilderness boundary. Even so, Sheep Corral Canyon offers an enjoyable, fast, and straightforward entry into the remote, scenic heart of the lower Gila River canyon. From the Sheep Corral Trailhead, walk north through the large forest camp to pick up the Sheep Corral Canyon Trail (231) on the left side of its namesake canyon just below the camp.

Sheep Corral Canyon

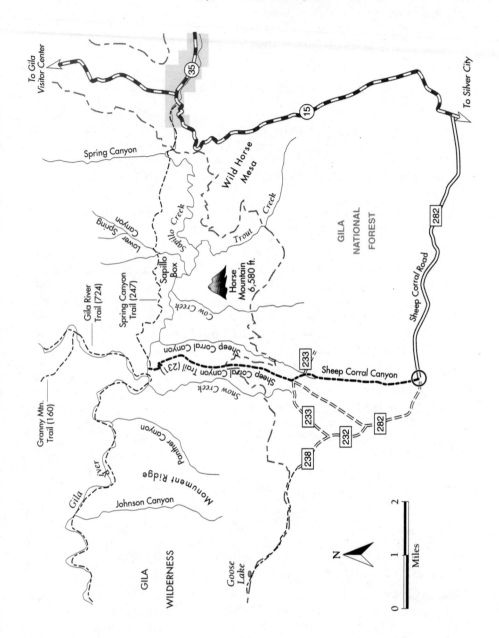

Crossing the Gila River just below the mouth of Sheep Corral Canyon.

The upper 0.5 mile of the canyon is narrow with steep sides rising more than 400 feet. The trail follows the moderate grade of the upper drainage through a mixed pine forest for about 2 miles. It then crosses the gully and climbs steadily to the wide level ridge between Sheep Corral Canyon and Snow Creek, where it intersects a jeep trail. For the next couple miles the trail drops gradually to the north, with occasional views westward of rugged rock outcrops above Snow Creek and beyond to the Gila River valley.

The wilderness boundary is located at the end of the jeep road close to where the flat ridge begins to drop steeply toward Sapillo Creek. The trail angles to the gentler right (east) side of the ridgeline and loses about 700 feet per mile over the following 2 miles. Several sets of switchbacks are interspersed with steeper pitches. Lower Sapillo Creek is reached at mile 6, where a drift fence and gate adjoin the signed junction with the Spring Canyon Trail (247). Turn left (west) for the 0.2-mile stroll to the mouth of Sapillo Creek on the Gila River. The valley is wide here with low-lying ledges and a monumental jagged "hook" of dark volcanic rock across the river. Rock cairns and sycamores mark this low bluff entrance to Sapillo Creek and its fabled box canyon above.

Options: From the Spring Canyon Trail junction, turn right (east) and walk upstream for about 1.5 miles to the lower end of the Sapillo Box (see Hike 36). Compared with the arduous Spring Canyon Trail, the Sheep Corral Canyon Trail is a shorter and easier way to reach the Gila River for a downstream hike (see Hike 38) or upstream to the Gila Bridge (refer to Hike 37).

While in this south-central edge of the wilderness you may want to check out other potential but problematic hikes in the Pinos Altos Range. Some of the trails shown on the Gila Forest map northwest of Sheep Corral are actually rough four-wheel-drive and ATV trails. A jeep trail shown as FR 282 and Trail 238 extends for more than 4 miles from Sheep Corral all the way to the wilderness boundary on Goose Lake Ridge. This point is 2 or 3 miles southeast of the Goose Lake stock pond and close to the upper end of Monument Ridge. Recent forest fires make trail finding difficult at best. For example, the unofficial Monument Ridge Trail shown on the Gila Wilderness map starts out as a good trail for a mile or so only to vanish on the ridge.

36 Sapillo Box

Highlights:	Dramatic overlooks into the box of Sapillo Creek canyon; solitude in a remote and rugged corner of the wilderness.
Type of hike:	Out-and-back long day hike or overnighter.
Total distance:	19.4 miles.
Difficulty:	Strenuous.
Best months:	March through November.
Maps:	Forest Service Gila Wilderness map (1984); Copperas Peak and Granny Mountain USGS quads.

Special considerations: Lots of steep up and down on a hot, south-facing trail with possible water at only one location 3.5 miles in, but no water for 8 miles is more likely.

Finding the trailhead: From Silver City drive 25 miles north on New Mexico Highway 15 or 17 miles south of the Gila Visitor Center on NM 15 to milepost 25. The unsigned trailhead is on the south side of the highway about 0.2 mile west of the junction of NM 15 and NM 35. The parking area is located on private land owned by the Heart Bar Cross Ranch and is posted against camping.

Parking and trailhead facilities: Large parking area with no other facilities. Camping at the privately owned trailhead is not allowed. Water (to be treated) is available from nearby Sapillo Creek.

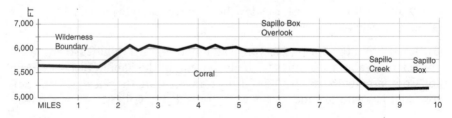

Key points:

- 0.0 Sapillo Creek Trailhead for Spring Canyon Trail (247).
- 1.3 Gila Wilderness boundary.
- 4.7 Corral.
- 5.9 Sapillo Box overlook.
- 7.1 Drift fence.
- 8.2 Bottom of Sapillo Creek.
- 8.7 Mouth of Sheep Corral Canyon.
- 9.7 Sapillo Box.

The hike: The hot, dry Spring Canyon Trail is not for the faint of heart or the faint of joint. For the first 6 miles the trail weaves in and out of complex topography cut by closely spaced ravines and side canyons. The payoff is the breathtaking view into the colossal canyon of the lower Sapillo Creek box. Well-conditioned hikers can make the nearly 20-mile round trip in a day, but the more reasonable option is an overnighter.

To begin the hike, cross the highway and ranch gate to a trail that starts out as an old road but soon becomes a well-beaten path. A large alcove on the right (north) at mile 0.3 signals the beginning of the upper Sapillo Creek canyon with cliffs and overhangs. Stream crossings are numerous but can usually be rock-hopped. Shortly after reaching the wilderness boundary at mile 1.3, the trail begins climbing out of the bottom on the north side. Be sure and fill up your water bottles here. The next water may be a tough 7 miles beyond.

For the next 0.9 mile the rocky trail winds in and out of gullies to a high pinyon-juniper ridge 350 feet above the creek. The trail then drops rapidly on shelf rock before shooting straight up to another windblown ridge. After 3.5 miles and a steep descent, you'll reach a small rocky draw with a grassy bottom that usually carries water in the early spring. Gird your loins for another 270-foot ascent to a ridge with an old Gila Wilderness/Spring Canyon Trail sign that may still be lying on the ground. The following 0.6 mile brings a constant series of 150-foot ups and downs to an old corral and ancient sign falsely claiming a distance of only 3 miles to the Gila River. Rises and falls continue for another half mile to a long-awaited contour stretch on a softer, gentler grade. Finally, at mile 5.9 the trail passes above a grassy swale, sloping to a rocky overlook into the spectacular volcanic chasm of the Sapillo Box. The trail continues down to a new stock fence and gate and then climbs to a long contour with continuous views into the mysterious dark recesses of the chasm. As the trail winds around a major side ridge, canyon views are replaced by panoramic mountain vistas to the west.

The Spring Canyon Trail descends 150 feet over the next 0.8 mile to a second drift fence at mile 7.1. After a short climb the trail plunges in places down a bed of loose rock and gravel, losing some 600 feet over another mile to the lovely sycamore bottom of lower Sapillo Creek. Although rough and rocky, the trail is cut into the steep slope and makes a direct descent to the bottom—a refreshing change after the endless up-and-down and in-and-out nature of the first 6 miles. A large rock cairn marks the stream crossing in

Sapillo Box

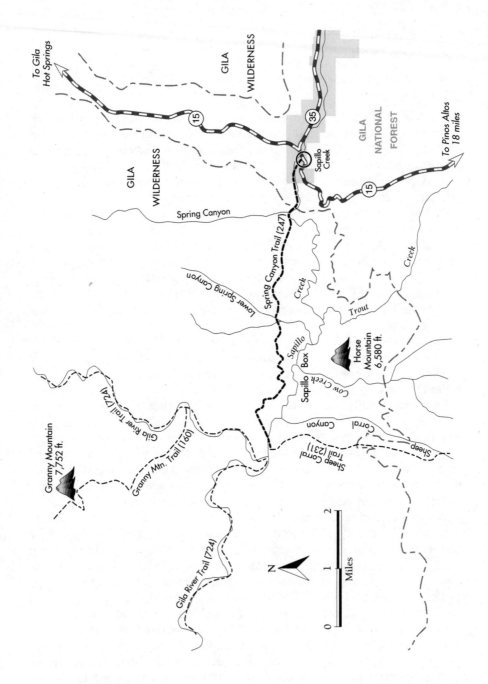

this sycamore grove at mile 8.2. Be sure and memorize this unsigned spot for the return journey.

From here the lower end of the Sapillo Box is located about 1.5 miles up Sapillo Creek. A primitive but well-defined cow path leads upstream across grassy flats with a diverse mix of riparian vegetation. The brushy bottom is a good place to look for javelinas or a host of raptors, circling overhead. After 0.4 mile, several large alcoves appear next to a drift fence and gate followed shortly by Sheep Corral Canyon entering the south side of Sapillo Creek. Another easy mile on the often obscure cow path brings you to the sheer 100-foot-high black volcanic walls of the box. Retrace your route from here or be prepared to wade some deep pools to explore the narrow box canyon upstream.

Options: The Spring Canyon Trail crosses Sapillo Creek a couple of times in the short 0.3-mile stretch to the broad valley of the Gila River. By all means walk down to this remote stretch of the Gila if for no other reason than to round out the out-and-back to an even 20 miles. See Hike 37 for a 25-mile shuttle trip from Sapillo Creek upriver to the Gila Bridge. A similar shuttle hike distance and duration downriver is described in Hike 38. Refer to Hike 35 for a shuttle route on the Sheep Corral Canyon Trail (231) from lower Sapillo Creek. Although the Sheep Corral Canyon Trailhead is higher than the Sapillo Creek Trailhead, this route is a bit easier and a couple of miles shorter than returning by way of the Spring Canyon Trail.

37 Sapillo–Gila Bridge

Highlights:	Dramatic overlooks into the box of Sapillo Creek canyon; solitude in a remote and rugged corner of the wilderness; pleasant hot springs; spectacular volcanic cliffs and formations in the rugged Gila River canyon.
Type of hike:	3- to 4-day backpacking trip; shuttle.
Total distance:	24.5 miles.
Difficulty:	Strenuous.
Best months:	May through November.
Maps:	Forest Service Gila Wilderness map (1984); Copperas Peak, Granny Mountain, Little Turkey Park, and Gila Hot Springs USGS quads.

Special considerations: Lots of steep up and down on a hot, south-facing trail with possible water at only one location 3.5 miles in, but no water for 8 miles is more likely. Do not attempt this route if water levels on the upper Gila River are unsafe for crossing. As with all hot springs, do not dunk your head and nose underwater. A warm-water amoeba, *Naegleria fowleri*, can enter the brain through the nasal passages and can cause a rare form of meningitis.

Finding the trailheads: Sapillo Creek Trailhead: From Silver City drive 25 miles north on New Mexico Highway 15 or 17 miles south of the Gila Visitor Center on NM 15 to milepost 25. The unsigned trailhead is on the south side of the highway about 0.2 mile west of the junction of NM 15 and NM 35. The parking area is located on private land owned by the Heart Bar Cross Ranch and is posted against camping.

Gila Bridge Trailhead: Drive north of Silver City on NM 15 and turn right (east) onto a gravel road signed Grapevine forest camp between mileposts 37 and 38 just before crossing the Gila River Bridge. The turnoff is also about 4 miles south of the Gila Visitor Center. Drive 0.1 mile down the steep, rocky gravel road, turning left at the sign for Gila River Trailhead for the Gila River Trail (724) and the end of the road at the river.

The one-way shuttle driving distance between trailheads is about 12.5 twisting mountain miles, all of which are paved.

Parking and trailhead facilities: Sapillo Creek Trailhead: large parking area with no other facilities. Camping at the privately owned trailhead is not allowed. Water (to be treated) is available from nearby Sapillo Creek.

Gila Bridge Trailhead: large gravel parking area and kiosk. Camping and vault toilets are available in the adjacent no-fee Grapevine forest camp. The Gila River is the only available source of water. Of course, the water must be treated, as is the case with all open water sources in the Gila country.

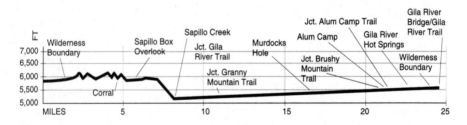

Key points:
0.0	Sapillo Creek Trailhead and Spring Canyon Trail (247).
1.3	Gila Wilderness boundary.
4.7	Corral.
5.9	Sapillo Box overlook.
8.2	Bottom of Sapillo Creek.
8.3	Junction with Sheep Corral Canyon Trail (231).
8.5	Junction with Gila River Trail (724).
10.5	Junction with Granny Mountain Trail (160).
16.5	Murdocks Hole.
21.0	Junction with Brushy Mountain Trail (403).
21.2	Alum Camp.
21.5	Junction with Alum Camp Trail (788).
22.7	Gila River Hot Springs.
24.4	Gila Wilderness boundary.
24.5	Gila Bridge Trailhead for Gila River Trail (724).

164

Sapillo–Gila Bridge

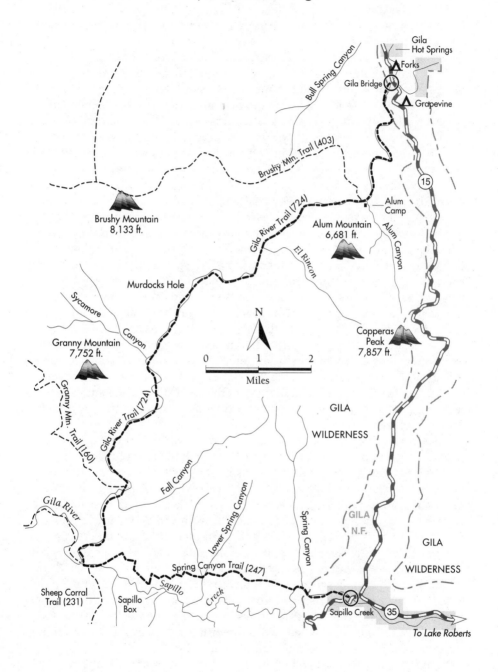

Gila
Hot Springs

Forks

Gila Bridge

Grapevine

Bull Spring Canyon

Brushy Mtn. Trail (403)

15

Alum
Camp

Gila River Trail (724)

Alum Mountain
6,681 ft.

Alum Canyon

Brushy Mountain
8,133 ft.

El Rincon

Murdocks Hole

Sycamore

Canyon

Copperas
Peak
7,857 ft.

Granny Mountain
7,752 ft.

N

Granny Mtn. Trail (160)

Gila River Trail (724)

0   1   2

Miles

GILA

WILDERNESS

Fall Canyon

Lower Spring Canyon

Spring Canyon

Gila River

GILA
N.F.

GILA

WILDERNESS

Spring Canyon Trail (247)

Sheep Corral
Trail (231)

Sapillo
Box

Sapillo

Creek

Sapillo Creek

35

To Lake Roberts

The hike: Between the hot, dry Spring Canyon Trail and the wet, slow Gila River Trail don't expect fast hiking on this one. In fact, turn the slowness into a plus as a way to more fully savor the canyon majesty. For the first 6 miles the Spring Canyon Trail weaves in and out of complex topography cut by closely spaced ravines and side canyons. The payoff is the breathtaking view into the colossal canyon of the lower Sapillo Creek box.

To begin the hike, cross the highway and ranch gate to a trail that starts out as an old road but soon becomes a well-beaten path. A large alcove on the right (north) at mile 0.3 signals the beginning of the upper Sapillo Creek canyon with cliffs and overhangs. Stream crossings are numerous but can usually be rock-hopped. Shortly after reaching the wilderness boundary at mile 1.3, the trail begins climbing out of the bottom on the north side. Be sure and fill up your water bottles here. The next water may be a tough 7 miles beyond.

For the next 0.9 mile the rocky trail winds in and out of gullies to a high pinyon-juniper ridge 350 feet above the creek. The trail then drops rapidly on shelf rock before shooting straight up to another windblown ridge. After 3.5 miles and a steep descent, you'll reach a small, rocky draw with a grassy bottom that usually carries water in the early spring. Gird your loins for another 270-foot ascent to a ridge with an old Gila Wilderness/Spring Canyon Trail sign that may still be lying on the ground. The following 0.6 mile brings a constant series of 150-foot ups and downs to an old corral and ancient sign falsely claiming a distance of only 3 miles to the Gila River. Rises and falls continue for another half mile to a welcomed contour stretch on a softer, gentler grade. Finally, at mile 5.9 the trail passes above a grassy swale, sloping to a rocky overlook into the spectacular volcanic chasm of the Sapillo Box. The trail continues down to a new stock fence and gate and then climbs to a long contour with continuous views into the mysterious darkness of the chasm.

The Spring Canyon Trail descends 150 feet over the next 0.8 mile to a second drift fence at mile 7.1. After a short climb the trail plunges in places down a bed of loose rock and gravel, losing some 600 feet over another mile to the lovely sycamore bottom of lower Sapillo Creek. Although rough and rocky the trail is cut into the steep slope and makes a direct descent to the bottom—a refreshing change after the endless up-and-down and in-and-out nature of the first 6 miles. A large rock cairn marks the stream crossing in this sycamore grove at mile 8.2. If time permits hike 1.5 miles up Sapillo Creek to the lower end of the Sapillo Box (see Hike 36).

The signed junction with the Sheep Corral Canyon Trail (231) taking off to the left is 0.1 mile downstream from where the Spring Canyon Trail meets Sapillo Creek. Another 0.2 mile brings you to the open valley of the Gila River. The trail junction is marked only with a rock cairn and an arching sycamore framing this low bluff exit of Sapillo Creek.

Turn right (north) and head up the Gila River. After about a quarter mile the trail climbs a brushy pinyon-juniper bench on the right (east) with old blazes, only to fade out as it steepens to nowhere. It's best to stay in the river bottom, crossing alternating alluvial benches. The trail is often faint, but the walking is fairly easy. After 2 miles (mile 10.5) the signed Granny Mountain Trail (160) heads north from the left side of the river just past an old corral. Continue right toward the Gila Bridge, crossing broad flats with a mix of cottonwood, ponderosa pine, and juniper overseen by multicolored bluffs of red, gray, white, buff, and black. The riparian off-and-on trail tends to hug the foot of steep slopes. Once in a while a rock cairn or blaze will reassure you that you're on the proper path. The trail tends to vanish at the many stream crossings, in part because hikers need to go up or downstream in search of a shallow crossing. Look ahead to the highest, driest bench and you'll soon intercept the elusive trail.

An impressive cliff dominates the west side at mile 12. The trail is often hidden by windblown sand where it crosses open benches, especially in rough cobblestone near the river. About 4 miles above Sapillo Creek, long benches give way to short benches in a tighter canyon, which means more stream crossings. Sycamores in the intimate canyon contrast with pinyon-juniper hillsides dotted with dark cliffs stacked like layers on a cake. For the following 2 or 3 miles the canyon deepens up to a dramatic spot where the river splits around a huge rock, creating an island. The left (west) branch is the only place on the main Gila where sheer cliff walls define both sides.

Another mile brings the rugged amphitheater of Murdocks Hole ("Murtocks" on the USGS quad map). For at least a mile the hole is wedged by rock formations of every size and shape. Narrow side canyons tempting rigorous off-trail exploration enter from the left (north). As the valley widens again the trail greatly improves, at crossings and across long benches. The canyon continues to narrow and widen with ever-changing variety. The river is a sparkling serpentine wonder with alternating rapids, lengthy rock gardens, and 90-degree bends into deep, dark pools guarded by sheer cliffs. A huge slide of sulfur-colored rock bracketed by bright red outcrops dominates the right (south) slope at mile 20. A grassy bench leads for more than a mile to the Brushy Mountain Trail (403) on the left (north) side at mile 21. Upstream to the right, the trail passes by an unsigned cutoff trail to Alum Camp, crosses the river, and joins the Alum Camp Trail (788) at mile 21.5.

Continue left (north) at the Alum Camp Trail junction. The good trail soon makes a sharp bend to the right with a prominent rocky ridge jutting eastward from the left. After rounding the bend and before making a second river crossing about 1.3 miles above the Alum Camp Trail junction, look for evidence of the Gila River Hot Springs across the river. The telltale sign is sulfur-colored rock. Cross the river, and upon reaching the bench look for a use trail back to the right (southeast) next to a large rock cairn. The use trail follows a gravel bar downstream about 0.1 mile to three spring-fed pools. They sit at the foot of a steep hillside near the east bank of the river. The two lower pools are lined with rocks, one of which is filled with scum. The other is large enough for two people and is endowed with a smooth sandy floor ideal for soaking. The temperature of the pool is delightfully warm and will be especially appreciated after several days of slogging along the Gila River.

As you continue upstream, the mostly well-defined river trail makes seven more crossings before reaching the exit trailhead at the Gila River Bridge. Two sets of high cliff faces just below the bridge give the hike a rugged seclusion to its conclusion.

Options: A steep exit to the Alum Camp Trailhead is possible, but trading the Gila River Hot Springs for a 1,000-foot climb may not be such a good idea. The same is true if the route is done in reverse. Hot springs at the beginning of any hike is less appreciated than toward the end. But, more important, the long dry trek on the rough Spring Canyon Trail will seem even more difficult after 16 miles of river grade trail. The best hike variation may be to begin the trip on the steeper but easier 6-mile-long Sheep Corral Canyon Trail (231) to the Gila River (see Hike 35).

38 Sapillo–Lower Gila

Highlights:	Dramatic overlooks into the box of Sapillo Creek canyon; solitude in a remote and rugged corner of the wilderness; spectacular river valley and side canyons; majestic rock formations and Indian ruins.
Type of hike:	3- to 4-day backpacking trip; shuttle.
Total distance:	26.5 miles.
Difficulty:	Strenuous.
Best months:	May through November.
Maps:	Forest Service Gila Wilderness map (1984); Copperas Peak, Granny Mountain, and Canyon Hill USGS quads.

Special considerations: Lots of steep up and down on a hot, south-facing trail with possible water at only one location 3.5 miles in, but no water for 8 miles is more likely. Due to flood danger on the Gila River, the trip should be avoided during spring runoff and after heavy rains. High-water river crossings are dangerous and probably impossible.

Finding the trailheads: Sapillo Creek Trailhead: From Silver City drive 25 miles north on New Mexico Highway 15 or 17 miles south of the Gila Visitor Center on NM 15 to milepost 25. The unsigned trailhead is on the south side of the highway about 0.2 mile west of the junction of NM 15 and NM 35. The parking area is located on private land owned by the Heart Bar Cross Ranch and is posted against camping.

Lower Gila River Trailhead: From Silver City drive 20 miles northwest on U.S. Highway 180 to mile post 89 and the turnoff for the town of Gila. Turn right (north) on NM 211. Drive north 4 miles to Gila and continue north on NM 153 for 4 more miles to the end of the pavement and the beginning of Forest Road 155. An ominous sign at this point warns of wet-weather hazards and difficulties for low-clearance vehicles. With cautious driving FR 155 is negotiable by most vehicles. Only flood conditions or snow make it impassable. Continue northeast on the rocky, unimproved FR 155 for about 6 miles to its boulder-blocked end on the east bank of the Gila River just below Crow Canyon.

The one-way shuttle driving distance between trailheads is about 62 miles, of which 6 are unpaved.

Parking and trailhead facilities: Sapillo Creek Trailhead: There is a large parking area with no other facilities. Camping at the privately owned trailhead is not allowed. Water (to be treated) is available from nearby Sapillo Creek.

Lower Gila River Trailhead: Undesignated trailhead parking is available along the side of the road near the trailhead. Camping is permitted nearby along the river but there are no trailhead facilities. The only water source is the Gila River.

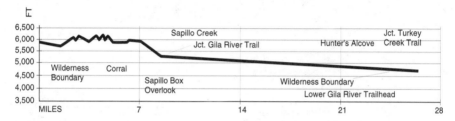

Key points:

    0.0   Sapillo Creek Trailhead and Spring Canyon Trail (247).
    1.3   Gila Wilderness boundary.
    4.7   Corral.
    5.9   Sapillo Box overlook.
    8.2   Bottom of Sapillo Creek.
    8.3   Junction with Sheep Corral Canyon Trail (231).
    8.5   Junction with Gila River Trail (724).
    22.5   Prehistoric hunter alcove.
    24.5   Gila Wilderness boundary.
    25.4   Mouth of Turkey Creek; junction with Turkey Creek Trail (155).
    26.5   Lower Gila River Trailhead and Gila River Trail (724).

The hike: This lower river exploration has some tough stretches, beginning with the endlessly up-and-down Spring Canyon Trail, and the going is slow. Hike this and any of the other trips along the Gila River only if you have enough time to enjoy it. With pesky cobblestones, sticker patches, phantom trails that wash out every few years, and endless crossings on a slippery stream bottom, you can expect to average about 1 mile per hour at best, but the scenery, setting, and solitude are worth it!

To begin the hike cross the highway and go through a ranch gate to a trail that starts out as an old road but soon becomes a well-beaten path. A large alcove on the right (north) at mile 0.3 signals the beginning of the upper Sapillo Creek canyon with cliffs and overhangs. Stream crossings are numerous but can usually be rock-hopped. Shortly after reaching the wilder-

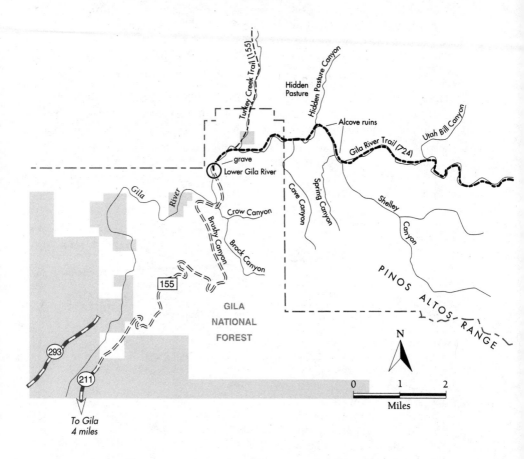

ness boundary at mile 1.3, the trail begins climbing out of the bottom on the north side. Be sure and fill up your water bottles here. The next water may be a tough 7 miles beyond.

For the next 0.9 mile the rocky trail winds in and out of gullies to a high pinyon-juniper ridge 350 feet above the creek. The trail then drops rapidly on shelf rock before shooting straight up to another windblown ridge. After 3.5 miles and a steep descent, you'll reach a small rocky draw with a grassy bottom that usually carries water in the early spring. Gird your loins for another 270-foot ascent to a ridge with an old Gila Wilderness/Spring Canyon Trail sign that may still be lying on the ground. The following 0.6 mile brings a constant series of 150-foot ups and downs to an old corral and ancient sign falsely claiming a distance of only 3 miles to the Gila River. Rises and falls continue for another half mile to a welcomed contour stretch on a softer, gentler grade. Finally, at mile 5.9 the trail passes above a grassy swale, sloping to a rocky overlook into the spectacular volcanic chasm of the Sapillo Box. The trail continues down to a new stock fence and gate and

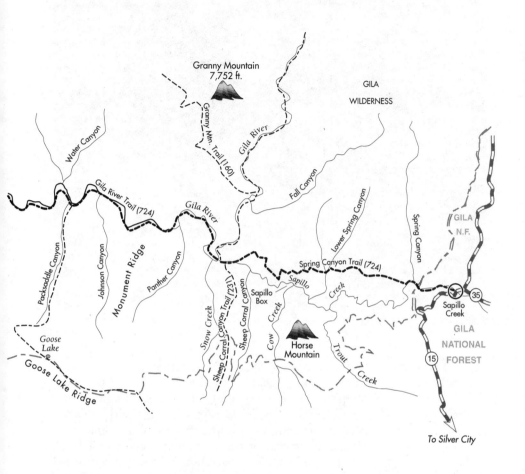

Granny Mountain
7,752 ft.

GILA

WILDERNESS

Water Canyon

Granny Mtn. Trail (160)

Gila River

Gila River Trail (724)

Gila River

Fall Canyon

Lower Spring Canyon

Spring Canyon

GILA

N.F.

Packsaddle Canyon

Johnson Canyon

Monument Ridge

Panther Canyon

Snow Creek

Sheep Corral Canyon Trail (231)

Sheep Corral Canyon

Sapillo Box

Sapillo

Creek

Cow Creek

Spring Canyon Trail (724)

Sapillo Creek

GILA

NATIONAL

35

Goose Lake

Horse Mountain

Trout Creek

15

FOREST

Goose Lake Ridge

To Silver City

then climbs to a long contour with continuous views into the mysterious dark recesses of the chasm.

The Spring Canyon Trail descends 150 feet over the next 0.8 mile to a second drift fence at mile 7.1. After a short climb the trail plunges in places down a bed of loose rock and gravel, losing some 600 feet over another mile to the lovely sycamore bottom of lower Sapillo Creek. Although rough and rocky the trail is cut into the steep slope and makes a direct descent to the bottom—a refreshing change after the endless up-and-down and in-and-out nature of the first 6 miles. A large rock cairn marks the stream crossing in this sycamore grove at mile 8.2. Continue down Sapillo Creek another 0.3 mile and turn left (west) on the Gila River Trail (724) for the remaining 18 miles down the Gila River. If time permits before heading downriver, explore the lower end of the Sapillo Box (see Hike 36).

Travel down the broad Gila valley is slow. There are patches of blazed trail, but at each river crossing the trail is lost on the sand and cobblestone beach in the sticky bushes, so after each crossing you have to look for it

Backpacking near Murdock's Hole.

again. This trip is very unpleasant for dogs; their feet seem to attract thorns and briars along the bank. Impressive cliffs and canyons guard the wide river. The rock formations are enchanting, and you will find traces of pre-historic activity. For the first few miles below Sapillo Creek the river valley is wide with brushy slopes climbing to distant rocky rims. The bottom is brushy and heavily vegetated, especially below the narrow notch of Hells Canyon entering from the right (north). Every so often the river trail is marked by cairns or tree blazes across benches. Ridgelines punctuated by dark volcanic cliffs are peppered with shallow caves and lower overhangs.

River bends continue to tighten with deeper and steeper side slopes downriver to mile 22.5 where Indian ruins shown on the USGS quad are notched into canyon alcoves. The first ruin is high on the rock slope of a ridge and difficult to find, let alone reach The second large river grade alcove used prehistorically as a hunter cave is hidden by dense vegetation on the north (right) side of the river. Please respect these and all other cultural sites, leaving them untouched for the ages. Downstream the canyon is pock-eted with more alcoves and ascending layers of cliffs jutting high above the river.

The trail exits the wilderness boundary 2 miles below the alcove ruins and turns into a soft sand and gravel doubletrack for the remaining 2 miles to a rock barricade that marks the trailhead. Unfortunately, the final mile or so of sandy doubletrack has been degraded by off-road vehicles, not the best way to end a long wilderness backpack. But the serenity, solitude, and scenery of the Lower Gila River will leave you with a longing to return.

Options: This route can certainly be hiked in reverse, but the long, dry trek on the rough Spring Canyon Trail will seem even more difficult after 18 miles of river grade trail. A more user-friendly hike variation is to begin the trip on the steeper but easier 6-mile-long Sheep Corral Canyon Trail (231) to the Gila River (see Hike 35).

39 Alum Camp

Highlights:	Colorful canyon formations; expansive vistas from upper end of trail; remnants of historic cow camp.
Type of hike:	Short out-and-back day hike or overnighter.
Total distance:	3.5 miles.
Difficulty:	Moderate.
Best months:	March through November.
Maps:	Forest Service Gila Wilderness map (1984); Gila Hot Springs USGS quad.

Special considerations: River crossings can be difficult to impossible during periods of high runoff.

Finding the trailhead: Drive north from Silver City on New Mexico Highway 15 and look for a large gravel pullout on the crest of a hill on the left (west) side of the highway between mileposts 35 and 36. The trailhead is about 7 miles south of the Gila Visitor Center. The unsigned Alum Camp Trailhead for the Alum Camp Trail (788) is marked only with a small metal wilderness boundary sign at the start of the trail.

Parking and trailhead facilities: Large gravel parking area; no trailhead camping; no water and no other facilities.

Key points:

0.0 Alum Camp Trailhead for Alum Camp Trail (788).
0.5 Wilderness boundary sign.
1.3 Junction with Gila River Trail (724).
1.8 Alum Camp.

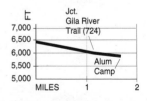

The hike: The hike begins high on the south rim of the Gila River canyon with magnificent views both up and down the valley. The good but rocky trail switchbacks steeply down a hillside mantled with pinyon-juniper and cholla cactus to an old wilderness boundary sign at 0.5 mile. It then makes a more gradual descent of a grassy ridge to a signed junction with the Gila River Trail (724). Turn left (south) and head downstream along the sycamore-lined riverbank. The trail crosses the river after 0.2 mile, but a sandy and somewhat brushy use trail stays on the left (east) side of the stream. This east side route to Alum Camp avoids crossing the river, especially useful

Alum Camp

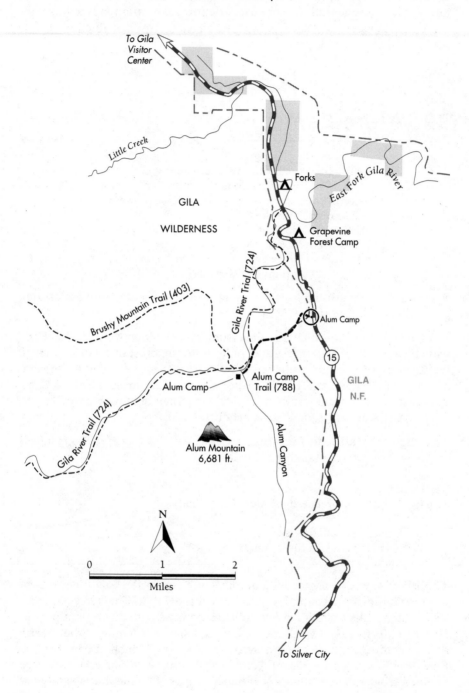

To Gila Visitor Center

Little Creek

GILA

WILDERNESS

East Fork Gila River

Forks

Grapevine Forest Camp

Gila River Trial (724)

Brushy Mountain Trail (403)

Alum Camp

15

GILA N.F.

Alum Camp

Alum Camp Trail (788)

Gila River Trail (724)

Alum Mountain 6,681 ft.

Alum Canyon

To Silver City

N

0   1   2

Miles

during high water. The old cow camp is perched on a left (south) side meadow about 0.5 mile below the trail junction. It sits close to the river and just beyond the mouth of Alum Canyon. The remains of the camp include a corral, foundation, and stone chimney. From the camp a good cutoff trail crosses the river and joins the main Gila River Trail. Despite its proximity to NM 15, the site is well insulated from the sound of the highway by the deep barrier of the canyon. Alum Camp is a pleasant day hike destination in its own right but would also make a good base camp for further exploration.

Options: Refer to Hike 41 for the trip upriver to the Gila River Hot Springs. The springs can be enjoyed during a shuttle hike to the Gila River Bridge or as a separate out-and-back from Alum Camp. A longer hike downstream to Murdocks Hole is about 9 miles round trip from the camp on mostly good trail. For a 1- to 3-mile round-trip exploration of scenic Alum Canyon, follow a distinct use trail up the right (west) side. Rugged cliffs rise high above the east side of the canyon after about 0.5 mile and continue for a considerable distance.

The Alum Camp Trail 788 begins at the wilderness boundary high above the Gila River.

40 Brushy Mountain

Highlights:	Gila River canyon; sweeping mountain vistas; solitude in a remote part of the wilderness.
Type of hike:	2- to 3-day backpacking trip; shuttle.
Total distance:	17 miles.
Difficulty:	Strenuous.
Best months:	April through November.
Maps:	Forest Service Gila Wilderness map (1984); Gila Hot Springs and Little Turkey Park USGS quads.

Special considerations: Gila River may be impassable during periods of high runoff. Steep, hot climb on the lower end of the lightly used Brushy Mountain Trail, which is also difficult to find in several places near Brushy Mountain. No pumpable drinking water along dry 10-mile stretch from the Gila River to Little Turkey Creek.

Finding the trailheads: Alum Camp Trailhead: From Silver City drive north on New Mexico Highway 15. The unsigned Alum Camp Trailhead for Alum Camp Trail 788 is located between mileposts 35 and 36 at the crest of the hill south of the Gila River Bridge and also 7 miles south of the Gila Visitor Center. Look for a large gravel parking area on the left (west) side of the highway.

Woody's Corral Trailhead: From Silver City drive north on NM 15 and turn left (west) after milepost 42 toward Gila Cliff Dwellings National Monument and Scorpion campgrounds. This junction is 0.3 mile south of the Gila Visitor Center. Drive 0.5 mile to Woody's Corral Trailhead for Miller Spring Trail 160 on your left (south).

The one-way shuttle driving distance between trailheads is 7 miles.

Parking and trailhead facilities: Alum Camp Trailhead: large gravel parking area. There is no water or other facilities. Woody's Corral Trailhead: large gravel parking area with undeveloped campsites, water, kiosk, and a vault toilet.

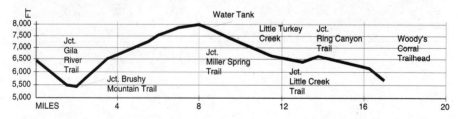

Key points:
0.0 Alum Camp Trailhead for Alum Camp Trail (788).
1.3 Junction with Gila River Trail (724).
2.0 Junction with Brushy Mountain Trail (403).
8.5 Water tank on Brushy Mountain.

Brushy Mountain

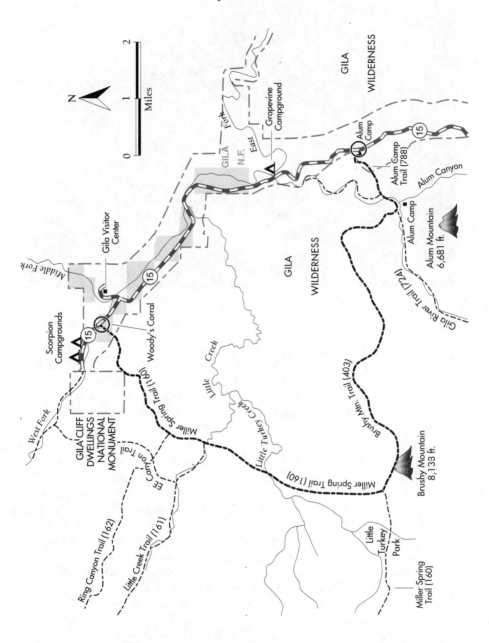

9.5   Junction with Miller Spring Trail (160).
11.5   Little Turkey Creek crossing.
13.0   Junction with Little Creek Trail (161).
13.7   Junction with Ring Canyon Trail (162).
17.0   Woody's Corral Trailhead.

The Gila River near Alum Canyon.

The hike: From riverbottom to mountaintop, this hike samples a wide diversity of landscapes within the Gila Wilderness. The trip begins on the Alum Camp Trail with a spectacular view down the Gila River valley. The trail, marked only with a small metal wilderness sign, switchbacks steeply down to its junction with the Gila River Trail (724) at mile 1.3. Turn left (south) along the sycamore-lined bank to a river crossing within another 0.3 mile. After climbing out of the gravelly stream bottom the trail meets the unsigned cutoff trail to Alum Camp. Continue right on the main Gila River Trail to the signed junction with the Brushy Mountain Trail (403) at mile 2 in a pinyon-juniper flat. Turn right (north) on the lightly used Brushy Mountain Trail, which is faint in places but generally easy to follow. The hardest part of the entire hike takes place over the next 1.5 miles as the trail gains nearly 1,200 feet on a loose gravel surface. As the ridge begins to mellow out, grab a shady spot under a pinyon pine and enjoy a grand view of the Gila River canyon, especially downriver. The primitive path is enjoyable as it makes a more gradual climb past huge alligator juniper mixed with oak and pines of the pinyon and ponderosa persuasions. The faint trail stays on the ridge and is easy to follow with occasional blazes and walk-around downfall. At mile 6 the trail passes through a stock fence and gate, climbs on to a narrow saddle, and then achieves its high point of 8,000 feet at mile 8. Open ponderosa-pine parks allow vistas on both side of the ridgeline trail. Sign of wildlife is abundant, particularly elk, bear, coyote, and mountain lion, along with the constant chattering of gray-colored squirrels to keep you company.

The needle-cushioned trail reaches a rainwater cistern at mile 8.3. A recent lightning-caused burn has obscured the trail, which is further confused by cut logs and a fireline that cuts downhill to the right. Go to the right (downhill) side of the fence surrounding the water tank and look for a small blaze on a pine tree. The unmarked trail continues downhill to the west along the gentle broad slope of a pine park. After another mile the signed junction is reached with the Miller Spring Trail (160), leading straight ahead another 0.8 mile to Little Turkey Park. Go right (north) at the junction where the Miller Spring Trail makes a sharp 45-degree turn to the right (northeast) and gently descends a pine ridge. The trail is rocky and deeply furrowed in spots. After another 2 miles the trail finally crosses Little Turkey Creek, the first pumpable source of drinking water since leaving the Gila River 10 miles back. The trail then sidehills to a ridge that drops through an open grassy park, leading to a rocky ravine on down to Little Creek. Parklike campsites can be found on both sides of the stream both above and below the trail junction.

From this idyllic meadow the trail climbs a volcanic ravine northward bound by a lava bluff on its west side. The Ring Canyon Trail (162) is reached at the top of the ridge 0.8 mile above Little Creek in a pine park. Stay on the Miller Spring Trail, which then follows the ridge above Cliff Dwellers Canyon on the north, reaching an old gated stock fence after another 2 miles. The final 1.3 miles to Woody's Corral crosses a grassy pinyon-juniper mesa before descending on a rock-stepped zigzag course to the trailhead.

Options: Alum Camp: For a short side hike to Alum Camp see Hike 39. Brushy Mountain: From the water tank at mile 8.3, climb left (southwest) to the main ridge and continue off-trail another 0.5 mile up the gently graded ridge to the indistinct top of Brushy Mountain. The mountain lives up to its name, with trees and brush blocking most of the view southward to the Gila River, but you've come this far so why not reach the high point?

Little Turkey Park: From the Miller Spring Trail junction at mile 9.5, take the gentle but rocky trail to the left another 0.8 mile to the spacious pine park and grassy meadow. A tiny mud pond in the center of the park defines the head of Little Turkey Creek.

41 Gila Forks

Highlights:	Hot springs; colorful canyon rock walls and formations; expansive views from above.
Type of hike:	Day hike; shuttle.
Total distance:	4.3 miles.
Difficulty:	Easy (in low water); moderate (if higher water makes river crossings more difficult).
Best months:	Year-round.
Maps:	Forest Service Gila Wilderness map (1984); Gila Hot Springs USGS quad.

Special considerations: Lots of river crossings. Check water levels ahead of time to ensure safe passage. If hitching between trailheads, don't count on a ride during off-season weekdays.

Finding the trailheads: Alum Camp Trailhead: Drive north from Silver City on New Mexico Highway 15 and look for a large gravel pullout on the crest of a hill on the left (west) side of the highway between mileposts 35 and 36. The trailhead is about 7 miles south of the Gila Visitor Center. The Alum Camp Trailhead for Trail 788 is unsigned, marked only by a small metal wilderness boundary sign at the start of the trail.

Gila River Trailhead: From Silver City drive north on NM 15 and turn right (east) onto a gravel road signed Grapevine forest camp between mileposts 37 and 38 just before crossing the Gila River Bridge. Drive 0.1 mile down the steep gravel road, turning left at the sign for the Gila River Trail (724) and the end of the road at the river.

The shuttle driving distance between the two trailheads is only 2 paved miles.

Parking and trailhead facilities: Alum Camp Trailhead: large gravel parking area; no camping; no water and no facilities. Gila River Trailhead: large gravel parking area, kiosk, camping, and vault toilets available in adjacent no-fee Grapevine forest camp. The Gila River is the only available water source. The river water must be treated.

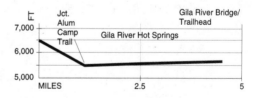

Key points:

0.0	Unsigned Alum Camp Trail (788) with wilderness boundary sign.
0.5	Wilderness boundary sign.
1.3	Junction with Gila River Trail (724).
2.5	Gila River Hot Springs.
4.3	Gila River Bridge and Gila River Trailhead.

Gila Forks

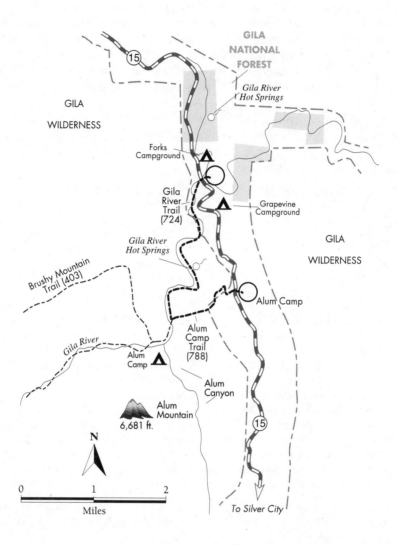

The hike: The start of the hike opens to a spectacular panorama down the Gila River valley. The otherwise good trail becomes rocky as it drops steeply through pinyon-juniper woodlands lined with cholla cactus. The grassy ridge trail then leads to a signed junction at 1.3 miles. The sign indicates a distance of 2.8 miles upriver to the bridge. Turn right (north) at this junction and head upstream. The distinct river grade trail soon makes a sharp bend to the right with a prominent rocky ridge jutting eastward from the left. After rounding the bend and before making a second river crossing about 1.3 miles above the trail junction, look for evidence of the Gila River Hot

Springs across the river. The telltale sign is sulfur-colored rock. Cross the river, and upon reaching the bench look for a use trail back to the right (southeast) next to a large rock cairn. The use trail follows a gravel bar downstream about 0.1 mile to three spring-fed pools. They sit at the foot of a steep hillside near the east bank of the river. The two lower pools are lined with rocks, one of which is filled with scum. The other is large enough for two people and is endowed with a smooth sandy floor ideal for soaking. The temperature of the pool is delightfully warm, providing a wonderful respite during a cold day or a hot hike.

As you continue upstream the mostly well-defined river trail makes seven more crossings before reaching the exit trailhead at the Gila River Bridge. Two sets of high cliff faces just below the bridge give the hike a rugged seclusion to its conclusion.

Option: Investigate the remains of Alum Camp, a 1-mile round trip from the trail junction (see Alum Camp Hike 39). The shuttle can be equally enjoyed in reverse from north to south with the main difference being a rocky uphill exit instead of a wet-foot river slog.

42 Gila River Hot Springs

Highlights:	Wonderful hot springs and scenic volcanic cliffs in the upper Gila River canyon.
Type of hike:	Out-and-back day hike.
Total distance:	3.6 miles.
Difficulty:	Easy (during low water); moderate (if higher water makes crossings more difficult).
Best months:	Year-round.
Maps:	Forest Service Gila Wilderness map (1984); Gila Hot Springs USGS quad.

Special considerations: Do not attempt this route if water levels on the upper Gila River are unsafe for crossing. As with all hot springs, do not dunk your head and nose under water. A warm-water amoeba, *Naegleria fowleri*, can enter the brain through the nasal passages and can cause a rare form of meningitis.

Finding the trailhead: Drive north of Silver City on New Mexico Highway 15 and turn right (east) onto a gravel road signed Grapevine forest camp between mileposts 37 and 38 just before crossing the Gila River Bridge. The turnoff is also about 4 miles south of the Gila Visitor Center. Drive 0.1 mile down the steep rocky gravel road, turning left at the sign for Gila River Trailhead for the Gila River Trail (724) and the end of the road at the river.

Parking and trailhead facilities: Large gravel parking area and kiosk. Camping and vault toilets are available in the adjacent no-fee Grapevine

Gila River Hot Springs

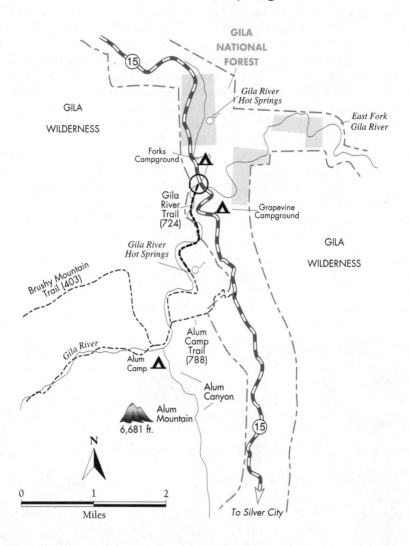

forest camp. The Gila River is the only available source of water. Of course, the water must be treated, as is the case with all open-water sources in the Gila country.

Key points:

    0.0   Signed Gila River Trailhead.
    0.1   Gila Wilderness boundary.
    1.7   Use trail to Gila River Hot Springs.
    1.8   Gila River Hot Springs.

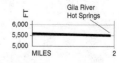

The hike: This upper stretch of the Gila River immediately below the bridge can provide quick year-round access to the off-river hot springs. The gradient is virtually flat, dropping only 40 feet to the springs. However, the Gila River Trail (724) crosses the river seven times between the bridge and hot springs, so low water is essential for this route. The trail is well defined by use, especially along forested benches above gravel bars. Two sets of high cliffs on alternate sides of the river necessitate river crossings at the start. After five more crossings, 1.8 miles and just before dropping to river crossing number eight, look for an unmarked use trail branching to the left (southeast) next to a large rock cairn. The use trail leads across a gravel bar on the east side of the river for 0.1 mile to the hot springs, located at the foot of a steep hillside.

This pleasantly warm spring has been minimally developed with rocks lining two lower pools and a tiny tublike pool above. A steady stream of hot water gushing from a natural rock spigot feeds the pools. One of the lower pools is full of scum, but the other has a smooth sandy bottom perfect for stretching out in. It is large enough for two serious soakers. The view of high bluffs and rock formations in this upper stretch of the river is an added attraction. Retrace your route to complete this relaxing Gila respite.

Option: To reduce the number of one-way river crossings from seven to two, take the Alum Camp Trail (788) down to the river, turn right, and head upstream another 1.3 miles to the hot springs for an up-and-down 5-mile round trip. Refer to Gila Forks (Hike 41) for more details.

Soaking in the Gila River Hot Springs.

43 Murdocks Hole

Highlights: Pleasant hot springs and spectacular volcanic cliffs and formations in the rugged Gila River canyon.
Type of hike: Out-and-back overnight backpacking trip.
Total distance: 16 miles.
Difficulty: Moderate (in low water).
Best months: April through November.
Maps: Forest Service Gila Wilderness map (1984); Gila Hot Springs and Little Turkey Park USGS quads.

Special considerations: Do not attempt this hike when river crossings are unsafe during high water levels. Do not dunk your head and nose under water in any hot springs. A warm-water amoeba, *Naegleria fowleri*, can enter the brain through nasal passages and can cause a rare form of meningitis.

Finding the trailhead: Drive north of Silver City on New Mexico Highway 15 and turn right (east) onto a gravel road signed Grapevine forest camp between mileposts 37 and 38 just before crossing the Gila River Bridge. The turnoff is also 4 miles south of the Gila Visitor Center. Drive 0.1 mile down the steep rocky gravel road, turning left at the sign for the Gila River Trail (724) and road's end at the river.

Parking and trailhead facilities: Large gravel parking area and information board. Camping and vault toilets are available in the adjacent no-fee Grapevine forest camp. The Gila River is the only water source. Of course, the water must be treated, as is the case with all open water in the Gila country.

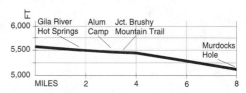

Key points:

0.0   Upper Gila River Trailhead at Gila Bridge for Gila River Trail (724).
0.1   Gila Wilderness boundary.
1.8   Gila River Hot Springs.
3.0   Junction with Alum Camp Trail (788).
3.5   Junction with Brushy Mountain Trail (403).
8.0   Murdocks Hole.

The hike: This route has lots of river crossings, especially during the first few miles. However, with the aid of Neoprene socks and a sturdy pair of river shoes, the trip is a joy during low water. But when the river is raging, look for a user-friendlier upland hike instead.

The well-worn river trail quickly enters the wilderness and crosses the Gila seven times in the 1.8 miles between the bridge and hot springs. Just before crossing number eight look for an unmarked use trail branching to

Murdocks Hole

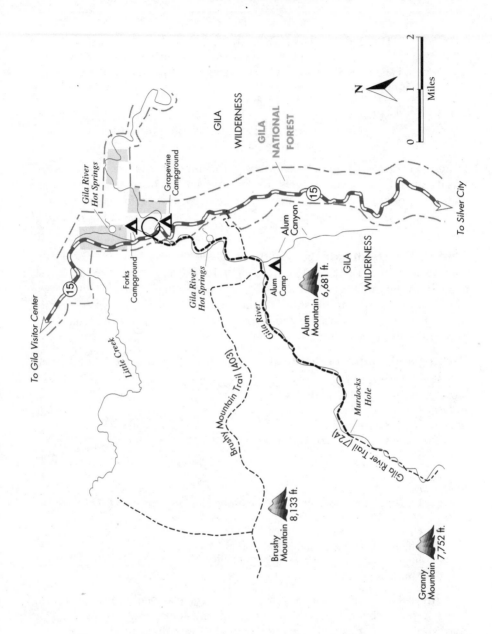

Enjoying a tranquil stretch of the Gila River below Murdocks Hole.

the left (southeast) adjacent to a large rock cairn. If you want to soak on the way to or from Murdocks Hole, follow the use trail on the east side of the river for about 100 yards to the hot springs. One of the small rock-lined pools has a sandy bottom ideal for two compatible soakers.

The trail continues another 1.3 miles around a sharp river bend to the left, crosses the river, and then follows the west side to the signed junction with the Alum Camp Trail (788). Continue to the right across the river to a grassy flat with an unsigned trail branching left to Alum Camp. If time allows, hike across the river 0.1 mile to the rustic ruins of Alum Camp. An old cow trail leads up the red rock entrance to Alum Canyon, inviting further discovery.

As you continue downriver, the Gila River Trail joins the Brushy Mountain Trail (403) on a grassy bench at mile 3.5. Stay on the main left-hand trail, which crosses grassy benches for more than a mile on the north side of the canyon with only a brief stretch of rough cobblestone. A striking yellow rockslide bracketed with bright red outcrops appears on the left (south) side of the river. The good trail continues as the wide valley closes in and opens up with over changing variety. Even the river crossings seem easier. After a narrow stretch the valley widens at mile 7, especially on the left (east) slope. Rugged side canyons enter from the right (west) slope, inviting rigorous off-trail exploration. The crossings and bench segments of the trail are distinct with occasional old blazes on alligator juniper. For the next mile the canyon is especially impressive. Jagged rock formations of every conceivable shape and size preview the rugged volcanic amphitheater of Murdocks Hole at mile 8. The name given on the USGS quad map is Murtocks Hole. Either way, the cliff-lined hole is more than 2,000 feet directly below and south of Brushy Mountain and could be a good resting spot. During the seemingly longer hike back upriver to the bridge, you might enjoy a soothing soak in the hot springs even more than on the way in.

Options: By all means explore farther downriver, out-and-back any distance, but be prepared for a rougher and more difficult trail to follow below Murdocks Hole. You can also continue down to Sapillo Creek on a reverse shuttle route for Hike 37 or do a reverse of Hike 29 another 26 miles down the Gila River past Turkey Creek.

44 Little Creek

Highlights:	Short hike to a wilderness stream; views of Brushy Mountain.
Type of hike:	Out-and-back day hike or overnight backpacking trip.
Total distance:	8 miles.
Difficulty:	Easy.
Best months:	March through November.
Maps:	Forest Service Gila Wilderness map (1984); Little Turkey Park USGS quad.

Special considerations: None.

Finding the trailhead: To reach the Woody's Corral Trailhead, turn left (west) from New Mexico Highway 15 just north of the mile 42 milepost toward the Gila Cliff Dwellings National Monument and Scorpion campgrounds. This intersection is 0.3 mile south of the Gila Visitor Center and 42 miles north of Silver City on NM 15. Drive 0.5 mile to Woody's Corral Trailhead for Trail 160 on your left (south). Turn left into the parking area.

Parking and trailhead facilities: There is a large gravel parking area with vault toilet and water. Camping is permitted at the trailhead, and the Scorpion campgrounds (no fee) are across the road. There is an information kiosk at the trailhead. There is no garbage service available in the Gila Hot Springs corridor, so be prepared to carry all your trash out with you.

Key points:

0.0   Woody's Corral Trailhead.
3.3   Junction with Ring Canyon Trail (162) to
      McKenna Park.
4.0   Little Creek crossing and the meadow; junction
      with Little Creek Trail (161).

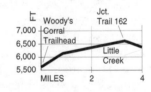

The hike: This short day hike takes you to a wilderness meadow along a delightful rocky stream. From the Woody's Corral Trailhead, take the Miller

Little Creek

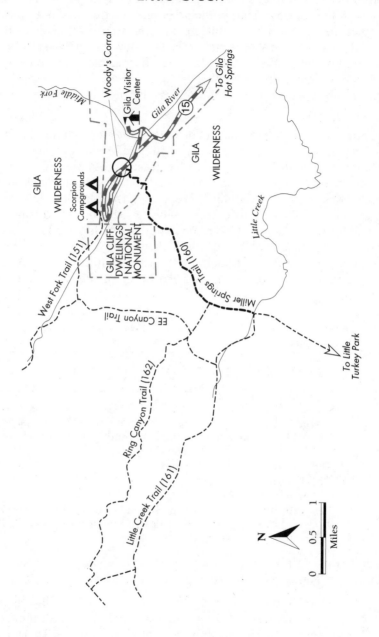

Springs Trail (160). The first 0.8 mile goes sharply uphill on a rock-stepped zigzag course to the mesa above Cliff Dweller Canyon. The clear trail travels then across a grassy pinyon-juniper mesa, rising gradually to a ponderosa pine park. The area experienced a number of fires in recent years, leaving the grass and ponderosa flourishing.

At the intersection with the Ring Canyon Trail (162), go north to McKenna Park on Miller Springs Trail, which descends swiftly down a volcanic ravine. On the right is a huge bluff of lava that stopped flowing at this spot and hardened in place. At the end of the lava flow you arrive at Little Creek, a pleasant brook that is easy to step over. If your plans are to camp, there are numerous campsites on both sides of the creek.

After your visit, return to the trailhead by the same trail, or by the EE Canyon route (see "Options").

Options: You can ramble on down Little Creek on a day hike from the meadow. This adventure begins on a faint trail created by horse parties. Within a mile the horse path heads left (east) across the dry mesa toward the corral. To continue beyond that you'll have to bushwhack along the stream, bouldering and wading. There is a spectacular volcanic gorge about 2 miles down. This is an arduous trip—quite strenuous—and is not recommended for backpacking. It's best done in early spring in a low-water year, before the streamside brush and willows have grown to dominate the banks.

A more gentle option to extend the Little Creek hike is described in Hike 45, the Little Creek Loop. Also, see Hike 46 for an alternate return trip via EE Canyon.

45 Lower Little Creek Loop

Highlights:	Streamside meadow; creek valley of pine parks, oak, and pinyon-juniper on rolling ridge; variety of volcanic formations.
Type of hike:	Day hike; loop.
Total distance:	18.2 miles.
Difficulty:	Strenuous.
Best months:	March through May and October through November.
Maps:	Forest Service Gila Wilderness map (1984); Little Turkey Park USGS quad.

Special considerations: No water beyond Little Creek crossing. Possible lightning on Thousand Mile Ridge during summer storms.

Finding the trailhead: To reach the Woody's Corral Trailhead, on New Mexico Highway 15, turn left (west) after milepost 42 toward the Gila Cliff Dwellings National Monument and Scorpion campgrounds. This junction is 0.3 mile south of the Gila Visitor Center and 42 miles north of Silver City. Drive 0.5 mile to the Woody's Corral Trailhead for Trail 160 on your left (south). Turn left into the parking area.

Parking and trailhead facilities: Large gravel parking area; water and vault toilet; Information board. Camping permitted. No garbage service.

Lower Little Creek Loop

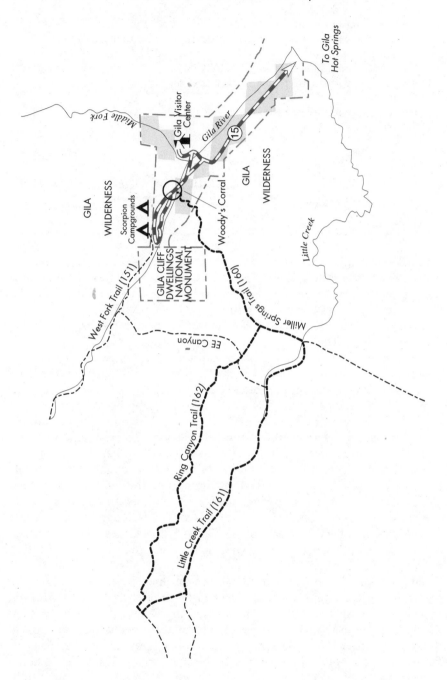

Key points:

0.0   Woody's Corral and Miller Springs Trail (160).
3.3   Junction with Ring Canyon Trail (162).
4.0   Little Creek crossing; junction with Little Creek Trail (161).
5.0   Junction with cut-over trail to Ring Canyon and EE Canyon Trails.
8.5   Junction with cut-over trail to Ring Canyon and Thousand Mile Ridge.
9.5   Junction with Ring Canyon Trail (162).
14.4 Junction with cut-over trail from Little Creek.
14.5 Junction with EE Canyon Trail.
14.6 Junction with Miller Springs Trail (160).
18.2 Woody's Corral.

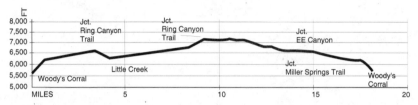

The hike: This hike merits a strenuous rating because of its length and the lack of water after mile 4. It is not recommended for the hot summer months for the same reasons. In addition, the ridge above Cliff Dweller and EE Canyons is highly vulnerable to lightning. In a recent year, five fires erupted in a cluster of lightning strikes near the trail intersection of Miller Springs and Ring Canyon Trails.

The Lower Little Creek Loop can be shortened by doing this hike as a day hike from a base camp on Little Creek. Then the 11-mile loop is rated moderate, for lack of water on the route (see Hike 44).

From the Woody's Corral Trailhead, follow the Miller Springs Trail up the bluff of volcanic rock. Within a mile you will be on the grassy rolling pinyon-juniper mesa above the hectic Gila corridor. The trail climbs gradually to the fragmented ridges at the head of Cliff Dweller Canyon, to the intersection with the Ring Canyon Trail. You will be coming through this junction on the Ring Canyon Trail at the end of the loop trip. For now, continue straight on Miller Springs Trail. The ponderosa pine parks display extensive evidence of fire activity in this area. The trail descends through a narrow ravine of lava to emerge on the bank of Little Creek. Cross the creek to pick up the Little Creek Trail on your right. After filling your water bottles, head up Little Creek.

The pleasant Little Creek Trail follows an open pine bench along the south side of the stream, which disappears in the rocky bottom within a mile. The first cut-over trail on your right, 1 mile above the creek crossing, goes up to Thousand Mile Ridge. For a miniature version of the loop (3 miles total distance from a camp at Little Creek), you can turn right here. For the longer loop, continue up the Little Creek valley. The valley is home to bear, mountain lion, and coyote, each of which has left scat on the trail. Periodically the footpath splits, only to rejoin later, so you can't go wrong regardless of which one you choose.

Hiking off-trail down lower Little Creek canyon.

A signed junction at 4.5 miles from the stream crossing is where you turn right (north). This cut-over trail climbs up a draw, steepening toward the upper end. It reaches the top of the ridge and meets the Ring Canyon Trail in 1 mile. Turn right here to Woody's Corral. Continue along the ridgetop trail as it winds through the pinyon-juniper oak woodland with open views both north and south. In places the trail is closed in with brush but still enjoyable to hike. Evidence of wild turkeys is ubiquitous. There are lovely places to pause and gaze at the canyons of the West Fork with their white cliffs of ashflow conglomerate.

Toward the end of the ridge, there are two trail junctions in rapid succession. The first, on the right, is the cut-over trail from Little Creek, followed quickly by the EE Canyon Trail on the left. Continue straight on the ridge to the Miller Springs Trail junction. Here you turn left and follow the trail back to Woody's Corral, unless you have established a camp at Little Creek, in which case you turn right to get to camp.

Option: To avoid retracing the first 3.3 miles of the hike, you can turn down EE Canyon and then go down the West Fork Trail (see Hike 46 for details).

46 EE Canyon Loop

Highlights:	Diverse terrain and scenery with modest elevation gain in a compact day loop; steep-walled canyons; ridgetop vistas.
Type of hike:	Day hike; loop.
Total distance:	8.3 miles.
Difficulty:	Moderate.
Best months:	March through November.
Maps:	Forest Service Gila Wilderness map (1984); Little Turkey Park USGS quad.

Special considerations: The one crossing of the West Fork may be difficult to impossible during high water; the final mile of the route involves walking the paved state highway back to Woody's Corral Trailhead.

Finding the trailhead: On New Mexico Highway 15 turn left (northwest) after mile post 42 toward Gila Cliff Dwellings National Monument and Scorpion campgrounds. This junction is 0.3 mile south of the Gila Visitor Center and 42 miles north of Silver City. Drive 0.5 mile to Woody's Corral Trailhead for Trail 160 on the left (south). Turn left into the trailhead.

Parking and trailhead facilities: Large gravel parking area, kiosk, vault toilet, and water at trailhead. Camping permitted. No garbage service.

Key points:

0.0   Woody's Corral Trailhead.
3.3   Ring Canyon Trail (162).
3.8   EE Canyon Trail Junction.
5.5   Junction with west branch of EE Canyon.
6.0   Junction with West Fork Gila River Trail 151.
7.3   Gila Cliff Dwellings National Monument.
8.3   Woody's Corral Trailhead.

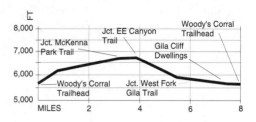

The hike: The popular EE Canyon loop is a good warm-up with the added attraction of year-round vehicular access to the trailhead. From the corral take Trail 160, known as the Miller Spring Trail. During the first 0.8 mile the zigzag trail gains 400 feet on a rock-stepped path. It continues across a grassy pinyon-juniper mesa through an old stock fence. After gaining the ridge, the trail wraps around the head of Cliff Dweller Canyon in an open ponderosa pine park. At 3.3 miles the Miller Springs Trail intersects the Ring Canyon Trail (162), which leads northwest for another 14 miles to McKenna Park. Turn right (northwest) and follow this easy ridgeline trail 0.5 mile to the EE Canyon Trail junction. The sign reads "West Fork 2.3 miles." Make another right (north) and begin the moderate descent into the densely forested upper draw of EE Canyon. Its moist north-facing aspect provides a diverse mix of Douglas-fir, oak, juniper, and ponderosa pine. After about 1.6 miles the canyon narrows with 70-foot cliffs of white volcanic tuff and columns of dark, angular rock just before joining a major side canyon entering from the left (west). This west branch is enticing, inviting at least a short visit.

The good trail continues down the sandy wash of lower EE Canyon, soon entering a recently burned flat surrounding its junction with the West Fork Gila Trail (151) after another 0.5 mile. Turn right (southeast) toward the Gila Cliff Dwellings National Monument. The trail crosses the bench and sidehills down to the only river crossing on the route. This is a scenic spot with a red volcanic band adding a splash of color to the far (north) side of the valley. The river is lined with fresh beaver dams and cuttings. The valley bottom trail continues downstream another 0.5 mile to the Gila Wilderness boundary and the enclave of the national monument. Another easy 0.5 mile brings you to both the West Fork Gila Trailhead and the Gila Cliff Dwellings National Monument Visitor Center and trailhead at the end of NM 15. Another mile down the paved road completes the circle to Woody's Corral.

Options: The loop can be lengthened 2 miles by continuing south to the Little Creek junction of Trails 160 and 161, then up Little Creek 1 mile to the cutoff trail leading north up to the ridge and junction with EE Canyon. For a short and interesting off-trail side trip, hike up the west tributary of EE Canyon 5.5 miles into the loop. This west branch is wilder and deeper with angular rock cliffs and overhangs 100 to 150 feet high. The sandy wash

EE Canyon Loop

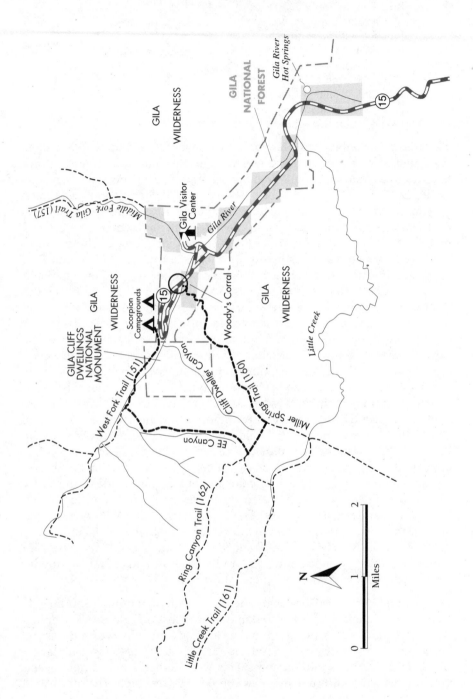

GILA
WILDERNESS

GILA
NATIONAL
FOREST

Gila River
Hot Springs

15

Gila Visitor
Center

Middle Fork Gila Trail (157)

Gila River

Woody's Corral

GILA
WILDERNESS

Little Creek

15

Scorpion
Campgrounds

GILA
WILDERNESS

GILA CLIFF
DWELLINGS
NATIONAL
MONUMENT

Cliff Dweller Canyon

Miller Springs Trail (160)

West Fork Trail (151)

EE Canyon

Ring Canyon Trail (162)

Little Creek Trail (161)

N

0   1   2
Miles

Fresh beaver cuttings along the West Fork Gila River just above the Gila Cliff Dwellings.

offers easy walking for about a mile to the upper forks of the canyon. A third option is to look for the Grudging Grave located about half a mile southeast of the EE Canyon–West Fork Trail junction. The grave is off-trail about 0.3 mile due south of where the trail crosses the West Fork Gila River (refer to Hike 49 for details). Lastly, don't overlook the easy and highly educational 1-mile loop hike to the Cliff Dwellings National Monument.

47 Granite Peak

Highlights:	Lovely ponderosa pine parklands; grassy flat of Little Spring; tuff formations; panoramic mountain vistas.
Type of hike:	3- to 4-day out-and-back backpacking trip.
Total distance:	32 miles.
Difficulty:	Moderate.
Best months:	April through October.
Maps:	Forest Service Gila Wilderness map (1984); Little Turkey Park and Diablo Range USGS quads.

Special considerations: Long stretch without water between miles 4 and 13. The upper portion of Granite Peak Trail may be blocked by snow into late spring.

Finding the trailhead: To reach the Woody's Corral Trailhead north of Silver City on New Mexico Highway 15, turn left (west) after milepost 42 toward the Gila Cliff Dwellings National Monument and the Scorpion campgrounds. This junction is 0.3 mile south of the Gila Visitor Center. Drive 0.5 mile to the Woody's Corral Trailhead on your left (south) and turn left into the parking area.

Parking and trailhead facilities: Large parking area with undeveloped trailhead camping, water, kiosk and a vault toilet. The no-fee Scorpion campgrounds are nearby. There is no garbage service in the Gila corridor; be prepared to carry all your trash out with you.

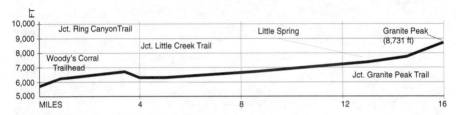

Key points:
- 0.0   Woody's Corral Trailhead and Miller Spring Trail (160).
- 3.3   Junction with Ring Canyon Trail (162).
- 4.0   Little Creek; junction with Little Creek Trail (161).
- 5.0   Cutover trail to Ring Canyon and EE Canyon Trails.
- 8.5   Cutover trail to Ring Canyon Trail.
- 13.0 Little Spring; junction with Turkey Creek Trail (155).
- 14.5 Turkey–Little Creek Divide; junction with Granite Peak Trail (150).
- 16.0 Granite Peak (8,731 feet).

The hike: This long out-and-back route samples the best of Gila mountain meadows, brooks, high pine parks, volcanic tuff, and serrated ridges. The views from the isolated apex of Granite Peak are sensational.

The Miller Spring Trail (160) gains 400 feet in less than a mile, up a rock-stepped lava ridge to a rolling pinyon-juniper mesa. The trail continues climbing as it wraps around the head of Cliff Dweller Canyon, where it joins the ridgetop Ring Canyon Trail. From this fire-scarred ridge the trail drops through a steep-walled volcanic ravine to the pleasant stream of Little Creek. After hopping across the creek, turn right (northwest) on the Little Creek Trail (161) and begin an enjoyable but dry 9-mile hike to Little Spring. Little Creek will probably be dry a short distance above the crossing, so be sure and fill your water bottles before moving on. Campsites abound in this area. The trail up Little Creek traverses a gentle, open pine-forested valley. The Little Creek Trail splits in several places, only to join later, so the choice is simply whether to remain along the bottom or sidehill a short distance above the drainage. Two crossover trails leading up to the Ring Canyon Trail are signed on your right (north). The well-blazed Little Creek Trail leads on up to the gloriously refreshing sight (and site) of Little Spring. The narrow notch of the upper north tributary to Little Creek will be flowing here through a

Granite Peak

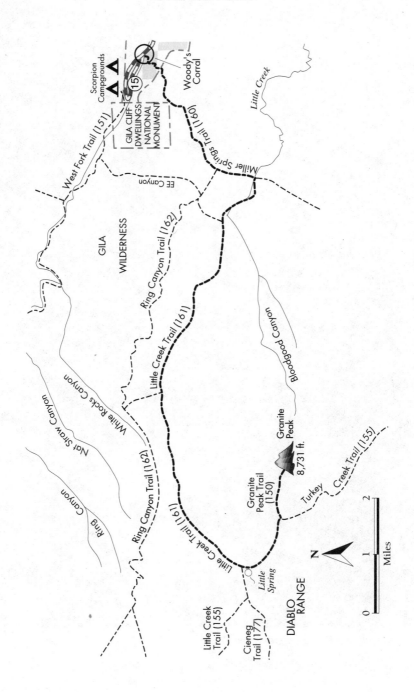

Scorpion Campgrounds

Woody's Corral

Little Creek

West Fork Trail (151)

GILA CLIFF DWELLINGS NATIONAL MONUMENT

Miller Springs Trail (160)

EE Canyon

GILA WILDERNESS

Ring Canyon Trail (162)

Little Creek Trail (161)

Bloodgood Canyon

Nat Straw Canyon

White Rocks Canyon

Ring Canyon

Ring Canyon Trail (162)

Granite Peak
8,731 ft.

Granite Peak Trail (150)

Turkey Creek Trail (155)

Little Creek Trail (161)

Little Spring

Little Creek Trail (155)

Cieneg Trail (177)

DIABLO RANGE

N

Miles
0   1   2

Looking southwest from the top of Granite Peak.

wide-open grassy flat overseen by towering pines. Little Spring "oasis" provides an ideal base camp for a 6-mile round-trip day hike to Granite Peak.

A sign at the edge of the meadow near the creek points to various locations including Turkey Creek 2 miles to the south. Cross the small stream and head south on the Turkey Creek Trail (155) to the dividing ridge between Little Creek and Turkey Creek. The trail crosses several side gullies of exposed volcanic tuff rock and then climbs up a narrow gully bound by pocketed mounds of white tuff on the left (east) side. An open pine forest thickly carpeted with needles leads up to the high saddle and signed junction with the Granite Peak Trail (150). Turn left (east) on Granite Peak Trail and follow the cairns as it crosses a small ravine. The trail starts out in good condition but soon becomes more faint from low usage. Thorny brush and downfall is especially prevalent where the trail passes through a north-side burn. The trail climbs steadily through a forest of pine and Douglas-fir, with stands of aspen on higher, moist north-facing slopes. Great mounds of white ashflow tuff mark the heads of canyons feeding back toward Little Creek. Most of the rocky ridgeline of Granite Peak is tree-covered, but a few open vistas exist. The views back to the north are especially striking with much of the Gila Wilderness mountains laid out like a giant map. Remnants of the old Granite Peak lookout can still be found anchored into crevasses along the serrated summit ridge. Retracing the route to the Woody's Corral Trailhead presents ever-changing perspectives, from mountaintops to stream bottoms and everything in between.

Options: Several loop trips are possible from Little Spring. A short loop to the West Fork Gila River Trailhead next to the Gila Cliff Dwellings National Monument is possible by way of EE Canyon (see Hike 46). A longer loop, adding 4 to 5 miles, to take the Little Creek Trail (155) northwest to the Ring Canyon Trail (162). Turn east on the high, dry Ring Canyon Trail to either EE Canyon or onto the Miller Spring Trail to Woody's Corral. By early summer water is definitely limited on this long dry stretch.

48 Little Creek–White Creek Flat Loop

Highlights:	Remote ponderosa parks on the slopes of the Diablo Range; dramatic canyons of the West Fork Gila River.
Type of hike:	5- to 6-day backpacking loop.
Total distance:	39.5 miles.
Difficulty:	Strenuous.
Best months:	May through October.
Maps:	Forest Service Gila Wilderness map (1984); Little Turkey Park, Diablo Range, Lilley Mountain, and Woodland Park USGS quads.

Special considerations: Long stretches without water on the first half of the hike. Many stream crossings on the West Fork, which may be hazardous during spring runoff.

Finding the trailheads: To reach the Woody's Corral Trailhead where the hike begins, on New Mexico Highway 15, turn left (west) after milepost 42 toward the Gila Cliff Dwellings National Monument and the Scorpion campgrounds. This turn is 42 miles north of Silver City and 0.3 mile south of the Gila Visitor Center. Drive 0.5 mile to the Woody's Corral Trailhead on your left (south). Turn left into the parking area.

For the exit trailhead at the West Fork, continue straight 1 mile beyond Woody's Corral to the end of the road at the monument parking lot and the West Fork Trailhead. Shuttle distance is 1 mile, an easy walk.

Parking and trailhead facilities: Both trailheads have large parking areas. Woody's Corral has water, a kiosk, and a vault toilet; the West Fork has a vault toilet. The Scorpion campgrounds (no fee) are halfway between the two trailheads. There is no garbage service in the Gila corridor; be prepared to carry all your trash out with you.

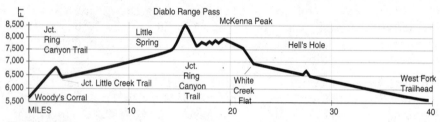

Key points:

0.0	Woody's Corral Trailhead and Miller Spring Trail (160).
3.3	Junction with Ring Canyon Trail (162).
4.0	Little Creek; junction with Little Creek Trail (161).
5.0	Cut-over trail to Ring Canyon and EE Canyon Trails.
8.5	Cut-over trail to Ring Canyon Trail.
13.0	Little Spring; junction with Turkey Creek Trail (155).
13.7	Junction Cieneg Trail (177).
17.0	Junction with Ring Canyon Trail (162).
19.0	McKenna Park; junction with Turbo Canyon Trail (158).
19.5	Junction with Mogollon Creek Trail (153).
22.0	White Creek Flat; junction with West Fork Trail 151.
27.5	Hells Hole; junction with bypass trail 785.
28.0	Junction with Hells Hole Trail (268).
36.0	Junction with Big Bear Canyon Trail (28).
38.5	Junction with EE Canyon Trail.
39.5	West Fork Trailhead.

The hike: This loop hike in the heart of the Gila takes you through a wide variety of ecosystems, from mountain meadows and streams to ridges and high ponderosa parks to the roaring canyon of the West Fork, and eventually its gentle riparian woodland at the Gila Cliff Dwellings National Monument. The loop can be done in reverse as well.

202

Little Creek–White Creek Flat Loop

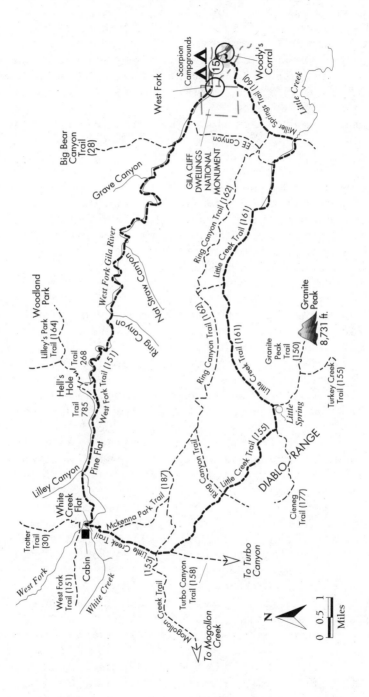

From the Woody's Corral Trailhead, the Miller Spring Trail climbs 400 feet within the first mile, up the rock-stepped lava ridge to a rolling mesa of pinyon-juniper and grass. Rising still, the trail bends around the head of Cliff Dweller Canyon and stays on the crest of the ridge where it meets the Ring Canyon Trail. The ponderosa groves near the intersection have been cleansed by lightning fires in recent years; the grand old trees are scarred but flourishing. From the ridge the trail drops through a ravine to Little Creek. The steep right wall of the ravine is a mass of lava that chilled and stopped moving at this spot.

After crossing Little Creek, turn right (northwest) and begin a waterless 9-mile stretch to Little Spring. The creek will be dry within a mile of the crossing, so fill your bottles here. To break up the first day of the backpack, you can settle in this area for the night.

The trail up the length of Little Creek to the spring travels through the gentle terrain of an open pine forest. In places the trail splits, only to join later, so you can select either branch. The two crossover trails up to the ridge are signed on your right. Little Spring is a welcome sight, not only because it has water but also because the wide open grassy area beneath the towering pines is an ideal campsite.

From Little Spring it is another 9-mile hike to the next reliable water, at the West Fork. With full water bottles, pick up the Little Creek Trail going west from the green. The trail sign may be on the ground, crushed by a huge ponderosa trunk. Rising into a ravine, the trail splits with the Cieneg Trail (177) to Mogollon Creek, while the Little Creek Trail (155) curves right and begins its climb toward McKenna Park. Stay right on Trail 155. In a 1.5 miles you will reach an unnamed pass in the Diablo Range (8,650 feet) before descending to the Ring Canyon Trail junction. You can't count on the spring adjacent to this junction. The trail to White Creek Flat rolls on, up and down on the low ridges coming off the Diablo Mountains, feathering into McKenna Park. The trail is well used and easy to follow. Ancient log cuts of fallen timber punctuate the route and are easy to see in the distance. The pine forest with a grassy carpet stretches on all sides; McKenna Park seems to go on forever.

On the western edge of the park the trail intersects the Turbo Canyon Trail near an old elk wallow. Turn north (right) toward White Creek Flat. There are two more signed junctions before the West Fork; at each continue north to the river. The final descent to the West Fork is rather steep and rocky, but you have terrific views of the canyons of White Creek and the West Fork from the switchbacks.

White Creek Flat has a Forest Service cabin and corral at the spacious wet meadow. Campsites ring the meadow and are also scattered along the riverbank. If you have scheduled a layover day, you would certainly enjoy it here!

The West Fork Trail crosses the river downstream from the meadow. On the river's north bank a sign indicates that the river trail is closed; a 1.5-mile detour has been constructed high on the north bank to bypass the gorge and canyon where flooding has erased the former trail. There are several sections

A perfect campsite at Little Spring.

along the West Fork where new trail segments rise above the river bottom. These stretches allow your feet to dry out, but campsites tend to be limited where trails follow contours of the forested slopes above the bottom.

At the mouth of Lilley Canyon the trail crosses to the south side and continues on a straight line for almost a mile. The canyon walls rise as you go downstream. After a narrow gorge the contorted contours of Hells Hole's volcanic cliffs erupt. Surrounded by lofty mountains the depths of Hells Hole seem exceptionally dramatic. The trail splits at Hells Hole. Stay to the right on the main trail, which climbs almost 200 feet up and over a point of land jutting northward into the mouth of Hells Hole Canyon. The second junction is to the Hells Hole Trail that climbs up to Woodland Park to the north. There are several campsites in the area.

Downstream of Hells Hole the river canyon becomes immediately dramatic, with more crossings as gorge after gorge drives the trail from one side of the stream to the other. Canyon walls shoot up 200 to 300 feet from the streambed. This is not a place to be in a flood. The pocked igneous towers with cone heads crowd the skyline. The narrow bottom supports stands of ponderosa pine, fir, and oak. Campsites are less numerous and smaller. After a mile of incessant crossings below Hells Hole, another new section keeps you high and dry on the south bank for more than a mile. After this interlude of dry feet, the canyon bottom widens and the trail drops back to stream level. In this lower section the riparian foliage includes ash, box elder, maple, oak, and sycamore. The trail is now a soft woodland path with intermittent cobblestone beaches, and the inevitable stream crossings. The lofty spires continue above, a fantasy sculpture garden silhouetted against the sky.

One mile downstream from the Graves Canyon ravine are the ruins of a solitary cliff dwelling on the south wall of the canyon. There are resting places on the opposite bank. From here to the trailhead the trail shows considerably more traffic and is marked with cairns. A short-cut on the south bank below the cliff dwelling bypasses the junction with the Big Bear Trail to the north. A new section then climbs above the river on the south bank, staying high for the junction with EE Canyon, and dropping only in the last mile for the final stream crossing of the journey. The trail then stays north of the river on dry land through a corner of the national monument and down to the trailhead.

Options: From a camp at Little Spring it is a 6-mile round trip to climb Granite Peak (8,731 feet) (see Hike 47). On your way down the West Fork, you can stop and pay your respects at the Grudging Grave, on the south bank near the last river crossing (see Hike 49).

49 Grudging Grave

Highlights:	Historic Gila gravesite; scenic stretch of the lower West Fork Gila River.
Type of hike:	Half-day; out-and-back.
Total distance:	2 miles.
Difficulty:	Easy.
Best months:	April through November with year-round accessibility.
Maps:	Forest Service Gila Wilderness map (1984); Little Turkey Park USGS quad.

Special considerations: River crossing prohibitive during periods of high wate. Unsigned off-trail route to gravesite.

Finding the trailhead: Drive to the end of New Mexico Highway 15, 44 miles north of Silver City, and park at the Gila Cliff Dwellings National Monument Visitor Center. The signed trailhead for the West Fork Gila River Trail (151) is located at the far end of the large parking lot. Allow at least 2 hours to travel from Silver City to the visitor center on this slow, winding, paved road.

Parking and trailhead facilities: The visitor center has a large parking area, kiosk, and vault toilets. Camping is not allowed at the trailhead, but the two Scorpion campgrounds are only 0.2 mile back down NM 15. Water is available at both campgrounds.

Grudging Grave

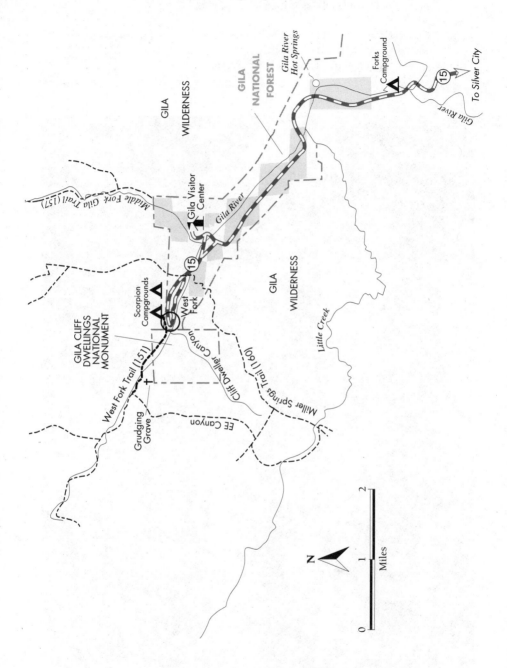

Key points:

- 0.0   Trailhead for West Fork Gila River Trail (151) near Gila Cliff Dwellings National Monument Visitor Center.
- 0.5   Signed Gila Wilderness boundary and gate at the north end of the monument.
- 0.9   Leave trail after first and only river crossing.
- 1.0   Grudging Grave.

The 1883 gravesite of William Grudging on a secluded bench above the West Fork Gila River.

The hike: Follow the heavily used West Fork Gila River Trail (151) to the first crossing of the West Fork. You'll have to rock-hop across a wet side channel along the way. Upon reaching the south side of the West Fork, look for a faint trail leading south toward the first low bench above the river. The forest is open, having been burned recently, so walk south for about 0.1 mile even if the actual path eludes you. Head toward a small draw to your left and look for a large dead oak tree. The marked headstone and foot stone of William Grudging's grave lies directly below the old dead oak, an appropriate final resting place for an early Gila settler. The tombstone tells the sad tale of the 37-year-old Grudging being "waylayed and murdered by Tom Wood" on October 8, 1883. It seems that the Grudging brothers believed that Wood had rustled their cattle. They killed Wood's son and a Mexican man whom they mistook for Wood in a nearby canyon. After killing both Grudging brothers in revenge, Woods hid out in the mountains for a couple of years before being acquitted. The Grudging cabin shown on the USGS quad was burned to the ground in a recent forest fire. Return by way of the West Fork Gila River Trail to complete this glimpse at a colorful bit of Gila history.

Options: To savor the mystique of a much earlier period of human occupation, take the easy 1-mile loop trail to the Gila Cliff Dwellings National Monument. The kiosk and river bridge are located next to West Fork Trailhead. The cave structures are amazingly well preserved and will leave you with a sense of awe about the Mogollon people who lived here for a brief time 700 years ago. The visit is well worth the $3-per-person entrance fee.

50 Cliff Dwelling

Highlights:	Short day hike up the Middle Fork; rugged canyon with remains of cliff dwelling.
Type of hike:	Day hike or overnight backpacking trip; out-and-back.
Total distance:	6 miles.
Difficulty:	Easy in low water.
Best months:	April through November.
Maps:	Forest Service Gila Wilderness map (1984); Little Turkey Park USGS quad.

Special considerations: There are only a couple of river crossings, but the trip is rated as strenuous (or even impossible) if the river is high.

Finding the trailhead: To reach the West Fork Gila River Trailhead at the Gila Cliff Dwellings National Monument, turn left (west) at milepost 42 on New Mexico Highway 15, 42 miles north of Silver City. From the Gila Visitor

Center, this junction is 0.3 mile south on NM 15. The turn is marked with a sign for the monument and the Scorpion campgrounds. Drive to the end of the road at the Gila Cliff Dwellings National Monument parking area and the West Fork Trailhead.

Parking and trailhead facilities: There is a large paved parking area. There is also a vault toilet and an information kiosk. No camping is permitted at the trailhead; the Scorpion campgrounds (no fee) are only 0.2 mile back down NM 15. There is no garbage service in the Gila Hot Springs corridor, so be prepared to carry your trash out with you.

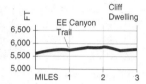

Key points:

    0.0   Gila Cliff Dwellings National Monument Trailhead on the West Fork.
    0.5   Gila Wilderness boundary.
    1.0   Junction with EE Canyon Trail.
    2.7   Junction with Big Bear Canyon Trail 28 on north side of West Fork.
    3.0   Cliff dwelling.

The Gila Cliff Dwellings—home to the Mogollon people 700 years ago.

210

Cliff Dwelling

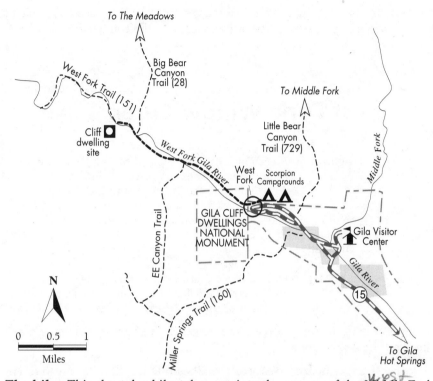

To The Meadows

Big Bear
Canyon
Trail (28)

West Fork Trail (151)

To Middle Fork

Cliff
dwelling
site

Little Bear
Canyon
Trail (729)

West Fork Gila River

Middle Fork

West
Fork

Scorpion
Campgrounds

GILA CLIFF
DWELLINGS
NATIONAL
MONUMENT

Gila Visitor
Center

EE Canyon Trail

Gila River

N

15

Miller Springs Trail (160)

To Gila
Hot Springs

0   0.5   1

Miles

The hike: This short day hike takes you into the canyon of the Middle Fork
Gila River, to the site of a remote cliff dwelling. There are numerous campsites along the river in the vicinity of the cliff dwelling, so the trip can be
done as an overnight backpack. This trail has moderate to heavy use, with
both hikers and horse parties enjoying trips up the West Fork.

From the trailhead at the monument parking area, go upstream on the
trail that parallels the river. The monument boundary is marked with a
stock fence and gate; this barrier also marks the wilderness boundary. The
trail then winds westward on the floodplain, eventually crossing the river.
The West Fork crossings are easy at low water and moderate at other times.
Only during flood conditions is the trip hazardous. After the crossing, the
trail stays on the southwest bank until shortly before reaching the cliff dwelling site. This new section of the trail is not shown on the topo map. It stays
high above the river, making the distance a bit longer but avoiding a multitude of crossings.

Follow the trail to the second crossing. The cliff dwelling is adjacent to a
large cave on the left (west) after the second crossing. The origin of this
dwelling, so far from the village 3 miles away in Cliff Dweller Canyon, is a
puzzle to archeologists, so you can wonder about this, too, as you explore.

Perhaps this was a honeymoon hideaway or a religious retreat for members of the Mogollon tribe.

After your journey to the past along the West Fork, return to the trailhead by the same route.

Option: To complete your historical tour of the West Fork, see Hike 49 and stop at the Grudging Grave on your way back to the trailhead.

51 West Fork–Willow Creek

Highlights:	Ascend entire length of the West Fork Gila River with its dramatic canyons and gorge, to Turkeyfeather Pass; drop to the forested intimacy of Iron Creek; arrive at Willow Creek Trailhead.
Type of hike:	5- to 7-day backpacking trip; shuttle.
Total distance:	32.5 miles.
Difficulty:	Strenuous.
Best months:	May through October.
Maps:	Forest Service Gila Wilderness map (1984); Little Turkey Park, Woodland Park, Lilley Mountain, Mogollon Baldy, and Negrito Mountain USGS quads.

Special considerations: Stream crossings. High spring runoff may make the West Fork hazardous.

Finding the trailheads: West Fork Trailhead: Drive 42 miles north of Silver City on New Mexico Highway 15; turn left (west) at sign for Gila Cliff Dwellings National Monument, and drive 1 mile to the end of the road and the parking area. The turn is also 0.3 mile south of the Gila Visitor Center.

Willow Creek Trailhead: From Glenwood, drive 4 miles north on U.S. Highway 180. Turn right (east) on NM 159, also known as Bursum Road, toward Mogollon. NM 159 changes from paved to improved gravel after 9 miles. Drive east a total of 25.5 miles to the Willow Creek Recreation Area. Turn right (south) and drive past the Willow Creek campground to the Iron Creek Lake Trail (151). Bursum Road is closed in the winter and often remains snow blocked into May. In early spring Forest Road 141 out of Reserve and FR 28 south of Negrito provide access to this trailhead.

The total shuttle distance, via Silver City is 137.5 miles.

Parking and trailhead facilities: At the West Fork Trailhead, there is a large paved parking area. The nearby monument has a vault toilet. No camping is permitted; the closest camping area is the Scorpion campgrounds (no fee), 0.4 mile down the road. At the Willow Creek Trailhead, there is a grassy parking area and a vault toilet. Camping is permitted at the trailhead; there are also two campgrounds nearby.

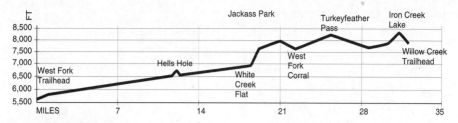

Key points:

0.0	West Fork Trailhead.
1.0	Junction with EE Canyon Trail.
2.8	Junction with Big Bear Trail (28).
12.0	Hells Hole; junction with Woodland Park Trail (268) and Bypass Trail (725).
17.5	White Creek Flat and cabin; junction with Little Creek Trail (155).
17.8	Junction with Trotter Trail (30).
18.2	Junction with discontinued West Fork Trail; trail to Jackass Park.
19.2	Junction with White Creek Trail (152).
19.4	Junction with another access to White Creek Trail (152).
23.5	West Fork Corral.
23.6	Junction with West Fork Corral Trail (814).
26.3	Junction with Jerky Mountain Trail (164).
26.5	Turkeyfeather Pass; junction with Turkeyfeather Mountain Trail (102).
28.5	Iron Creek; junction with Cooper–Clayton Trail (141).
31.0	Junction with Iron Creek Mesa Trail (173).
31.4	Iron Creek Lake; junction with Iron Creek Lake Trail (172).
31.5	Willow Creek Trailhead.

The hike: This through-hike takes you up the length of the West Fork, then up Turkeyfeather Creek and over the pass into the Iron Creek valley. From there it is a short climb over the Iron Creek Lake ridge before dropping into Willow Creek. Like any river travel in the Gila, the journey cannot be done hurriedly. River miles are always long. Moreover, the dramatic West Fork canyon requires you to pause and enjoy the scenery.

Water, obviously, is plentiful, except for the dry stretch through Jackass Park (mile 18 to mile 22) and the trip over Turkeyfeather Pass. Campsites, likewise, are frequent, which enables you to divide the trip into moderate segments. At a reasonable pace you can take three days to reach White Creek Flat; from there another day will put you at West Fork Corral, which has excellent campsites. With your lightened pack you can reach the northern trailhead on day five. Of course, if you have more time, you can dawdle along the West Fork and focus on enjoying the canyon instead of rushing upstream. A pair of sacrifice boots is essential for wading, with Neoprene socks if cold feet are a problem.

From the trailhead, the trail stays east of the river for the first 0.9 mile. During this dry warm-up you pass through a gate, leaving the monument and entering the wilderness. Here the West Fork valley is wide and flat. After the first crossing, the trail climbs to a bench on the south bank, and stays 80 feet above the river for almost a mile. Here you will find the junction with EE Canyon Trail. Sections of the West Fork trail have been re-routed away from the river due to incessant repairs after floods. On these

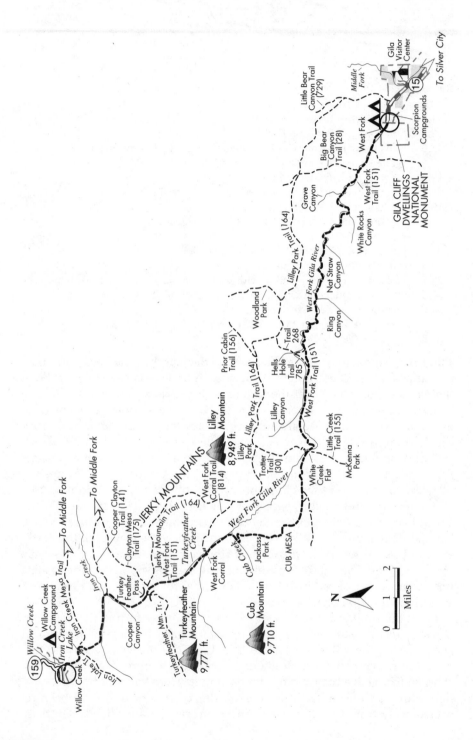

higher routes you usually have vistas of the curving river below. Some of the new trail segments are longer than the original path, so the old mileage estimates may be incorrect.

Eventually you drop back to the riverbottom and begin the pattern of frequent stream crossings, with stretches of cobblestone beaches intermingled with earthen woodsy paths. The junction with the Big Bear Canyon Trail is on the north side of the river; it is likely you will miss it since there is an inviting shortcut on the cobblestones on the south bank, avoiding two stream crossings. Just above that intersection you will find two caves on the south canyon wall. This is the site of a solitary cliff dwelling. In this wider section of the West Fork, the riparian foliage includes ash, boxelder, maple, oak, and sycamore. Towering above are the lofty spires of the canyon walls, creating a fantasy sculpture garden on the skyline.

Above the cliff dwelling site, the canyon soon becomes narrow, reducing the woodland and increasing the crossings. There are intermittent campsites along the river. About 5 miles from the trailhead, the trail climbs onto the south bank and stays above the stream for more than a mile. During this section there are no campsites adjacent to water. Do not wait until the last vestige of daylight to seek a campsite. Upstream from the stretch of dry trail, the canyon deepens, the walls close in, and the West Fork becomes a gorge. This is not a place to be in high water. The trail zigzags across the river frequently, and each twist in the canyon provides a breathtaking view of intricate volcanic conglomerate walls. Pocked igneous towers soar to the sky, with cone heads on the top. Although narrow, the river bottom supports stands of ponderosa pine, fir, and oak.

Twelve miles from the trailhead the canyon widens as you approach Hells Hole, a canyon on the north side of the West Fork. After being confined to the narrow chasm, you will be delighted with the contorted contours of the craggy cliffs of Hells Hole and its ring of lofty mountains. Here a trail cutoff leads to the right, climbing out of the canyon and up to the mesa to Woodland Park. The trail continues straight on the West Fork, then climbs over a low ridge and drops back to the water just upstream of Hells Hole. Here is the junction with a second cut-over trail, completing the triangle of trails. Hells Hole is a delightful spot to stop and explore. There are several campsites on the ponderosa flats along the West Fork just downstream from Hells Hole. If it's a windy or rainy evening you might prefer the alcove campsite located on the eastern leg of the Hells Hole triangle, right on the river.

Between Hells Hole and White Creek Flat the trail stays above the river in two sections. The first one is on the south side in the long straight section of Pine Flat. After a crossing below the mouth of Lilley Canyon, where there are campsites, a 1.5-mile new trail segment climbs 200 feet above the river gorge. The roar of the waterfalls below and a view of the gorge will make you appreciate the new trail location. After the detour the trail drops back to the river just south of White Creek Flat.

The White Creek Flat cabin is surrounded by a lush meadow. The trail to McKenna Park goes up the canyon wall south of the cabin. There are ponds and braided streams at the confluence of White Creek and the West Fork.

Crossing the West Fork Gila River 10 miles above the trailhead.

Continuing on the West Fork Trail across the West Fork, the Trotter Trail intersection is 0.3 mile west of the cabin. Above this junction, on the south side of the river, is the sign warning West Fork travelers that the original West Fork trail is no longer maintained and is not recommended for livestock. Actually, it is not recommended for anybody; the narrow valley has been ravaged by floods, and the Forest Service finally gave up. Here the West Fork Trail now goes left and climbs to Cub Mesa on a long detour to the West Fork Corral at the mouth of Turkeyfeather Creek.

Fill your water bottles before this portion of the trail. It's almost 6 miles before you will reach water again. Shortly after reaching the mesa, the White Creek Trail goes off to your left and the West Fork Trail gradually curves north, dropping through the head of Packsaddle Canyon. When you reach flat Jackass Park the trail straightens out to take the shortest line northward. The zigzagging returns as it drops through Cub Creek and returns to the West Fork.

The upper West Fork valley is a forested ravine, with dense conifers cloaking the steep hillsides. In a mile, you reach the site of the West Fork Corral, a broad, grassy spot surrounded by the forest. This is the best campsite until you reach Iron Creek, 5 miles away over Turkeyfeather Pass. It is also the last water until you get to Cooper Canyon right above Iron Creek, except for lightly running Turkeyfeather Spring halfway to the pass.

From the West Fork Corral, the route goes up Turkeyfeather, a rocky, dry trail. The pass is a broad ponderosa park on the ridge between the Mogollon and the Jerky Mountains. Continuing onward over the pass you drop quickly down Cooper Canyon, which becomes a tight ravine before it reaches Iron Creek. Iron Creek is the site of a Gila trout-reintroduction program, so fishing is prohibited. The trail turns west at Iron Creek, going upstream on the north bank through spacious ponderosa groves. Just across Iron Creek is a mystical spruce-fir forest, draped with mosses and dense with centuries of downfall. The trail stays on the north bank and then turns sharply north and climbs to the mesa.

Iron Creek Lake forms a reflecting pool surrounded by ponderosa and grass. The former stock pond is too muddy for human use, however. The trail, a former jeep track that's now a wide, rocky path, passes the lake and descends to the busy world of the Willow Creek Recreation Area and the trailhead. What a contrast with the solitude of the West Fork!

Options: Because of the length of the car shuttle, it may be advisable to organize this trip with another party. Hike from the two trailheads and plan a key exchange at a midpoint. Reliable friends are important for this to be successful. This trip can also be done in the reverse direction. Along the route you may wish to visit the Grudging Grave (Hike 49), or explore the Jerky Mountains on a layover day at the West Fork Corral (Hike 83).

52 Adobe Canyon

Highlights: Accessible off-trail hike up a picturesque canyon.
Type of hike: Out-and-back day hike.
Total distance: 4 miles.
Difficulty: Easy.
Best months: March through December.
Maps: Forest Service Gila Wilderness map (1984); Little Turkey Park and Woodland Park USGS quads.

Special considerations: Although a spring may be found, the canyon is usually dry from late spring on. A map and land navigation skills are required for the moderate loop options.

Finding the trailhead: The TJ Corral Trailhead is about 43 miles north of Silver City on New Mexico Highway 15, and 1 mile from the Gila Visitor Center on the road to the Gila Cliff Dwellings National Monuments. Turn right (east) at the sign for Trail 729 just before reaching the Scorpion ampgrounds.

Parking and trailhead facilities: Large parking area, kiosk, a trailhead sign, corral, and water.

Key points:

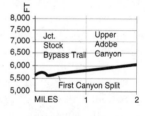

0.0   TJ Corral Trailhead for Little Bear Canyon Trail (729).
0.2   Junction for Stock Bypass Trail.
0.3   Enter Adobe Canyon.
0.6   First fork in the canyon.
1.5   Second fork in the canyon.
2.0   Upper Adobe Canyon.

The hike: This short off-trail excursion provides a sense of adventure with the advantages of year-round vehicular access to the trailhead and a wide, low-gradient canyon floor suitable for casual strolling. Among other places, the trailhead sign points toward Little Bear Canyon. The heavily used Little Bear Canyon Trail (729) climbs gently to a signed junction with the stock bypass trail at 0.2 mile. The main trail continues right (north) up the slope to the Middle Fork Gila River by way of Little Bear Canyon. From the junction turn left and drop into the sandy bottom of lower Adobe Canyon. Low sandstone walls define the canyon up to and beyond the first set of forks at 0.6 mile. Continue left up the main fork. The nearly level canyon twists and turns with cow trails cutting the bends and bypassing rock and log obstacles in the bottom. After about 1.5 miles the canyon steepens at the second major fork with higher ridges on both sides. Either branch can be climbed. The steeper fork to the left reaches the more gently sloped uplands quicker, whereas the main fork to the right provides a longer canyon hike. To complete this 4-mile round-trip canyon exploration, turn around after about 0.5 mile up the main right-hand branch as the going becomes rougher and rockier.

Adobe Canyon

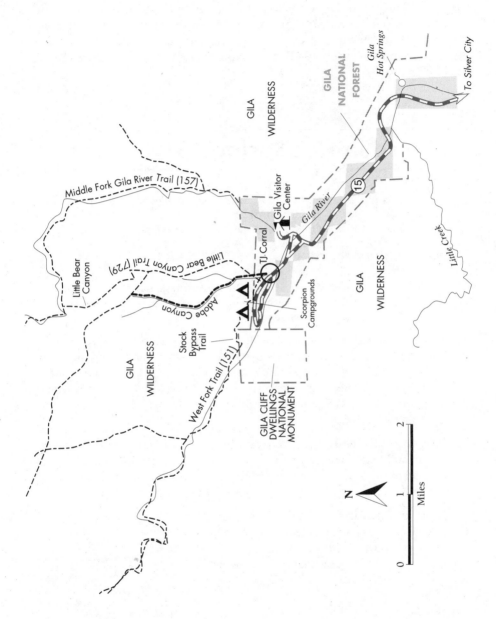

Options: Take the first right-hand fork at 0.6 mile and follow it north for another 0.8 mile where the head of the draw intersects the Little Bear Canyon Trail. Turn right (south) and take the Little Bear Trail back to the TJ Corral Trailhead for a loop of about 3 miles. For a longer day loop of anywhere between 5 and 9 miles, continue up the main upper right-hand branch of Adobe Canyon to about the 2-mile mark. Look for a good spot to climb out of the canyon and head for the top of the main east ridge about 400 feet above the canyon floor. Upon reaching the up-and-down ridge, turn left (north) and continue for about 0.5 mile until intersecting a good Forest Service trail. This is the Lilley Park Trail (164). Turn right (east) and you will shortly meet the Little Bear Canyon Trail. From this junction you can head either north down the slot canyon of Little Bear to the Middle Fork (see Hike 53) or south on the Little Bear Canyon Trail another 2 miles back to the trailhead.

53 Jordan Hot Springs

Highlights:	Fastest, most direct route to a popular hot springs in a spectacular river canyon.
Type of hike:	Out-and-back day hike or overnighter.
Total distance:	12 miles.
Difficulty:	Moderate.
Best months:	May through November.
Maps:	Forest Service Gila Wilderness map (1984); Little Turkey Park, Gila Hot Springs, and Woodland Park USGS quads.

Special considerations: Stay clear of the narrow Little Bear Canyon during flash flood weather; river crossings may be dangerous during high runoff, which is often caused by the same thunderstorms that produce flash flooding. Keep your head and nose out of hot springs water. A warm-water amoeba, *Naegleria fowleri*, can enter the brain through nasal passages and can cause a rare type of meningitis.

Finding the trailhead: The TJ Corral Trailhead is 43 miles north of Silver City on New Mexico Highway 15, and 1 mile from the Gila Visitor Center on the road to the Gila Cliff Dwellings National Monument. Turn right (east) at the sign for Trail 729 just before reaching the Scorpion campgrounds.

Parking and trailhead facilities: Large parking area, trailhead sign, kiosk, water, and corral. Camping is available at the nearby Scorpion campgrounds.

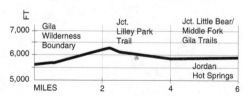

Key points:

0.0	TJ Corral Trailhead and Little Bear Canyon Trail (729).
0.2	Junction with stock bypass trail.
0.3	Gila Wilderness boundary.
2.0	Junction with Lilley Park Trail (164).
4.0	Mouth of Little Bear Canyon and the junction with Middle Fork Gila River Trail (157).
6.0	Jordan Hot Springs.

Jordan Hot Springs

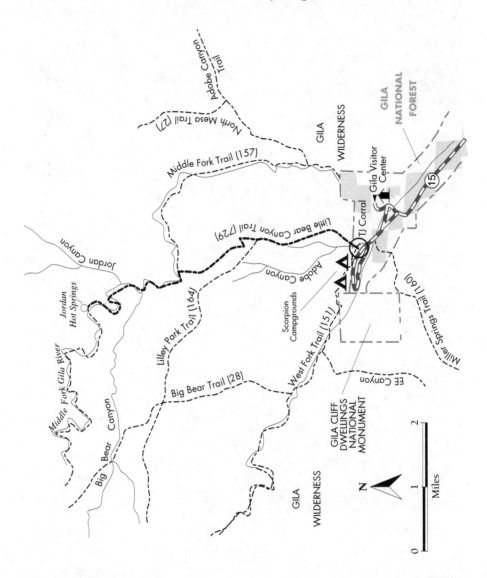

The hike: Despite its hard-to-reach remoteness, Jordan Hot Springs is one of the more popular thermal features in the Gila Wilderness. The semideveloped pools are pleasantly warm and surrounded by canyon majesty. Many places in the Gila offer profound wilderness solitude, but this isn't one of them. It is certainly possible to visit the hot springs on a long day hike, but if you do you'll wish that you were staying overnight.

The heavily used Little Bear Canyon Trail (729) intersects the West Fork Gila stock bypass trail at 0.2 mile. Turn right (north) to the wilderness

A determined beaver has been at work on this huge old cottonwood on the Middle Fork Gila River.

boundary. The trail climbs open pinyon-juniper grasslands, passes through a stock fence, and then sidehills along a rocky stretch for the next mile. At mile 1.7 a steep, rocky trail blocked by logs climbs straight up the ridge. Stay right, reaching the junction with the Lilley Park Trail (164) at mile 2. The Little Bear Canyon Trail continues up to the divide and a sweeping overlook between the West and Middle Forks. It then drops steeply across the head of Little Bear Canyon to rolling woodlands. The soft dirt trail and sandy wash provide easy passage into the canyon. For the next mile down to the Middle Fork Gila River the trail weaves in and out of the wash wherever it's blocked by rock ledges or boulders. Several large alcoves are carved into the left (west) side of the canyon. The deepest slot canyon is in the lower half mile. Sheer walls that close in with soaring rock columns on both sides bind the tight, sandy wash of the canyon.

A spacious flat near the mouth of Little Bear Canyon supports a diverse mix of cottonwood, juniper, ponderosa pine, and Douglas-fir. Some of the highest sheer cliffs in the Middle Fork Canyon appear on the right (east) side just above Little Bear Canyon. After crossing the Middle Fork at the mouth of Little Bear Canyon, continue left (upstream) for the next 2 miles to Jordan Hot Springs. With an average of seven cold river crossings per mile you'll be a lot happier with Neoprene socks. The canyon achieves monumental proportions with spires, hoodoos, goblins, balancing rocks, and caves. The unsigned hot springs are about 0.3 mile beyond (above) the mouth of Jordan Canyon on the right (east) side of the canyon and 50 feet above the river. A striking cliff stabs the sky across the narrow valley.

To find the hot springs, look for a well-worn use trail climbing past several overused campsites to the springs. In order to safeguard the wild values of this special place, the Forest Service prohibits camping within 400 yards of the springs. There are several good campsites upstream and across the river. If you miss the lower end of the short hot springs trail, look for the outlet of the springs flowing through the cobble on the east side of the Middle Fork and then backtrack to the trail. This wonderful stairstep set of three large crystal clear pools is understandably a major destination. The upper pool is larger, deeper, and a bit warmer than the others. A soothing hot soak after or during a long tough day on the trail sure hits the proverbial spot!

Option: For a 14-mile loop, return by hiking 8 slow miles down the Middle Fork, with roughly 50 river crossings, to the Middle Fork Trailhead next to the Gila Visitor Center (see Hike 56). Walk or hitch the mile of road on NM 15 back to the TJ Corral Trailhead.

54 Middle Fork Hot Springs

Highlights:	Easily accessible hot springs in scenic surroundings.
Type of hike:	Out-and-back day hike.
Total distance:	1 mile.
Difficulty:	Easy (during periods of low water).
Best months:	Year-round.
Maps:	Forest Service Gila Wilderness map (1984); Gila Hot Springs USGS quad.

Special considerations: Do not attempt river crossings when water levels are high. Do not dunk your head or nose in the hot springs. A warm-water amoeba, *Naegleria fowleri*, can enter the brain through the nasal passages and can cause a rare form of meningitis.

Finding the trailhead: Follow the signs to the Gila Visitor Center, located 42 miles north of Silver City on New Mexico Highway 15. Drive through the far end of the visitor center parking lot and turn right. The signed Middle Fork Gila River Trailhead is less than 0.2 mile on the left.

Parking and trailhead facilities: Limited parking on a gravel surface and kiosk. There are no facilities, water, camping, or garbage service at the trailhead.

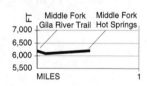

Key points:
- 0.0 Trailhead for Middle Fork Gila River Trail (157).
- 0.5 Middle Fork Hot Springs and Gila Wilderness boundary.

The hike: Walk down the old roadbed past the gate to the first river crossing at 0.2 mile near the entrance to the lower Middle Fork canyon. After another 0.2 mile the trail splits, with a steep, rocky, high-water route continuing left. Take the riverbottom trail to the right leading to the second crossing. The hot springs emerge from a cleft in the rock on the right (east) side of the river at 0.5 mile. The water comes out at a scalding 130 degrees F but is cooled to a pleasantly warm temperature in several tiny, shallow pools next to the river. The signed wilderness boundary is immediately upstream adjacent to a narrow, rocky section of the trail.

Option: The hot springs can be enjoyed as a short side trip before or after touring the Gila Visitor Center or as a relaxing respite during a longer hike up or down the Middle Fork Gila River.

Middle Fork Hot Springs

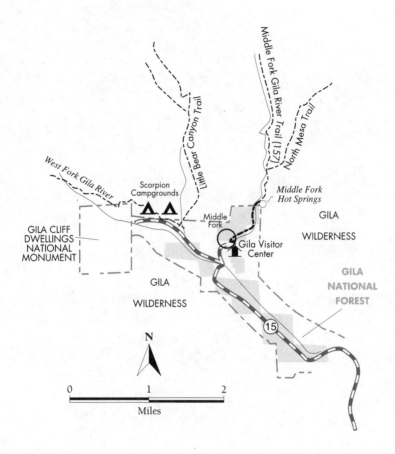

Scorpion Campgrounds

West Fork Gila River

Little Bear Canyon Trail

Middle Fork Gila River Trail (157)

North Mesa Trail

GILA CLIFF
DWELLINGS
NATIONAL
MONUMENT

Middle Fork

Middle Fork
Hot Springs

GILA

WILDERNESS

Gila Visitor
Center

GILA

WILDERNESS

GILA
NATIONAL
FOREST

15

N

0   1   2
Miles

55 Whiterocks

Highlights:	Day hike to startling mounds of white ashflow tuff, a geologic adventure.
Type of hike:	Out-and-back day hike or 2-day backpacking trip from base camp on the Middle Fork.
Total distance:	14 miles.
Difficulty:	Strenuous.
Best months:	April through November.
Maps:	Forest Service Gila Wilderness map (1984); Gila Hot Springs and Burnt Corral Canyon USGS quads.

Special considerations: High water in the Middle Fork would make the trip hazardous. There is no water available after leaving the Middle Fork.

The first river crossing above the Middle Fork Trailhead.

Finding the trailhead: To reach the Middle Fork Trailhead, follow the signs to the Gila Visitor Center, 42 miles north of Silver City on New Mexico Highway 15. Drive through the visitor center parking lot. Turn right at the sign for the Middle Fork Trailhead and drive 0.2 mile to the trailhead on your left, above the river.

Parking and trailhead facilities: There is a limited gravel parking area and an information kiosk at the trailhead. There are no other facilities. Trailhead camping is not permitted. The nearest public camping is at the Scorpion campgrounds (no fee) 1 mile away, on the road to the Gila Cliff Dwellings National Monument. There is no garbage service in the Gila Hot Springs corridor, so be prepared to take your trash home with you.

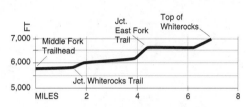

Key points:
- 0.0   Middle Fork Trailhead.
- 0.8   Middle Fork Hot Springs
- 1.5   Junction with North Mesa Trail (27).
- 4.0   Junction with Adobe Canyon Trail (804) to East Fork Gila River.
- 6.6   Junction with Whiterocks Trail (771).
- 7.0   Whiterocks.

The hike: This excursion to the Whiterocks can be done as a long day hike from the Middle Fork Trailhead. For a less strenuous outing, without the pressure of sunset pushing you, you can backpack up the Middle Fork and camp along the river and do the 11-mile hike as a day hike. This schedule will permit you to lounge in the hot springs en route.

From the trailhead head up the trail along the Middle Fork. There are several wet-foot crossings before you reach the dry portion of the hike, so wear your waders and carry your dry boots. At 1.5 miles, turn east on the North Mesa Trail (27). The trail climbs up the east side of the Middle Fork canyon to a grassy rolling pinyon-juniper mesa. The trail heads north, toward the higher mesa, and climbs quickly and steeply to the mesa edge. While you pause to catch your breath, enjoy the panoramic view of the Middle Fork canyon rim. Just beyond the rim is the junction with the East Fork Trail via Adobe Canyon. Turn left toward Whiterocks. Do not be misled by the mileage estimate. Your destination is 3 miles from the junction.

The trail north is marked with cairns and is grooved into the earth of the mesa. Watch for the Whiterocks on the horizon to the northeast. At 2.6 miles from the junction on the mesa you will reach an old corral, followed by a couple of empty stock tanks. The trail to Whiterocks is an unsigned trail beyond the corral on your right. Immediately at the corral there is another unsigned pathway. This one goes to an old cow camp and deadends, so it is not the trail you want. On the correct trail you will see the Whiterocks through the pines and arrive at their base in 0.5 mile.

Both the wilderness map and the Burnt Corral Canyon topo map have

Whiterocks

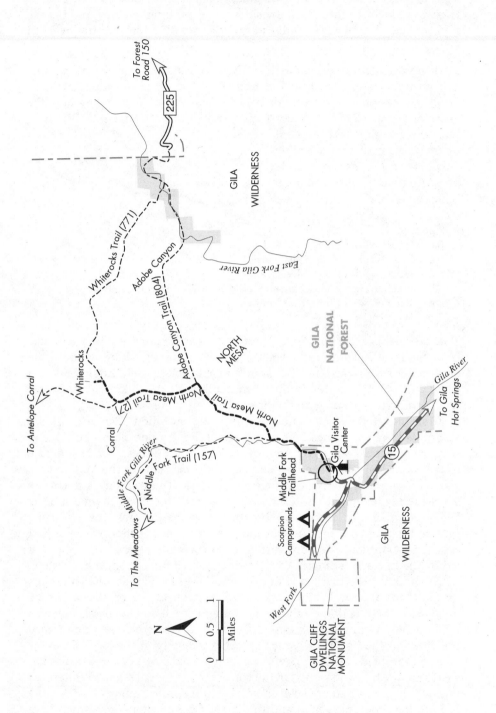

To Forest Road 150

225

GILA WILDERNESS

Whiterocks Trail (771)

Adobe Canyon

Adobe Canyon Trail (804)

East Fork Gila River

NORTH MESA

GILA NATIONAL FOREST

Whiterocks

North Mesa Trail (27)

North Mesa Trail

To Antelope Corral

Corral

Middle Fork Gila River

Middle Fork Trail (157)

Middle Fork Trailhead

Gila Visitor Center

Gila River

To Gila Hot Springs

15

To The Meadows

Scorpion Campgrounds

GILA WILDERNESS

West Fork

GILA CLIFF DWELLINGS NATIONAL MONUMENT

N

0   0.5   1
Miles

the Whiterocks in the wrong location. They are north of the trail, not south. Luckily the geologic feature stands out in this largely greenworld so you can't miss them. The dramatic white tuff has a sandstone texture with chunks of lava embedded in it. The peaks rise like ghosts of stiff egg whites, with hollow eye sockets. This island of geologic anomaly looks like it landed from another planet. The Whiterocks are fun to climb around on, so allow yourself plenty of time to explore before you have to head back. Return to the trailhead by the same route. Watch for elk on both the upper and lower mesas if it is early evening.

56 Little Bear Canyon Loop

Highlights:	Spectacular river canyon with massive cliffs and unusual rock formations along with a narrow slot canyon.
Type of hike:	2- to 3-day backpacking loop.
Total distance:	10 miles.
Difficulty:	Strenuous.
Best months:	May through November.
Maps:	Forest Service Gila Wilderness map (1984); Little Turkey Park, Woodland Park, Burnt Corral Canyon, and Gila Hot Springs USGS quads.

Special considerations: Constant river crossings may be dangerous during high runoff; do not enter the narrow slot canyon during flash flood weather. The same thunderstorms that can suddenly raise river levels may also cause flash flooding. If sampling the hot springs, do not dunk your head or nose in the water. A warm-water amoeba, *Naegleria fowleri,* can enter the brain through the nasal passages and can cause a rare form of meningitis.

Finding the trailhead: Middle Fork Trailhead: Follow the signs to the Gila Visitor Center, located 42 miles north of Silver City on New Mexico Highway 15. Drive through the far end of the visitor center parking lot and turn right. The signed Middle Fork Gila River Trailhead is less than 0.2 mile on the left.

TJ Corral Trailhead: From Silver City drive about 42 miles north on NM 15 and turn left toward the Gila Cliff Dwellings National Monument at the junction to the Gila Visitor Center. After about 0.5 mile turn right (east) into the trailhead marked with a Trail 729 sign just before reaching the Scorpion campgrounds.

The road distance between the two trailheads is about 1 mile.

Parking and trailhead facilities: Middle Fork Gila Trailhead: A small parking area with a kiosk and trailhead sign but no water, garbage service, or other facilities. TJ Corral Trailhead: Large parking area with trailhead sign, kiosk, water, and corral. Garbage service is not provided in the Gila corridor, so be prepared to haul out your trash. Camping is available at the nearby Scorpion campgrounds.

Key points:

- 0.0 Trailhead for Middle Fork Gila River Trail (157).
- 0.5 Middle Fork Hot Springs and Gila Wilderness boundary.
- 1.5 Junction with North Mesa Trail (27).
- 6.0 Junction with Little Bear Canyon Trail (729).
- 8.0 Junction with Lilley Park Trail (164).
- 9.7 Exit wilderness boundary.
- 9.8 Junction with West Fork stock bypass trail.
- 10.0 TJ Corral Trailhead.

The hike: The spectacular Middle Fork Gila River canyon offers a scenic, winding trail with almost no perceptible ascent. However, with at least six river crossings per mile, the travel is slow and arduous and can therefore be best enjoyed as an overnighter. If you bring Neoprene socks along for thermal protection you'll wonder how you could possibly make the trip without them. The loop can be hiked from either direction, but we recommend starting up the Middle Fork when you're fresh. In so doing you'll better appreciate the rugged grandeur of the lower canyon.

The trail drops to the river and crosses twice before reaching the wilderness boundary at 0.5 mile. The Middle Fork Hot Springs emerges from a cleft in the rock on the right (east) side just before the boundary sign. Unfortunately, the pleasant river-level pools are better appreciated at the end than at the beginning of a long hike, but hey, why not take a few minutes for a quick soak anyway? Overhangs with layered cliffs of dark volcanic rock capped with lighter tuff provide a colorful contrast on both sides of the river. At 1.5 miles, the trail crosses the river and meets the signed junction with the North Mesa Trail (27) to Whiterocks.

It doesn't take long for the canyon to envelop you in its wildness. You'll be soothed by the sound of the river as it twists through this convoluted land of cliffs and caves. White caps atop dark cliffs alternate from side to side with the highest escarpments rising more than 400 vertical feet on the left (west) side. Somewhere around mile 2.7 a steep-walled canyon enters from the left, tempting your exploratory instinct. Gigantic white-trunk sycamores stand out in a mixed conifer-hardwood forest. Great volcanic ramparts jut out from more gently arching brushy slopes. Unworldly rock shapes can be anything your imagination permits, from castle turrets to goblins. Monumental columns, spires, and cliffs of dark Gila conglomerate resemble sharks' teeth guarding the inner sanctum of the Middle Fork.

Little Bear Canyon joins the Middle Fork from the left (south) after 6 serpentine miles. The sign reads 4.3 miles to TJ Corral and issues a warning about dangerous flash floods in the slot canyon of Little Bear during the rainy season. Hawks soaring high among the spires enrich this magical set-

Little Bear Canyon Loop

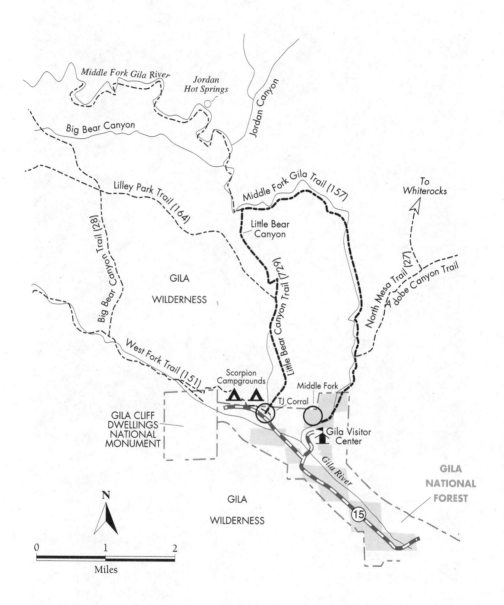

ting. The narrow sandy bottom of Little Bear Canyon quickly closes in with sheer walls of multicolored rock formations. The deepest and most intimate slot canyon is in this lower stretch for the next 0.5 mile. Rock ledges and boulders force the soft dirt trail in and out of the sandy wash. After about 1 mile the trail passes through rolling pine woodlands and then contours more steeply around the head of Little Bear Canyon to an expansive overlook on the divide between the Middle and West Forks of the Gila River. A short

Backpacking in lower Middle Fork Gila River canyon.

gentle descent is then made to a signed junction with the Lilley Park Trail (164) 2 miles south of the Middle Fork. Continue south (left) as the trail descends pinyon-juniper grasslands for the next 1.3 miles to a stock fence. Exit the wilderness at the bottom of a large, sloping park and reach a junction where the stock bypass trail heads to the West Fork. Turn left for the short drop to the TJ Corral Trailhead. Turn left onto NM 15 and walk down the highway for 1 mile to the Middle Fork Gila Trailhead if you left your car there.

Option: If time and energy permit, continue your river slog upstream to Jordan Hot Springs, located 2 miles and 15 river crossings above the mouth of Little Bear Canyon (see Hike 56 for details).

57 Meadows–Big Bear Loop

Highlights:	Spectacular river canyon with towering rock formations; solitude in the remote heart of the Middle Fork; hot springs; broad mountain vistas.
Type of hike:	4- to 5-day backpacking loop.
Total distance:	24.6 miles.
Difficulty:	Strenuous.
Best months:	May through November.
Maps:	Forest Service Gila Wilderness map (1984); Gila Hot Springs, Burnt Corral Canyon, Woodland Park, and Little Turkey Park USGS quads.

Special considerations: Numerous river crossings should not be attempted when water levels are high. Do not dunk your head or nose in any hot springs. A warm-water amoeba, *Naegleria fowleri*, can enter the brain through the nasal passages and can cause a rare form of meningitis. There are no water sources along the 10-mile return leg of the loop, so plan accordingly.

Finding the trailheads: Middle Fork Gila River Trailhead: Follow the signs to the Gila Visitor Center, located 42 miles north of Silver City on New Mexico Highway 15. Drive through the far end of the visitor center parking lot and turn right. The signed Middle Fork Gila River Trailhead is less than 0.2 mile on the left.

TJ Corral Trailhead: The trailhead is about 43 miles north of Silver City on NM 15, and about 1 mile from the Gila Visitor Center, on the road to the Gila Cliff Dwellings National Monument. Turn right (east) at the sign for Trail 729 just before reaching the Scorpion campgrounds.

Parking and trailhead facilities: Middle Fork Gila River Trailhead: small parking area, trailhead sign, and kiosk. There is no water or other facilities. TJ Corral Trailhead: large parking area, trailhead sign, kiosk, water, and corral. Camping is available at the nearby Scorpion campgrounds.

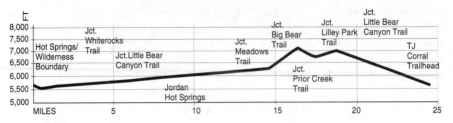

Key points:

0.0   Middle Fork Gila River Trailhead for Middle Fork Trail (157).
0.5   Middle Fork Hot Springs and Gila Wilderness boundary.
1.5   Junction with North Mesa Trail (27).
6.0   Junction with Little Bear Canyon Trail (729).
8.0   Jordan Hot Springs.
14.5   The Meadows and junction with Meadows Trail (53).
14.6   The Meadows and junction with Big Bear Trail (28).
16.1   Junction with Prior Creek Trail (156).
18.6   Junction with Lilley Park Trail (164).
22.6   Junction with Little Bear Trail (729).
24.6   TJ Corral Trailhead.

The hike: This is not the kind of hike to hurry through, even if you could. The going is inherently slow, not only because of countless and constant stream crossings but also because you'll want to pause often to savor and photograph the canyon majesty. The Meadows can be reached in two days, but if you plan on taking three you'll enjoy the trip a lot more. The return upland leg of 10 miles to the TJ Corral can be backpacked in one long day.

The Middle Fork Gila River Trail (157) crosses the river a couple of times before reaching the hot springs and adjacent wilderness boundary at 0.5 mile. The shallow river-level pools are pleasantly warm and certainly offer an excuse to drop your pack for a while. Colorful layered cliffs with alcoves oversee the river up to the North Mesa Trail junction. Continue left along the forested stream bottom. Soon the deepening canyon will captivate you with the soothing sounds of river music. Crossings average at least six per mile and are marked with rock cairns and good campsites. Massive white-trunk sycamores stand out in the mixed conifer-deciduous woodland. Fantastic rock shapes can be anything your imagination desires, from white castle turrets to dark spires stabbing the sky. By mile 5 the canyon achieves its most spectacular, neck-craning proportions. Soaring cliffs and columns of dark Gila conglomerate resemble sharks' teeth guarding the inner sanctum of the Middle Fork. At mile 6 Little Bear Canyon enters from the left (south) signed for the TJ Corral. A spacious flat supports a diverse mix of cottonwood, juniper, ponderosa pine, and Douglas-fir.

More columns, hoodoos, goblins, balancing rocks, and caves, along with continual crossings, mark the next 2 miles to the fabled Jordan Hot Springs. These three stairstep pools are well worth a visit while en route to the Meadows. Look for them above the mouth of Jordan Canyon high on the right (east) side of the Middle Fork. If you miss the lower end of the short hot springs trail, look for the outlet of the springs flowing through the cobble

Meadows–Big Bear Loop

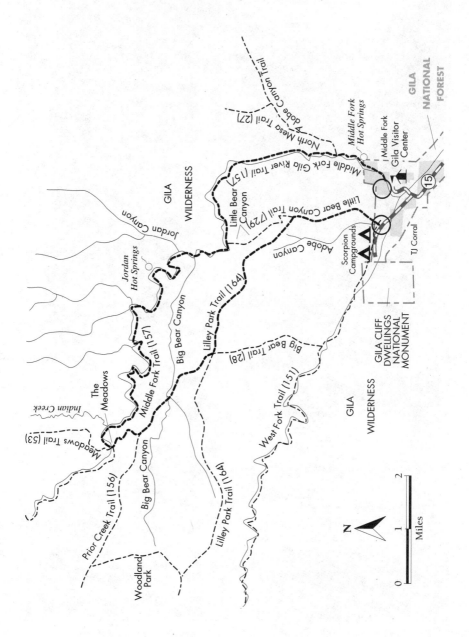

The only dry foot crossing of the Middle Fork Gila River between the Middle Fork Trailhead and The Meadows is across this huge ponderosa-pine bridge.

on the east side of the Middle Fork. If you decide to spend the night here, camp at least 400 yards upstream from the hot springs to help safeguard the wilderness integrity of this popular destination.

The canyon continues to deepen above the hot springs with higher cliffs, jagged minarets, and freestanding clusters of rock columns. Trout and, sadly, introduced carp, dart in dark emerald pools overseen by sheer walls hundreds of feet high. The walls are gloriously framed by arching sycamores and cottonwoods. Deep pools bound by cliff walls tend to be on the outer curves of the endless river bends. The trail is distinct across benches but often disappears across gravel bars. Simply scan the far bank for the trail and take the path of least resistance to it. The signed 8.5-mile distance from Little Bear to the Meadows seems much farther in this serpentine chasm with its constant river crossings and rough gravel bars.

Sizable warm spring ponds just below the Meadows cause a tricky spot on the trail. Upon reaching the larger pond, cross on the beaver dam to pick up the old trail on the right (north) side of the Middle Fork. The trail climbs through rocky woods about 0.2 mile to a signed junction for Meadows Trail (53) that heads uphill to the right (north) to Double Springs. Continue left another 0.1 mile to the wide-open grassland of the Meadows. The flat is surrounded by brushy rock-strewn hills that rise more than 1,000 feet to the distant rims. Clumps of huge ponderosa pine shade perfect campsites on benches near the river.

To continue the loop, use the convenient "bridge" of a gigantic pine tree that has fallen across the stream, the only dry crossing of the countless stream slogs up to this point. Big Bear Trail (28), marked with a cairn, takes off up the south side of the canyon. The original trail used to gain the 1,140 feet to the south rim in 1 steep mile but has since been graded with switchbacks that lengthen the distance to 1.5 miles. The switchbacks seem to go on forever, with plenty of resting spots for viewing the Middle Fork and the lower canyon of Indian Creek to the north.

When the trail finally tops out on the south rim, it meets the Prior Creek Trail (156). Continue left (southeast) on the Big Bear Trail as it gently descends a grassy pine mesa. After about a mile it begins to drop more steeply into the midsection of Big Bear Canyon. After paralleling the south side of the drainage for about 0.5 mile it gains 300 feet over the next mile to its junction with the Lilley Park Trail (164). Turn left (east) on the Lilley Park Trail. This pleasantly graded 4-mile stretch follows a narrowing up-and-down ridge to the broad, pinyon-juniper mesa intersection with the Little Bear Canyon Trail (729). Turn right (south) for the final 2-mile stretch down pinyon-juniper grasslands. Shortly after leaving the wilderness boundary, turn left at the stock bypass trail junction to reach the TJ Corral. If you've left your vehicle at the Middle Fork Trailhead, whoever loses the toss gets to walk 1 more mile to the Gila Visitor Center on NM 15.

Options: When you reach the mouth of Little Bear Canyon at mile 6 consider stashing your pack and hiking a mile or so up the narrow slot canyon on Little Bear Trail (729) (see Hike 56). But if you hear distant thunder, remember the danger of flash floods, and save the canyon for another day.

A variation of the loop route is to continue south on the Big Bear Trail (28) from its junction with the Lilley Park Trail. The West Fork of the Gila River is reached after 2 miles with another 2.5 miles downstream to the West Fork Trailhead next to the Gila Cliff Dwellings National Monument. A reduction in total loop distance of about 1.5 miles is more than offset by several additional river crossings and an extra mile of walking on NM 15 to retrieve your car from the Middle Fork Trailhead.

58 Meadows–Hells Hole Loop

Highlights:	Explore the canyons of the Middle and West Forks, crossing from the meadows to Hells Hole via Prior Cabin.
Type of hike:	5- to 7-day backpacking trip; shuttle.
Total distance:	36.5 miles.
Difficulty:	Strenuous.
Best months:	May through November.
Maps:	Forest Service Gila Wilderness map (1984); Little Turkey Park, Woodland Park, and Lilley Mountain USGS quads.

Special considerations: Many stream crossings. Both forks are hazardous during spring runoff and any time of high water.

Finding the trailheads: Middle Fork Trailhead: Follow signs to the Gila Visitor Center, 42 miles north of Silver City on New Mexico Highway 15. Drive through the visitor center parking lot. Turn right at the sign for the Middle Fork Trailhead and drive 0.2 mile to the trailhead on your left, above the river.

West Fork Trailhead: Turn left (west) at milepost 42 on NM 15 toward the Gila Cliff Dwellings National Monument and Scorpion campgrounds. From the visitor center, turn right (west), 0.3 mile south of the visitor enter on NM 15. Drive to the end of the road, 1 mile from the turn, to the monument parking lot and the West Fork trailhead.

The one-way shuttle driving or walking distance between trailheads is 1.8 miles.

Parking and trailhead facilities: At the Middle Fork Trailhead there is limited parking on a gravel lot; there is an information board, but no other facilities. Camping is not permitted. The Scorpion campgrounds (no fee) are about halfway between the two trailheads on the road to the monument and the West Fork. At the West Fork trailhead, there is a large paved parking area and a vault toilet. There is no garbage service in the Gila corridor, so be prepared to take all your trash with you.

Key points:

0.0	Middle Fork Trailhead and Middle Fork Trail (157).
1.5	Junction with North Mesa Trail (27).
6.0	Junction with Little Bear Canyon Trail (729).
14.5	The Meadows; junction with the Meadows Trail (53) and Big Bear Canyon Trail (28).
16.0	South rim; junction with Prior Creek Trail (156).
19.0	Junction with Woodland Park Trail (12).
19.5	Prior Cabin; junction with Chicken Coop Canyon Trail (29).
21.8	Junction with Lilley Park Trail (164).
23.0	Junction with Hells Hole Trail (268).
24.5	West Fork Gila River; junction with West Fork Trail (151).
33.8	Junction with Big Bear Canyon Trail (28).
35.5	Junction with EE Canyon Trail.
36.5	West Fork Trailhead.

The hike: This is a popular loop trip that can be done in either direction. You get to visit the canyons of both forks of the Gila, so you don't have to choose one over the other. The overland crossover takes you by the Prior Cabin, where there is a spring. It is about the same distance (10 miles) to cross through Woodland Park, but this latter route does not have water available.

Be prepared for endless wet-foot crossings. Sturdy footwear is essential for backpacking in the river bottoms. Neoprene socks are a boon to those with cold feet problems. A sturdy walking stick is also an asset in the swift current. Do not attempt the trip when the water in either river is high, during spring runoff, or after heavy rains.

From the Middle Fork Trailhead, the path drops quickly to the river where the crossings begin. At the wilderness boundary, 0.5 mile from the trailhead, there is a hot spring on the east side of the river, right by the bank. As you continue upstream, the layered cliffs on either side of the valley provide a ribbon of color. After a crossing you will come to the North Mesa Trail sign on the east side. Continue upstream.

The dramatic canyon walls of the Middle Fork are endlessly enchanting the entire length of the river. Jutting ramparts, turrets, mushrooms, cone heads—the variety of shapes will challenge your vocabulary; words are not sufficient to describe the geologic wonders of the Middle Fork. In the canyon bottom a ribbon of mixed conifer and deciduous trees runs along the river. Campsites are plentiful, usually near the crossings.

Little Bear Canyon is on the south just after a particularly stunning display of volcanic spires and columns. It is worth it to drop your pack and

Meadows–Hells Hole Loop

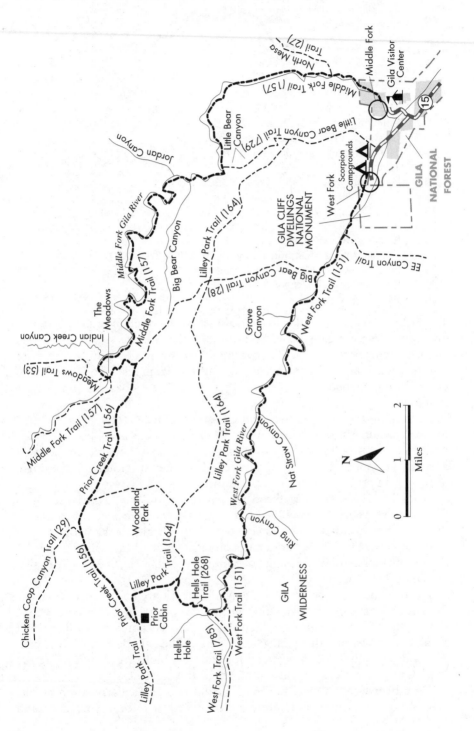

take a quick 2-mile side trip up Little Bear but not if there has been heavy rain in the region. It's a narrow slot canyon, with vertical walls reaching to the sky. The Little Bear Trail is the main route to Jordan Hot Springs, 2 miles up the Middle Fork from its mouth, so you can expect to encounter hikers in this area.

From Little Bear to the hot springs the trail crosses the river more than a dozen times. The springs are actually 0.3 mile beyond the mouth of Jordan Canyon, on the north bank above the river. A heavily used trail goes by the soaking pools, while the official trail on the riverbank is barely visible, so it would be hard to miss the springs (see Hike 53 for details). Campsites are plentiful all along the Middle Fork, so avoid camping near the busy hot springs.

The magnificent display of volcanic geology and erosion continues to the Meadows. The winding river has a multitude of carp, an introduced species that has grown numerous at the expense of trout. You will notice schools of bold carp in the deep pools, as well as darting through the riffles at crossings.

Below the Meadows, the trail becomes indistinct due to erosion on the south bank. Warm springs ponds are on the north bank; cross the beaver dam at the foot of the large pond to pick up the trail on the north bank where it climbs through aspen to the wooded junction with the Meadows Trail (53). Continue on the main river trail another 0.1 mile to the wide-open grassland flat of the Meadows. The flat is surrounded by brushy rock-strewn hills that rise more than 1,000 feet to the distant rims. Clumps of huge pine shade ideal campsites. Bring insect repellent; the mushy meadow is a rich breeding area for mosquitoes.

After enjoying the Meadows, cross the Middle Fork on the huge pine tree that makes a convenient bridge. This is the only dry crossing on the river. The prone tree trunk points at the location of the Big Bear Canyon Trail (28), which takes off up the south canyon wall. A cairn also marks the trail. Whether going up or down, you will find this trail tough with a heavy pack. The sign indicates a mile, but it is definitely longer. The original trail had few switchbacks, and the addition of switchbacks over time hasn't been reflected in the mileage estimates. Hikers have modified some of the signs. The trail climbs sharply from the canyon floor to a hanging valley that has been blasted with a hot fire that exploded the boulders. Then it switchbacks interminably to the canyon rim, climbing 1,100 feet in 1.5 miles. There are plenty of pausing points for vistas of the Middle Fork and the rugged canyon of Indian Creek running to the north.

At the rim is the intersection with the Prior Creek Trail (156) on the right. Turn right (west) toward Prior Cabin, 3.5 miles away. The rolling ponderosa park makes hiking easy. The intersection with the Woodland Park Trail (12) is 0.5 from the cabin—Woodland Park Trail is an alternate route to Hells Hole. Continue on to the cabin, with its nearby spring. After refreshments, hike up the gently sloped Prior Creek drainage to the southwest to the intersection with the Lilley Park Trail (164). Turn left (east) toward Woodland Park and the Hells Hole Trail. The Lilley Park Trail skirts the rugged depths

"Organ pipe" formations rise above the West Fork Gila River below Hells Hole.

of Hells Hole Canyon to the trail junction in a little more than a mile. Turn right on the Hells Hole Trail. The descent is as dramatic and swift as was the climb out of the Meadows. The trail leaves the ponderosa pine park to arrive at the lush riparian zone of the West Fork. Along the way are wonderful views of Hells Hole Canyon and the rift of the West Fork.

Many campsites dot the West Fork Trail near the Hells Hole intersection. You will pass an alcove campsite adjacent to the river, most inviting if it is a cold or rainy evening. Heading on down the West Fork, the canyon closes in just downstream of Hells Hole. For the next 10 miles the narrow canyon walls limit your view of the sky but provide an awesome display of geology. Pocked igneous towers tickle the skyline with their pointy fingers. Much narrower than the Middle Fork, the abrupt canyon walls cause the river to bounce from side to side. The trail shifts frequently too. Campsites are infrequent and smaller. If it is growing late, do not delay in selecting your site. It may be an hour before you see the next one. Sections of the West Fork Trail have been relocated to the higher benches when possible, due to repeated flooding and exhaustion of the Forest Service trail crews. These higher sections allow your feet to dry out but are limited in camping opportunities.

Gradually, the forested strip along the river bottom changes into a deciduous woodland of oak, sycamore, maple, ash, and boxelder, with fewer conifers. In this lower part of the river you will come across a solitary cliff dwelling. Downstream of the Graves Canyon mouth, the dwelling is high on the south canyon wall, with several campsites on the opposite bank. From here to the trailhead, the West Fork is more heavily traveled. Frequent cairns mark the route. The intersection with the Big Bear Canyon Trail is just beyond the cliff dwelling site, but it is easy to miss since the more popular trail is in the cobblestone bottom taking a shortcut across the south bank where the Big Bear Trail junction is on the north side.

In the final 1.8 miles, the trail has been elevated to the south bench, where it remains above the stream until it passes the EE Canyon Trail. After this junction, the trail returns to the river for the final crossing. The last 0.9-mile stretch is dry, on the north side, cutting across a corner of the monument to reach the trailhead.

Options: A side trip to Whiterocks is an exciting geologic opportunity (see Hike 55). Consult Hikes 53 and 54 on hot springs etiquette and medical notes prior to enjoying this special feature of the Gila Wilderness. See Hike 77 for an outing from the Meadows toward Yellow Mountain. On your way to the West Fork Trailhead, you may want to visit the Grudging Grave (see Hike 49).

59 The Forks via Trotter

<table>
<tr><td align="right">Highlights:</td><td>Soaring elegant cliffs in the Middle Fork and the West Fork; rolling meadows and ridges on the Trotter Trail.</td></tr>
<tr><td align="right">Type of hike:</td><td>8 to 10 day backpacking trip; shuttle.</td></tr>
<tr><td align="right">Total distance:</td><td>57 miles.</td></tr>
<tr><td align="right">Difficulty:</td><td>Strenuous.</td></tr>
<tr><td align="right">Best months:</td><td>April through November.</td></tr>
<tr><td align="right">Maps:</td><td>Forest Service Gila Wilderness map (1984); Gila Hot Springs, Burnt Corral Canyon, Lilley Mountain, Little Turkey Park, and Woodland Park USGS quads.</td></tr>
</table>

Special considerations: Many stream crossings on the forks of the Gila. Do not attempt this trip in high water, either during spring runoff or after heavy rains. Hot springs may contain the amoeba *Naegleria fowleri*, which can cause meningitis if it comes in contact with your nose or mouth.

Finding the trailhead: For the Middle Fork Trailhead, follow signs to the Gila Visitor Center, 42 miles north of Silver City on New Mexico Highway 15. Drive through the visitor center parking lot. Turn right at the sign for the Middle Fork Trailhead and drive 0.2 mile to the trailhead on your left above the river.

For the West Fork trailhead, on NM 15 turn right (west) 0.3 south of the visitor center toward the Gila Cliff Dwellings National Monument and the Scorpion campgrounds. This junction is 42 miles north of Silver City on NM 15, at milepost 42. Drive 1 mile to the end of the road at the monument parking area and the trailhead for Trail 151.

The shuttle distance is 1.8 miles between trailheads.

Parking and trailhead facilities: At the Middle Fork Trailhead, there is limited parking. There is an information board but no other facilities. Camping is not permitted at the trailhead. The closest campground is at the Scorpion campgrounds (no fee) near the West Fork Trailhead. At the West Fork there is a large paved parking lot, a vault toilet, and an information board. No camping is permitted. Note that there is no garbage service in the Gila corridor, so be prepared to carry your trash out with you.

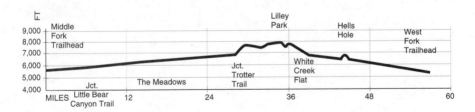

244

Key points:

0.0	Middle Fork Trailhead and Middle Fork Trail (157).
0.5	Middle Fork Hot Springs.
1.5	Junction with North Mesa Trail (27) to Whiterocks.
6.0	Junction with Little Bear Canyon Trail (729).
8.0	Jordan Hot Springs.
14.5	The Meadows; junction with Meadows Trail (53) and Big Bear Canyon Trail (28).
21.6	Junction with Garcia Spring Trail (730).
21.9	Junction with Homestead Trail (101).
23.4	Junction with Canyon Creek Trail (31).
26.9	Junction with Flying V Canyon Trail (708).
28.2	Junction with Aeroplane Mesa Trail (705).
28.4	Trotter Meadow; junction with Trotter Trail (30).
29.6	Junction with Flying V Canyon Trail (706).
31.5	Papineau grave.
31.9	Junction with Clear Creek Trail (165).
32.9	Junction with Chicken Coop Canyon Trail (29).
35.3	Lilley Park Spring.
35.8	Lilley Park; junction with Lilley Park Trail (164).
37.6	Overlook above White Creek Flat.
38.8	West Fork; junction with West Fork Trail (151).
39.0	White Creek Flat; junction with Little Creek Trail (155).
44.5	Hells Hole bypass trail (785).
45.0	Hells Hole; junction with Hells Hole Trail (268).
54.5	Junction with Big Bear Canyon Trail (28).
56.0	Junction with EE Canyon Trail.
57.0	West Fork Trailhead and Gila Cliff Dwellings National Monument.

The hike: This is the whopper of loop hikes on the forks of the Gila. You can do the trip in either direction, enjoying the dramatic canyons of one fork, crossing on the Trotter Trail, and then visiting the soaring depths of the other fork. The journey on the Middle Fork is the longer of the two, so we recommend going up that river first. You could be tired of river crossings by the end of the week, and the trek down the West Fork is a straighter line to the parking lot. In either direction, be prepared for stream crossings with a sturdy pair of sacrifice boots for hiking and crossing. If cold feet are a problem (the water is cold), Neoprene socks can make the trip more pleasant. Trekking poles or a walking stick can make crossing the swift streams with a heavy pack a lot easier.

River travel in the Gila forks is slow. The trails wind up and down and sideways, with frequent crossings to interrupt the hiking rhythm. Do not make the mistake of underestimating the time required to enjoy a trip on the rivers. It is easily a five-day journey to Trotter Meadow, especially if you stop to enjoy the hot springs en route or explore some of the side canyons. After crossing to White Creek Flat, it's a three-day trip to the trailhead. Rough weather or a rising river can require you to modify your schedule. We spent a freezing day in our tent at White Creek Flat in early April while a blizzard blew down the valley. Slogging down the river in those conditions was not possible.

The Forks via Trotter

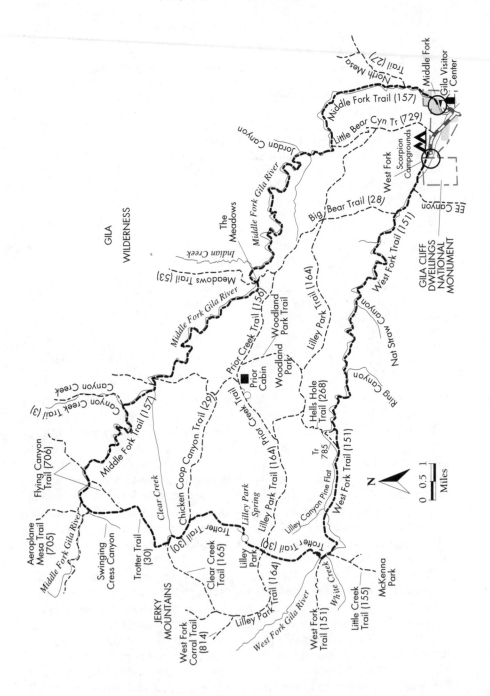

Starting at the Middle Fork Trailhead, the trail slopes down to the riverbank where the pattern of crossing begins. The layered cliffs of the canyon rise above; the lighter sandstone capped with dark volcanic rock provides a colorful contrast with the greenery of the river valley. The lower Middle Fork hot springs, also known as Light Feather Hot Springs, is 0.5 mile from the trailhead, at the wilderness boundary, right next to the trail. It may be a bit early in the trip to stop and soak. As you continue on up the canyon, the trail is easy to follow. Crossings are often marked with cairns so you can spot the next trail segment on the opposite bank. Campsites are frequent, often at crossings, nestled under the sycamores.

In the vicinity of Little Bear Canyon, the Middle Fork cliffs are extraordinary. South of the junction, great columns, spires, and sheer cliffs of dark Gila conglomerate soar high above the river like sharks' teeth. The Little Bear Trail, on the left, leads up the slot canyon to the mesa in 1 mile. Drop your pack and explore this dramatic chasm. Heed the warning regarding the flash flood danger in Little Bear. The 4-foot-wide canyon can become a raging torrent.

Continuing up the Middle Fork from Little Bear you may encounter other parties since the famed Jordan Hot Springs lie 2 miles upstream. There are more than two dozen crossings before you reach the hot springs. The canyon in this stretch is remarkable, with hoodoos, goblins, balancing rocks, and caves along the intricate volcanic walls. At the hot springs the official trail continues in the river bottom while the more heavily used trail goes up the north bank to the hot springs about 50 feet above the river. Campsites are heavily impacted around the springs in spite of the Forest Service efforts to forbid camping within 400 feet of the springs. Take note, too, of the warning regarding meningitis from the amoeba *Naegleria fowleri*, which is to be taken seriously. After a stop at the inviting pools, continue on upstream before camping.

The winding canyon continues to provide spectacular scenery on its way to the Meadows. Crossings are endless, but campsites are frequent where the bottom widens. Constant crossings and lumpy gravel bars make the journey arduous. Above the angular rock columns, spires and cliffs provide a constant source of awe. The variety is infinite. South of the Meadows the trail becomes indistinct due to severe erosion on the south bank. Stay on the north side along the warm ponds from a tepid spring. Upon reaching a larger pond, cross the beaver dam to pick up the old trail on the north side. The trail climbs slightly away from the river as it approaches the Meadows, first meeting the Meadows Trail (53) in the rocky woods, and then dropping to the grassy flatland of the Meadows itself. The wide, open grassland flat is surrounded by brushy, rock-strewn hillsides that rise more than 1,000 feet to the distant rugged rims. Clumps of huge pines shade ideal campsites on the perimeter and along the stream. This is a popular destination, and you can expect to have company here.

Above the Meadows ponderosa pine becomes the dominant species in the riparian forest. The trail traverses brushy sections, indicating less traffic. Campsites, also, are less numerous. The inspiring geology display con-

A spring snowstorm carpets White Creek Flat, location of the Forest Service White Creek Guard Station.

tinues up the canyon. In the limestone formations, caves and alcoves dot the canyon walls, some at ground level, others far above. Deep river pools harbor schools of carp, an unfortunate alien species that has driven out the native trout.

At Flying V Canyon an expansive meadow spreads out on the river bottom. This vast flat is a good place to spot elk in the evening as they head for water along the willow-lined stream. Old cabin ruins are in a heap near the mouth of Flying V Canyon, evidence of an early settler's optimism. From the meadow the trail to Trotter has only one crossing, right next to a huge streamside alcove. This has been used for centuries by travelers seeking shelter from the wind and rain. Trotter Meadow is just ahead. It's an open grassland surrounded by a mix of cottonwood and pine. The cabin shown on the topo map no longer exists, having burned years ago.

From Trotter Meadow, it is 10.5 miles over to the West Fork, via the Trotter Trail. Even in a dry year it is likely you will find water in Clear Creek, which you cross in 3.5 miles. Lilley Park Spring, at around 7 miles, also has water in its protected enclosure, although the flow may be light. The junctions on the crossover trail are numerous, but the trail is well signed and distinct. Just keep heading south, skirting Lilley Mountain to the west. The trail is up and down, along ridge crests and through sloping mountain meadows, with ponderosa forests, pine parks, and mixed dense growth on shady northern slopes in Chicken Coop Canyon. A startling sight, perhaps, is the grave of an early trapper, Papineau, right next to the trail on the ridge between Swinging Cross and Clear Creek Canyons. He was buried on the spot where he was slain by Apaches.

South of Lilley Park the trail breaks out of the woodland on the ridge to a promontory point above White Creek Flat. After enjoying the view, you have a very steep descent via a long series of lengthy, slightly graded switchbacks down the hillside. The denuded slope was blasted by forest fire, so you have a good view all the way down to the West Fork. You will arrive in the valley just north of the flat and the cabin. Turn left and thread your way through the braided stream and the beaver ponds to the meadow near the Forest Service cabin. Campsites dot the forest edge around the grassy flat.

The West Fork Trail has been rerouted away from the stream bottoms in several places between White Creek and the trailhead. The Forest Service, tired of annual reconstruction after floods, has moved sections to higher benches when possible. The old mileage signs have not been corrected to reflect the new routes. From the flat you will encounter a new section right away. The gorge and falls below White Creek have forced the trail to the forested slope north of the river for 1.5 miles. At the mouth of Lilley Canyon, it returns to the river bottom, then it stays on a pine bench on the south side while the canyon walls rise ever higher above. After the narrow canyon the contorted contours of Hells Hole's volcanic cliffs are a startling sight.

There's a trail split at Hells Hole, with a triangular bypass route available. Going downstream, continue on the right, climbing over the ridge that protrudes into Hells Hole from the south. Near the eastern leg of the triangle are several pine-shaded campsites. If the weather is unpleasant you might want to camp at the alcove along the river—take the eastern Hells Hole Trail north 0.2 mile to find it.

The West Fork canyon changes after Hells Hole, becoming more narrow and more rugged. Canyon walls shoot 200 to 300 feet straight up from the streambed. The slender riverbottom supports stands of pine, fir, and oak on the limited soil, while above, the pocked igneous towers, with cone heads, create a fascinating skyline. The narrow gorge drives the trail back and forth across the river. Campsites are less frequent, so don't delay stopping if it is growing late. It may be an hour until you find the next site. Sections of the newer trail along the pine benches also limit camping. These high, dry sections are a speedy respite from endless crossings but do not provide camping opportunities.

About a mile downstream from the dry mouth of Graves Canyon, watch for a large cave on the south canyon wall of the West Fork. This is the site of a solitary cliff dwelling. From here the river trail shows considerably more traffic, with frequent cairns marking crossings. A new section of the trail goes high on the south bank below the dwelling, climbing 80 feet above the river. Just beyond the EE Canyon Trail junction it drops back down for the final crossing before the trailhead. The trail crosses the valley and stays on the north side of the meandering stream. You will cross a corner of the Gila Cliff Dwellings National Monument, marked by a fence, and finally arrive at the trailhead, concluding a lengthy adventure in the wild Gila forks.

Options: Side trips along the way are wonderful opportunities to dry out your feet. Whiterocks (Hike 55) and Little Bear Canyon (Hike 56) are below the Meadows. At the Meadows you can investigate the north trail (Hike 77) or the south one to Prior Cabin (Hike 58). From White Creek Flat, visit McKenna Park (Hike 48). On the West Fork, explore Hells Hole (Hike 58) and visit the Grudging Grave (Hike 49).

60 Middle Fork–Gilita

Highlights:	A complete traverse of the country, from south to north, on the longest continuous trail in the Gila Wilderness, with deep fish-filled pools, spectacular canyons and rock formations, hot springs, and historic artifacts in the wild remote reaches of the Middle Fork.
Type of hike:	6- to 8-day backpacking trip; shuttle.
Total distance:	40 miles.
Difficulty:	Strenuous.
Best months:	May through November.
Maps:	Forest Service Gila Wilderness map (1984); Gila Hot Springs, Burnt Corral Canyon, Woodland Park, Lilley Mountain, Loco Mountain, and Negrito Mountain USGS quads.

Special considerations: There are more than 100 river crossings on this route, which may be dangerous and perhaps impassable during high runoff. Higher-elevation forest roads and trailheads may be blocked by snow into late spring. Do not dunk your head or nose in any of the hot springs. A warm-water amoeba, *Naegleria fowleri,* can enter the brain through the nasal passages and cause a rare form of meningitis.

Finding the trailheads: Middle Fork Trailhead: Follow the signs to the Gila Visitor Center, located 42 miles north of Silver City on New Mexico Highway 15. Drive through the far end of the visitor center parking lot and turn right. The signed Middle Fork Gila River Trailhead is less than 0.2 mile on the left.

Gilita Creek Trailhead: Drive 4 miles north of Glenwood on U.S. Highway 180. Turn right (east) on NM 159, also known as the Bursum Road, toward Mogollon. NM 159 changes from paved to improved gravel after 9 miles. Drive east 27 miles to the signed Gilita Creek Campground. The Middle Fork Gila River Trail (157) begins at the eastern end of the campground with one shallow stream crossing to drive through just above the trailhead.

The one-way shuttle driving distance between trailheads is 139 slow, winding miles, 124 of which are paved.

Parking and trailhead facilities: Middle Fork Gila River Trailhead: limited parking on a gravel surface and kiosk. There are no facilities, water, camping, or garbage service at the trailhead. Gilita Creek Trailhead: a no-fee forest camp with ample parking, vault toilet, kiosk, trailhead sign, and water from the creek (must be treated).

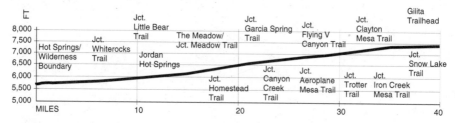

Key points:

0.0	Middle Fork Gila River Trailhead for Middle Fork Trail (157).
0.5	Middle Fork Hot Springs and wilderness boundary.
1.5	Junction with North Mesa Trail (27).
6.0	Junction with Little Bear Canyon Trail (729).
8.0	Jordan Hot Springs.
14.5	The Meadows and junction with Meadows Trail (53).
21.6	Junction with Garcia Spring Trail (730).
21.9	Junction with Homestead Trail (101).
23.4	Junction with Canyon Creek Trail (31).
26.9	Junction with Flying V Canyon Trail (706).
28.2	Junction with Aeroplane Mesa Trail (705).
28.4	Junction with Trotter Trail (30).
30.9	Junction with Clayton Mesa Trail (175).
31.0	Junction with Iron Creek Mesa Trail (171).
34.0	Junction with Snow Lake Trail (142).
40.0	Gilita Creek Trailhead.

The hike: With the longest continuous trail in the Gila on a route that brings new discoveries around every river bend, this trip has it all. Because many visitors use side trails to access specific points to and from the river, there are several remote stretches with very little human traffic, especially above the Meadows. The 2,000-foot elevation gain from the Middle Fork Trailhead to the Gilita Creek Campground is spread evenly over 40 miles so that the climb is hardly noticeable. In fact the only time you're aware of climbing is when the trail gains and loses a quick 100 feet by going over or around a headwall or cliff face. An upriver route is suggested so that the more rugged and spectacular lower canyon is experienced early on, when you're fresh. As the country opens up more in the upper reaches you'll be able to make better time to the exit trailhead when the "going to the barn" syndrome begins to kick in. For some, the long, slow shuttle drive between trailheads may be more formidable than the hike. See if you can find another party to exchange car keys with halfway through the route. It'll save valuable time better spent hiking.

After a couple of stream crossings, the Middle Fork Trail reaches a shallow set of hot springs pools along the east shore of the river just below the wilderness boundary at 0.5 mile. The temperature is pleasant for soaking

Middle Fork–Gilita

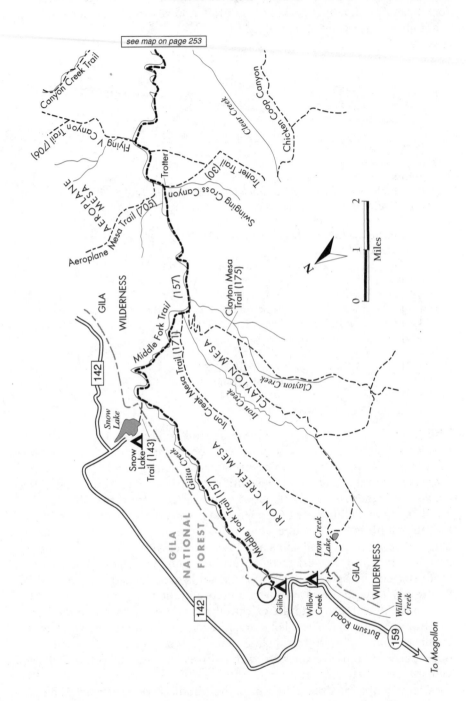

see map on page 253

Canyon Creek Trail

Flying V Canyon Trail (706)

Clear Creek

Chicken Coop Canyon

Trotter

Trotter Trail (30)

Swinging Cross Canyon

AEROPLANE MESA

Aeroplane Mesa Trail (705)

Clayton Mesa Trail (175)

Miles

GILA WILDERNESS

Middle Fork Trail/ (157)

(171)

CLAYTON MESA

Clayton Creek

142

Iron Creek

Iron Creek Mesa Trail (171)

Snow Lake

Snow Lake Trail (143)

IRON CREEK MESA

Gilita Creek

Middle Fork Trail (157)

GILA NATIONAL FOREST

Iron Creek Lake

GILA WILDERNESS

142

Gilita

Willow Creek

Willow Creek

Bursum Road

159

To Mogollon

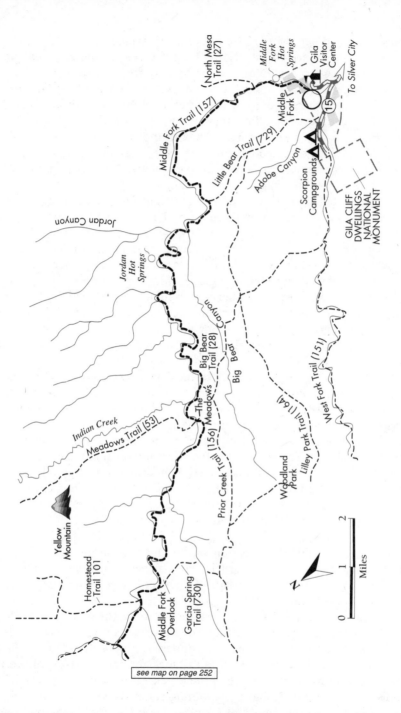

see map on page 252

and the next hot springs is a long, slow 8 miles upstream. A rugged canyon pocketed with several large alcoves previews more to come as the trail intersects the North Mesa Trail at 1.5 miles. Continue left through a diverse riparian forest overseen by cliffs rising more than 400 feet on the left (west) side. Crossings average six per mile and are typically marked with a rock cairn and good campsite. Huge white-trunk sycamores are especially distinctive in the mixed forest. By the time you reach mile 5 the canyon has attained its most spectacular, neck-craning dimensions thus far. Great columns, spires and cliffs of dark Gila conglomerate seem to snarl above the river like sharks' teeth guarding the inner sanctum of the Middle Fork. Little Bear Canyon enters from the left (south) at mile 6 with a trail signed for the TJ Corral, an easy 4 miles compared with the slow 6 miles you've already slogged. You'll find the going slow, not only because of countless and constant stream crossings but also because you'll want to stop often to savor the majesty of these wild, rugged surroundings.

Some of the highest cliffs define the right (east) side of the river just above the spacious flat near the mouth of Little Bear Canyon. A geologic wonderland of spires, hoodoos, goblins, balancing rocks, and caves marks the next 2 miles, along with constant river crossings, to the popular Jordan Hot Springs. The highest of the three large crystal clear pools is also the largest and deepest, with the warmest soaking temperature. The springs are perched about 50 feet above the river on the right (east) side of the canyon. Look for a well-worn trail. To protect the wild quality of this special place, the Forest Service prohibits camping within 400 yards of the springs.

As you continue upstream the canyon deepens further with soaring cliffs, jagged minarets, and freestanding columns. Fish dart in dark, mysterious pools closed in by walls perfectly framed by sweeping sycamores and cottonwoods. The deepest pools are on the outer curves of the endless river bends. The trail tends to be well defined along higher benches but often disappears across gravel bars. Scan the far bank for the trail and take the path of least resistance to it. Don't even try to pinpoint your location in this serpentine chasm. Throw speed to the wind and revel in the joy of this ever-changing journey. The trail loses itself near sizable warm ponds just below the Meadows. Upon reaching the larger pond, cross on the beaver dam to pick up the old trail on the right (north) side of the river. The trail climbs through rocky woods about 0.2 mile to a signed junction with the Meadows Trail (53) that heads uphill to the north 5.5 miles to Double Springs. Continue left to the expansive opening of the Meadows at mile 14.6. The large, grassy flat is surrounded by brushy, rock-strewn hills that rise more than 1,000 feet to distant rims. Clumps of giant pine trees shade perfect campsites near the stream.

The canyon takes on a gentler character above the Meadows. Cliffs are still imposing but appear as distant outcrops on sloping brushy hillsides. The riparian forest is dominated by ponderosa pine. After 0.7 mile the canyon again closes in with vertical fault block formations rising above deep pools, alternating from one side to the other. After another 2 miles the trail climbs 80 feet above a chasm containing stairstep waterfalls and emerald pools just beyond the mouth of Chicken Coop Canyon. Large rock monuments continue to mark the rough, rocky, but well-defined trail. Formations of every imaginable shape dot the slopes on both sides.

At mile 17.5 the trail passes through a pine park guarded by the longest continuous cliff wall thus far, extending more than 0.3 mile on the left (south) side. The sheer face towers at least 400 vertical feet. River crossings as well as established campsites become less frequent above Chicken Coop Canyon with long stretches of soft dirt trail across open pine benches. This marvelous canyon could be hiked every year of one's life, and every time would be like the first time. Every river bend presents a whole different world. Around mile 21 the trail climbs steeply 50 feet where a long stretch of the river is oriented north to south. After another 0.5 mile, note the signed junction of the Garcia Spring Trail (730) at the end of a long ridge on the south side across from a huge, fractured rock wall.

For the most dramatic trail-accessible view of the Middle Fork gorge, drop your pack and follow the Garcia Spring Trail southward. After about 1.5 miles the trail crosses just above a prominent rock ledge. Cliffs drop from the ledge 500 vertical feet to the Middle Fork with volcanic buttresses rising hundreds of feet higher to the mesa of Yellow Mountain across the river.

Continuing up the Middle Fork the canyon becomes more subdued but is still rugged above Clear Creek. The "Homestead" Trail (101) meets the Middle Fork directly across from the mouth of Clear Creek and 0.3 mile above the Garcia Spring Trail junction. This faint path makes a relatively easy ascent to the north rim. The next 1.5-mile stretch up to Canyon Creek is pocketed with a wonderland of stream-level grottoes. The trail climbs high on a steep west-facing slope dotted with hoodoos and beehive-shaped formations. In places the trail is faint and brushy from low use with fewer rock cairns.

The Canyon Creek Trail (31) leads north 4.3 miles to private land on Forest Road 917. The bouldery stream of Canyon Creek flows year-round but goes beneath a wide, sandy wash in the lower end only to emerge near the canyon mouth. The Canyon Creek Trail largely coincides with the rocky streambed and is difficult to follow in spots. After 0.8 mile, the trail enters the most narrow and rugged part of the canyon, followed by a pleasant 0.5 mile along pine benches. The lightly used trail reaches an open grassy meadow with gigantic cottonwood trees at 1.3 miles. This is a good turn-around point for a 2.5-mile round-trip leg stretcher from the river.

Above Canyon Creek rocky spires rise from deep pools. The trail crosses a grassy flat and then traverses rocky stream bottoms as the rough-hewn canyon again closes in. River crossings are tricky here because of the incredibly slippery surface of polished bedrock. When crossing look for gravel bottoms or passages across broken rock. A long, easy length of trail occurs 1.5 miles above Canyon Creek across a south-side pine park. Massive cliffs pocketed with caves define the opposite side of the canyon. Between miles 25 and 26 the river has carved grottoes and overhangs that likely provided shelter for aboriginal hunters. At mile 27 the mouth of Flying V Canyon meets the most extensive meadows on the Middle Fork, surrounded by a distant rim of low pine-clad ridges. This vast, grassy flat is a good place to see elk as they head for water in the evening. Old cabin ruins at the east entrance to Flying V Canyon tell a silent tale of the past. From the signed junction in the meadow, the Flying V Canyon Trail (706) heads 5 miles north to the main FR 142, although the upper segment is lightly used and hard to locate from the road.

The next stretch of trail to Trotter is the best yet, with only one crossing in 1.3 miles to the junction with Aeroplane Mesa Trail (705) next to a huge alcove. The good Aeroplane Mesa Trail climbs steeply 1 mile north to the mesa and then another 3 miles to the trailhead on FR 142. (See Hike 78 for details about this fast, direct route into the upper Middle Fork.)

Continue left on the Middle Fork Trail to Trotter Meadow, which is reached after another 0.2 mile at mile 28.4. The meadow is a large, open grassy flat with a mix of ponderosa pine and cottonwood. The cabin shown on the quad no longer exists. A sign at the mouth of Swinging Cross Canyon points west to Lilley Park (7.5 miles) and north on the main Middle Fork to Clayton Creek. The willow-lined stream meanders along the edge of Trotter flat with low pine hills and rock bluffs across the river in contrast to the rugged canyon downstream. The good Middle Fork Trail continues another 2.5 miles up the pleasant widening valley to Clayton Creek. There is a trail junction on each side of the gravelly streambed in a wide, grassy meadow surrounded by densely forested hills. The first trail climbs left (south) to Clayton Spring and beyond, and the second heads left to the muddy pond of Iron Creek Lake.

Stay right on the main trail toward Snow Lake. After another 0.5 mile the trail reaches another large grassy meadow containing interesting ruins of old settler cabins. Then the canyon narrows dramatically, followed by several stream crossings and intervening pine parks. Below the mouth of Gilita Creek the valley widens with extensive slopes of talus rock on both sides. The unsigned junction with the Snow Lake Trail (142) is reached at mile 34 just inside the wilderness boundary about 1 mile south of Snow Lake. Look for a cairn before crossing Gilita Creek. The Middle Fork Trail turns left here, climbing gently along a rocky pine bench above the south side of Gilita. The next 6 miles of trail, with an average elevation gain of 100 feet per mile, are lightly used and rarely maintained. There will be logs to climb over, thorny brush to avoid, and numerous crossings of the small, lovely stream, so once again it's best to not be in a hurry.

After about 2 miles the canyon deepens with higher cliffs, alcoves, and even an eroded hole-in-the-rock wall. In places, the primitive needle-cushioned trail crosses grassy flats in between dark volcanic ledges and outcrops in the steep-gradient, V-shaped valley. Large, old ponderosa pine and Douglas-fir give way to a primeval spruce-fir forest. At times the trail climbs high in rough talus rock to bypass a cliff. The Gilita forest camp and trailhead are located just outside the wilderness boundary. Despite its proximity to roads, Gilita Creek is wild and secluded enough to provide a fitting conclusion to this grand 40-mile exploration of the Middle Fork Gila River.

Options: The hike can be shortened by 5 miles and made somewhat easier by exiting to the Snow Lake Trailhead (see Hike 79). A similar possibility and distance is to hike up as far as Trotter Meadow and to then exit by way of the Aeroplane Mesa Trail to FR 142 (see Hike 78). The main option is to hike the route downstream from Gilita Creek, an equally enjoyable way to experience this untamed artery of the Gila.

61 SA Canyon

Highlights:	Narrow scenic canyon with alcoves notched into cliffs above deep pools.
Type of hike:	Out-and-back day hike.
Total distance:	2 to 6 miles.
Difficulty:	Easy.
Best months:	Year-round.
Maps:	Forest Service Gila Wilderness map (1984); Gila Hot Springs USGS quad.

Special considerations: Moderate off-trail rock scrambling and wading may be required.

Finding the trailhead: Drive north from Silver City on New Mexico Highway 15 and turn right (east) between mileposts 37 and 38 onto a gravel road signed Grapevine forest camp just before crossing the Gila River Bridge. This turnoff is also about 4 miles south of the Gila Visitor Center. Drive down the steep gravel road, turn right (southeast), and follow the road about 0.4 mile to the upper end of the Grapevine forest camp. Park before crossing the East Fork of the Gila River near the rocky unsigned entrance to SA Canyon on the immediate south.

Parking and trailhead facilities: No-fee Grapevine forest camp, vault toilets; water must be treated if taken from the East Fork Gila River; ample parking; no sign at the trailhead.

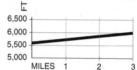

The hike: SA Canyon is a major tributary to the East Fork Gila River just above the Gila forks. It is a classic example of one of those close, easily accessible places overlooked by people camping next door or hiking to more distant spots. The surprisingly rugged canyon forms part of the Gila Wilderness boundary immediately east of NM 15. No sign or trail will lead you into the canyon, only a sense of adventure. The canyon mouth is reached from the last Grapevine campsite on the right (south). The streambed is usually dry for the first 0.3 mile, straight down from the sights and sounds of the ridgetop highway. Soon the steep-walled narrow chasm envelopes you with a feeling of remoteness and solitude. A small stream is encountered after 0.3 mile with moderate ledge and rock-hopping to a large pool at 0.4 mile. Take along wading shoes and explore this intimate canyon for as long as your energy holds out. The main branch of SA extends southeast for more than 6 miles to the Copperas Tank adjacent to NM 15. Caves, cliffs, alcoves, and deep pools await the explorer willing to trade wet feet for discovery.

Option: A long, strenuous, off-trail shuttle route up SA Canyon to the south end of the Military Trail 709 continuing to the Military Road Trailhead on NM 15 about 6 miles south of the Gila River Bridge. (See Military Trail Hike 64 for details.)

SA Canyon

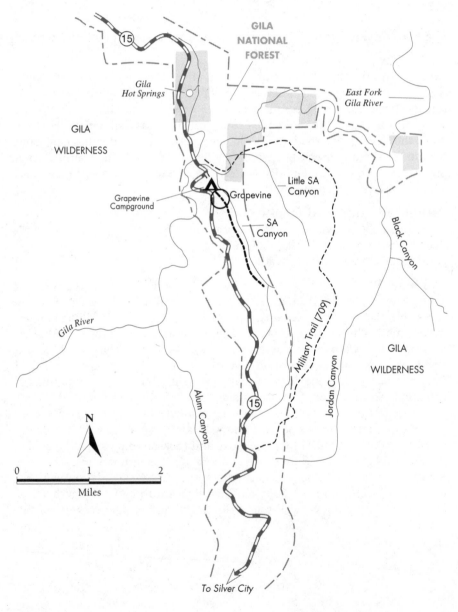

62 Lower Black Canyon

Highlights:	A day hike loop from a busy campground to a remote river canyon; vistas of East Fork cliffs.
Type of hike:	Day hike loop.
Total distance:	12.7 to 15 miles.
Difficulty:	Strenuous.
Best months:	April through November.
Maps:	Forest Service Gila Wilderness map (1984), Gila Hot Springs USGS quad.

Special considerations: Stream crossings on the East Fork. Long, dry stretch (4.2 miles) without water. Exposure to storms and lightning on ridge. Off-trail segments.

Finding the trailhead: To reach the Grapevine forest camp, drive 4 miles south of the Gila Visitor Center on New Mexico Highway 15. Turn left (east) at the Grapevine forest camp immediately south of the Gila River Bridge, between mileposts 38 and 37. From Silver City, drive 37.5 miles north on NM 15 to the Grapevine forest camp and Gila River Trailhead. Turn right (east). From either direction, continue 0.1 mile on the improved gravel road to the river's edge; turn right (east) at the sign for the campground. Follow the road through the campground and park before the East Fork River crossing.

Parking and trailhead facilities: There is ample undesignated parking at the no-fee campground. There is a vault toilet. Water from the East Fork must be treated. There is no signed trailhead.

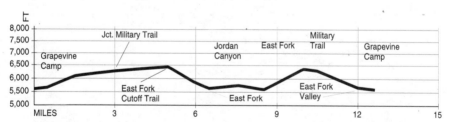

Key points:

- 0.0 Grapevine forest camp and East Fork Gila River crossing.
- 0.4 Open gate; enter private land.
- 3.0 Junction with Military Trail (709).
- 4.0 Junction with cutoff trail to East Fork valley.
- 6.6 Mouth of Black Canyon.
- 7.6 Junction with Jordan Canyon.
- 8.8 Junction with East Fork cutoff trail.
- 10.2 Junction with Military Trail (709).
- 10.7 Junction with horse trail.
- 12.2 Junction with East Fork valley road.
- 12.7 East Fork Gila River crossing and Grapevine forest camp

Lower Black Canyon

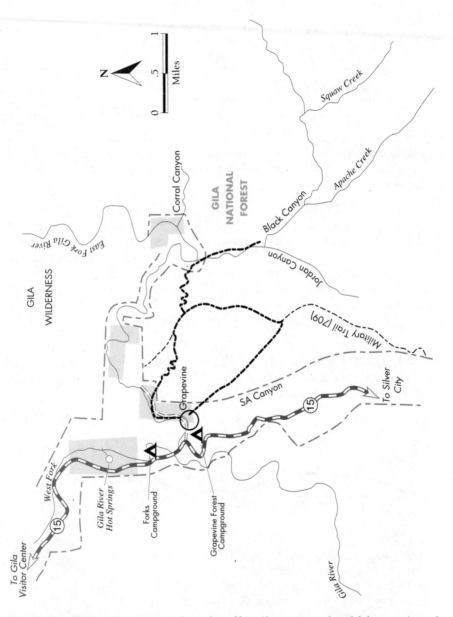

The hike: This adventure is largely off-trail, so you should be equipped with a topo map and a compass. It also cuts across corners of private property in the East Fork valley, so it is important to leave all gates as you find them and pack out all your trash.

From the East Fork at the end of the Grapevine forest camp, follow the doubletrack gravel road, crossing the river twice. Wind along the edge of

Hiking along the East Fork Gila River.

the valley, where you will enter private land. At the second open fence, turn right and take the faint-use path up the hill to the mesa top. Angle east to pick up an old wagon trail with a doubletrack path still visible in the brush and grass. When the wagon trail turns south at a cairn, continue straight up the steep slope on the game trail. The route switchbacks and climbs steadily as the dense pinyon-juniper gives way to more open grasslands near the ridgetop. Vistas of the East Fork valley are plentiful; when you reach the ridge summit, the highway can be seen to the west, two ridges away. Continue along the crest of the ridge, curving gradually southeast and getting farther away from the highway. The country is open, with only intermittent trees, so it is easy to keep your bearings. A stock fence cuts across the ridgetop shortly before you encounter the Military Trail, 3 miles from the trailhead.

Turn left (northeast) and follow the old military wagon doubletrack for 2 miles as it traces the crest of the ridge above the East Fork. After 2 miles, a heavily used horse trail goes sharply downhill to the right (east) to the valley of the East Fork. This junction might be marked with a log across the Military Trail to divert traffic to the East Fork cutoff. Turn onto the unsigned, rocky horse trail and follow it down the steep hillside. It reaches an intermediate bench where it bends southward and then drops through another steep, rocky section in a ravine to reach the East Fork bottom, 1.4 miles from the turnoff on the ridge. There are stock fences with gates in the bottom; be sure they are closed and latched after you pass.

Continue south along the oxbow bend of the East Fork to the mouth of Black Canyon. The trail up the canyon begins at a stock gate on the east side of the perennial stream. The trail crosses the stream repeatedly as it wanders up the wide riparian bottom of cottonwood, cedar, pine, and juniper. The trail is no longer maintained by the Forest Service, so it is lightly used and primitive but is kept open by cattle and horse parties. The drainage is bound by distant rock bluffs. Occasionally a low cliff is undercut by the stream. You will reach the mouth of Jordan Canyon after about a mile, at a sharp left turn of Black Canyon. There is a dense riparian forest at the junction. Jordan is trail-less and invites adventuresome explorers to investigate. The use trail in Black Canyon continues 1.5 miles farther to the junction with Apache Creek. When your time or energy is dwindling, it is time to turn around and retrace your steps to the East Fork, and then climb the steep, rocky hillside back to the Military Trail on top.

At the Military Trail, turn right (northwest). After 0.5 mile, a well-used horse trail turns off to the left (west) where the military doubletrack continues straight and eventually fades from disuse. Take the horse trail, steeply switchbacking down the rocky hillside, crossing two benches and a faint dirt road and eventually dropping to the valley floor of the East Fork, 1.5 miles after leaving the Military Trail on the ridge. In the valley, the horse trail joins the doubletrack road to the campground. Follow it downstream in front of the private residence, pass through the two open fences, and return to the campground.

Options: This trip could be done as an overnight backpack in order to explore further up Black Canyon. Do not camp on private land in the East Fork valley. Another extension of the basic trip is to do it as a point-to-point backpack to the Rocky Canyon forest camp on FR 150 (North Star Mesa Road) on the east side of the Gila Wilderness. Hike up Black Canyon and follow Apache Creek to Big Timber Canyon. The old trail goes all the way to Brannon Park then up the Rocky Canyon Trail to the campground. This 25-mile trip takes two to three days (see Hike 69 for further information).

63 Grapevine–Middle Fork

Highlights:	Loop trip in remote East Fork; winding Adobe Canyon; across North Mesa to Middle Fork and its hot spring.
Type of hike:	3- to 4-day backpacking trip; shuttle.
Total distance:	21 miles.
Difficulty:	Strenuous.
Best months:	April through November.
Maps:	Forest Service Gila Wilderness map (1984); Gila Hot Springs and Burnt Corral Canyon USGS quads.

Special considerations: Stream crossings on East Fork and Middle Fork. The hike crosses private land along the East Fork. Leave all gates as you find them, and do not camp on private land. If you are hiking in a large party, contact landowners in advance (get current names and phone numbers from the visitor center).

Finding the trailhead: For the Grapevine Trailhead, drive 4 miles south of the Gila Visitor Center on New Mexico Highway 15. Turn left (east) at Grapevine forest camp immediately south of the Gila River Bridge, between mileposts 38 and 37 on NM 15. This turn is 37.5 miles north of Silver City on NM 15. Drive 0.1 mile on the improved gravel road, turning right at the sign for the campground. Follow the road through the campground. Park before the East Fork crossing.

For the exit trailhead on the Middle Fork, follow signs to the Gila Visitor Center, 0.3 north of milepost 42 on NM 15. Drive through the visitor center parking lot. Turn right at the sign for the Middle Fork Trailhead and drive 0.2 mile to the trailhead on your left above the river.

The shuttle distance is 5 miles.

Parking and trailhead facilities: At the Grapevine Trailhead, there is undesignated parking in the campground, which has a vault toilet. At the Middle Fork is limited parking and an information board but no other facilities. Camping is not permitted at the Middle Fork Trailhead.

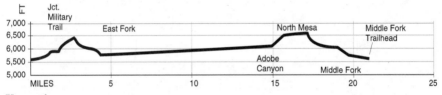

Key points:

    0.0 Grapevine forest camp and East Fork crossing.
    0.5 Horse trail to mesa.
    2.0 Junction with Military Trail (709).
    2.5 Outfitter trail to East Fork oxbow.
    3.9 East Fork valley.
   14.9 Junction with Adobe Canyon Trail (804).
   17.0 Junction with North Mesa Trail (27).
   19.5 Middle Fork; junction with Middle Fork Trail (157).
   21.0 Middle Fork Trailhead.

The hike: From the busy Gila corridor this trip takes you into a seldom-visited region of the Gila, the East Fork. It is not easy to get to the East Fork because portions of the valley are private property. As a result, the route from Grapevine goes up and over the Military Trail (709) to avoid the ranches in the bottom.

From the river crossing at the end of the Grapevine campground, hike up the dirt doubletrack. There are two stream crossings as well as two gates. Leave all gates as you find them as country etiquette requires. Stay on the road on the stream bottom as it winds below a private home. When the road bears to the right around a bluff, watch for a well-traveled horse trail that climbs up to the right. Take this unsigned trail up 80 feet to the bench.

263

Grapevine–Middle Fork

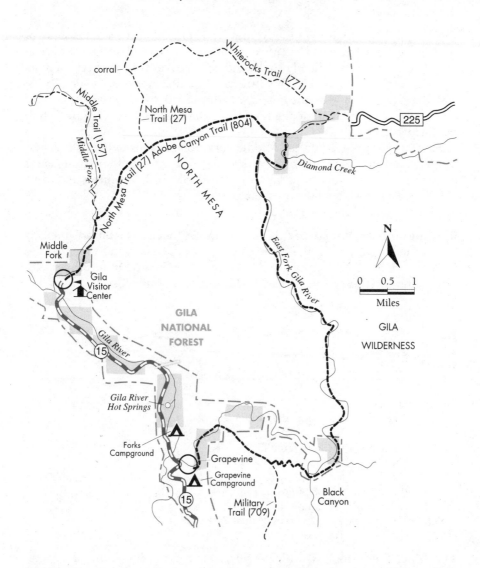

Continue on it across the bench and on up another steep slope. The trail is easy to follow on the sparsely vegetated mesa. At the top of the rise it joins the Military Trail, an old doubletrack established by the army 100 years ago.

Go southeast on the Military Trail, which rises along the crest of the ridge, for 0.5 mile. On your left a well-defined but unsigned trail goes sharply down the slope toward the East Fork valley. There may be a log or some other obstacle on the Military Trail to divert traffic down the outfitter trail to the East Fork. Turn left and take this steep, rocky trail down to the river. It drops sharply via switchbacks to a grassy bench, then bends right and

Hiking along the East Fork Gila River.

dives down a rugged ravine to emerge on the sandy bank of the East Fork above Black Canyon. The river bends in a dramatic oxbow here, leaving two humps of land, like a camel, on the peninsula in the middle.

The East Fork valley is broad and open, bracketed by volcanic cliffs. The river meanders from side to side, creating steep banks where it carves the sandy soil out from under the cottonwood groves. The hike upstream to Adobe Canyon involves wandering with the river, slogging through many crossings, and a bit of route finding since the river constantly remodels its bed. Pieces of trail will be visible and then will vanish where the river has modified the bank. River miles are slow miles, so allow at least two days for the hike to Adobe Canyon. The open, 100-yard-wide river bottom provides instant campsites. Toppled old cottonwoods are evidence of the strong winds that roar down the valley, so you might avoid camping beneath the big old trees if the weather is threatening.

Diamond Creek comes in from the right about half a mile below the Adobe Canyon Trail (804). The wide canyon mouth of Diamond Creek is a signal that the next sharp angle in the East Fork is the location of the Adobe Canyon exit. The Adobe Canyon Trail sneaks off to the left without any sign or fanfare; it is easy to hike on by it and end up at the Trails End Ranch, 2 miles farther upstream. This 4-mile extension of the hike should be avoided if possible.

Adobe Canyon and the subsequent hike across North Mesa go much faster than the river bottom journey did. The harder surface is a delight after the soft sand, and the trail is relatively straight instead of wandering. Your feet will also enjoy this interlude of dryness. In Adobe Canyon the trail is on the right side of the rocky canyon outwash, shifting to the left at a drift fence across the canyon at 0.1 mile. Climb the fence and continue up the canyon 0.8 mile to an open drift fence and a collection of rusty old stock watering equipment. There's a spring in a cleft in the west canyon wall, the source of stock water years ago. A cairn marks the trail's left turn to go up to the mesa. The steep trail climbs 400 feet in 0.7 mile to arrive at the mesa's edge. While you recover from the climb, saunter 50 feet over to the right to a rise. There's a smashing view across North Mesa to the Whiterocks, 2 miles away as the raven flies, rising like an apparition from the pinyon-juniper greenery of the mesa.

Return to the main trail and follow its gently undulating path across the mesa, by North Tank near an old corral, to the junction with the North Mesa Trail on the western edge, above the Middle Fork valley. From here it is 2.5 miles down to the Middle Fork (and 3 miles up to the Whiterocks if you decide to include them in your trip). The North Mesa Trail goes over the edge, through a stock fence, and down the steep edge of the mesa. There are magnificent views of the rolling upper benches of the Middle Fork valley. Evening is an excellent time to see deer and elk on the grassy meadows or along the forested edge.

The trail takes you southward across the lower bench, rolling through rutted ravines. Finally it drops sharply 200 feet down the east wall of the Middle Fork, arriving at the stream bank, 1.5 miles above the trailhead by the visitor center. There are several campsites at the trail junction.

As you turn left to go down the river, you have several crossings before arriving at the trailhead. You might want to stop at the Middle Fork hot springs on the river's east bank half a mile above the trailhead. Avoid getting the hot water on your face. There is a danger of meningitis from the amoeba *Naegleria fowleri* that lurks in warm water and can enter your brain through your nose.

Beyond the hot springs the canyon narrows and the cliffs soar skyward, providing a very different river experience from the canyon of the East Fork. After the final crossing the trail climbs the south slope to the parking area near the visitor center.

Options: Extend your trip with an out-and-back ramble up Black Canyon at the southern end of the East Fork oxbow (see Hike 62 for details). To visit Whiterocks, you can continue up the East Fork to the Whiterocks Trail (771), which climbs to North Mesa near Cement Canyon. In addition to the volcanic tuff formation along the trail on the edge of the canyon above the East Fork, this trail goes to the Whiterocks (4 miles); after exploring the mounds of tuff, continue west to the North Mesa Trail, which you take south to the Middle Fork (see Hike 71).

64 Military Trail

Highlights: Solitude of lightly used ridge (except in hunting season); vistas of eastern Gila Wilderness to the Black Range of the Aldo Leopold Wilderness; dramatic canyon walls of the East Fork.
Type of hike: Day hike; shuttle.
Total distance: 8 miles.
Difficulty: Moderate.
Best months: April through November.
Maps: Forest Service Gila Wilderness map (1984); Copperas Peak and Gila Hot Springs USGS quads.

Special considerations: No water available on trail until the first East Fork crossing (7.8 miles). Wear orange during hunting season. Like all ridge trails, the Military Trail should be avoided in summer electrical storms. There are two wet-foot crossings of the East Fork.

Finding the trailhead: To reach the entrance trailhead, drive 32 miles north of Silver City on New Mexico Highway 15 to the trailhead on the right (east) side of the highway. From the Gila Visitor Center, drive 10 miles south on NM 15 to turn left (east) to the Military Trail (709) trailhead. From the highway the trailhead is 0.1 mile on the left via the improved gravel road.

For the exit trailhead at the Grapevine forest camp, drive 5.5 miles north on NM 15 to turn right (east) at sign immediately before the Gila River Bridge. The turn is between mileposts 37 and 38 on the highway. Descend on the improved gravel road 0.1 mile to campground sign; turn right (east), following the road through the campground to the East Fork, 0.3 mile from the highway.

The shuttle distance is about 6 miles.

Parking and trailhead facilities: At the Military Trail Trailhead is a large gravel parking area. Camping is permitted, but there is no water. There is an information board, although the trail itself is not signed. At the Grapevine Trailhead, there is a campground (no fee) with vault toilets. Water is available from the river (to be treated). There is plenty of parking both in the campground and at the East Fork Trailhead immediately adjacent to the camping area.

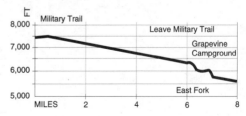

Key points:
- 0.0 Military Trail Trailhead (709) on NM 15.
- 0.2 Gila Wilderness boundary.
- 6.0 Leave the Military Trail; horse trail to East Fork.
- 7.8 East Fork crossing.
- 8.0 Grapevine forest camp.

Military Trail

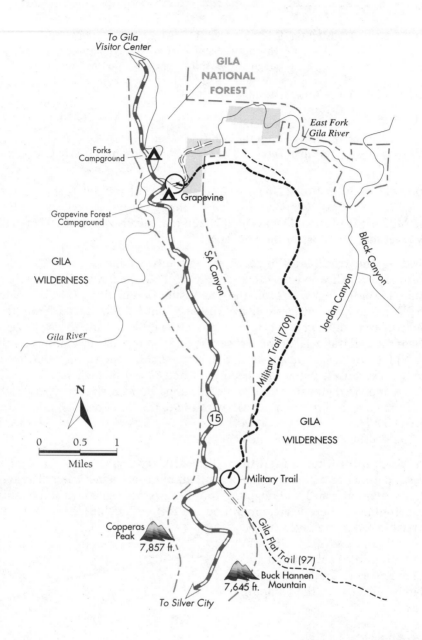

To Gila
Visitor Center

GILA
NATIONAL
FOREST

East Fork
Gila River

Forks
Campground

Grapevine

Grapevine Forest
Campground

GILA

WILDERNESS

SA Canyon

Jordan Canyon

Black Canyon

Gila River

Military Trail (709)

N

0   0.5   1
Miles

15

GILA

WILDERNESS

Military Trail

Gila Flat Trail (97)

Copperas
Peak
7,857 ft.

Buck Hannen
Mountain
7,645 ft.

To Silver City

The hike: This outing is excellent for a cool spring day. The pinyon-juniper forest along the ridge provides a bit of shade yet allows excellent vistas of the surrounding countryside. In the fall, likewise, the scenery is outstanding. The ridge, however, is heavily used during hunting season, so it is advisable to wear hunter's orange to make yourself conspicuous in the heavy cover.

For most of this hike you follow the old Army doubletrack built in the late nineteenth century to supply military outposts on the Gila River. As a consequence, this is a rocky trail that stays on the crest of the ridge. The Army wagons must have had to travel very slowly, and carrying gunpowder or other explosives must have been nerve-racking. A bent piece of an iron wagon rim lying along the track attests to the arduous nature of the journey. Side trails are numerous, created by cattle and hunters, but the doubletrack is persistent and always clear on the ground.

The Military Trail (709) does not actually start at the trailhead—it is 0.2 mile to the north. From the parking area, follow the path beneath the power line right-of-way leading north. At 0.2 mile the utility poles turn northwest at an open stock gate where the Military Trail begins. Turn right through the fenceline, which is also the wilderness boundary. The 100-year-old doubletrack takes you up to the high point on the ridge, then straight along the descending crest between SA and Jordan Canyons. The rocky pathway makes for slow hiking in the first third of the trip. The forest gives way to the more open grassy ridge as the elevation drops below 7,000 feet. There are scenic detours to overlooks of Jordan Canyon created by curious hunters and hikers; the Military Trail continues its track toward the East Fork valley.

At mile 6 there is a decisive fork in the trail, with the military doubletrack continuing north and a more heavily used trail descending to the left (west). The old doubletrack leads to private land along the East Fork and hasn't been used for many years. The more dominant horse trail on the left bypasses the private inholdings along the river valley, and will take you to the Grapevine forest camp. Turn left on the rocky trail to the west. It switchbacks steeply down the hillside, crosses two benches and a dirt doubletrack and then drops again to the valley of the East Fork. In the valley it joins the dirt road that leads left (west) to the Grapevine camp. Stay on the road through the private land along the river. There are two crossings of the East Fork before the trailhead at the campground; both are gravel-bottomed, low-water crossings.

Option: After embarking on the Military Trail you can take SA Canyon back to the Grapevine forest camp. This is an arduous outing, requiring a map and a compass. Numerous game and cattle paths lead to SA Canyon along the ridge, 1.5 miles from the trailhead, but this is an off-trail adventure from the ridge all the way down SA to the campground on the East Fork (see Hike 61 for details).

65 Gila Flat

Highlights:	Ashflow tuff formations; panoramic views in the lower (southern) stretch; solitude in a portion of the wilderness that is lightly visited (except during the fall hunting season).
Type of hike:	Day hike; shuttle.
Total distance:	9.8 miles.
Difficulty:	Moderate.
Best months:	March through November.
Maps:	Forest Service Gila Wilderness map (1984); Copperas Peak and North Star Mesa USGS quads.

Special considerations: No pumpable water. Slow, rocky trail in places.

Finding the trailheads: Military Trail and Gila Flat (97) Trailheads: Drive 32 miles north of Silver City on New Mexico Highway 15 to the trailhead turnoff on the right (east). From the Gila Visitor Center drive 10 miles south on NM 15 and turn left (east) to the trailhead. Bear right at the corral and drive 0.4 mile on a rough four-wheel-drive road to the signed trailhead for the Gila Flat Trail (97).

Exit (south) trailhead for the Military Road Trail (96): From the junction of NM 15 and NM 35 drive 6 miles east on NM 35 to a sign for the turnoff to trail 96 on your left (north) at milepost 21.5. A short dirt road leads to the trailhead just north of the highway.

The shuttle driving distance between trailheads is about 14 miles.

Parking and trailhead facilities: Military Trail and Gila Flat Trailheads: limited parking at signed trailhead with a turnaround, undeveloped campsites with no water, and no other facilities.

Military Road (96) Trailhead (south): limited parking at signed trailhead, no camping, water, or other facili-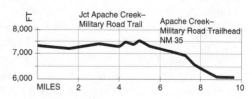
ties. The nearest public campgrounds are at Lake Roberts 1.5 miles west on NM 35 and at the no-fee Sapillo forest camp 1 mile east on NM 35

Key points:

0.0	Trailhead for Military Road and Gila Flat Trails (97).
4.0	Junction with Apache Creek Trail (96) and fenced stock pond.
5.7	Gated corral.
9.8	Military Road Trail (96) exit on NM 35.

The hike: A north-to-south direction with a mostly downhill route is recommended for this long shuttle hike. The rewards include scenic views into Railroad and Rocky Canyons and northeast to the distant Black Range. Carry plenty of water on this high, dry mesa-ridge excursion. The trailhead sign

Gila Flat

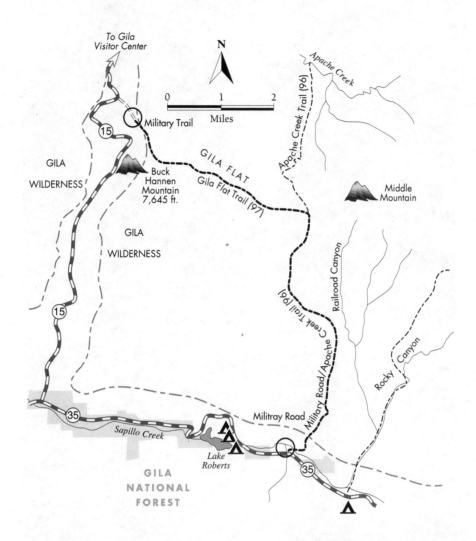

To Gila
Visitor Center

N

0   1   2
Miles

15

Military Trail

GILA
WILDERNESS

GILA FLAT

Gila Flat Trail (97)

Buck
Hannen
Mountain
7,645 ft.

GILA

WILDERNESS

15

Apache Creek

Apache Creek Trail (96)

Middle
Mountain

Railroad Canyon

Apache Creek Trail (96)

Rocky Canyon

Military Road/Apache

35

Sapillo Creek

Militray Road

Lake
Roberts

GILA
NATIONAL
FOREST

35

points south to NM 35, 9.8 miles away. The trail immediately enters the wilderness and is barricaded to prevent illegal entry by off-road vehicles. At first the historic Military Road is evident with a good trail surface thanks to removal of the rough volcanic rocks. The trail gently climbs and drops to the north slope of prominent Buck Hannen Mountain (7,645 feet). After following a rocky ridge, the trail passes by a small stock pond on the right (south) at 1.4 miles. Gila Flat is mantled with pinyon pine, alligator juniper, and a few clumps of ponderosa pine. The trail alternates from remnants of the old wagon road and a singletrack trail to smooth dirt surfaces and a rocky way. A stock fence parallels the trail on the left (north) side. Signs of coyote, mountain lion, and black bear are abundant.

The Military Road Trail (97) near Buck Hannen Mountain is "straight as an arrow".

The only trail junction on the route is reached at 4 miles in a pine forest, by going around the left side of a fenced stock pond shown as Thirtytwo Tank on the USGS quad. This is the end of the Gila Flat Trail and the start of the south segment of the Military Road Trail (96). The sign points left to Apache Creek (3.5 miles) and right to NM 35 (6 miles). Actually the trail continues straight ahead to Apache Creek. The Military Road Trail to NM 35 turns right (south) next to a prominent blaze on a pine tree.

After climbing about 100 feet with a stock fence on the right (west) along with intermittent cow paths, the old wagon roadbed becomes more distinct. The trail continues steeply uphill and passes another fenced stock pond at mile 5.5. This may be a confusing spot. Cut around the right (west) side of the pond to pick up the wagon-road trail and stock fence on the left (east). The trail soon meets a corral. Pass through the gate on the left and continue southeast on the rocky route. Lake Roberts comes into view at mile 6 along with great vistas of the Black Range as the rocky trail makes a long descent. Another 1 to 1.5 miles brings fabulous views of Rocky Canyon, followed by an overlook into the ashflow tuff cliffs of Railroad Canyon. After descending a long ridge, the trail reaches an open, grassy flat with an old sign pointing back to Apache Creek. A use trail heads left up the draw. Continue right as the well-defined trail crosses grassy benches and the draw to a canyon opening at 9.5 miles. Turn right at the canyon mouth and follow the large rock cairns to the signed exit trailhead on the north side of the highway.

Options: Apache Creek can be explored from the junction of the Gila Flat Trail and Military Road Trail 4 miles into the hike. At first, the 3.5-mile-trail to Apache Creek is tricky to find because of a maze of cow paths. From the signed junction head straight up a shallow gully, looking for the occasional blaze on a pine tree or snag. After a gentle climb the trail gradually swings to the left (north) and down a steep grade, parallel to a stock fence on the left. From the first saddle, the Apache Creek Trail climbs a hill and then descends a long ridge northward to the midsection of Apache Creek. An unofficial and unmaintained trail continues down Apache Creek to Black Canyon. Apache Creek can thus be explored as an out-and-back hike of 7 to 10 miles round trip from Gila Flat or as part of a longer and more strenuous Black Canyon shuttle hike.

66 Purgatory Chasm

Highlights:	A broad mesa and a dramatic canyon of winding slickrock.
Type of hike:	Day hike loop.
Total distance:	2.2 miles
Difficulty:	Easy.
Best months:	Year-round.
Maps:	Forest Service Gila Wilderness map (1984); Copperas Peak USGS quad.

Special considerations: Do not take this hike during periods of intense rainfall; the canyon is susceptible to flash flooding.

Finding the trailhead: From the intersection of New Mexico Highway 15 and NM 35, 25 miles north of Silver City, turn east on NM 35 and continue 4 miles. The trailhead for Trail 779 is marked on the left (north) side of NM 35. It is opposite the Lake Roberts boat launch and picnic area.

Parking and trailhead facilities: There is a large gravel parking area just east of the trailhead sign on the gravel outwash north of the highway. There are no other trailhead facilities. The closest campgrounds are at Lake Roberts (fee) and at the Sapillo forest camp (no fee), 3 miles east of the trailhead on NM 35.

Key points:

- 0.0 Trailhead on NM 35.
- 0.4 Boundary of Gila Wilderness.
- 1.6 Head of Purgatory Chasm.
- 2.2 Trailhead on NM 35.

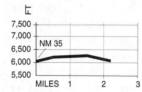

The hike: This nifty nugget of a Gila hike is a perfect combination of the various landscapes that attract visitors to this country with a sampler of a riparian woodland, a pinyon-juniper mesa grassland, and a winding canyon of sculptured rock. And it's all very convenient to a paved road. This canyon wonderland does not deserve its hellish name.

The hike starts off as a nature trail with about half a dozen signs, most touting the products of the national forest. There's an ominous "Stay on the Trail" sign where the trail splits at a Y. Bear right here, and do the loop in a counterclockwise direction, saving the best for last. The Y coincides with the wilderness boundary. The educational messages of the nature trail end.

The wilderness trail leads up to an overlook of a curving sandstone canyon. Here one wonders if this is Purgatory Chasm. Without signs or commentary, the trail winds back westward across the flat grassy mesa. Then it turns south and drops into the head of a winding slot canyon, unnamed on the topo map, as are so many wondrous places in this complicated terrain. Now you've reached the focal point of the hike.

Even in dry years there is a trickle of water in Purgatory. You will encounter

Purgatory Chasm

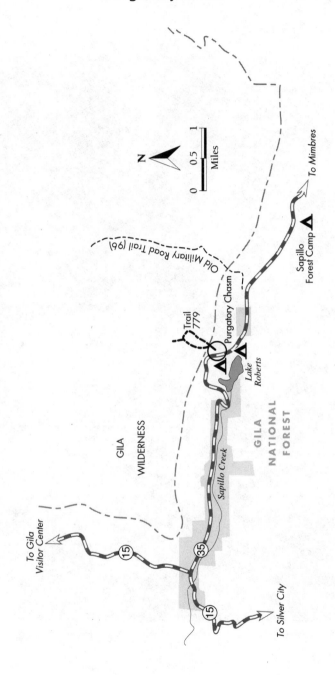

Upper Purgatory Chasm.

isolated pools in the upper canyon. The local wild creatures visit them, leaving their footprints on the sandy canyon bottom.

The journey through the canyon is enchanting. The earlier sign about staying on the trail has no meaning for this part of the trip. Explore in any direction, either on the footpath or on the canyon bottom. Do not embark on this outing if there have been recent rainstorms; the trailhead sign regarding danger of flash flooding is to be taken seriously. The canyon itself testifies to the power of water in this arid land.

You will emerge from the canyon wonderland at the junction; return to the parking area by the same trail you came in on.

67 Rocky Canyon

Highlights:	Rugged, steep-walled canyons; panoramic vistas; remote midsection; historic homestead site.
Type of hike:	Long day hike; shuttle.
Total distance:	11.3 miles.
Difficulty:	Moderate.
Best months:	April through November.
Maps:	Forest Service Gila Wilderness map (1984); North Star Mesa USGS quad.

Special considerations: There is no water throughout most of this hot, south-facing trail with the exception of lower Rocky Canyon near the beginning of the hike. Several steep, rocky trail sections.

Finding the trailhead: Rocky Canyon Trailhead: From the intersection of New Mexico Highway 15 and NM 35, 25 miles north of Silver City and 17 miles south of the Gila Visitor Center, drive 8 miles east of the intersection to the signed Trail 700 trailhead on the left (north) side of the road. The trail begins at a hiker's maze gate just north of the highway.

Rocky Canyon Forest Road Trailhead (exit): From the intersection of NM 15 and NM 35, drive east on NM 35 for 13 miles to Forest Road 150 (North Star Mesa Road) on your left (north). Signs at the junction warn of rough road and suggest a four-wheel-drive, high-clearance vehicle; there is no food, lodging, or gas for 120 miles. Actually, FR 150 is a rough, slow, improved gravel road negotiable, with care, by two-wheel-drive passenger vehicles. Drive 11 miles north on FR 150 to the Rocky Canyon forest camp and Trail 700 on your left (west).

The one-way car shuttle between the two trailheads is 19 miles, 8 of which are paved.

Parking and trailhead facilities: Rocky Canyon Trailhead: a sizable dirt parking area with no facilities, camping, or water. The closest public camping is the Sapillo forest camp directly across NM 35, 0.7 mile down a gravel road, with picnic tables and portable toilets. Water is not available at this no-fee site.

Rocky Canyon Forest Camp Trailhead: Ample trailhead parking at the campground. The no-fee forest camp has portable toilets and picnic tables but no water.

Key points:

0.0	Rocky Canyon Trail Trailhead for Rocky Canyon Trail (700).
0.7	Signed boundary of Gila Wilderness.
2.6	Trail climbs left (northwest) out of Rocky Canyon.
7.5	Cow camp/corral/lower Brannon Park.
8.3	Junction with Big Timber Trail (95) pointing toward Apache Creek.
11.0	Junction with Caves Trail (803).
11.3	Rocky Canyon Forest Camp Trailhead for Rocky Canyon Trail (700).

The hike: Rocky Canyon offers one of the better shuttle day hikes in the east end of the Gila Wilderness. Portions of the trail receive moderate use, particularly on the north end from the Rocky Canyon forest camp. Despite a mostly uphill route from south to north, this direction is recommended. The modest difference in elevation between the two trailheads of less than 2,000 feet is spread over a long distance, and you'll appreciate having the sun at your back if you take this trip during the warmer months.

The trailhead sign for the Rocky Canyon Trail (700) accurately indicates 8.3 miles to Brannon Park, which is actually the distance to the first trail junction just beyond the park, and another 3 miles to the exit trailhead on FR 150. After passing through the hiker's maze gate and bypassing a small reservoir, the signed Wilderness boundary is reached at mile 0.7. The trail follows the bottom of Rocky Canyon, well marked by rock cairns, and sometimes sidehills along forested benches. The mouth of Railroad Canyon appears on the left (northwest) around mile 1.9, inviting side exploration. The blazed trail continues up the diverse riparian bottom of Rocky Canyon with its rims of Gila conglomerate rising 200 to 300 feet in places. The tiny stream flows here beneath grassy banks early in the season.

The trail climbs northwest out of Rocky Canyon at mile 2.6 on a dividing ridge of conglomerate rock with exceptional views into both Rocky Canyon and the small side canyon on the left (west). This narrow chasm is blocked by a 10-foot pouroff 0.1 mile up. Beyond, erosion has exposed rolling mounds of gray volcanic conglomerate in contrast to caps of golden hillsides. Traces exist of an abandoned trail from this point on up the bottom of Rocky Canyon.

After leaving the canyon, Rocky Canyon Trail steadily climbs a pinyon-juniper ridge with unusually dense cholla cactus. As the mesa broadens, sign of elk increases. Cross a stock fence at mile 4.4, followed by a 400-foot drop into a ravine. Cow paths branch off from the trail. Look for rock cairns as well as tree blazes as the trail reenters the forest. After passing a muddy

Rocky Canyon

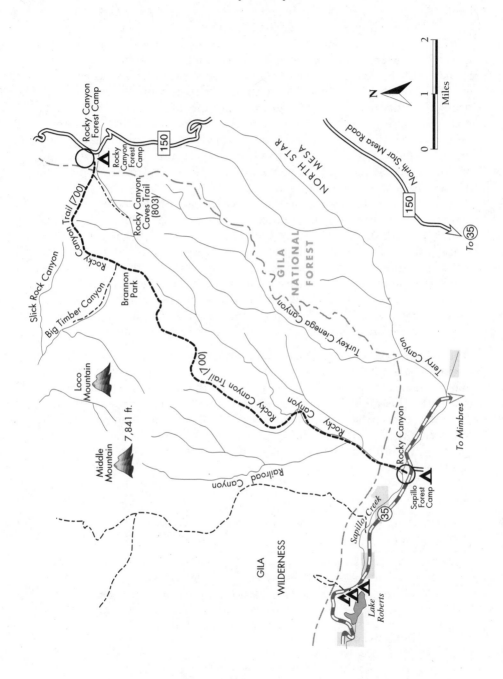

spring and several low side draws that may have early season water, the trail gradually ascends a drainage. It then steepens up the right fork to a boulder-strewn slope and onto mixed woodland underlain by exposed white bedrock. This lightly used midsection is well marked with blazes and cairns.

At mile 7.5 a cow camp with a corral and gate in a ponderosa-pine park marks the lower end of Brannon Park. This large 7,400-foot-high grassy meadow still displays some evidence of early homesteading. The trail weaves around the left (northwest) side of the park, then gently climbs a small spring-fed gully to a signed trail junction at mile 8.3. The sign reads "State Road 61, 3 miles" but has been replaced by the forest road designation for FR 150. The sign points northwest toward Big Timber Canyon indicating 4 miles to Apache Creek. In fact, the elusive Big Timber Trail is nowhere to be seen near this junction. (If you want to explore Big Timber Canyon on down to Apache Creek refer to Hike 69.)

As you hike to the northeast, the Rocky Canyon Trail becomes rocky as it gradually climbs a gully to the mixed woodland high point of the hike at 9.5 miles. After turning southeast along the ridge, the trail sidehills to the south with sweeping views into upper Rocky Canyon framed by green pine forests to infinity. Before dropping to a grassy pine flat the trail becomes rough as it plummets with a tread of loose rock. The signed junction with the Rocky Canyon Caves Trail (803) appears on the right (south) side of Rocky Canyon at mile 11. A final 0.3 mile of crossing back and forth up Rocky Canyon brings you to the forest camp and FR 150 trailhead.

Options: If time allows take an adventurous out-and-back hike up Rocky Canyon above the 2.6-mile point where the trail climbs out of the canyon. You'll find traces of the abandoned pack trail that is now little more than a cow path. This midsection of the canyon is both scenic and secluded. Big Timber Canyon (Hike 69) and the Caves (Hike 68) can also be visited as side hikes from the main shuttle route. The Rocky Canyon hike can also be enjoyed from north to south, especially if the shuttle driving direction is more compatible with your travel plans.

68 Caves

Highlights:	Unusually dense concentration of rock formations, caves, and deep alcoves, some inaccessible.
Type of hike:	Half day out-and-back.
Total distance:	2 miles.
Difficulty:	Easy.
Best months:	April through November.
Maps:	Forest Service Gila Wilderness map (1984); North Star Mesa USGS quad.

Caves

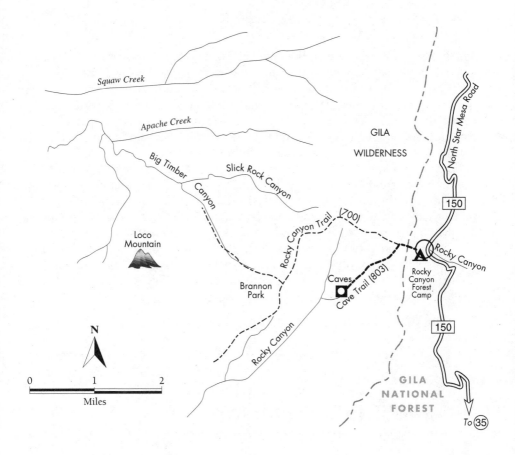

Special considerations: Early season access may be difficult on the rough, two-wheel-drive Forest Road 150 (North Star Mesa Road). Steep dropoffs adjacent to the caves.

Finding the trailhead: From the intersection of New Mexico Highway 15 and NM 35, 25 miles north of Silver City and 17 miles south of the Gila Visitor Center, drive 13 miles east on NM 35 to FR 150 (North Star Mesa Road) and turn left (north) on FR 150. Signs at the junction warn of rough road and suggest a four-wheel-drive, high-clearance vehicle; there's no food, lodging, or gas for 120 miles. Actually, this rough, slow, improved gravel road is negotiable, with care, by two-wheel-drive passenger vehicles. Drive 11 miles north on the North Star Mesa Road to the Rocky Canyon forest camp and Trail (700) signs on your left (west). The signed trailhead is located at the lower end of the forest camp.

Parking and trailhead facilities: There is plenty of room for trailhead parking at the campground. The no-fee Rocky Canyon forest camp has portable toilets and picnic tables but no water.

Key points:

0.0 Trailhead at Rocky Canyon Forest Camp and Rocky Canyon Trail (700).
0.3 Signed junction with Cave Trail (803).
1.0 Caves.

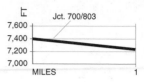

The hike: A trailhead sign at the lower end of the forest camp identifies the trail as the Rocky Canyon Trail (700). It also points to the Cave Trail (803) junction 0.3 mile beyond. Sure enough, 0.3 mile down Rocky Canyon the main trail continues straight (right) and the signed Cave Trail turns left, continuing down Rocky Canyon as it turns to the southwest. The needle-carpeted indentation of the lightly used trail is faint but marked by old tree blazes every so often as it weaves back and forth across the rocky stream bottom. If you lose the trail, simply walk down the open parklike benches that line the stream course. The first set of low overhangs and alcoves appear on the right (north) side about 0.8 mile below the trail junction. Larger cliffs, caves, and alcoves extend downstream on both sides of the canyon for another 0.3 mile. Most of the overhangs are easily accessible, but a few require moderate rock climbing and boulder-hopping skills. One could spend hours exploring the intricately pocketed rocks. Prehistoric Mimbres hunters surely took advantage of these natural shelters. Take care to leave this special place as you found it.

Option: You can extend this short day hike by continuing past the caves down Rocky Canyon.

69 Big Timber Canyon

Highlights: A remote wilderness canyon on the eastern side of the Gila.
Type of hike: Out-and-back day hike.
Total distance: 14 miles.
Difficulty: Strenuous.
Best months: April through November (depending on snowfall).
Maps: Forest Service Gila Wilderness map (1984); North Star Mesa USGS quad.

Special considerations: Forest Road 150 (North Star Mesa Road) may be blocked by snow into the spring. Seasonal washouts also make the road impassable until the road crew arrives with the machinery. Call the Gila Wilderness Ranger District to find out if the road is open to Rocky Canyon forest camp.

Finding the trailhead: From the New Mexico Highway 15/NM 35 intersection, 25 miles north of Silver City and 17 miles south of the Gila Visitor Center, drive east 13 miles on NM 35 to FR 150 (North Star Mesa Road) on your left (north). Signs at the junction warn of a rough road and suggest a four-wheel-drive, high-clearance vehicle; there's no food, lodging, or gas for 120 miles. FR 150 is a rough, slow, improved gravel road, negotiable with care by two-wheel-drive passenger vehicles. Drive 11 miles north on North Star Mesa Road to Rocky Canyon forest camp and Trail 700 signs on your left. Turn in here, at the Rocky Canyon forest camp.

Parking and trailhead facilities: There is a large gravel and grass parking area at the trailhead. Rocky Canyon forest camp (no fee) has portable toilets and picnic tables. There is no water.

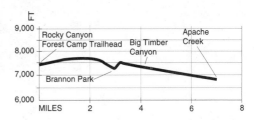

Key points:

    0.0   Trailhead at Rocky Canyon forest camp.
    0.2   Turnoff to the Caves.
    3.0   Brannon Park; junction with Big Timber Trail (95) to Apache Creek.
    7.0   Confluence of Big Timber and Apache Creeks.

The hike: While the trail to Brannon Park has moderate traffic during the busy summer and fall seasons, you can be ensured of solitude down Big Timber Canyon. This remote canyon leads to Apache Creek, and from there you can hike down Black Canyon to the East Fork of the Gila for a longer backpacking trip. Big Timber Canyon is an entry into a wilderness wonderland.

At the west end of the campground, pick up the trail to Brannon Park and follow it up out of the canyon to the south-facing slope of pinyon-juniper. Quickly you climb to the high point of the hike (7,720 feet) on the ridge; from there it is a long, rocky slope to the intersection in Brannon Park. The Big Timber sign clearly states that the trail to Apache Creek deadends in 4 miles; this kind of misinformation discourages traffic down Big Timber, keeping the canyon pristine. The lack of traffic has also caused the trail from Brannon Park to vanish, lost in a maze of cattle tracks.

From the trail sign, go northwest of the signpost to the stock fence, about 0.2 mile to the west. The fence runs north over the ridge and drops into the head of the Big Timber drainage. Follow the fence until you encounter a streambed, about 0.4 mile from the junction. Follow the streambed, eventually crossing the fenceline, and you will pick up traces of an old trail, both the groove on the earth and the weeping blazes. Make a mental note of the route for your return trip.

By about 0.5 mile down the drainage, water seeps create pools in the main creek bed; water is available in Big Timber even in a dry year. The old trail becomes easier to find the farther down the canyon you go. The Big Timber valley is narrow enough to keep the trail near the creek. The tinkling water in the creek is the only noise in the stillness of the remote canyon. We ran into some wranglers out looking for their cattle in early spring, and they were astonished to see anyone in the valley.

Big Timber Canyon

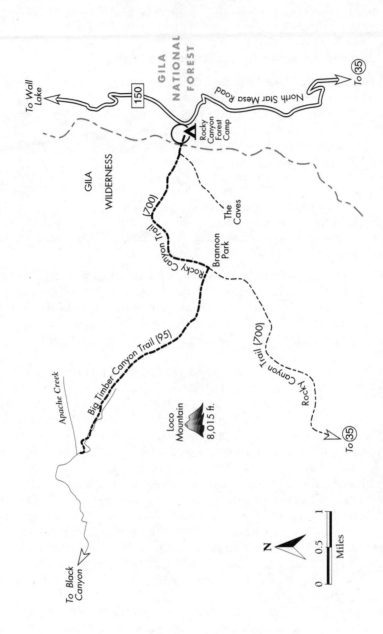

The faint Big Timber Canyon Trail marked by an old blaze in a pine tree.

The trail goes all the way to Apache Creek, where you can continue your exploration if time permits. Then return the way you came, taking care to follow the main stream channel all the way to the stock fence at the head of the drainage before angling right along the fenceline to return to the junction at Brannon Park. From here it's a mellow roll up the ridge and back to the campground by the same route you came in.

Options: The old topo map refers to the Big Timber Trail as the Brannon Park Trail; it starts down at the mouth of Apache Canyon. For a longer outing you can therefore follow the trail all the way through Black Canyon to the East Fork Gila. From there, hike over to the Grapevine campground and trailhead (see Hike 62) for a two- to three-day, 25-mile backpack adventure.

70 Upper Black Canyon

Highlights: A primitive path winding along a pleasant babbling brook in gentle terrain nestled in a remote canyon.
Type of hike: Out-and-back day hike.
Total distance: 8.6 miles.
Difficulty: Moderate.
Best months: May through November.
Maps: Forest Service Gila Wilderness map (1984); Middle Mesa USGS quad.

Special considerations: High water can make the lower canyon gorge impassable. During early spring, check with the Forest Service on the condition of Forest Road 150 (North Star Mesa Road).

Finding the trailhead: From the New Mexico Highway 15/NM 35 intersection, 25 miles north of Silver City and 17 miles south of the Gila Visitor Center, drive 13 miles east on NM 35 to FR 150 (North Star Mesa Road) on your left (north). Signs at the junction warn of rough road and suggest a four-wheel-drive, high-clearance vehicle; there is no food, lodging, or gas for 120 miles. Actually, FR 150 is a rough, slow, improved gravel road, negotiable, with care, by two-wheel-drive passenger vehicles. Drive 20 miles north on FR 150 to the unsigned Black Canyon forest camp. Turn left (west) at the pond. Pass by the upper forest camp and continue 0.5 mile to the lower forest camp at the end of the road in a grassy meadow. There's a steep stream crossing between the two forest camps. You may wish to park before crossing and begin the hike from there.

Parking and trailhead facilities: There is plenty of room for parking along with portable toilets and no-fee campsites. The only available water (to be treated) is from Black Canyon Creek.

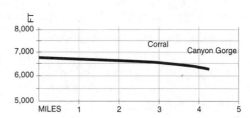

Key points:
0.0   Lower Black Canyon Forest Camp and trailhead for Black Canyon Trail (94).
3.0   Corral.
4.3   Canyon gorge.

The hike: This mellow east-side entry point into the Gila Wilderness provides an increasingly rugged and remote canyon experience with each passing mile. The unsigned trail begins from the lower right (north) side of the forest camp meadow. A somewhat confusing sign pointing in the wrong direction to "Forest Trail" should be ignored. The Gila Wilderness boundary is reached after 0.1 mile. For the first 0.7 mile the soft dirt trail stays on the north side of the stream in the pleasant pine-forested valley. The trail then

286

Upper Black Canyon

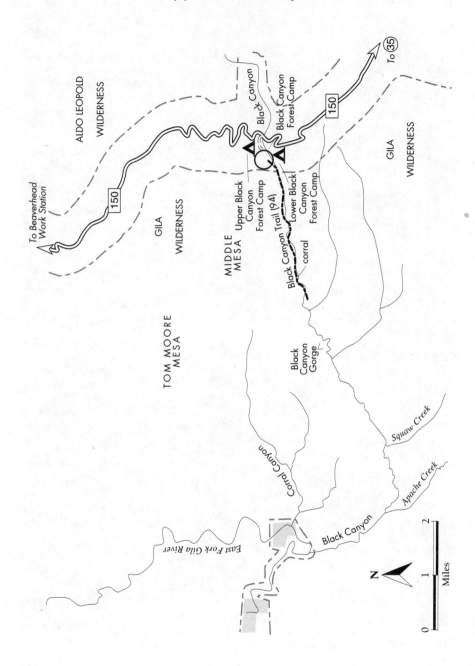

To 35

150

ALDO LEOPOLD WILDERNESS

Black Canyon

Black Canyon Forest Camp

150

GILA WILDERNESS

To Beaverhead Work Station

GILA WILDERNESS

Upper Black Canyon Forest Camp

Lower Black Canyon Forest Camp

MIDDLE MESA

Black Canyon Trail (94)

corral

TOM MOORE MESA

Black Canyon Gorge

Squaw Creek

Apache Creek

Corral Canyon

East Fork Gila River

Black Canyon

N

0   1   2
Miles

Hiking down the upper reaches of Black Canyon.

crosses the creek repeatedly as the valley narrows. Remnants of the brushy old pack trail are sometimes lost in washouts or intermingled with old cow paths. Several huge gravel fans meet the canyon bottom from the right (north) side. There are no rock cairns and only a few tree blazes between miles 1 and 3.

After 3 miles, note an old corral on the north side as the valley opens to a grassy flat. This is close to the end of the Black Canyon Trail (94) as depicted on the Gila Wilderness Map. Ironically, the trail actually improves beyond the corral. A major side canyon enters from the left (south) at mile 3.4. The canyon deepens with higher dark walls, but grassy benches alternating along the rocky stream allow easy hiking for another mile to the upper end of a narrow dead end gorge. From here the abandoned Black Canyon pack trail climbs steeply up the left (south) slope gaining 250 feet in 0.2 mile, then drops and climbs in and out of a ravine before descending to the canyon floor after another 0.5 mile. The upper end of the gorge is a good out-and-back day hike destination. The return back up Black Canyon is like an entirely different route. You'll find trail segments you missed on the way down and every turn will present a new canyon vista, from cottonwood groves in meadows to rock slides to interesting volcanic rock formations.

Option: The trail down Black Canyon below the corral is no longer an official, maintained Forest Service trail. In places, brush, debris and rockfall obscure the remnants of the old trail. After climbing up and around the gorge between miles 4 and 5 it is still possible to hike down the canyon all the way to the East Fork of the Gila River. This strenuous route of about 13 miles to the East Fork is best accomplished as an overnight backpack shuttle. See Hike 62 for information about the route from the East Fork to the exit trailhead at the Grapevine forest camp.

71 Trails End–Whiterocks Loop

Highlights:	Views of vast canyons and cliffs in lightly used area of wilderness; explore exotic formations of white volcanic tuff.
Type of hike:	Day hike; loop.
Total distance:	12.9 miles.
Difficulty:	Moderate.
Best months:	March through November.
Maps:	Forest Service Gila Wilderness map (1984); Burnt Corral Canyon USGS quad.

Special considerations: Wet-foot crossings on the East Fork. Long, dry stretches on North Mesa. Forest Road 150 (North Star Mesa Road) may be accessible only from the north, via Wall Lake, until late spring.

Finding the trailhead: To reach the Trails End Trailhead, from New Mexico Highway 35 drive 32 miles north on FR 150 (North Star Mesa Road, improved gravel) to turn left (west) onto FR 225. From where the pavement ends at Wall Lake to the north it is 7 miles south on FR 150 to the FR 225 intersection. Turn west on FR 225, an improved gravel road, and drive 5.5 miles. The trailhead is on the red earth mesa above the East Fork, 0.5 mile before the Trails End Ranch gate. There is a pullout on the right (west) side of FR 225.

Parking and trailhead facilities: The trailhead has a large parking area but no other facilities. Camping is not permitted. The closest public land is a mile east of the junction of FR 150 and 225, near the trailhead for Diamond Creek Trail (40) into the Aldo Leopold Wilderness.

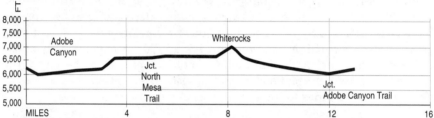

Key points:

   0.0   Trails End Trailhead and Adobe Canyon Trail (804).
   0.5   Junction with Whiterocks Trail (771).
   5.1   Junction with North Mesa Trail (27).
   7.7   Junction with Whiterocks Trail (771).
   8.1   Whiterocks, north of the trail.
 12.4   Junction with Adobe Canyon Trail (804).
 12.9   Trails End Trailhead.

The hike: This day hike loop begins at the new trailhead above the East Fork. From this vantage point you can view the spectacular cliffs of the East Fork valley and the walls of Cement Canyon to the northeast. You also have a preview of the trail stretching over the bench and down to the banks of the East Fork. Follow the earth pathway, marked with cairns, downward. The trail crosses the road at the ranch gate near the fenced family cemetery, and continues across the bench and down the bluff to the East Fork bottom. A conspicuous cairn marks the trail at the foot of the bluff for the return to the trailhead.

    Under normal conditions, the stream crossings on the East Fork are not challenging, but the knee-deep stream requires appropriate footwear. Just beyond the first crossing is the junction with the Whiterocks Trail (771). For a quick out-and-back trip to the Whiterocks formation, you can take this route, a 9-mile round trip. For the longer loop, continue down the broad East Fork valley. The valley is wide, with volcanic cliffs rising sharply at the edges. The bottom consists of grassy flats, with patches of grand old cotton-woods punctuating the river's edge. The trail turns up Adobe Canyon on the east, 2 miles from the trailhead, where the East Fork doglegs sharply south. There is no sign; Adobe Canyon is a continuation of the East Fork Trail.

Trails End–Whiterocks Loop

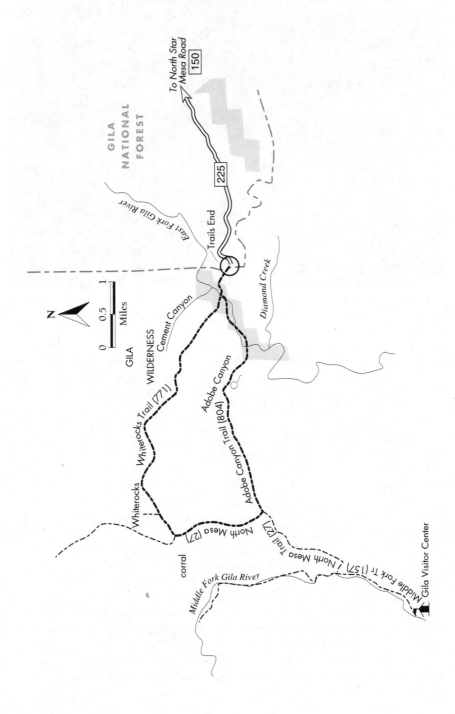

Glassing the broad East Fork Gila River valley from the gleaming white rocks of lower Cement Canyon.

The trail wanders up the canyon, often in the bottom, but periodically climbing the rocky walls. At the head of Adobe is a collection of rusty stock-watering equipment. In a cleft in the west canyon wall you'll find the remains of the spring that supplied the water. Here cairns mark the trail's ascent to North Mesa. It's a steep, rocky climb. While you recover at the top, wander over to the rise on the right (north) of the trail for a wonderful view of the Whiterocks, rising like an apparition from the pinyon-juniper greenery of North Mesa. From here, more adventuresome hikers, armed with topo map and compass, can navigate in a straight shot northwest to the formation, reducing the trip by about 2 miles.

The trail route continues across the mesa. Disregard wandering cattle trails, and watch for elk in the shadows of the pines. At the western edge of North Mesa, you reach the junction with the trail from the Middle Fork, which is called North Mesa Trail (27). Turn north (right) and continue on the trail for 2.6 miles, where an old corral will be on your left, followed by two old stock ponds. It is here that the unsigned trail to Whiterocks (771) goes to the right (northeast). You will also be able to spot the Whiterocks formation rising beyond the pine trees. Turn right, and in 0.5 mile you will be at the foot of the bizarre formations. Note that the rocks are incorrectly located on both the topo and wilderness maps; they are north of the trail. The grainy surface and the pointy sculptures invite climbers; it is a moonscape in the forest.

After your exploration, continue on the Whiterocks Trail eastward, back to the lip of the mesa above the East Fork. Here you will want to pause and explore the similar volcanic tuff formations above Cement Canyon. It is a short descent to the East Fork valley floor, where you return to the main trail. After the river crossing, follow it back to the trailhead on the mesa.

Option: In addition to the two abbreviated versions suggested above, the Whiterocks trip can be extended by continuing on to the Middle Fork (see Hike 55 for details).

72 Trails End–Middle Fork

Highlight:	Overland backpacking trip from East Fork to Middle Fork, avoiding a 70-mile drive.
Type of hike:	2- to 3-day backpacking trip; out-and-back
Total distance:	15.2 miles.
Difficulty:	Moderate.
Best months:	March through November.
Maps:	Forest Service Gila Wilderness map (1984); Burnt Corral Canyon and Gila Hot Springs USGS quads.

Special considerations: Stream crossings.

Finding the trailhead: To reach the Trails End Trailhead, drive north on Forest Road 150 (North Star Mesa Road), an improved gravel road, 32 miles to left turn at FR 225 to Trails End. From the north, drive 7 miles south of Wall Lake on FR 150 to turn right at FR 225. Drive 5.5 miles on FR 225, an improved gravel road. The trailhead is on the red earth mesa above the East Fork, 0.5 mile before the Trails End Ranch gate. There is a pullout on the right (west) side of FR 225.

Parking and trailhead facilities: There is a large parking area, but no other facilities at the trailhead. Camping is not permitted. The closest public land suitable for camping is a mile east of the junction of FR 150 and 225 near the trailhead for the Diamond Creek Trail (40) into the Aldo Leopold Wilderness.

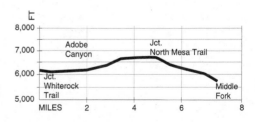

Key points:
- 0.0   Trails End Trailhead and Adobe Canyon Trail (804).
- 0.5   Junction with Whiterocks Trail (771).
- 5.1   Junction with North Mesa Trail (27).
- 7.6   Junction with Middle Fork Trail (157).

Trails End–Middle Fork

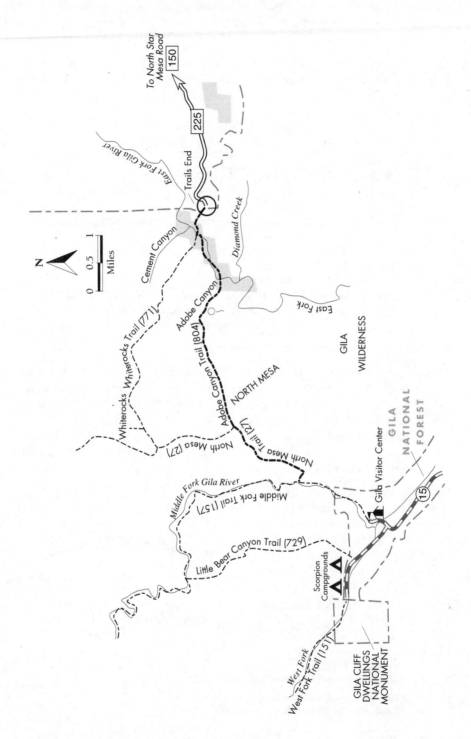

A gigantic cottonwood tree was laid apart like a banana peel from the powerful winds that sometimes roar down the East Fork of the Gila River valley.

The hike: This is a nifty, efficient shortcut that gets you into the heart of the Gila forks, omitting hours (and miles) of driving. Once you reach the Middle Fork, you can extend your trip infinitely. You can continue 8 miles up the Middle Fork to Jordan Hot Springs (see Hike 57), or to one of the cross-over routes to come down the West Fork (see Hikes 56, 58, and 59) for a loop trip. Or from a base camp on the Middle Fork, you can travel to the Gila Visitor Center and the Gila Cliff Dwellings National Monument. The Scorpion campgrounds (no fee) are adjacent to the monument.

From the vantage point of the trailhead, you can see the trail across the bench below, dropping to the river bottom and crossing the East Fork beyond. Follow this new segment of the trail downward. You will cross the old road, passing the ranch gate and the fenced family cemetery. The cairned pathway continues over the bluff edge and down to the river. A large cairn marks the trail for the return trip.

The river crossing is not hazardous. With a gravel bottom, it is usually no more than calf deep, but you will need sturdy wading footwear for this hike. After crossing the East Fork, you will encounter the Whiterocks Trail (771) on your right. A delightful side trip 0.3 mile up this trail takes you to an enchanting world of volcanic tuff formations and views of Cement Canyon. To continue to the Middle Fork destination, continue on downstream in the broad East Fork valley. The river has carved a 100-yard, flat valley, edged with cliffs of volcanic conglomerate. Large cottonwoods are sentinels along the way, except for the ones toppled by the fierce Gila winds.

The river bends sharply south and the trail turns up Adobe Canyon on the right side of the valley 1.5 miles from the first East Fork crossing. At the head of Adobe you will find rusty stock-watering equipment. A spring is located in a cleft in the west canyon wall. Here the trail climbs sharply up to North Mesa. Cairns mark the footpath across the mesa to the intersection with North Mesa Trail (27) on the western edge, above the vast Middle Fork valley. Turn left and follow North Mesa Trail down the steep hillside to another grassy rolling pinyon-juniper bench. The trail takes you southward before descending over the final canyon wall to arrive at the Middle Fork Trail (157). There are several campsites near the intersection.

When your explorations of the Middle Fork are complete, return to the Trails End Trailhead by the same route.

Option: In addition to lengthening the trip on the Middle Fork or the West Fork, you can also include a visit to the Whiterocks on your return, making this a loop trip (see Hike 71 for details).

73 Black Mountain

Highlights:	The lofty Black Mountain Lookout; sweeping views of the Gila Wilderness.
Type of hike:	Out-and-back day hike.
Total distance:	8 miles.
Difficulty:	Moderate.
Best months:	May through November.
Maps:	Forest Service Gila Wilderness map (1984); Black Mountain USGS quad.

Special considerations: Forest access roads to trailhead may be blocked by snow into May at higher elevations.

Finding the trailhead: From the junction of New Mexico Highway 35 and Forest Road 150, drive 45 miles north on FR 150 along the eastern edge of the Gila Wilderness. Turn left (west) on paved NM 59, also designated as FR 141 (Black Mountain Mesa Road) 1 mile south of the USDA Forest Service Beaverhead Work Center. Continue west for 5 miles to the sign for Trail 773 on the left (south). Turn left (south) on the unnumbered improved gravel road and drive about 1 mile to the Wolf Hollow forest camp and end-of-road trailhead.

Parking and trailhead facilities: The Wolf Hollow Trailhead and no-fee forest camp have plenty of graveled parking with camping and a vault toilet, but there is no water.

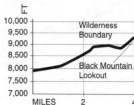

Black Mountain

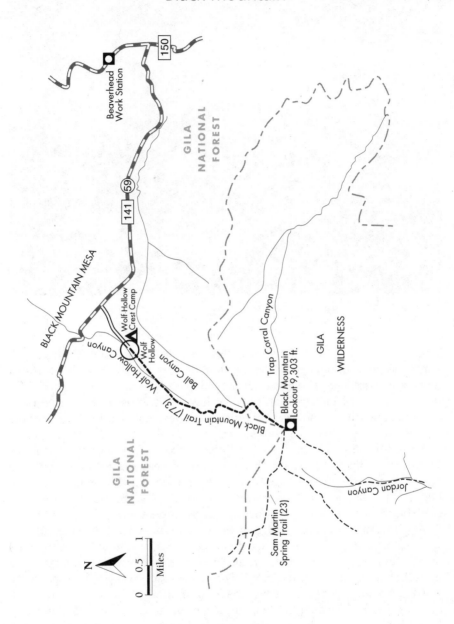

Key points:

0.0	Wolf Hollow Trailhead for Black Mountain Trail (773).
3.0	Gila Wilderness boundary.
3.9	Junction with Sam Martin Spring Trail (23).
4.0	Black Mountain Lookout and junction with Jordan Trail (26).

Westward to the lofty Mogollon Range from the Black Mountain Lookout.

The hike: With much of the elevation to 9,303-foot Black Mountain already gained at the trailhead the 4-mile hike to the lookout is a pleasurable highcountry ramble. The good but narrow pack trail is well maintained for the actively used lookout but not overdeveloped. Most of the route is located in contiguous roadless land outside the designated wilderness, but the country still retains its wild character.

The trailhead sign simply reads "Wilderness Boundary 3 Miles." The Black Mountain Trail (773) contours through a pine forest, reaching a stock fence after 0.3 mile, then climbs gently to a second fence at 1.1 miles. The well-blazed trail joins a ridge above Wolf Hollow after a long steady climb, followed by several switchbacks through a mixed pine forest.

As you continue up the ridge, it then contours around the head of Bell Canyon, reaching the wilderness boundary in a prominent wooded pass overlooking Trap Corral Canyon at 3 miles. A patchwork of burned and unburned forest stretches eastward. The gently graded trail then drops southward to a lower pass before switchbacking another 0.5 mile up to the lookout. Just before reaching the lookout, a sign points ahead for the Sam Martin Spring Trail (23). The lookout is perched on the rounded knob of Black Mountain another 100 feet up the hill. A small cabin sits next to the lookout and is normally staffed by May 15, depending on the fire season. A sign on the south side of the lookout points downhill to Jordan Trail (26), 4.3 miles. The Sam Martin Spring Trail winds around the right (north) side of the lookout and continues down the west ridge of Black Mountain.

With the exception of the fall hunting season, the Black Mountain Trail is lightly used. If you venture up to Black Mountain before the trail has been cleared for the lookout you may be climbing over a lot of downfall. The person staffing the lookout told me that she had cut out 26 trees the week before so that the pack train could get through. If the lookout is staffed during your visit, you can ask to climb the steep ladders to the top for a clear 360-degree view. Otherwise, hike a short distance down the west ridge on the Sam Martin Spring Trail for an open vista to the south. You'll see the entire Gila Wilderness stretched out like a giant map. Especially impressive is the view of Gila's rooftop—the Mogollon Mountains.

74 Black Mountain–Christie

Highlights:	Black Mountain, the northern sentinel of the Gila; sweeping mountain vistas.
Type of hike:	Day hike; shuttle.
Total distance:	7.5 miles.
Difficulty:	Moderate.
Best months:	May through November.
Maps:	Forest Service Gila Wilderness map (1984); Canyon Creek Mountains and Black Mountain USGS quads.

Special considerations: Forest access roads to the trailheads may be blocked by snow into May at higher elevations. No pumpable drinking water is available on the hiking route.

Finding the trailhead: Wolf Hollow Trailhead: From the junction of New Mexico Highway 35 and Forest Road 150 drive 45 miles north on FR 150 along the eastern edge of the Gila Wilderness. Turn left (west) onto paved NM 59, also designated FR 141 (Black Mountain Mesa Road) 1 mile south of the USDA Forest Service Beaverhead Work Center. Continue west for 5 miles to the sign for Trail 773 on the left (south). Turn left (south) on the unnumbered improved gravel road and drive about 1 mile to the Wolf Hollow forest camp and end-of-road trailhead.

Christie Canyon Trailhead: From the turnoff for the Wolf Hollow Trailhead continue west on NM 59 another 4 miles to the junction with FR 142 at the stop sign. Turn left (southwest) and drive 2 miles to FR 142C on the left. Turn left (south) on the unimproved rocky road and go another 2 miles to the unsigned trailhead by a stock pond. This is the exit point and parking spot for the shuttle hike. The road turns east at this point and becomes increasingly rougher, so you'll know if you've driven too far.

Parking and trailhead facilities: Wolf Hollow Trailhead: The no-fee forest camp has plenty of graveled parking space with camping and a vault toilet, but there is no available water. Christie Canyon Trailhead: Trailhead camping and ample parking space are available, but there are no facilities or pumpable water.

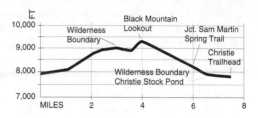

The one-way shuttle driving distance between trailheads is about 9 miles, 4 of which are paved.

Key points:
- 0.0   Wolf Hollow Trailhead for Black Mountain Trail (773).
- 3.0   Gila Wilderness boundary.
- 3.9   Junction with Sam Martin Spring Trail (23).
- 4.0   Black Mountain Lookout and junction with Jordan Trail (26).
- 4.7   Junction with Cassidy Spring Trail (25).
- 6.0   Junction with Sam Martin Spring Trail and unsigned Christie Canyon Trail.
- 6.1   Leave Gila Wilderness boundary.
- 6.6   Christie stock pond.
- 7.0   Christie Canyon.
- 7.5   Christie Canyon Trailhead.

The hike: This enjoyable day shuttle along the northern perimeter of the Gila Wilderness begins and ends at about the same elevation, with the Black Mountain high point at its midpoint. Added features include a short commute between trailheads and views of an endless mountain panorama across most of the wilderness. The first 3 miles of the Black Mountain Trail (773) to the signed wilderness boundary gain a fairly evenly distributed 1,200 feet. The wooded 9,000-foot boundary pass opens to a grand mosaic of burned and unburned forest in Trap Corral Canyon. The trail then drops gently southward to another gap before climbing the final 0.5 mile to the 9,303-foot Black Mountain Lookout. The lookout is staffed during the fire season, commencing by May 15, often sooner. The foot of the lookout is closed in by trees, so take advantage of any invitation you might receive to climb the tower for a better view. The lookout view across the forks of the Gila and onto the Mogollon Range is breathtaking.

Just before you reach the lookout tower, a trail sign points to the Sam Martin Spring Trail (23), which wraps around the right (north) side of the tower. Another signed trail leading south to the Jordan Trail (26) is located on the south side of the lookout. Take the Sam Martin Spring Trail as it drops down the west ridge of Black Mountain. An expansive view opens to the south after 0.1 mile. The old roadbed is gradually reverting to a singletrack trail. It is steep, rocky, and blocked by downfall in places but easy to follow. At mile 4.7, a signed junction directs you left to the Cassidy Spring Trail (25) adjacent to a fence on the right (north). Continue right (northwest) on the Sam Martin Trail, which quickly crosses the fence and drops to a recent burn. The old road trail continues its steep descent with rock cairns appearing every so often. At mile 6 a tiny sign on a ponderosa pine reads "Sam Martin Trail" to the left (west). The main trail sign is buried beneath a fallen pine tree. Stay on the more obvious doubletrack trail to the right. It descends

Black Mountain–Christie

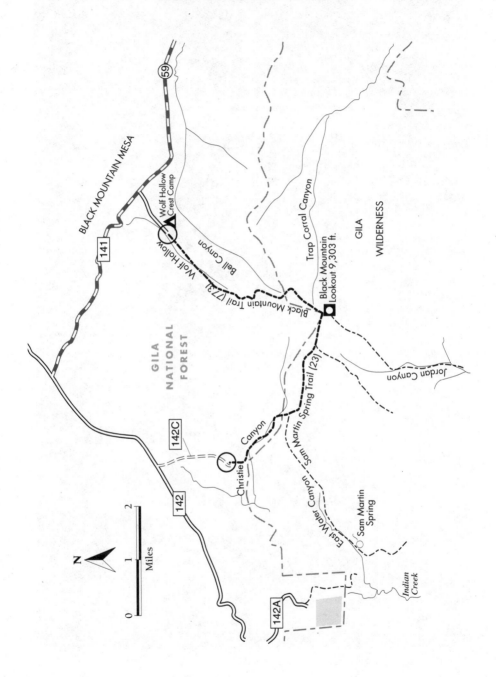

- 59
- BLACK MOUNTAIN MESA
- Wolf Hollow Crest Camp
- 141
- Wolf Hollow
- Bell Canyon
- Black Mountain Trail (772)
- Trap Corral Canyon
- GILA WILDERNESS
- Black Mountain Lookout 9,303 ft.
- Jordan Canyon
- GILA NATIONAL FOREST
- Sam Martin Spring Trail (23)
- 142C
- Christie Canyon
- East Water Canyon
- Sam Martin Spring
- 142
- 142A
- Indian Creek
- N
- Miles
- 0   1   2

The Black Mountain Lookout (9,303 feet elevation).

a hill exiting the wilderness boundary 0.1 mile north of the Sam Martin Trail junction.

For the final 1.5 miles to the trailhead follow the doubletrack to the right (east) of a stock pond in a wide grassy valley. The old roadbed drops into the middle reaches of Christie Canyon, then climbs around a wide mesa ridge to another parallel draw immediately north. Look for the trailhead in this low dip on the prairie next to the Gillette stock tank.

Option: For a longer shuttle hike of 15 miles with a much longer shuttle drive between trailheads consider heading south from Black Mountain to the Gila Visitor Center. The basic route from the junction on the south side of the lookout is to head down Jordan Canyon to Whiterocks and on down to the lower Middle Fork Gila River. The downhill shuttle is high and dry until reaching the Middle Fork near the end of the hike.

75 Black Mountain–Indian Creek

Highlights:	Black Mountain, the northern sentinel of the Gila; expansive mountain vistas and secluded canyons.
Type of hike:	Day hike; shuttle.
Total distance:	11.5 miles.
Difficulty:	Strenuous.
Best months:	May through November.
Maps:	USFS Gila Wilderness Map (1984); Canyon Creek Mountains and Black Mountain USGS quads.

Special considerations: Forest access roads to the trailheads may be blocked by snow at higher elevations into May. There is no water during the first 9 miles.

Finding the trailhead: Wolf Hollow Trailhead: From the junction of New Mexico Highway 35 and Forest Road 150 drive 45 miles north on FR 150 on the eastern edge of the Gila Wilderness. Turn left (west) onto paved NM 59, also designated FR 141 (Black Mountain Mesa Road) 1 mile south of the USDA Forest Service Beaverhead Work Center. Continue 5 miles west to the sign for Trail 773 on the left (south). There is no sign for the no-fee Wolf Hollow forest camp. Turn left (south) on the unnumbered improved gravel road and drive about 1 mile to the Wolf Hollow forest camp and end-of-the-road trailhead.

Horse Camp Trailhead: From the Wolf Hollow trailhead turnoff on NM 59 (FR 141) continue on NM 59 another 4 miles to the junction with FR 142 at the stop sign. Turn left (southwest) on the improved gravel road FR 142 and drive about 8 miles to FR 142A. Make a left (south) turn onto FR 142A (improved gravel) and drive about 2 miles to the signed trailhead for the Horse Camp Trail on the left (east) located on the north boundary of the private inholding.

The one-way shuttle driving distance between the two trailheads is about 15 miles.

Parking and trailhead facilities: Wolf Hollow Trailhead: The no-fee Wolf Hollow forest camp has a vault toilet and lots of graveled space for parking. Water is not available. Horse Camp Trailhead: Limited trailhead camping and a large parking area are available, but there are no facilities and no water.

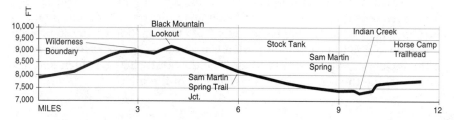

Key points:

0.0	Wolf Hollow Trailhead for Black Mountain Trail (773).
3.0	Gila Wilderness boundary.
3.9	Junction with Sam Martin Spring Trail (23).
4.0	Black Mountain Lookout and junction with Jordan Canyon Trail (26).
4.7	Junction with Cassidy Spring Trail (25).
6.0	Junction with Sam Martin Spring Trail and unsigned Christie Canyon Trail.
7.4	Upper Dutch stock tank.
9.0	Sam Martin Spring.
9.2	Trail sign pointing to Whiterocks, Black Mountain, and Double Springs.
9.7	Indian Creek.
10.0	Unsigned junction—head north up the ridge.
11.5	Horse Camp Trailhead.

The hike: This great excursion across the northeast end of the Gila Wilderness offers wide variety, from mountaintops to mesas. Some of the ending segments of the route are rarely visited, adding a bit of challenge to the art of trail finding. The first 4 miles to the 9,303-foot Black Mountain Lookout are a delight. The well-graded trail gains 1,200 feet over the course of 3 miles to a wooded gap marking the wilderness boundary. This is a good viewpoint, with a mosaic of burned and unburned forest unfolding across Trap Corral Canyon to the east. The Black Mountain Trail then drops gently to another saddle before making the final 0.5-mile switchback ascent to the lookout tower. Two signed trails wrap around the lookout. The one to the right (north) drops down the west ridge of Black Mountain toward Sam Martin Spring, the other heads south into Jordan Canyon. For the middle segment of the shuttle hike, take the Sam Martin Spring Trail (23). But first check out the lookout. It's staffed by May 15 or earlier depending on the arrival of the fire season. Trees close in the actual summit of Black Mountain. If the friendly lookout person invites you up to the tower, you'll be treated to an amazing 360-degree view. The entire Gila Wilderness stretches southward. The vista across the forks of the Gila to the lofty Mogollon Range is especially impressive.

Black Mountain–Indian Creek

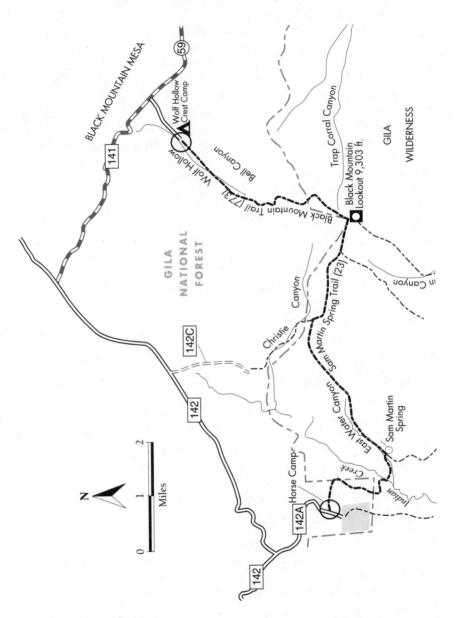

The segment of the Sam Martin Trail that drops along the west ridge of Black Mountain is actually an old roadbed that is slowly recovering to a singletrack trail. If you missed the view from the tower you'll still see the country southward from an open stretch along the ridge 0.1 mile below the lookout. At mile 4.7 you'll reach the junction with the Cassidy Spring Trail. Continue straight (right) into a recent burn where the trail becomes steep and rocky with downfall. Cairns lead the way on down to mile 6 where an obscure sign points left (west) to Sam Martin Spring. The main junction sign is buried beneath a fallen tree in a grassy pine woodland where the ridge widens and flattens. There is an occasional blaze, but this is a confusing spot. The key is to stay on the broad ridge as it turns to the southwest. A well-worn cow path cuts the trail at right angles about 0.5 mile below the junction. The cow path looks deceptively like the main trail. Continue straight and soon you'll pick up a more distinct trail with cairns and blazes. After steeply descending a rocky ridge, the trail passes by a small stock pond on the left at mile 7.4 shown as the Upper Dutch Tank on the USGS quad. Becoming more primitive, the trail continues its descent of the shallow East Water Canyon and adjacent pine benches to Sam Martin Spring at mile 9. Immediately below the spring an old unsigned wagon trail climbs to the left (south). This is the Jordan Canyon Trail (26) that could be taken across a mesa 11.5 miles to Whiterocks continuing on to the Middle Fork Gila River.

The Sam Martin Trail is indistinct at this point as it crosses to the west side of the gully. An abandoned trail continues down East Water Canyon to Indian Creek. It used to follow Indian Creek all the way down to the Middle Fork Gila River until rockslides took out the trail back in 1941. If time and energy permit, the lower end of East Water Canyon is well worth an off-trail side trip. The deep chasm is wedged tightly between colorful rock turrets, cliffs, and spires.

The unmarked Sam Martin Trail leading west out of East Water Canyon is directly across the gully from the metal stock tank. Head uphill to the right (west) to a signed trail junction at mile 9.2. The sign tells you that you've traveled 5.5 miles from Black Mountain with another 1.5 miles to Double Springs. The trail has since been rerouted around the privately owned Double Springs Ranch, becoming distinct as it passes through a stock fence and gate at mile 9.4 next to a superb overlook into the rugged lower East Water Canyon. The trail angles down to the wide, and likely dry, Indian Creek valley, then climbs nearly 200 feet to an unsigned point on a prominent ridge. The new trail heads right (north) up this steep ridge. Only a rock cairn marks this junction of trail and ridge. You've gone too far if you reach a signed trail junction pointing back to Sam Martin Spring. Head straight up this ridge, gaining 200 feet in 0.2 mile. Continue north as the narrow mesa gradually widens. The trail may be obscure to nonexistent. Continue parallel to a fence on your left (west). After 1 mile the rocky trail turns left (west) as it enters a forest marked with old blazes. The Horse Camp Trailhead is finally reached after another 0.5 mile. The sign says 1.5 miles to Sam Martin Spring, but with the trail relocation you can add at least 1 hard mile to the distance.

Options: The hard-to-find places on the Sam Martin Trail are easier to locate if the shuttle is done in reverse. The tradeoff is that you would have your back to the better scenery.

A longer but no more strenuous shuttle hike leads south from Black Mountain Lookout down Jordan Canyon to Whiterocks and on down the

Middle Fork Gila River to the Gila Visitor Center. These 15 or so miles are dry until you reach the lower Middle Fork toward the end of the hike.

A rugged, essentially off-trail, out-and-back exploration of Indian Creek is also possible from this hike. This can be done as a short side trip during the hike or preferably as a separate day hike from the Horse Camp Trailhead.

76 Sam Martin Spring

Highlights:	Rugged, deep canyons in the remote northern reaches of the wilderness.
Type of hike:	Out-and-back day hike.
Total distance:	5 miles.
Difficulty:	Moderate.
Best months:	May through October.
Maps:	Forest Service Wilderness map (1984); Canyon Creek Mountains and Woodland Park USGS quads.

Special considerations: Forest roads may be blocked by snow at higher elevations into late spring. No water between the trailhead and Sam Martin Spring. Steep climb back to the trailhead.

Finding the trailhead: From the junction of New Mexico Highway 35 and Forest Road 150 drive 45 miles north on FR 150 along the eastern edge of the Gila Wilderness. Turn left (west) on paved NM 59, also designated FR 141 (Black Mountain Mesa Road) 1 mile south of the USDA Forest Service Beaverhead Work Center. Continue west on NM 59 for 9 miles to its junction with F R 142 at the stop sign. Turn left (southwest) and drive 8 miles to FR 142A on your left (south). Turn left (south) on FR 142A and drive 2 miles to the signed Horse Camp Trailhead on the left at the northern boundary of the Double Springs Ranch.

Parking and trailhead facilities: There is no water, and the only facilities are a large parking area and limited trailhead camping.

Key points:
- 0.0   Horse Camp Trailhead and Sam Martin Spring Trail (23).
- 1.5   Junction of new trail with Sam Martin Spring Trail.
- 1.8   Indian Creek valley.
- 2.3   Trail sign for Sam Martin Spring.
- 2.4   East Water Canyon and unsigned junction with Jordan Canyon Trail (26).
- 2.5   Sam Martin Spring.

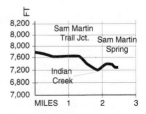

The hike: Except for the fall elk-hunting season, East Water Canyon and Indian Creek are lightly visited. This may be partly due to the trails starting

Sam Martin Spring

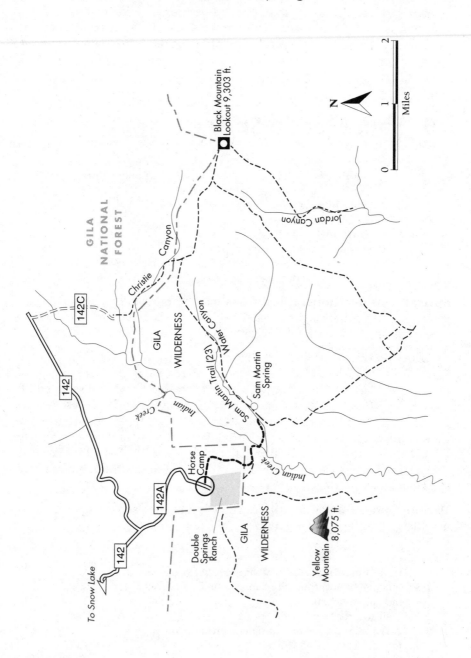

out on private land with uncertain access. However, the Forest Service has recently built a new trail from the Horse Camp Trailhead just east of the Double Springs Ranch. As a result the canyons and trails in this region can be accessed entirely from public land. Sam Martin Spring is located just above the rugged lower portion of East Water Canyon, a major tributary to Indian Creek, a northern branch of the Middle Fork Gila River.

The trail starts out in a pine-fir forest, evenly losing 200 feet over 0.5 mile as it heads southeast to an open mesa above Indian Creek. Follow the rock cairns as the obscure-to-nonexistent trail heads south across the rocky mesa. If all else fails, a stock fence parallels the route on your immediate right (west). After a fairly flat 0.8 mile the trail plummets 200 feet straight down the ridge to the well-defined Sam Martin Spring Trail (23). Only a rock cairn marks the unsigned junction, so fix this spot in your memory for the return. If you turn right you'll end up at the Double Springs Ranch. Continue left (east) on the good Sam Martin Trail. It drops to the wide gravelly bottom of Indian Creek and then regains the elevation to a ridgetop overlook into the rocky confines of East Water Canyon at mile 2.1. The trail passes through a gated drift fence and then contours quickly to a trail junction sign that is actually about 0.1 mile uphill from the real junction. The sign points in various directions to Whiterocks, Double Springs, and Black Mountain. Continue downhill toward a metal stock tank in the bottom of East Water Canyon. Keep the tank in mind for the return trip because this unsigned spot is where the trail heads uphill to the misplaced junction sign mentioned above. The unsigned wide wagon road of a trail to Whiterocks (Trail 26) cuts sharply uphill to the right. A trickle of water in the gully along with the old Sam Martin Spring is immediately up the shallow, rocky canyon to the left.

With a couple of steep uphill pitches, two unsigned junctions discussed above, and a long stretch of faint trail on the mesa, the return leg of the route is a bit more challenging.

Options: From Sam Martin Spring a 7.5-mile shuttle hike can be continued to the Christie Canyon Trailhead (see Hike 74) or 11.5 miles to the Wolf Hollow Trailhead by way of Black Mountain (see Hike 75). For a vigorous side trip, the rugged Indian Creek Canyon can be accessed by walking down the drainage from the trail crossing at mile 1.8 or by hiking about 0.8 mile down East Water Canyon from just below Sam Martin Spring to Indian Creek. The serpentine canyon becomes increasingly narrow and steep-walled after another mile. Heavy rains washed out the early day Indian Creek pack trail in 1941. Although remnants of the trail remain, the canyon offers a strenuous, mostly off-trail adventure.

77 The Meadows

Highlights:	A direct, relatively fast route into the heart of the Middle Fork Gila River country; high elk numbers on mesa; sweeping mountain vistas; rugged canyon formations; warm (not hot) springs.
Type of hike:	Long out-and-back day hike or overnighter.
Total distance:	15.2 miles.
Difficulty:	Strenuous.
Best months:	May through November.
Maps:	Forest Service Gila Wilderness map (1984); Canyon Creek Mountains and Woodland Park USGS quads.

Special considerations: No water en route to the Middle Fork Gila River. Vehicular access to higher-elevation trailhead may be blocked by snow into late spring.

Finding the trailhead: From the junction of New Mexico Highway 35 and Forest Road 150 drive 45 miles north on FR 150 along the eastern edge of the Gila Wilderness. Turn left (west) on paved NM 59, also called FR 141 (Black Mountain Mesa Road) 1 mile south of the USDA Forest Service Beaverhead Work Center. Continue 9 miles west on NM 59 to its junction with FR 142 at the stop sign. Turn left (southwest) and drive 8 miles to FR 142A on your left (south). Turn left (south) on FR 142A and drive 2 miles to the signed Horse Camp Trailhead on the left at the northern boundary of the Double Springs Ranch.

Parking and trailhead facilities: A large parking area and limited trailhead camping with no water or other facilities.

Key points:

0.0	Horse Camp Trailhead.
1.5	Unsigned junction with the Sam Martin Spring Trail (23).
2.0	Trail sign pointing to Meadows Trail (53).
2.3	Cross-country to the Meadows Trail.
4.2	High point of trail along east slope of Yellow Mountain.
7.6	The Meadows.

The hike: The Meadows are a key destination for hiking, camping, and fishing on the wild Middle Fork Gila River midway between the Gila Visitor Center and the isolated northern boundary of the wilderness. It takes two or three days of spectacular but slow going to reach the Meadows from the visitor center. If time is limited, the upland Meadows Trail (53) can shorten the hiking time to a half day. The broad mesa south of Yellow Mountain is a good place to see elk and other wildlife as well as glimpse into the twisting maze of lower Indian Creek.

The Meadows

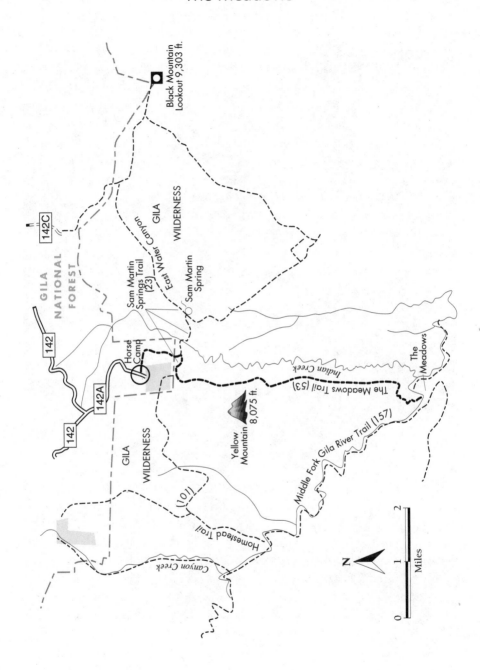

The Meadows on the Middle Fork Gila River.

The hike begins on a recently constructed trail around the east side of the Double Springs Ranch. An older blazed trail heads southeast for 0.5 mile and then turns south across an open mesa before plummeting 200 feet down a steep ridge to an unsigned intersection with the Sam Martin Spring Trail (23) at mile 1.5. The trail across the mesa may be faint to nonexistent with only an occasional small rock cairn. A parallel stock fence on your right (west) will help guide you south to southwest to the Sam Martin Trail. Simply stay on the ridge as it narrows downward, and remember the rock cairn at the base of the slope for the return hike. Turn right (northwest) toward the Double Springs Ranch, reaching a trail sign within 0.5 mile. At this point you are in the south end of the ranch. The landowner allows hiker access except during the fall hunting season. The sign points right (west) toward the Meadows Trail (53), but the trail is missing. Head southwest across the gully and swales of ponderosa pine toward the far ridge to pick up the Meadows Trail after about 0.3 mile of going cross-country. Cross the stock fence that parallels the trail and turn left (south).

The trail winds through several ravines and contours across alternating woodlands and meadows as it climbs along the east slope of Yellow Mountain. Signs of elk, coyote, mountain lion, and bear are abundant. The trail then drops to the broad mesa. There is a confusing spot at mile 5.5 in a gully where several cattle and game trails intersect. Take the left-hand trail next to a small rock cairn. Despite level ground, hiking is slowed by volcanic rocks embedded in the trail. After another 0.8 mile the pinyon-juniper opens to good views into the rugged lower reaches of Indian Creek. The trail soon passes through an old drift fence next to an overlook directly above the Meadows. It then loses 860 feet over the final brushy mile to the Meadows with several steep rocky pitches along the way. The signed junction with the Middle Fork Gila River Trail (157) is just above a tree-enclosed campsite on the north side of the river. A warm (not hot) spring feeds a pond about 0.3 mile downstream on the left (north) bank of the Middle Fork. The open grassy expanse of the Meadows is a pleasing anomaly in an otherwise narrow chasm both above and below. Stately pines shade grassy bench campsites near the river with great volcanic pillars rising overhead.

Options: Longer shuttle backpacks can be made upstream or downstream (see Hike 60) or up and over to the West Fork Gila River canyon (see Hikes 57, 58, and 59). A long three- to four-day backpack loop of about 25 miles is possible by continuing up the Middle Fork to Clear Creek and then north on the "Homestead" Trail (101) to the Double Springs Ranch. This trail provides an easier climb out of the river canyon. Be sure to request permission to cross the private land en route to the Horse Camp Trailhead ahead of time. While hiking to or from the Meadows, consider a short side climb to the top of 8,075-foot Yellow Mountain. A good route is up the southeast slope from the high point on the Meadows Trail. The 20-minute, 360-foot walk-up to the east end of the mountain opens to a broad view of ridges, mesas, and canyon tops across much of the Gila Wilderness.

78 Aeroplane Mesa

Highlights:	A quick, short route to the Middle Fork from the north, providing access to a vast area of wilderness trails and outings.
Type of hike:	2- to 3-day backpacking trip; out-and-back.
Total distance:	8.5 miles for basic journey to Trotter Meadow.
Difficulty:	Easy.
Best months:	May through October.
Maps:	Forest Service Gila Wilderness map (1984); Loco Mountain USGS quad.

Special consideration: There is one crossing of the Middle Fork.

Finding the trailhead: To reach the Loco Mountain Trailhead, drive 4 miles north of Glenwood on U.S. Highway 180. Turn right (east) on New Mexico Highway 159 (Bursum Road) toward Mogollon. NM 159 is paved for the first 9 miles and then is improved gravel. Drive east on NM 159 a total of 30 miles to Forest Road 142. Turn right (east) and drive 12 miles to the sign for Trail 705 at the new trailhead facility adjacent to FR 142, about 5 miles east of Snow Lake.

Parking and trailhead facilities: There is a large gravel parking area. Other trailhead facilities are being developed; plans include vault toilets and an information board. There is no water. Camping is permitted at the trailhead.

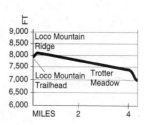

Key points:
- 0.0   Loco Mountain Trailhead on FR 142.
- 4.0   Middle Fork; junction with Middle Fork Trail (157).
- 4.3   Trotter Meadow; junction with Trotter Trail (30).

The hike: The trail across Aeroplane Mesa is the shortest route into the Middle Fork. The high point of the trip occurs in the first 0.5 mile from the trailhead, and thereafter the trail slopes gradually to the rim of the Middle Fork canyon. There it descends 400 feet to the river. The trail junction with the Middle Fork Trail (157) is on the north side of the stream. There is also a large alcove in the cliff at the trail junction. From the junction Trotter Meadow is 0.3 mile upstream. Turn right (north) on the Middle Fork Trail; there is one crossing before the meadow.

The meadow is an ideal location from which to base your further exploration of the wilderness. Loop trips up the river and over to Iron Creek and Turkeyfeather Pass, or up through the Jerky Mountains are lengthy possibilities. Shorter day hikes are also possible, out-and-back on the Middle Fork, or up the Trotter Trail to Lilley Park. When your time to enjoy the wilderness is close to an end, retrace your steps up to Aeroplane Mesa and return to the trailhead by the same route.

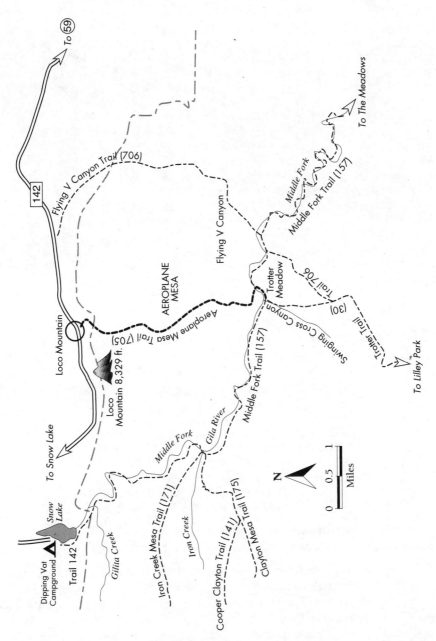

Options: See Hikes 59 and 60 for details on excursions from the Trotter campsite; see Hike 83 for the Jerky Mountains. With a Gila Wilderness map you can incorporate these trips in an itinerary from Trotter Meadow. The options are infinite.

The view northeast to Aeroplane Mesa from the Trotter Trail.

79 Trotter

Highlights:	Scenic cliffs and formations in upper canyon; historic cabin ruins; meandering trout stream; pleasant pine parks and meadows.
Type of hike:	Out-and-back day hike or overnighter.
Total distance:	13.2 miles.
Difficulty:	Moderate.
Best months:	May through November.
Maps:	Forest Service Gila Wilderness map (1984); Loco Mountain and Lilley Mountain USGS quads.

Special considerations: Forest roads and trailhead may be blocked by snow into late spring. Do not attempt river crossings during high runoff.

Finding the trailhead: From Glenwood drive 4 miles north on U.S. Highway 180 and turn right (east) on New Mexico Highway 159, (Bursum Road). Drive east on Bursum Road for 30 miles to Forest Road 142. Turn right (east) on FR 142 and drive 7 miles to Snow Lake. The trailhead, marked with a small sign, is adjacent to the dam on the west side of the lake below the Dipping Vat campground.

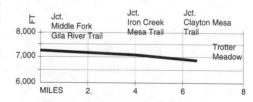

Trotter

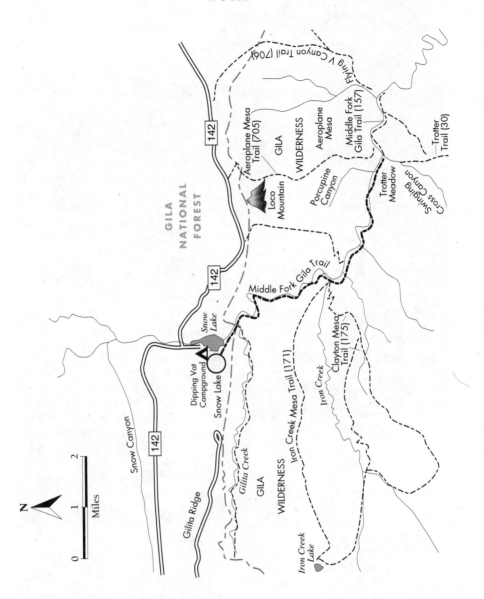

Parking and trailhead facilities: Large gravel parking area, vault toilets, and water pumps (summer only) at the adjacent fee campground.

Key points:

- 0.0 Snow Lake Trailhead for Snow Lake Trail (142).
- 1.0 Junction Middle Fork Gila River Trail (157).
- 4.0 Junction Iron Creek Mesa Trail (171).
- 4.1 Junction Clayton Mesa Trail (175).
- 6.6 Trotter Meadow and junction with Trotter Trail (30).

A soft dirt trail parallels the Upper Middle Fork 1.5 miles below Gilita Creek.

The hike: This trip samples the best of the upper canyon and valley of the Middle Fork Gila River and is sure to bring you back for further exploration downriver. Historic cabin ruins in wide meadows surrounded by rugged canyon rims are among the many "photo ops" between Snow Lake and Trotter Meadow.

The Snow Lake Trail (142) leads south past the lake along the outlet stream for a mile to the mouth of Gilita Creek, entering from the right (west). The Middle Fork of the Gila River starts from the intersection of these two small streams. The Middle Fork gains velocity and volume through an increasingly rugged canyon for another 34 wilderness miles to the Gila Visitor Center. The upper 6 of these serpentine miles to Trotter Meadow are a delight. Trotter and other closer meadows are fine destinations for a long day hike and even more enjoyable for camping along the river. After crossing the mouth of Gilita Creek, look for the Middle Fork Trail (157) in the brush. The junction is unsigned but marked with rock cairns. The Middle Fork Trail continues left (south) down the main drainage. It crosses a pine park, climbs talus rock on the right (west) side, and then crosses the river a few times. These upper reaches of the Middle Fork have an unusual rugged yet mellow feel to them. The trail then ascends a rocky slope on the right side of a dramatically narrowing canyon. Suddenly the valley widens to a large, grassy flat with historic cabin ruins 2.5 miles below Gilita Creek.

Wide, grassy meadows surrounded by forested hills continue for another 0.5 mile to the Iron Creek Mesa Trail junction in a cottonwood grove. The next junction is immediately across Iron Creek where the Clayton Mesa Trail climbs steeply to the right (west) and the main Middle Fork Trail continues left (south). The Middle Fork canyon closes in here with high cliffs, beginning an alternating series of widening and narrowing for the next 2.5 miles down to the expansive Trotter Meadows.

The Trotter cabin shown on the USGS quad no longer exists. The meadow consists of a huge, open, grassy flat with an interesting mix of water-loving cottonwoods and dry-loving ponderosa pines. The lower forested draw of Swinging Cross Canyon joins the meadow from the south, signaling the start of the Trotter Trail to White Creek Flat on the West Fork Gila River. The pleasant meadow is bound by low pine-clad hills and rock bluffs across the willow-lined stream. Along the Middle Fork the surroundings are gentle—the sort of place where you can identify birds, key flowers, settle into a good book, and watch the river flow by for hours.

Option: Instead of retracing your route upriver to Snow Lake, consider a shorter shuttle hike of 10.8 miles on the Aeroplane Mesa Trail (705). From Trotter hike downstream 0.2 mile to the junction of the Aeroplane Mesa Trail adjacent to a large alcove on the left (north) side of the river. This good trail gains a steep mile northward to Aeroplane Mesa and then crosses the mesa for another 3 miles to the trailhead on FR 142. The exit trailhead is about 5 miles east of Snow Lake.

80 Snow Lake–Willow Creek

Highlights:	Rugged upper canyon with a blend of parks and meadows;, meandering trout stream; historic cabin ruins; wildlife viewing opportunities; scenic mountain vistas.
Type of hike:	2- to 3-day backpacking trip; shuttle.
Total distance:	14 miles.
Difficulty:	Moderate.
Best months:	May through November.
Maps:	Forest Service Gila Wilderness map (1984); Loco Mountain and Negrito Mountain USGS quads.

Special considerations: Forest roads and trailheads may be blocked at higher elevations by snow into late spring. Avoid river crossings if water levels are high. Water might not be available along a lengthy stretch of the mesa trail.

Finding the trailheads: Snow Lake Trailhead: From Glenwood drive 4 miles north on U.S. Highway 180 and turn right (east) on New Mexico Highway 159 (Bursum Road). Drive 30 miles east on Bursum Road to Forest Road 142. Turn right (east) on FR 142 and drive 7 miles to Snow Lake. The trailhead for the Snow Lake Trail (142) is adjacent to the dam on the west side of the lake below the Dipping Vat campground.

Willow Creek Trailhead: Drive 4 miles north of Glenwood on US 180 and turn right (east) on NM 159 (Bursum Road). Drive east on Bursum Road 25.5 miles to the Willow Creek Recreation Area. Drive past the Willow Creek campground to the signed trailhead for the Middle Fork Gila River Trail (157) to Iron Creek Lake and beyond.

Special note: If Bursum Road to the west is still blocked by snow in the early spring, vehicular access to the trailheads is possible on FR 141 out of Reserve and FR 28 south of Negrito Work Camp. Refer to the Gila National Forest map (1997) for route information.

The one-way shuttle driving distance between trailheads is about 11.5 miles.

Parking and trailhead facilities: Snow Lake Trailhead: Large gravel parking area with vault toilets and well water at the adjacent fee campground (summer only). Willow Creek Trailhead: Parking on the edge of a grassy meadow, vault toilet, kiosk, and trailhead sign; water available from Willow Creek (to be treated). Trailhead camping is allowed, and there are two nearby campgrounds on Willow Creek.

Snow Lake–Willow Creek

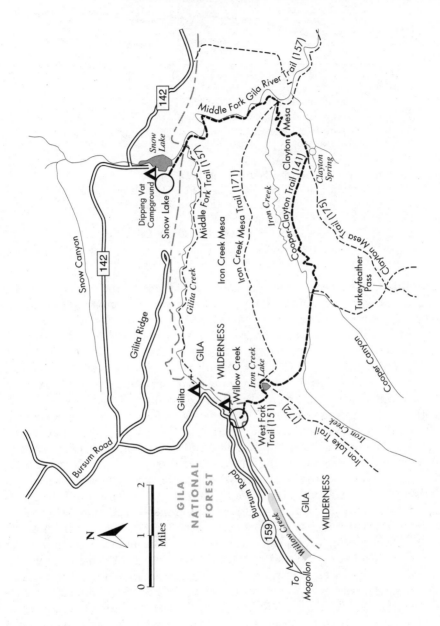

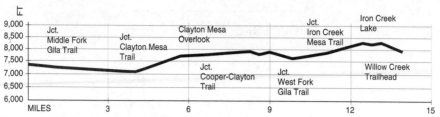

Key points:

   0.0   Snow Lake Trailhead for Snow Lake Trail (142).
   1.0   Junction with Middle Fork Gila River Trail (157).
   4.0   Junction with Iron Creek Mesa Trail (171).
   4.1   Junction with Clayton Mesa Trail (175).
   5.6   Clayton Mesa overlook.
   6.7   Junction with Cooper–Clayton Trail (141).
 10.0   Junction with West Fork Gila River Trail (151) on Iron Creek.
 11.7   West Fork Gila River Trail leaves Iron Creek.
 12.5   Junction with Iron Creek Mesa Trail (171).
 12.9   Iron Creek Lake and junction with Iron Creek Lake Trail (172).
 14.0   Willow Creek Trailhead.

The hike: This sweep across the north-central end of the Gila Wilderness offers a pleasant transition from deep river canyons to broad grassy meadows to high mesas to open pine parks and babbling brooks. Along the way you may thrill to flushing a turkey and hear, if not see, elk fading into the thick forest.

The Snow Lake Trail (142) heads south above the west side of the lake's outlet for a mile to a wide opening at the mouth of Gilita Creek. Gilita flows from the west (right) and joins the Snow Lake outlet to become the Middle Fork Gila River. After crossing Gilita Creek look for rock cairns marking the unsigned junction with the Middle Fork Gila River Trail (157) in the brushy bottom. Continue straight (south) on the Middle Fork Trail. Pine park benches, talus slopes, a deep narrowing canyon, and river crossings mark the next 2.5 miles to a large grassy expanse with historic cabin ruins. With forested hills above, the meadow continues for another 0.5 mile to the Iron Creek Mesa Trail (171) junction in a cottonwood grove. The Clayton Mesa Trail (175) is only 0.1 mile beyond, just across Iron Creek. This is a striking spot with cliffs towering over a canyon that closes in again below the junction.

Before turning right (west) on the Clayton Mesa Trail, make sure you're carrying enough water. The next 6 miles to Iron Creek are apt to be high and dry. The trail at the junction is somewhat indistinct. Take a hard 45-degree turn to the right and follow the tree blazes across the pine park to where the trail becomes clear. For the next 1.5 miles the trail switchbacks steadily up to Clayton Mesa. For the most part the trail surface is good, but low use has resulted in side-sloping along parts of the trail along with thorny brush and downfall in burn areas. Upon reaching the mesa rim, drop your pack and feast your eyes into the trail-less canyon of lower Iron Creek on down to the Middle Fork. The view from this open rock ledge is sensational!

For the next mile the trail rolls across level pine woodlands and then

322

A field of wild iris appears in the ponderosa pines along Iron Creek Trail 151 not far from Willow Creek campground.

makes a short rocky descent to lush open meadows below Clayton Spring. This is a favored elk pasture, so approach cautiously for a possible sighting of the elusive wapiti. The Cooper–Clayton Trail (141) junction is just above and beyond Clayton Spring, which will most likely be dry. The junction may be unsigned and is easy to miss because the dominant Clayton Mesa Trail continues left over a low ridge to Clayton Creek and on to Turkeyfeather Pass. If you inadvertently bypass the junction and end up on the pass it's not the end of the world. In fact, you've added an interesting 4 miles to your route (see "Option" below). If you are able to locate the Cooper–Clayton Trail take it to the right (northwest) to Clayton Mesa. After crossing the mesa the trail weaves in and out of several side ravines before making a steep descent to the mouth of Cooper Canyon on Iron Creek at mile 10. Iron Creek is well sheltered by a dense spruce-fir forest, providing essential habitat for the reintroduced endangered Gila cutthroat trout. There are plenty of intimate campsites along the small stream, particularly along its north bank on open pine park benches.

The signed trail junction with the West Fork Gila Trail (151) is located at the Cooper Canyon mouth. Turn right (west); hop across Iron Creek, and head upstream along the north side of Iron Creek through pleasant pine parklands. After 1.7 miles the West Fork Trail leaves the creek with a sharp bend to the right (north). The trail steepens, gaining 400 feet in 0.8 mile to its junction with the upper end of the Iron Creek Mesa Trail (171). Continue left to and around the small stock pond of Iron Creek Lake. Just beyond the lake the Iron Creek Lake Trail (172) heads south to the lofty Mogollon Mountains. Stay right (west) on the West Fork Trail for the final 1.1 miles to the exit trailhead on Willow Creek. The trail makes a slight climb and then drops steadily on an old doubletrack for 0.8 mile to the rocky brook of Little Turkey Creek just before the signed trailhead.

Option: To lengthen the loop by 4 miles with a corresponding increase in scenic diversity, take the Clayton Mesa Trail (the main trail to the left near Clayton Spring) to the subalpine meadow of Turkeyfeather Pass (8,320 feet). Upper Clayton Creek usually has running water a short distance below the pass. Turn right at the first trail junction on the south side of the meadow toward Turkeyfeather Pass. Continue right (northwest) at the second junction for the 2-mile descent of Cooper Canyon to Iron Creek. From the pass the wide rocky trail narrows to a singletrack as it follows the gully of Cooper Canyon's east fork. The trail weaves through a moist spruce-fir forest and crosses the small stream many times with bypasses around large downed trees. A small spring with a water pipe buried under the trail enters from the right (west) 1.5 miles below the pass. High cliffs on the east side close in on the lower canyon just above Iron Creek.

81 Gilita Creek

Highlights:	Accessible yet wild canyon with perennial stream and a fishable trout population.
Type of hike:	Day hike; shuttle.
Total distance:	7 miles.
Difficulty:	Moderate.
Best months:	June through November.
Maps:	Forest Service Gila Wilderness map (1984); Negrito Mountain and Loco Mountain USGS quads.

Special considerations: Slow going on infrequently maintained trail, blocked in places by downfall and brush. Forest roads to higher-elevation trailheads are snowbound into late spring, especially if driving east from U.S. Highway 180. Many stream crossings.

Finding the trailheads: Gilita Creek Trailhead: Drive 4 miles north of Glenwood on US 180. Turn right (east) on New Mexico Highway 159, also known as the Bursum Road, toward Mogollon. NM 159 changes from paved to improved gravel after 9 miles. Drive east 27 miles to the Gilita Creek campground. The Middle Fork Gila River Trail (157) begins at the eastern end of the campground with one shallow stream crossing just above the trailhead.

Snow Lake Trailhead: From the junction of US 180 and NM 159, 4 miles north of Glenwood, drive 30 miles east on NM 159 to its junction with

Forest Road 142. Turn right (east) on FR 142 and drive another 7 miles to the Snow Lake campground. The trailhead is below the campground on the west side of the lake.

The one-way shuttle driving distance between the two trailheads is 10 miles.

Parking and trailhead facilities: Gilita Creek Trailhead: a no-fee forest camp with ample parking, vault toilet, a kiosk, and water that can be taken and treated from the creek. Snow Lake Trailhead: a fee campground with well water during the summer, large parking area, and vault toilets.

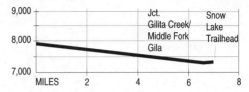

Key points:
  0.0   Gilita Creek Trailhead and Middle Fork Gila River Trail (157).
  6.0   Junction of Middle Fork Gila River Trail and Snow Lake Trail (142).
  7.0   Snow Lake Trailhead and Snow Lake Trail (142).

The hike: Depending on your direction, Gilita Creek is the beginning or end of the longest designated trail in the Gila Wilderness—41 miles down the Middle Fork to the Gila Visitor Center. The 7-mile hike to Snow Lake starts at the Gilita forest camp in a lush spruce-fir forest next to a sparkling trout stream. Gilita Creek loses an average of 100 feet per mile over its 6-mile length to the upper Middle Fork Gila River. As it descends, the country becomes increasingly rough, rocky, and dry within a modest elevation difference of only 600 feet

A trailhead sign refers to the special trout waters of the stream and the two-fish limit. It also recommends against stock use because of infrequent maintenance. The trail quickly crosses to the right (south) side, followed by repeated crossings. At times cliffs force the trail across talus slopes high above the stream. These rocky stretches also tend to be plagued by thorny brush. Old tree blazes appear off and on, but the first large rock cairn is 2.5 miles downstream. The rough spots are interspersed with pleasant sections of primitive needle-carpeted paths through ponderosa pine parklands. The trail is often obscure at stream crossings. Whenever the terrain closes in on the side you're on, simply cross and you'll soon find the trail on the other side. The canyon bottom hosts a diverse coniferous forest of big, old spruce, Douglas-fir, and ponderosa. Ledges and outcrops of dark volcanic rock confine the steep V-shaped valley. Big logs across the trail with catclaw nipping at your legs will slow your progress as the canyon deepens. Enchantment also deepens with small waterfalls, alcoves on higher cliffs, and even a distinctive hole in a wall of Gila conglomerate on the left (north) side about 4 miles down. After a difficult brushy stretch, the trail improves along the lowest 0.5 mile of the stream as it winds along a rocky pine bench on the right (south) side. The canyon opens at the confluence of Gilita Creek and the outlet of Snow Lake, signaling the beginning of the Gila River's Middle Fork.

Gilita Creek

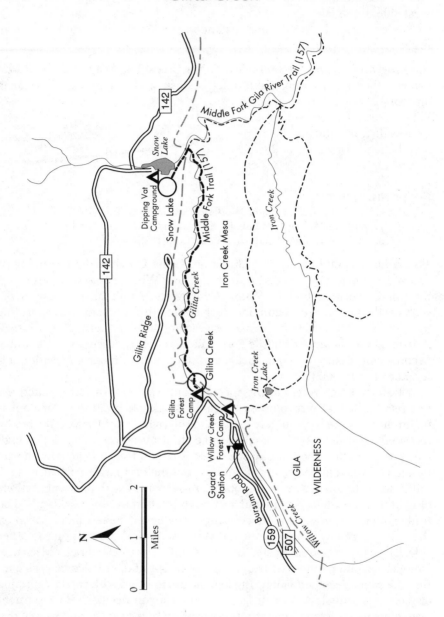

There is no sign at the junction. The trail drops to the stream in a willow thicket where rock cairns mark the T intersection. The Middle Fork Trail continues downstream to the right (south). Snow Lake is to the left (north) another mile upstream. The trailhead for the Snow Lake Trail (142) is next to the dam and below the campground on the west side of the lake.

Looking up Gilita Creek about 3 miles below the Gilita forest camp.

Options: Don't count on hitching in this remote country. If you don't have a shuttle driver, consider a longer and more strenuous out-and-back of 12 miles round trip to the mouth of Gilita Creek. Another possibility is to combine this hike with Hike 80 for a three-day shuttle backpack from Gilita to Willow Creek. Still a third option is a five- to seven-day shuttle backpack down the Middle Fork to the Gila Visitor Center, a reverse route for Hike 60.

82 Iron Creek

Highlights:	A short hike to a wilderness mountain stream in a conifer forest.
Type of hike:	Out-and-back day hike or overnight backpacking trip.
Total distance:	4.6 to 8 miles.
Difficulty:	Easy.
Best months:	May through October (depending on snow).
Maps:	Forest Service Gila Wilderness map (1984); Negrito Mountain USGS quad.

Special considerations: Avoid the weeks of hunting season, if possible.

Finding the trailhead: To reach the Willow Creek Campground Trailhead for Trail 151, drive 4 miles north of Glenwood on U.S. Highway 180. Turn right (east) on New Mexico Highway 159, also known as the Bursum Road, toward Mogollon. NM 159 changes from paved to improved gravel after 9 miles. Drive east a total of 25.5 miles to the Willow Creek Recreation Area, then turn right. Drive past the Willow Creek campground to the Iron Creek Lake Trail (151) parking area. Bursum Road is closed in winter and often remains snow-blocked into May. In early spring, Forest Road 141 out of Reserve and FR 28 south of Negrito provide access to this trailhead if Bursum Road is not open.

Parking and trailhead facilities: There is a large, grassy parking area, a vault toilet at the trailhead, and an informational kiosk. Water is available in the creek (to be treated). Trailhead camping is permitted.

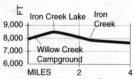

Key points:
- 0.0 Willow Creek Campground Trailhead.
- 1.1 Iron Creek Lake and junction with Trail 172 to Mogollon Baldy.
- 1.5 Junction with Iron Creek Mesa Trail (173).
- 2.3 Iron Creek.
- 4.0 Cooper Canyon and junction with Cooper–Clayton Trail (141).

Iron Creek

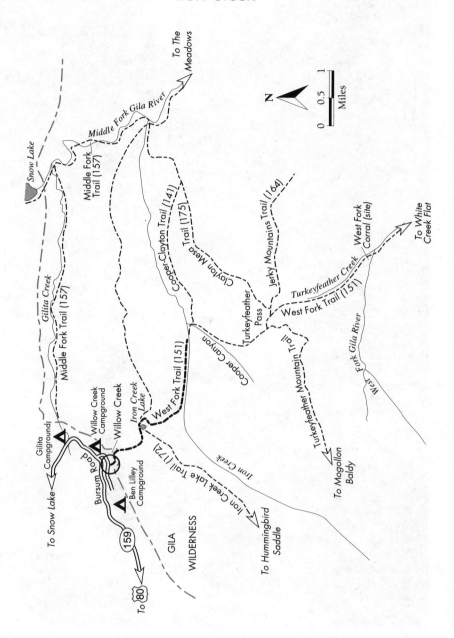

The hike: From a busy campground, this trip takes you to a mountain stream with ponderosa pine parks on one bank and a dark spruce and Douglas-fir forest on the other. From a base camp on Iron Creek you can explore Turkeyfeather Pass or embark on a longer journey to the West Fork Corral or the Jerky Mountains (see "Options" below).

Filtering water from Iron Creek along the West Fork Gila Trail (151).

From the trailhead, follow the trail along the little brook, cross the bank at the trail sign, and head up the wide trail toward Iron Creek Lake. This ancient jeep doubletrack is heavily used by hikers and horse parties. After passing through ponderosa pine meadows carpeted with wild iris, you will come to Iron Creek Lake and the trail junction on its western bank. The lake is an old stock tank; it is too muddy to pump.

The trail continues beyond the lake to the intersection with the Iron Creek Mesa Trail at the head of the ravine to Iron Creek. The trail signs on the tree at the junction have been altered by hikers who don't agree with Forest Service mileage estimates. Go right at the junction. The trail descends in a straight line to arrive at Iron Creek. The trail then parallels the creek on the sunny north bank down to the solitary crossing just before the junction with Cooper Canyon where it turns south to climb to Turkeyfeather Pass.

There are campsites along the Iron Creek trail as well as at the mouth of Cooper Canyon. No fishing is allowed in Iron Creek since it has been stocked with the reintroduced endangered Gila trout. With the open ponderosa meadows on the north, the valley presents a contrasting forest of darkness on the shady southern side. There the dense spruce-fir forest is draped with moss, its moist habitat protecting it from the fires that sweep the ponderosa pine parks.

After your outing on Iron Creek, return to the Willow Creek Trailhead by the same trail.

Options: For a day hike to Turkeyfeather Pass from a camp along Iron Creek, continue on Trail 151 up Cooper Canyon. In 2 miles you will be at the pass, marked with a sign. There is no water at the pass.

For a longer trip (10 miles round trip) continue over the pass, and stay on Trail 151 all the way down Turkeyfeather Creek to its confluence with the West Fork. Here there's a spacious meadow, site of an old corral (see Hike 83 for a longer loop).

83 Jerky Mountains Loop

Highlights:	Backpack to a base camp, then enjoy a long day hike through the remote mountains rising between the West and Middle Forks of the Gila; magnificent views; secluded mountain valleys and streams.
Type of hike:	3- to 5-day backpacking trip/day hike combination.
Total distance:	18 miles out-and-back (backpack); 14.5-mile loop (day hike).
Difficulty:	Strenuous.
Best months:	May through October.
Maps:	Forest Service Gila Wilderness map (1984); Mogollon Baldy Peak and Lilley Mountain USGS quads.

Special considerations: The day hike journey over the Jerky Mountains has a long 12-mile stretch without water, so carry several water bottles. The Jerky Mountains are highly vulnerable to lightning.

Finding the trailhead: To reach the Willow Creek campground trailhead, drive 4 miles north of Glenwood on U.S. Highway 180. Turn right (east) on New Mexico Highway 159, also known as Bursum Road, toward Mogollon. NM 159 changes from paved to improved gravel after about 9 miles. Drive east a total of 25.5 miles to Willow Creek Recreation Area. Turn right and drive past the Willow Creek campground 0.5 mile to the Iron Creek Lake Trail (151). Bursum Road is closed in the winter and often remains snow-blocked into May. In early spring, Forest Road 141 out of Reserve and FR 28 south of Negrito provide access to this trailhead.

Parking and trailhead facilities: At the trailhead there is a large grassy parking area. There is a vault toilet, an information board, and water is available in the creek (to be treated). Trailhead camping is permitted; two Forest Service campgrounds are nearby.

File 083--Jerky

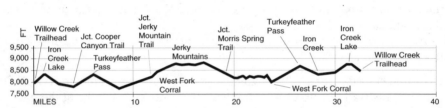

Key points:

    0.0   Willow Creek campground trailhead.
    1.1   Iron Creek Lake; junction with Trail 172 to Mogollon Baldy.
    1.5   Junction with Iron Creek Mesa Trail (173).
    2.3   Iron Creek.
    4.0   Cooper Canyon; junction with Cooper–Clayton Trail (141).
    6.0   Turkeyfeather Pass; junction with Turkeyfeather Mountain Trail (102).
    6.3   Junction with Jerky Mountain Trail (164).
    9.0   West Fork Corral; junction with West Fork Corral Trail (814).
   11.8   Junction with Jerky Mountain Trail (164).
   11.9   Junction with Clayton Mesa Trail (175).
   19.5   Junction with Clear Creek Trail (165) to Marrs Spring.
   20.0   Junction with West Fork Corral Trail (814).
   23.5   West Fork Corral; junction with West Fork Trail (151).
   26.5   Turkeyfeather Pass; junction with Turkeyfeather Mountain Trail (102).
   28.5   Iron Creek; junction with Cooper–Clayton Trail (141).
   31.1   Junction with Iron Creek Mesa Trail (173).
   31.5   Iron Creek Lake; junction with Trail 172 to Mogollon Baldy.
   32.5   Willow Creek campground trailhead.

The hike: This hike is a lollypop loop: The stem is the out-and-back 9-mile section to a base camp at the West Fork Corral, and the candy is the 14.5-mile loop trip over the Jerky Mountain Range, done as a backpacking trip. The backpack to the base camp could easily be divided into two days by

Jerky Mountains Loop

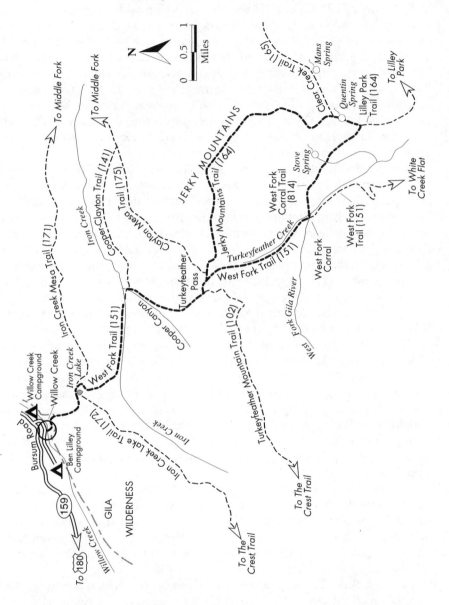

camping along Iron Creek the first night and then going over Turkeyfeather Pass to the West Fork on the second day. On your hike out, with a lighter pack, the 9 miles are less daunting.

From the Willow Creek Trailhead, the West Fork Trail (151) charges up the hillside above the valley, crosses a ponderosa pine mesa, and arrives at Iron Creek Lake, a muddy stock tank. From the lake the moderately used trail passes an intersection with the Iron Creek Mesa Trail (173), and then drops swiftly to Iron Creek, which it follows for 1.7 miles. There are campsites along Iron Creek as well as at the Cooper Canyon junction (see Hike 82 for details).

At the mouth of Cooper Canyon the trail climbs through the canyon to reach Turkeyfeather Pass. There often is water in Cooper Canyon. It's a cozy canyon with magnificent walls closing in on the trail in its lower portions. It widens at its head as the trail curls around to the flats of Turkeyfeather Pass. The pass is dry. The nearest water, should you wish to camp there, is back down Cooper, or on Clayton Creek, via Trails 164 and 175; both water sources are about a mile away. From the pass continue down Turkeyfeather Creek on the West Fork Trail. Three miles from the pass is the confluence of the West Fork and Turkeyfeather. Here there is a broad, grassy ponderosa flat with spacious campsites, the site of a historic corral.

From a comfortable camp on the West Fork you can take off on the Jerky Mountain trip with a light pack—except you need at least two full water bottles for the trip. Backtrack up Turkeyfeather Creek to the Jerky Mountain Trail below the pass. Turn right (east) here at the site of a dry lake. There's a second intersection on the east side of the lake. Disregard the mileages on these signs; Forest Service estimates run low. Turn right toward Marrs Spring. The trail scoots right up the ridge with a magnificent view of Turkeyfeather Mountain's forested summit across the valley of the West Fork. The trail continues to climb to an open ridge of pines and grasses, with vistas in every direction.

The Jerky Mountains' height and relative isolation between the forks of the Gila have made it a prime target for lightning. The multitude of fire-created openings makes for spectacular views of the country. The trail follows the undulating ridge that forms the crest of the Jerkies. Even with the burns the trail is easy to follow. After 4 miles of up-and-down travel, the trail begins its descent along a ridge on the southeastern side of the Jerkies, gradually sloping into a soft grassy swale of a valley to the intersection with the Clear Creek Trail to Marrs Spring. A small spring above the junction is likely to have water even in dry years. Bear right (southwest) at the junction and continue down the sloping valley, following Quentin Creek to a trail junction with the Lilley spring and Lilley Park Trail.

This junction is a tricky spot. The West Fork Corral Trail does not continue down the creek, although that's what the arrow on the sign suggests. Instead, from the sign take a sharp right and go up the hill. The trail is visible on the hillside if you look in that direction. Lots of hikers have wandered on down the creek, creating quite a noticeable path in the wrong direction. The mileage is off, too; from here it's 3.5 miles to the West Fork.

The West Fork Trail goes up and down over a long series of low ridges that slope down off the Jerkies. These foothills of the Jerkies cause you to relive your journey along the crest: up and down. Along the way you may encounter water in the springs that emanate from the mountain, even in a dry year, and there's water in the creek that trickles down from Stove Springs about halfway to the West Fork.

At 3 miles from the junction, the trail breaks out on the canyon edge above the West Fork. What a view! Pause on the promontory rocks and soak up the sweeping view of the densely forested West Fork. From here it's a drop via extremely lengthy switchbacks to the Middle Fork valley.

If your schedule permits a layover day, enjoy your respite in camp after the mountain loop. When your West Fork adventures have been completed, retrace your steps to the Willow Creek Trailhead via Turkeyfeather Pass and Iron Creek.

Options: This loop can be reversed, although it is easier to hike up Turkeyfeather Creek than it is to climb the canyon wall above the West Fork corral. A trek in the Jerkies can be incorporated in several hikes in the north Gila. See Hike 51 on the West Fork, where the Jerky loop is a side trip, or Hike 78 on the Middle Fork, where itis a destination for a trip from Trotter Meadow.

This hike can be expanded with a swing through the Mogollon Mountains. From the corral, continue down the West Fork Trail to White Creek Flat. From there take the trail to Mogollon Baldy (Trail 152). Travel north on the Crest Trail (182) to the Iron Creek Lake Trail (172) near Center Baldy, heading northeast back to Iron Creek Lake. This additional 30 miles requires at least two more days in the schedule (see Hike 2 for details on the Crest Trail).

Appendix A: For More Information

FOREST SERVICE OFFICES

USDA Forest Service
Southwestern Region
Public Affairs Office
517 Gold Avenue, SW
Albuquerque, NM 87102
(505) 842-3292

Gila National Forest
3005 East Camino del Bosque
Silver City, NM 88061
(505) 388-8201

Glenwood Ranger District
P.O. Box 8
Glenwood, NM 88039
(505) 539-2481

Wilderness Ranger District
Route 11, P.O. Box 50
Mimbres, NM 88049
(505) 536-2250

Gila Visitor Center
Route 11, P.O. Box 100
Silver City, NM 88061
(505) 536-9461

**Gila Cliff Dwellings
National Monument**
Route. 11, P.O. Box 100
Silver City, NM 88061
(505) 536-9461

**Aldo Leopold Wilderness
Research Institute**
P.O. Box 8089
Missoula, MT 59807
(406) 542-4190

General information about the Gila Wilderness is easily accessible on the Internet from the recreation website: www.recreation.gov

**PUBLIC LANDS
CONSERVATION GROUPS:**

Gila Watch
P.O. Box 309
Silver City, NM 88062
(505) 388-3449

**New Mexico Wilderness
Alliance**
P.O. Box 13116
Albuquerque, NM 87192
(505) 255-5966 ext. 106
Email: nmwa@earthlink.net

Wilderness Watch
P.O. Box 9175
Missoula, MT 59807
(406) 542-2048
Website: www.wilderness
watch.org
Email: wild@wilderness
watch.org

The Wildlands Project
1955 West Grand Road, Suite 148A
Tucson, AZ 85745
(520) 884-0875 or (520) 884-0962
Website: www.twp.org
Email: information@twp.org

The Wilderness Society
900 Seventeenth Street, NW
Washington, DC 20006-2506
(202) 833-2300
Website: www.wilderness.org

The Wilderness Society Wilderness Support Center
wsc@tws.org

The Wilderness Society
Four Corners Regional Office
7475 Dakin Street, #410
Denver, CO 80221
(303) 650-5818

Finding the Right Map

To explore the Gila Wilderness, you need two basic types of maps. First are the large-scale 1:24,000 topographic maps (with 40-foot contour intervals), listed in the map information for each hike. These detailed USGS quads are essential for on-the-ground route finding. Second, the 1984 1:63,360 Gila Wilderness map (with 200-foot contour intervals) shows trailhead access, numbered Forest Service trails, and major features. This small-scale map, along with the 1997 Gila National Forest map (half inch to the mile on a planimetric base) is useful for overall trip planning and for finding your way to trailheads and at trail junctions.

The Gila Wilderness map costs $5 and the Gila National Forest map is priced at $4. They can be obtained from the USDA Forest Service offices listed above. In addition, the Forest Service has published a plastic, spiral-bound book of 128 color maps covering the entire Gila National Forest. These maps are reproductions from the USGS 1:24,000 quad base series reduced to 1 inch = 1 mile. The book of maps costs $40.

The USGS quads sell for $4 each. They may be purchased from USGS Information Services, Box 25286, Denver, CO 80225, or by calling 1-800-HELP-MAP. The USGS charges a handling fee of $3.50 for each order mailed.

Appendix B: Further Reading

Campbell's Trading Post at Gila Hot Springs has an outstanding selection of titles on archeology, natural history, settlers, ranchers, hunters, explorers, and miners of the Gila Wilderness and southwestern New Mexico. Many of the books are published locally and are difficult to locate elsewhere. Listed here are several widely available books.

Bowers, Janice E. *100 Desert Wildflowers of the Southwest*. Southwest Parks and Monuments Association: Tucson, AZ, 1989.

_____. *Shrubs and Trees of the Southwest Deserts*. Southwest Parks and Monuments Association: Tucson, AZ, 1993.

Brown, David E., and Carmody, Neil B., editors. *Aldo Leopold's Southwest*. University of New MexicoPress: Albuquerque, NM, 1990.

Leopold, Aldo. *A Sand County Almanac*. Ballantine Books: New York, NY, 1966.

Little, Elbert L. *The Audubon Society Field Guide to North American Trees*. Alfred A. Knopf: New York, NY, 1980.

Lorbiecki, Marybeth. *Aldo Leopold: A Fierce Green Fire*. Falcon Publishing: Helena, MT, 1996.

MacCarter, Jane S. *New Mexico Wildlife Viewing Guide*. Falcon Publishing: Helena, MT, 1994.

Peterson, Roger Tory. *Field Guide to Western Birds*. Houghton Mifflin Co.: Boston, MA, 1990.

Taylor, Ronald J. *Sagebrush Country: A Wildflower Sanctuary*. Mountain Press: Missoula, MT, 1992.

Appendix C: Hiker Checklist

Hiking in the Gila Wilderness requires solid preparation. One of the first steps to being properly prepared is packing the right equipment for the type, season, and duration of the hike. We joke about carrying "80 pounds of light-weight gear," but in all seriousness, you must carry everything on your back. So, take only what you really need. Use the checklist below before your trip into Gila country to ensure you haven't forgotten an essential item.

CORE ESSENTIALS FOR DAY HIKES

- [ ] Day pack (or "day-and-a-half," climbing-style pack, if needed)
- [ ] Water: 2 quarts to 1 gallon per person per day in 1- to 2-quart Nalgene bottles
- [ ] Matches in a waterproof container
- [ ] Small first-aid kit: tweezers, adhesive bandages, antiseptic, moleskin/second skin/ spyroflex (for blister prevention), first-aid tape, prescriptions, antibiotics, ibuprofen or acetaminophen, antacid tablets, bee sting kit (over-the-counter antihistamine or epinephrine by prescription), knee or ankle wraps, snakebite kit
- [ ] Head net and insect repellent (in season)
- [ ] Sunglasses, sunscreen (with an SPF of 15 or more), and lip sunscreen
- [ ] Pocketknife
- [ ] Whistle and signal mirror
- [ ] Flashlight with extra batteries and bulb
- [ ] Lunch and high-energy snacks, with plastic bag for your trash
- [ ] Toilet paper in plastic bag
- [ ] Wilderness and topo maps and compass
- [ ] Rain gear that can double as wind protection (breathable, water-repellent parka or rain suit with pants or chaps)
- [ ] Warm shirt, fleece, or polypropylene top (for layering)
- [ ] Gear and accessories for overnight trips add the following:
- [ ] Backpack with waterproof pack cover and extra set of pack straps
- [ ] Tent with ground cloth (cut or folded to size of tent floor) and repair kit (including ripstop tape)
- [ ] Sleeping bag (rated to at least 10 degrees F or as season requires)
- [ ] Sleeping pad (self-inflating type is best)
- [ ] Walking stick or trekking poles
- [ ] Backpack stove, fuel bottle (filled), repair kit with cleaning wire
- [ ] Collapsible bucket (for settling silty water)
- [ ] Water filter (with brush to clean in the field) and iodine tablets for backup
- [ ] Cooking kit, pot gripper, cleaning pad
- [ ] Eating utensils, including a cup, fork, spoon, and bowl with cover (3-cup size)
- [ ] Trowel
- [ ] Several small drawstring grab bags for odds and ends
- [ ] Biodegradable soap, waterless hand sanitizer, small towel
- [ ] Toothbrush, toothpaste, dental floss
- [ ] Nylon tape or duct tape

- [ ] Nylon stuffsack with 50- to 100-foot nylon cord for hanging food and drying clothes
- [ ] Plastic bags and a few smaller zip-locked bags
- [ ] Small sewing kit
- [ ] Notebook, pencils
- [ ] Field guidebooks
- [ ] Compact binoculars
- [ ] Camera, film, lenses, filters, lens brush, and paper (or keep it light and simple with a "point and shoot")
- [ ] Fishing tackle (fly and/or spinning)
- [ ] Thermometer
- [ ] Watch
- [ ] Sufficient food, plus a little extra
- [ ] Clothing—quick-dry fabrics preferred
- [ ] Boots (medium weight recommended, broken in)
- [ ] Lightweight boots for wading streams that are sturdy enough for backpacking
- [ ] Neoprene socks (thermal protection for stream crossings)
- [ ] Several pairs of wool hiking socks and polypropylene or inner socks
- [ ] Extra underwear and shirt
- [ ] Shirt, sweater, pants, and jacket suitable to the season
- [ ] Warm skiing-style hat (balaclava, headband, or stocking cap)
- [ ] Hat, windproof with broad brim (for sun protection)
- [ ] Mittens or gloves (weight depends on the season)
- [ ] Hiking shorts
- [ ] Swimsuit
- [ ] Gaiters (especially when snow is present)
- [ ] Thermal underwear (wool or polypropylene/capilene, depending on the season)

Afterword

When we first contemplated our exploration of the Gila Wilderness, we could hardly contain our excitement. Here was a chance to learn more about an entirely different ecosystem than our northern Rockies home. What a challenge, we thought. We eagerly foresaw many interim hurdles along the way, such as the challenge of becoming intimate with this splendid corner of southwestern New Mexico and its secluded treasures beyond the roads. There would be the challenges of climbing rugged peaks; of safely crossing swift, swollen rivers; of negotiating narrow canyons; of learning enough about the interconnected web of Gila Wilderness geography, geology, and ecology to interpret some of its wonders for others to appreciate. In short, of field checking the best hikes this vast and varied land has to offer. These challenges called to us from blank spots on the wilderness map.

But we each face a far greater challenge—the challenge of wilderness stewardship, which must be shared by all who venture into wild country.

Wilderness stewardship assumes many forms, from political advocacy to a zero-impact hiking and camping ethic to quietly setting the example of respect for wild nature for others to follow. The political concessions that brought about passage of the 1980 New Mexico Wilderness Act, which included restoration of land to wilderness status first recognized by Aldo Leopold, have been made. The lines drawn represent a positive step forward in the unending battle to save what little remains of our diminishing wilderness heritage.

But drawing boundaries is only the first step. Now the great challenge is to take care of what we have. We can each demonstrate this care every time we set out on a hike. It comes down to respect for the untamed but fragile mountains, mesas, and canyons; for those wild denizens who have no place else to live; for other visitors; and for those yet unborn who will retrace our hikes in the new millennium.

During our often long and strenuous hikes through the Gila, we felt as though Aldo Leopold were hiking with us. We knew that if he could have shared his perspective with us, he would congratulate us not by the mountains we climbed but by what we pass onto others in an unimpaired condition.

About the Authors

Polly Burke and Bill Cunningham are partners in the long trail of life. Polly, formerly a history teacher in St. Louis, Missouri, now makes her home with Bill in Choteau, Montana. She is pursuing multiple careers in freelance writing, leading group trips in the wilderness, and working with the developmentally disabled. Polly has hiked and backpacked extensively throughout many parts of the country.

Bill is a lifelong "wildernut"—a conservation activist, backpacking outfitter, and field studies teacher. He has written several books and dozens of magazine articles about wilderness areas based on extensive on-the-ground knowledge. He is the author of *Wild Montana,* the first in Falcon Publishing's series of guidebooks to wilderness and unprotected roadless areas.

Polly and Bill recently coauthored Falcon's *Hiking California's Desert Parks* (1996), and *Wild Utah* (1998). *Hiking the Gila Wilderness* is their third coauthorship for Falcon, in a continuing series of joint exploration and writing projects.

The Wilderness Society

THE WILDERNESS SOCIETY'S ROOTS

When their car came to a screeching halt somewhere outside of Knoxville, Tennessee, the passengers were in hot debate over plans for a new conservation group. The men got out of the car and climbed an embankment where they sat and argued over the philosophy and definition of the new organization.

Three months later, in January 1935, the group met again in Washington, D. C. Participants in the meeting included Robert Sterling Yard, publicist for the National Park Service; Benton MacKaye, the "Father of the Appalachian Trail"; and Robert Marshall, chief of recreation and lands for the USDA Forest Service. "All we desire to save from invasion," they declared, "is that extremely minor fraction of outdoor America which yet remains free from mechanical sights and sounds and smells." For a name, they finally settled on The Wilderness Society.

Among the co-founders was Aldo Leopold, a wildlife ecologist at the University of Wisconsin. In Leopold's view, The Wilderness Society would help form the cornerstone of a movement needed to save America's vanishing wilderness. It took nearly 30 years, but President Lyndon B. Johnson finally signed The Wilderness Act of 1964 into law September 3rd, in the rose garden of the White House.

THE WILDERNESS SOCIETY TODAY

The founders called the organization The Wilderness Society, and they put out an urgent call, as we do today, for "spirited people who will fight for the freedom of the wilderness." Today, Americans enjoy some 104 million acres of protected wilderness, due in large part to the efforts of The Wilderness Society. The Wilderness Society is a nonprofit organization devoted to protecting America's wilderness and developing a nation-wide network of wild lands through public education, scientific analysis and activism. The organization's goal is to ensure that future generations will enjoy the clean air and water, wildlife, beauty and opportunity for renewal provided by pristine forests, mountains, rivers and deserts. You can help protect American wildlands by becoming a Wilderness Society Member. Here are three ways you can join: **Telephone: 1-800-THE-WILD; E-mail: member@tws.org or visit the website at www.wilderness.org; Write: The Wilderness Society, Attention: Membership, 900 17th Street Northwest, Washington, D.C. 20006.**